A Life in Shadow

6 Dec 08

To Sue

Best Wishes

[illegible]

ISBN: 1-4196-1123-2

To order additional copies, please contact us.
BookSurge, LLC
www.booksurge.com
1-866-308-6235
orders@booksurge.com

ALAN I. DAVIES

A LIFE IN SHADOW:
DIVINE SPARK OR CHEMICAL IMBALANCE?

2005

A Life in Shadow

ACKNOWLEDGMENTS

The single biggest source of facilitation to write this memoir came from my wife, Juliane. She kindly enabled me to dodge much of our household's daily chores. Julie shouldered this burden uncomplainingly even though she suffered a debilitating illness for a number of years during the eight-year writing process.

Another source of worthwhile help and solid support came from participants in two writers' critique groups who indulgently listened to my writing and then offered helpful suggestions. Here my thanks are directed exclusively to those genuine people who attended these groups with a serious desire to improve their own craft skills.

Worthy of particular mention is a neighbor and, I hope, a friend, who saved me through his generous donation of many hours of personal, patient instruction on my computer which, arriving late in my life, has held me hostage ever since. Jim Hurstell rode to my rescue more often than the United States' cavalry did in America's pioneer west.

Two friends from a senior tennis group also gave me frequent computer first aid. Maggie Katrek provided gentle, understanding ministrations when I became stuck in the treacle of the ever-changing text software programs. She solved the complexities of the digital age, and formatted the photos, when I had the bright idea to add photographs to leaven the dough. Maggie also expertly proofed the book.

Gary Evans, who as a teenager built a TV that worked, took me by the hand and led me expertly through the minefields of cyberspace when my original computer called it quits. These three saved me a lot of time had I gone the paper and pencil route, my natural habitat.

AUTHOR'S NOTE

This chronicle is true to the best of my memory. But human memory is flawed, influenced by emotion, and the overlay of more recent experiences. There may be people who remember details, characters, or events differently.

The dialogue quoted in this memoir is, of course, reconstructed. I do not claim these words were ever spoken exactly as I've written. These recreated conversations are included to suggest tone, tenor and overall substance between me and another person, especially in humorous situations. I do not remember the details of such exchanges, some having taken place as many as 65 years ago. Furthermore, probably all of the adult people mentioned in the chapters covering my childhood and early teen years are gone from this earth.

Geographic movement has characterized my life, across oceans and across continents. I've lost touch with most of the people I knew briefly along my meandering route. A majority of these disconnects were my fault, as I tended to be lazy when it came to keeping up friendships. I lay the blame on my itinerant life. But this probably is just a convenient excuse. As a result, corroboration and correction of my recollections has been largely confined to my siblings: their memories keener than mine. While all of the people mentioned did or do exist, I have changed their names (except for immediate family members) to avoid possible pain or embarrassment to them or their survivors.

PROLOGUE

In times past, only the powerful, wealthy, or wizened and wise undertook the writing of an autobiography. Although the accepted practice until relatively recently, as early as the 1750s the renowned English writer, Dr. Samuel Johnson, proclaimed: "There has rarely passed a life of which a judicious and faithful narrative would not be useful."

Nowadays it seems that, in addition to those who fill the above exalted categories, many senior citizens—and the numbers increase exponentially—are pecking out their life stories, judicious and faithful or not. Some of these sudden memoirists are even resorting to a recent do-it-yourself, fill-in-the-blanks guide for the production of their autobiographies: a sort of write by-the-numbers methodology. Dr. Johnson could not have foreseen what his words have wrought.

Regardless of how useful or useless it may be, I decided to undertake the daunting task of writing my autobiography and tossing it on the swiftly growing heap. The result of this decision is now before you, and written, it should be noted, without any artifices but in the old-fashioned way: one word after the other.

While I've been interested in writing since my teens, I'm merely another of the millions of senior citizens who, if more civic minded, would promptly pass from the earth. Instead, I/we hang around straining the Social Security System. Yet despite inner reservations about putting pen to paper to recount my life, my gut tells me that my time on earth has been somewhat different from the norm and therein lays the justification for plunging in. I hope you will come to agree.

Born during the Great Depression, my boyhood evolved in London, England, in the turbulent years of World War II. My teen years were spent in the war's immediate aftermath in a threadbare Britain. I emigrated to the United States at about the time it became de facto leader of the western world in the monumental struggle between capitalism and communism during the second half of the 20th century. Hopefully this historical background, and my life antics, will make this a memoir of interest, leavened with a few dollops of humor

It's long been my sense that people with the urge to write are often driven by ego. A recent NEWSWEEK magazine seemed to confirm my theory when book reviewer Sean Smith opined: "Most people's lives are fascinating only to themselves, but that doesn't stop newbie writers from churning out memoirs that showcase mostly their own narcissism." Ouch! So I readily concede the writing of an autobiography must be considered the ultimate vanity. Now you know the kind of person with whom you're dealing.

Having quoted a sage from England, where my life began, let me also quote New England's reclusive Emily Dickinson whose haunting poetry so stirred America, the land where I have now lived so long. This poignant poem stayed in my mind since first reading it many years ago:

I took my Power in my Hand—
And went against the World—
'Twas not so much as David—had—
But I was twice as bold—
I aimed my Pebble—but Myself
Was all the one that fell—
Was it Goliath—was too large—
Or was myself—too small? (1)

CHAPTER 1

Mom opened the door to our small bedroom, stepped quietly in house slippers across to my bed, and gently shook my shoulder. An inner dread had woken me earlier but I pretended to be asleep. Not wanting to face the day, I kept up my pretense until Mom shook me again with more vigor.

When I opened my eyes, Mom's diminutive stature formed a silhouette with right arm outstretched balancing some clothes on her hand. The backdrop illumination emanated from the hall overhead bulb, its worn Victorian cloth shade with four pretentious, imitation-silk corner tassels. She hadn't switched on the bedroom light to avoid disturbing Roy, my two-year old brother, asleep in a small bed, separated and parallel to mine.

"It's time to get up, Alan," she bent forward to whisper close to my ear. "Today is yo… excursion to the countryside."

"I … " I whined, angrily turning toward the wall, … the pillow.

… Mom remonstrated gently while placing the … beds. "You'll wake Roy. Now don't be so … that you'll be with your school friends and …

… go," I repeated, now more awake, and … ce.

… rk this morning," Mom responded, tak… hold, "he told me the Council says you … n, we have to do what the Council says."

I … ng, it was no school outing. In any cas… was not the kind that offered outings. … children were crowded in a building … , and could have been easily mistaken f… we worked with old and second-rate textbooks, f… only the most basic equipment.

"Stop being so naughty!" Mom snapped with fatigue in her voice. Roy stirred but didn't wake.

"No more arguing! You can be so difficult. Wash, get dressed and come downstairs quickly. Wear the clean clothes I put on the chair. Hurry or we'll be late getting to the station."

My suspicion told me this was not a day's outing, or even one of several days. I'd seen Mom packing a suitcase with sets of my underwear, shirts and socks, short trousers, and a jacket. Now today's clean clothes were piled neatly on the chair. Why was I putting on fresh stuff in the middle of the week? Clean clothes were for Mondays, and they had to last all week.

Even my cantankerous self sensed I was not going to win this one. Sometimes I could drive a wedge between Mom and Dad, but this time they were hanging tough together. And I'd never had to reckon with the Council before. I accepted defeat and followed orders.

Irritably I cat-licked my face and hands in our second-floor tiny bathroom with its cast-iron sink fixed to the wall below a frosted half-pane window. The enamel tub in this room was the moveable type and hung on a wall peg when not in use. Our one commode, with its fixed wood bench seat and overhead chain-operated cistern, hid in a 3x3 foot brick cubicle attached at the rear of the house on the ground level. We had to go outside to gain access to that amenity. A loo visit in the winter was a cold encounter of the worst kind.

As I put on the clean clothes, I stared woefully at my brother still asleep in the dark side of the room. I accepted he was too young to go on this so-called outing because he wasn't even in school yet. But what about Vera, my six-year older sister? Miss Fancy Pants enjoyed her own bedroom. She wasn't finished with school yet, although soon would be. Why didn't she have to go? For days she'd been full of her own importance because she'd been designated to stay with Roy while Mom took me to the meeting place for our school. Life was so unfair!

My breakfast of bread, butter and jam, washed down by hot tea with milk and sugar, made me feel better. During the meal, Mom kept up intermittent propaganda on the many positives why I should be happy to go with my classmates today. Finally it went into my thick head that Mom, Dad, and the Council, whatever that vague entity, were going to resist my resistance.

Soon Mom and I were trudging along drab Whitta Road with its mundane row houses on one side and the prison-like eight-foot high wall, topped with broken glass, surrounding the London Cooperative Society's depot, on the other. We were on our way to Manor Park Station to travel to central London. Mom carried the suitcase, heavy with my clothing for summer and winter. I didn't understand why she had packed so much, especially the cold season stuff, if I was going for only a few days.

I carried the government-issued child gas mask in a khaki cardboard square box, suspended round my neck on a string. I really didn't know what it was for, but I knew I looked like a sissy with this thing bouncing slightly on my chest. There had been another fight with Mom over this silly gadget. She had been adamant that I carry it with me at all times, even keeping the dumb thing next to my bed. She'd won this battle as well. My recent domestic battle scores were dismal.

We traveled for well over an hour on steam and underground trains to reach Paddington Station in central London, the main rail terminal serving western England. I'd sat pouting in a sullen silence for most of the journey, no doubt trying to give Mom a guilt trip for what I perceived as her incredible cruelty. It is quite likely Mom didn't need any help of this nature from me that morning.

A broiling sea of humanity, civilian and military, thronged huge, cavernous, smoky Paddington Station, with its Victorian wrought iron, fluted columns supporting a curved glass roof which imparted the impression of being in a cathedral. I'd never seen so many people in one place, and most had the little cardboard boxes round their necks. Suddenly I disliked mine less.

Service personnel from all three branches were on the move. The Army men sported canvas web harnesses, and some had rifles slung on shoulder straps. They all seemed to tote large duffel bags and other forms of baggage. Their military boots made so much noise as they clumped across the cement platforms. I figured they all must be strong, and momentarily forgot my unhappiness.

Mom found out that all school excursion children were assembling at several remoter platforms. There I recognized a couple of boys I knew and wanted to go to them. But Mom said before I could do that we had to line up and do something called "registering." It seemed we waited forever although I was distracted enough by all the activity to forget my anxious impatience. When we reached the table, several of our own teachers were seated on the other side filling in forms with our names, addresses, ages, something called gender, hair and eye color, even something called religious preference, and finally one called destination. Several of these categories I didn't know I had, but the last one I thought, ominously, I knew what it meant.

When our turn came, Mom produced a letter from that hated Council and the teacher wrote information on several forms. It seems I was a male gender, but I could have told them that long ago. As to religion, it startled me to find I had a preference for the Church of England. To the best of this eight-year-old's memory, the last time I was in a church was for baptism, but I really couldn't remember that at all.

Then something happened that seemed most foreboding. A teacher came around the table and tied a large, tan luggage label to my jacket lapel buttonhole. Aside from personal data, the destination line was filled in. It read "Cirencester, Gloucestershire." It dawned on me that I, along with a lot of other innocents, was being shipped off like a package to that strange-sounding place. Now I was surer than ever that I wanted no part of this pantomime. I wanted to go home.

Once registered, we jostled through the station's swarming crowd, most people present that particular morning because of this thing called World War II. As we approached the platform entrance to our special train, and because of departure time's approach, I suppose Mom felt it necessary to let me know finally that she would not be coming on the trip. I'd suspected this all along, but Mom had always evaded my direct questions. At last she'd confirmed my fears, and I responded with a flood that welled up from deep within, quickly smearing my face with salty tears and slime. Between the loud sobbing and a heaving chest, I kept proclaiming my regret for my entire past bad behavior and all I ever wanted was to stay at home with my Mom and Dad.

My noise attracted a uniformed monitor once we reached the platform control barrier. Mom handed her our documentation and said a few words to this lady who had a name and title plate fixed to her lapel. She knelt down and grasped my shoulders.

"Don't be so upset, little boy," she said to my downcast, sodden face. "These are times when our young ones must be brave. As brave as all these soldiers and sailors we see here today."

They're brave, I thought, because they've got guns and big boots. But all I managed, between continuing sobs, was my plea to go home, feeling certain of its eminent reasonableness.

She stood up and said something to Mom. They both took one of my hands and I was more or less dragged along despite my lachrymose objections. A railway guard at the train's tail end took the suitcase from Mom. A few of these men had formed a chain and were passing the luggage, each with its identity tag, into the goods wagon.

Now, as we walked beside the train looking for the carriages that would accommodate my school and particular class, I tried to control myself. Just when I felt I had things in hand, I'd think about my imminent separation from Mom and start sobbing again. But at the same time I dreaded my schoolmates seeing me in such a watery state.

Not many fathers were present because of military service or performing essential work requiring their full-time attendance. Some children stood close to their mothers, only a few tearful or looking most apprehensive. Other children, however, were talking with their classmates and seemed to have their emotions in check. Towards the front of the long train, I saw children from my very own class. I tried even harder to suppress the occasional sob that still found its way to the surface.

Shortly, station personnel came along directing each school group into their carriages and then class groups into assigned compartments. Mom stooped to give me a couple of quick kisses. This shattered my rickety emotional dam and the crying started again. Now my weeping was not deterred by the presence of schoolmates. Nothing had precedence over the fact I was about to be sent away from my parents. My overly sensitive nature manifested itself for that wartime crowd to see. My extreme embarrassment could not restrain it.

A surge of children trying to get window seats jostled me up the iron steps and into the carriage corridor. I didn't care about looking out because my vision was blurred by what seemed like unstoppable tears. My bursting chest hurt filled beyond capacity with a first-ever level of intense grief. When I reached my assigned compartment, a wall of small, shoving bodies pressed against the window. But by climbing on a seat I could see over their heads to Mom. I don't believe she could see me, and certainly not hear me, as I called out the same appellation of endearment coming from every child's tongue that morning.

A universal gasp came from its cargo of small humans as the train momentarily jolted when it lurched twice before settling into a smooth forward roll. Instantly every child on the train and every parent on the platform waved frantically and called out to each other even more loudly. Through the forest of swaying arms, I saw my mother for the briefest time before she was gone from my view. Weak with a previously unknown sadness, I slumped into a seat and covered my face to sob into my hands. Mom and Dad and the wicked Council were sending me into the countryside to be billeted with strangers just because of a war going on a long way away. My up-to-now happy world crumbled! I knew that I was but one in a trainload of children whose lives were about to similarly shatter, but my pain was the only pain that counted.

This chapter is, in fact, the product of my imagination. The reality is I have retained only one or two blurry memories of trivia from that long ago day and its forced journey. It is a fact I attended Salisbury Road Junior School, Manor Park, East Ham borough, crammed into London's East End. Under this voluntary but strongly encouraged evacuation program, the children of this school were sent to Gloucestershire, in the west of England, provided their parents consented. We were resettled near Cirencester, once site of a Roman garrison, only 85 miles from central London, and about 100 miles from home. But for me at the time it could have been 100 million light years away.

A psychiatrist once conjectured that perhaps emotional problems I encountered years later might have had their origins in that first enforced separation from my family. Perhaps I repressed memories of the journey because of their pain. If the doctor's theory is correct, and my gut feeling is he was on to something, it could explain a few events in my erratic life.

CHAPTER 2

It is, perhaps, an exaggeration to compare London's East End of the 1930s with the favelas of today's Rio de Janeiro. But this British contribution to world communities where their citizens lived brutish, hopeless lives ranked high in the league of man-made monuments to soulessness. The need for early London planners to inexpensively house a vast, dirt-poor population, which provided a source of cheap manual laborers and service workers for the burgeoning metropolis, overrode any consideration for the human spirit or aesthetics. Even now, in spite of recent urban renewal efforts, thousands of cramped, featureless streets spread east for miles from the edge of London's financial district, known as "the City."

These streets are monotonously lined with small, mean, back-to-back, two-story, brick row houses with front doors opening onto the public sidewalk. Passing traffic and pedestrian noise and dust seep into the houses even with windows and doors shut. Soothing domestic privacy is a luxury not afforded to the residents of these basic abodes. They tend to produce a hardened occupant on a par with the character brittleness of today's homeless.

Professor Sir Cyril Burt, a psychologist at University College, London, 1932-50, produced sensitive insights from his research on East End Cockney kids of that time (1). In the professor's words: "The vocabulary that the child absorbs is restricted to a few hundred words, most of them inaccurate, uncouth, or mispronounced, and the rest unfit for reproduction in the schoolroom. In the home there is no literature that deserves the title; and the child's whole universe is closed in and circumscribed by walls of brick and a pall of smoke."

On cold days, clay chimneys, jutting above gray/black slate roof tiles, puffed forth listless spirals of poisonous smoke from open-grate bituminous coal fires that inefficiently heated a single living/kitchen area within. This source of London's infamous yellow smog which descended for days when climatic conditions contrived to bring the nation's capital to a virtual halt.

It is only as this ugly urban outward sprawl nears the boundary of Essex County are the houses adorned with minuscule front gardens which, in slower and gentler times, allowed some occupants to grow a sprinkling of hardy plants and bushes to soften the harshness of the bleak streets. Nowadays, these gardens increasingly disappear under cement to make off-road parking for the motoring age of the common man.

In more recent years, the soft coals gave way to anthracite, a cleaner domestic heating fuel, and some houses converted to oil-fired central heating. Thus, the lethal effect of London's home heating has been largely eliminated. However, with a perversity that often stalks the work of humankind, automobile exhaust fumes now are a significant health risk. Further, the clutter of cars of varying degrees of disrepair parked along East End streets has surely done nothing for community attractiveness. One cannot help wondering about the common man's thoughts as he sits stymied in mega traffic gridlock on the tight little island's constipated highways. Is he any more mobile—socially or spatially—in his symbolic automobile than his father who could hardly move when a London pea souper settled in? It seems to me, as the old saw goes, one step forward and two back.

To be born in London's East End started one with an instant stigma in English society. It's the American equivalent of birth on the wrong side of the tracks. But while all societies have similar socially grading birthmarks, in England the birthmark was more like scar tissue. Certainly in America one could cross to the other side with greater facility.

With life's arbitrariness, I emerged into the world to join an English working-class family on 27 March 1932 at one of these row houses with a small front garden. In that year Sir James Chadwick, the Englishman pursuing the mind-bending discipline of modern physics at Cavendish Laboratory, Cambridge University, discovered the neutron. This is one of the fundamental particles of an atom, and led to the bomb of that name. Although I don't really believe these two events were related, the big boys were thinking small. I fitted in at a little over six lbs. and stretching all of 17 inches.

This debut occurred in Manor Park, a deceptively pleasant name for a solidly working-class area located at the eastern edge of London's jurisdiction. Presumably, when this district was named, a manor house and a park were located there, but had been long gone when I arrived.

The postal district immediately to the west, Forest Gate, to which we later moved, referred to its historic past as the gateway to Epping Forest, an extensive hunting preserve popular with successive monarchs. Over subsequent centuries many tracts of the forest were leveled to permit London's constant outward march. Nowadays the boundary of a greatly reduced Epping Forest is found about 30 miles north. All the wild boars are gone, and Royalty never visits.

During World War I, my father in 1915, at age 13, started work locally at the bottling and distribution center of a large national brewery. He was informally apprenticed to become a bricklayer, both the trade and workplace of his own father. The education of working class children had never been a significant consideration of the British government. "... only in 1880 did education become compulsory for children up to 10 years, extended at the end of the century to 12. These were days of acute poverty and they lived in depressing and unsanitary conditions..." (2)

Dad harbored dissatisfaction with his life prospects. At 17, he undertook the mandated learning necessary to become a London taxi driver, a big decision. Inherently shy, he displayed a lot of get-up-and-go by taking early charge of his life. He avoided the footsteps of his own father into a grim, dull life, exacerbated by heavy drinking encouraged by free beer available to brewery employees.

Becoming a London cabby entails learning the geography of the huge metropolis, at least the inner core segments. In the trade, this process is called "getting the knowledge," and Dad required about three years to complete. Without an automobile, on weekends, in the evenings, and during vacations, he walked or cycled the streets of London and studied maps. By my calculation, Dad passed the stiff Metropolitan Police-administered test and started as a cabby in 1922 at age 20. He never owned his own cab, always driving for a garage, known as "mushing," that maintained a fleet of some twenty. He continued chauffeuring humanity through London's twisting streets for more than 50 years, interrupted only by four years of Army service during World War II.

At the time he began driving, the clip-clop of horse-drawn Hansom cabs, which rang through London for over a century, was being silenced forever by the gasoline-operated motor taximeter cab that turned on its own radius in deference to the capital's narrow streets. These first motor cabs had no windshields and were open at the driver's side to accommodate ocean trunks for people journeying to the corners of Britain's then far-flung empire. My father wore goggles and bundled up against the cold winters. When it rained, he wrapped himself, up to his armpits, in a tarpaulin with his feet protruding below. He put in long hours behind the wheel of his cab to bring home money enough to keep food on the table. At some point he worked nights to improve his earnings of which two-thirds of the total were retained by the cab owner, and Dad received one third, plus tips.

Dad's mother, Annie Davies (1873-1952), was our proverbial family skeleton. A fairly common occurrence of the times, this sensitive woman found herself trapped in a marriage to an unthinking, heavy drinker. Over the years, her harsh domestic circumstances eroded her fragile spirit. Then, approaching menopause, she had her fifth child, a boy. When he reached age five, sometimes she would not let him go to school. Or, if she did, after he came home for lunch, she'd prevent him returning. Perhaps she clung to this child because he represented the only love and warmth in her life. This pattern of behavior went on for upwards of a year. Eventually an exasperated school authority successfully applied to have her committed to a mental hospital.

To the best of my recollection my parents never talked about her while Roy and I were in their presence. Grandma Davies was committed to a mental hospital in 1923/24 to remain there until she died in 1952 at age 79. Roy or I never visited her. I don't know the clinical nature of the malady that engulfed her. From what I've heard it could have been obsessive-compulsive disorder, depression, or even schizophrenia. As the years passed, she grew more disoriented. My sister, Vera, who used to visit her, said that in later years this paternal grandmother would brush imaginary insects from her nightgown sleeves.

The family tree on my mother's side also sprouted a few none-too-healthy branches. Her father, born in 1868, committed suicide in the kitchen gas oven in 1934, two years after my birth. Again, these two events are not to be assumed as related. I have no recollection of him, and this is probably just as well. According to family gossip, he never worked regularly because of seriously defective eyesight. My parent's June 1925 marriage certificate records him as a "house decorator." Hitler, too, did a stint at this calling, but Mom's Dad confined his demonism strictly to his personal domestic setting. Although he had no steady income, he fathered eight children, of which my mother was the youngest. He also found the funds required to spend great amounts of time and money at local pubs. My maternal grandmother, who took in ironing to help raise a few pennies while caring for her large brood, was forced on occasion to pawn her iron when things got really tight.

One story about my mother's parents says it all, or at least a great deal, about the downtrodden plight of working-class women in those days. No doubt with the domestic situation beyond desperate, this grandmother challenged her husband when he came home from the pub one night. She met him at the door and asked, probably with typical English politeness, if he knew "the lateness of the hour," holding up an alarm clock to make the point. It's reliably reported her husband, by way of clever response, snatched the clock from her hand and smashed it into her face shouting "that's the time if you really want to know." Not long before she died, my mother said I looked a lot like her father. I'm rather glad it's too late now to ask what she meant by this comparison.

My knowledge is scanty of my mother's employment after she left school at age 14 in 1917. Prior to marriage in 1925 she worked for a while in a small plant near the financial district hand-rolling cigars from imported Cuban-cured tobacco leaves. While it must have been an excruciatingly dull occupation, it was representative of the types of manual work then available to uneducated girls. In the tradition of the British working class, my mother stopped working outside the home once Vera, her first child, was born, a year after their civil ceremony wedding.

I have a listing of houses where my parents lived during their married lifetime. It comprises 17 addresses in and around east London. They never lived farther than about 25 miles from the same street on which they spent their childhood, met, and courted. This long list could lead one to assume they were constantly just one jump ahead of the rent collector. Mom once said, however, these frequent moves were motivated always by the effort to find the best accommodation for the least money. They could afford to purchase their own home only 22 years after marrying.

At one of these stops on life's journey we occupied the upstairs apartment (or flat in Britain) where I fell and rolled down, from top to bottom, a flight of wooden stairs leading to the garden. On yet another occasion, I broke a glass bottle and severed the tendon in the second finger of my left hand. I survived the fall, but the finger has never since properly closed. I made yet another attempt to destroy myself at about age three. As I explored the apartment, I discovered a box of Ex-lax. I couldn't remove the silver foil fast enough when I found each shiny packet contained chocolate, the king of foods, in bite-sized pieces. In nothing flat I'd devoured the lot. Mom told me I groaned for days.

In spite of this tendency to self-mutilation, in 1937 I started at the local junior state school for children 5-7 years, creatively named "4th Avenue School." From family comments I recall in later years, it appears I took to school on a par with others. There is even a faint recollection of having a piece of work hung on a classroom wall, which gave me good vibes. The fact I was pumped does indicate I had an interest in what was going on inside that Victorian building. I like to believe this memory might indicate a potential serious student, only to be thwarted by the impending global World War II. But probably, every kid's work hung on that wall!

It does seem I early displayed a hamish streak because I was cast in several class plays. In one I appeared as a blade of grass, a rabbit in another. The drama teacher must have finally decided I qualified to play a human and gambled on me to play a serf in a crowd scene from the Middle Ages. Subsequently, I appeared as Rumpelstiltskin, and also as Good King Wenceslaus' page. Later I performed as Scrooge in Christmas Carol. This apparent thespian talent had, I now suspect, more to do with my voice, which is naturally loud and carries far, rather than native acting talent. But my small stature eventually extinguished my promise for great attainment on stage and screen.

The first wreck on the road to dousing of theatrical ambitions came with the Scrooge role. In one scene I had to retrieve a bathrobe from a wall peg. During the play's only performance, with the entire school enrollment in attendance, it transpired I couldn't reach the garment. The stage carpenter had forgotten my lack of inches. I started boisterously jumping to dislodge the stupid thing, causing the scenery wall to sway, almost topple. This gymnastic display tended to destroy the proper portrayal of Scrooge as a rickety, irascible, old man. The audience broke into laughter, impolite and loud. I painfully recollect glancing to the wings where stood our drama teacher, hands covering face, her head rotating slightly in well-recognized denial.

But the real destruction of my acting ambitions came in 1945 at age 13. One of the few studios then producing movies in Britain geared up to film Charles Dickens' "Great Expectations," to be released in 1947. The studio put out an advertising short with a young John Mills (later Sir John Mills following a successful stage and film career), which I saw at a local cinema, seeking a boy to play the main character, Pip, as a child. John Mills played Pip as an adult. Boys wanting to be considered were invited to attend a selection review at an Odeon cinema in West London. Now with an extensive theatrical background, I fancied my chances. But the selection site was on the other side of London. Mom generously advanced the two shillings and six pence (Britain's pre-decimal currency) needed for the round-trip fare. Don't even ask what it costs today!

The cinema soon flooded with aspiring Pips on that fateful day. We were told to sit in the center block of front seats. Probably we boys were filled with as much nervous hope as we'd experience a few fears into the future on our wedding nights.

Once the selection process started, decisions came rapidly. All the Pips were told to stand, and two destiny-empowered females from casting walked up two aisles scanning each row and dismissing these too tall or short, or lacking the required Cambridge-Boys-Choir angelic aura. One swift glance and I struck out for inadequate height. I don't believe they even took account of my aura. The world lost a second Alex Guinness, albeit a short version and my mother lost her investment. But I've gotten ahead of myself. Yet to come is a world conflagration in which I did play a role, selected or not.

Mother at 21; father at 22, a year before they married. (Photo 1924).

Vera aged 8 and me aged 2. (Photo 1934).

CHAPTER 3

Family gossip has the arrival in 1938 of my brother, Roy, a third child, as an unintended addition. Knowledgeable, but obviously biased relatives, report my mother had cooled to the prospect of more children after my birth. Whatever the facts, a recollection persists from 1937/8 of hearing my parents talk about the possibility of war. Exact comments aren't recalled, but I was conscious of a certain constraint in their voices. A child's uncanny, indelible perception of its parent's emotional tension possibly registered their conversation with me.

Certainly such concern invaded millions of British households. After all, a mere 20 years had passed since WWI with its trench warfare horrors. Ordinary people were intensely concerned about the new gathering storm, to use Winston Churchill's words, even though few could articulate their fears with his eloquence. As the prospect of war came closer, families with the means began to leave the country for British Commonwealth nations and America. Others moved from the bigger cities, London in particular, to rural areas. About two million people, primarily middle class, evacuated at their own expense from larger conurbations (3).

The flight from London of one schoolteacher enabled my parents to rent their best living quarters so far. In mid 1939 we moved to a four-bedroom house in Forest Gate, the adjacent postal district. Although just another row house, it faced a large public common. A cemetery bordered the rear garden, separated by a six-foot brick wall. I know the height because I fell from it several times. The section of the council-owned cemetery immediately to the back of us contained older graves overgrown through neglect. This meant we had no houses in front or rear, providing spaciousness rare in East London, and I had two extensive play areas.

Our newly rented house, at 161 Capel Road, possessed one feature establishing that we had moved an inch up the social ladder. A chute, its grated entry just outside the front door, permitted the coal deliveryman to pour our heating bituminous directly into a cellar. He arrived, a sackful on his back, covered head-to-toe with coal dust and looking like a Negro minstrel, only eyes and teeth showing white. At our former residences he had to stomp through the house to tip his sack's contents into a storage bin in the rear. This front-garden chute was progress indeed!

Another telltale indication that the fleeing schoolteacher inhabited a world different from ours was a cache of twenty or so abandoned books found in a bedroom closet. I believe they were the first books possessed in our family because I can recall they were discussed. It remains in my memory as something of a noteworthy incident, even though I don't know if any members of our household read them. Much closer to my sphere of interest was the mature Morello cherry tree growing close to the house in the back garden. A fence, demarcating our property from the neighbor's, provided a convenient platform from which I could reach lower branches. I suspect my early passion for that Morello, with its shiny, gray-brown bark, revealed my inherited tree-climbing DNA.

When we moved into the house in early summer 1939, the cherries weren't ripe. While all Britain fretted about Armageddon inching ever closer, I was the happiest East London kid. Every day after school I was swiftly up in the Morello locked in my own war against a persistent enemy in the form of local sparrows and starlings that seemed to like the fruit as much as I did. However, I soon withdrew wounded from the battle: the sour cooking cherries worked with incredible efficiency.

That Morello served to inspire me to tackle several much taller trees standing just on the other side of the cemetery wall. Courtesy of the far end of that same fence, I could gain the top of the wall, balance along it, and reach the first of the high trees. I loved climbing them but lacked the intellectual curiosity to learn their types in whose branches I mounted. My small size and lightweight enabled me to ascend almost to their tops, well above the slate tile roofs of the row houses. From there I could see Wanstead, on the other side of the common, a solidly middle-class district with detached single-family homes. Our imposing, proper school headmaster lived there. I was not, of course, then conscious of the social stratification of British society. And while perhaps most of those born on the wrong side of the tracks remained there in contented, blissful ignorance, a few, including me, were destined to be lifelong protesters of its inequities.

On 3 September 1939 a solemn voice announced on the radio that Britain and France were at war with Germany because of its invasion of

Poland. I don't remember what was said in our house, and we kids were separated by six years between each one so that we were at significantly different comprehension levels. The government warned the nation to anticipate attack from the air because Hitler had used aircraft so effectively in his successful blitzkrieg on the European continent. Britain awaited with nerve-tingling dread the drone of German bombers.

One of the first manifestations that life was going to be different came when street night-lights stayed dark and people were ordered to "blackout" residences. In response, along with millions of others, my parents hung dark material on the inside of windows to block electric light at night from providing navigational aid to enemy aircraft. Although the bombing maelstrom did not immediately materialize, Mom and Dad decided to temporarily relocate under a national government evacuation program through the local council just in case.

Declining the East Ham Council's offer of rail tickets to get there, Dad rented his cab from its owner and drove Mom and us three children to Hemsby, the designated evacuation village about 10 miles north of Great Yarmouth, Norfolk, near the North Sea. The village clergyman had volunteered to take an evacuation family, and we were sent there. It appeared the good man was offering his Vicarage to a terrified London family to do his part for the nation in time of war. Even if God wasn't impressed, presumably village churchgoers and parish elders would be. In reality, Mom filled his vacant position for a cook (meal preparation and all kitchen cleaning) for him and his wife, and their two chaste, early-teen daughters. Mom, Roy and I moved into the large vicarage, its roof tiles encrusted with moss. Dad and Vera returned to London. My sister would be finishing school and starting work at age 14 in a few months.

What Mom didn't know was the religious family had recently lost its German housekeeper/cook/maid/scullery helper who had fled back to the Fatherland. Domestic servants had suddenly become scarce because more lucrative jobs were opening up as men were called to military service and women were finding a broader range of opportunities in an economy rapidly changing. No doubt desperate to prevent their cozy lifestyle from disappearing into the vortex of world events, what the vicar and his wife really had in mind was quick replacement of their probably conscientious, hard-working, and slavishly obedient German domestic. As I later came to see Mom's personality, she was not the person to step into those Teutonic shoes. While the vicar received an allowance for billeting us, his wife expected Mom to do all the cooking and washing-up for everyone in the Vicarage. My parents could justify this state of affairs only by the arrival of German bombs from the sky.

I can recall virtually nothing about the large brick Vicarage other than the huge, dark kitchen that housed the religious family's extensive collection of steel pots and pans. Mom spent a lot of time in that gloomy room. I did, too, but not, I confess, in the role of Mom's helper. Yet I recall one particular morning I selected a shiny cooking pot, put it on my head, and marched around the kitchen as a fearless British soldier. Hitler would have to tangle with me if he tried any funny business with us Brits! Suddenly Mrs. Vicar loomed large in the doorway. Apparently totally unimpressed by my military pride and preparedness, she launched a lightning, frontal attack, under which I caved in.

"You dirty little urchin! How dare you use my expensive saucepan in that disgusting way? You'll sicken my daughters with your horrible London germs!"

Mom received a lecture on discipline and was made to scour my tin helmet and put it back in its proper place. Mom, too, must have said something to me about my proper place. We remained with the religious family six weeks. Mom didn't relish the servant status, and I found the stiff atmosphere oppressive. On a Sunday not long after, Dad again rented his taxi for a day and drove to Hemsby. He loaded his family and their few suitcases and we returned to London. That the nation was officially at war with two of history's biggest dictators didn't bother me because I enjoyed the 125-mile journey through the countryside in a taxicab like a real middle-class person coming home from an East Coast vacation.

Many years later I learned the first German bomb to fall on Britain in World War II exploded near Great Yarmouth. A lone reconnaissance plane on its way back across the North Sea after surveying parts of East Anglia, future site of many RAF and USAF bases, released it. Ironically we had moved, at our own expense, to the very area where the first bomb struck!

Now back in London, I became eligible in March 1940 for admission to the next level of state co-educational school for children 8 to 11 years. I switched to Salisbury, the nearest junior elementary school, just about half a mile from our rented house. The four- or five-story drab brick building epitomized Victorian era construction. Located in a commercial area, not a single tree or bush grew in the school playground.

There were no toilets inside the building, at least for the pupils, with the boys' across the playground in a shed. We waited until break time to use it. Students were not allowed to raise a hand during class to be excused. This sanitary facility had a long trough urinal and we lined up without embarrassment, shoulder-to-shoulder, to relieve ourselves. Sometimes, if no male teachers on playground duty were nearby, we would step back to see who could achieve the highest pee arc. I never won either because of stature or inadequate propulsive thrust. Although annoyed, I never sought clarification whether my deficiency was architectural, mechanical, or mental.

While our old tattered and uninspiring school textbooks were in short supply, each classroom displayed a new-looking, wall-mounted, framed photograph of the current monarch. Also hanging on some walls were colored world maps, with the many British Empire nations highlighted in red. All this red represented the largest empire the world had ever seen, covering twelve million square miles, or one-fifth of earth's land surface. It contained nearly 400 million people, some quarter of the world's population (1). None of this did I then know. While the subtle brainwash inherent in the royal visage in each classroom then escaped me, I did fall prey to the red-splotched, patriotism-promoting atlases. I can distinctly recall being swept by a wave of boyish pride when I looked at these maps. A kind of cheerleader enthusiasm surged in me with the vague feeling I was somehow special by virtue of being a Brit, the world's big shots. Look at all that red! Little did I then realize how small the percentage of the British population privileged to benefit from the wealth generated by that vast empire. Conning people works best when they are young.

In the late spring of 1940, one or two air probes over the south coast took place and authorities again warned bombing would commence momentarily. The national government and London County Council now implemented its voluntary mass evacuation for school children. I've already reconstructed in chapter one my conjecture of the first day of the separation from my family. It would have been a long, traumatic day for this impatient boy.

If parents in large cities had equivocated up to now, they must have been convinced in unison. By the end of the war, more than three million children had relocated (2). Schools moved as complete units so that its children remained together in the new location to theoretically lessen the trauma of removal from their families. They would at least have the companionship of their own school acquaintances. Even so, for more sensitive children, this was an uncertain, scary time.

In the villages, the children were billeted in homes of people who volunteered and demonstrated to the local council that they had sufficient space. Billeting families received an allowance of ten shillings and six pence (in the former Sterling monetary system) for boarding and feeding one child and eight shillings and six pence for each additional evacuee (3). This mass migration of predominantly working-class children into rural, conservative and structured communities produced its share of friction. The big city children tended to be less disciplined and generally grungier than the local specimens. When these small displaced persons arrived at the local train station, bewildered and already missing their homes, they were put in the hands of local officials steeped in the politics of village life. Probably, over a pint at the local pub, these officials had been quietly advised by local wealthy families with large houses of their reluctance to open their doors to the refugees. It was in the tiny cottages of the farm hands, who could use the cash allowance, where the displaced children wound up. As an example, in one country town prominent citizens who failed to open their homes included the vicar, town clerk, bank manager, and even the chief billeting officer himself (4).

No doubt I brought to this extraordinary affair a genetic emotional make-up less stable than would have been desirable. Ironically, an uprooting intended to preserve that very life severed my eight-year olds sense of life continuity. Although the program obviously saved the lives of many children, it was a massive disruption for them and their families. In later life I wondered, cynically, if my generation had been saved for no other reason than this war might consume as many lives as its predecessor. We'd be needed for cannon fodder. To present a balanced view, it must be mentioned the national government, stretched to the breaking point conducting a worldwide war, found the time to prepare and distribute a guidance pamphlet about children who were bed-wetters. This pamphlet was for householders who took on the responsibility of billeting children who manifested this nervous problem. Years later I read of Sigmund

Freud's daughter, Anna, who conducted studies on the trauma children suffered when separated from their parents. She concluded that, no matter the danger, children below age three should not be removed from the natural family and its home setting (5).

In time, we learned Hitler delayed attacking Britain hoping his early, overwhelming military successes on the Continent would cause us to surrender. When Britain remained defiant, however, in spring 1940 the Luftwaffe launched an aerial bombardment of daylight raids against strategic British targets.

In preparation, a scrambling British government distributed an arched, corrugated-steel air raid shelter to individual households. The "Anderson shelter," named for the government minister whose department oversaw its design and production, quickly became the "the doghouse." It offered protection for up to six people from a near-miss high explosive bomb, but not a direct hit. Erection involved sinking it in the back yard into an 8x5 feet rectangle pit dug to a depth of 3.5-4 feet. The soil from the pit was then thrown over the top and tamped. There was no floor, and with Britain's rain-prone climate and high groundwater levels, standing water often developed; not an inviting sanctuary at the country's northern latitudes. Dad installed ours.

During the summer of 1940, in unusually glorious weather, the Royal Air Force wrestled with the Luftwaffe high in the skies above England's green fields. Although outnumbered, the RAF possessed swifter, more maneuverable planes, with perhaps better pilots. Britain's radar system, although primitive, gave some advance warning of approaching enemy aircraft. The RAF inflicted such heavy losses on the Luftwaffe that Hitler changed tactics. Starting in September, his squadrons of death arrived in darkness to drop thousands of tons of bombs on and round London and a few other cities. These were hideous times for the people crowded in the bigger cities. Relief came only when fog settled over coastal France and prevented the mighty Luftwaffe from taking to the air. While the destruction of strategic targets remained an objective, the Germans also hit randomly to terrorize the civilian population in the hopes it would now press its government to surrender.

Defending London had become the responsibility of anti-aircraft batteries, which had limited success, as RAF fighter planes could not operate in the hours of darkness. Night after night, week after week, month after month, squadrons of German Dorniers, Heinkels, Junkers and Messerschmitts left French airfields to drop their bombs almost freely on assigned targets in England (6). This relentless nightly onslaught stretched taut the nerves of the affected citizens. They felt so defenseless against the bombs raining down on them from planes that could be heard but not seen. Bad enough during the daytime, people now had to retreat to the bleakness of their air raid shelters in the pitch black. They put camp beds and old armchairs in them to improve their comfort. Candles were the main source of lighting. People who lived closer to central London, whose back-to-back houses had no rear garden, went to the basements of large buildings designated as public shelters. Those living near London's underground (subway) system bedded down on its platforms. Heart-stirring photos of these nightly subterranean dwellers, which portrayed the civilian hardships so poignantly, went around the world.

During the winter of 1940/41 citizens scurried to their doghouses almost every night while the air raids were in progress, returning to their houses only when the all-clear sirens sounded. Then a pot of tea, the traditional British beverage, was relished before going back to bed for an hour or two prior to facing another workday. I believe the solace in a cup of tea helped most British working-class civilians through the horrors of German aerial warfare.

It was not one of the grander moments in Britain's imperial history when a goodly portion of its city dwellers spent night after night cowering in their half-submerged tin bunkers. While this became almost a constant feature of their hard lives, the wealthy were snug in their thick stonewalled, solid country manors, mostly fortified with good Cognac. The bombing continued unabated until June 1941.

Alan (circa 1940/41) among cabbages in back yard at house on Capel Road, London E.7., England. Note the "thumbs up" stance. Life seemed to go downhill thereafter!

CHAPTER 4

My Salisbury Junior School went en masse to Gloucestershire, a pretty county, with wooded, gently rolling hills and open downs. It's an enchantingly English region as evidenced by its selection for the estates of several members of British Royalty. Wool merchants in the Middle Ages amassed great wealth that today is reflected in the magnificence of churches they built for the community and the beauty of gracious manorial houses they constructed for themselves. These structures were built from the eye-appealing, honey-colored, soft limestone quarried locally from the underlying rolling hills (1).

Probably because of random selection, I was not assigned to a village family. Six boys, me included, ranging in age from seven or eight to 12 or 13 years, were billeted at the Waterton estate of Sir Wilfred and Lady Margaret Snelling, near the village of Ampney Crucis, three miles east of Cirencester. Sir Wilfred Lawson Snelling was a solid member of the upper middle class. Educated at Harrow, one of England's leading private schools, followed by Balliol College, Oxford, he went to India with a commercial company at age 23 where he remained more than 20 years. Upon his return to England, at age 45, he became a director of Anglo-Persian Oil Company from which he retired in 1946 at age 72. In 1928 he received a knighthood (2).

While Waterton had all the trappings of a rich family's estate, including a manorial house, it operated a working farm. The labor force included two farm supervisors who qualified to live in cottages on the estate and were exempt from war service because of their vital work. A number of older farm hands lived in the village and rode bicycles daily to the estate. Another component of the farm workforce was four members of the Women's Land Army. These WLA sisters, looking dapper in their government-issued tan military jackets, jodhpurs, calf-high boots, and modified cowboy hats, also occupied one of the cottages. The WLA had its origin in the First World War, but was de-commissioned in 1918. When war clouds again raced towards Britain, the WLA was re-formed in June 1939 (3).

Because of his expertise in world oil supplies, at the beginning of the war Sir Snelling had been seconded to the national government ministry handling energy supplies. At that time Britain produced no petroleum, relying on imports. His oil market knowledge must have made him a vital member of the organization, and I assume his duties required his almost constant presence. I don't recall ever seeing him at the estate.

Sir Snelling's absence, however, didn't mean we boys moved into his manor house with its five storys and 12 chimneys. Along with other wealthy families, the Snellings presumably wanted to do their part for the war effort. Nevertheless, this didn't extend to six young east Londoners sleeping under the same roof. The farm workers' cottages were grouped together at some distance from the manor. Also dotted about here were several equipment barns, Shire horse stables, and a long row stable with stalls for eight saddle horses. The family had once owned such riding horses, but they'd been sold because of the emergency. We six boys were allocated to the vacant saddle horse stable, but fortunately not the stalls. On the second floor were a series of rooms once used to accommodate the grooms, now also gone. One large room was converted to a dormitory with six beds. We ate in a nook in the makeshift kitchen along the 2nd floor hallway. Another room held some beat-up, over-stuffed armchairs, and this served as our den/rumpus room. This equestrian building was to be home for the next 14 months, so different from my real one.

Although the local authorities arranged our billeting with admirable speed, it proved to be weeks before a hastily-organized village school opened to receive our variegated band of young refugees. An east London woman, who accompanied her own pubescent daughter into evacuation, got the job to take care of us. A rough, unkempt person, who frequently dangled a cigarette from her lips, remains in my memory. Presumably the government allowance paid for each of us went to the Waterton estate, and it, in turn, paid this woman and our living expenses.

While we waited for the school opening, when confined to the rumpus room on wet days, time dragged heavily for us normally active children. We stood at the rain-splattered windows looking down at the strange world of damp, muddy farmyard activity. Such days were sad. Too much time to think about home and family. There were no organized activities for us displaced school kids. I believe I remember a few board games in our quarters, sent from the Snelling manor. They must have been the property of the Snelling children who were now grown. But I can recall no books, possibly because we were viewed as non-reading types. Had there been books around, I probably wouldn't have used them. But without access and a little direction, most eight year-old boys don't gravitate to books. I soon fell into the idle mind and devil's playground trap.

Notwithstanding, our new locale and circumstances slowly became more familiar and comfortable. Individually we adjusted to this alien rural environment so different from our urban habitat. I now suspect that acclimation proceeded with a growing, if unrecognized, enthusiasm as the surrounding natural beauty impressed itself on our young minds. We roamed the countryside until school opened and then after school and on Saturdays, in an expanding radius from the estate.

In these countryside excursions, the older boys didn't want the younger ones tagging along. We usually broke into two groups of three each, those above 10 years and those below. We bonded like true orphans. Redolent orchards dotted the area with row after row of evenly spaced apple, pear, and plum trees. We looked for vulnerable spots in their defensive hedgerows or dry stonewalls where eight-year olds could gain access. And make a quick escape. I honed my skills as a tree climber. Once the fruit was ripe we returned to help ourselves, which is known, in best English slang, as "scrumping." We were chased away by several irate orchardists and learned to select our targets by the owner's lack of youthfulness and sprint capacity.

We wandered the village lanes, making idiotic remarks about the tiny thatched cottages with their small, irregular, lead-framed windows, like elf houses in picture books. We waded in the Ampney stream, flowing through the village. Once we cornered a water rat and with sticks beat the poor animal to death. We annoyed the locals by our noise and disrespect. They might well have preferred a German invasion to a trainload of undisciplined, uncouth and unwashed east London kids.

The Waterton estate farm pasteurized milk. It also devoted acreage for wheat and barley cultivation. The farm was not mechanized and these crops were cut by threshing machines drawn by Shire draft horses. Such Equus caballus specimens weighed up to 2,300 lbs. and stood 16 to 17 hands. Sometimes when the workers returned from the fields they would urge me to lead one of these powerful beasts of burden through the farm yard to its stable because my size contrasted rather noticeably with that of the horse. I made for farm worker entertainment, and clearly remember leading several of these behemoths while terrified they would suddenly bolt and I'd be squashed flat under their massive hooves. Fortunately, they were gentle giants.

Toward the end of the summer, when harvest time arrived in the cycle of farm life, the sweat, sounds and smells of the hard physical labor permeated the long days. We watched in fascination the entire farm crew and horses toiling in the fields. They cut the ripe grain crops in a neat, square pattern starting inward from the outer edges of the field. Eventually only a small square of tall, golden stalks remained. Dozens of wild rabbits were now hunkered down in the center, having migrated there in fear as the reaper came ever closer. Then horses and machines were moved to one side of the field, and we boys enviously watched the proceedings from there. A line of beaters marched into the standing crop to drive the terrified rabbits towards the opposite side. As soon as the rabbits broke cover in a frantic dash to escape, the senior male farm workers squeezed off barrages from their shotguns. Rabbits hit keeled over, flipped, and collapsed writhing for a few minutes before expiring. A second volley quickly dispatched those slightly wounded and still intent on escape. Few Lepus cuniculus won their freedom. Rabbit cooked in many ways was a staple for British families until the myxomatosis disease came to Britain from Australia around the mid-1950s and rabbit was banned from dining tables.

Until arriving on this farm, I had a tenuous understanding of the origination of the milk I'd poured so generously on my breakfast cereal at home. Basically I thought it was manufactured magically at the London Cooperative Society's dairy plant, around the corner from our house, because their milkmen delivered it to our front door. Now the startling truth was revealed to me when I saw the herd of passive cows grazing throughout Sir Snelling's pastures.

At first when crossing Waterton meadows and encountering these huge bovines, I was both awed and scared. But I soon realized these quadrupeds were docile, even a little dumb, as they stared at me languidly and without interest, only to return again to their ceaseless chewing. Then a great truth was revealed: their fear of me was greater than my fear of them. I discovered a new sport, just perfect for empty-headed London brats.

If one slapped their rumps they'd trot away a short distance, large udder swaying. A harder slap, or two, increased both speed and distance of their jog, and associated pendulousness. At last I'd found something much bigger than me I could dominate! It was a heady sensation for a small boy. Then one day a farm worker caught me industriously pursuing my ego-satisfying cow cowering. He snitched to a supervisor who, in turn, reported me to the Snelling Manor. That same day a peremptory summons came to appear at the "big house," as we called it. I can still recall walking with great trepidation up the wide tier of stone steps, bordered by an ornate, undulating low stone wall at each side, leading to the huge oak door and nervously pulling on the iron rod that jangled a bell inside. A uniformed maid stiffly ordered me to wait in the outer foyer. This appeared almost as big as our whole house in London, with a ceiling as high as a good medium tree.

It seemed to me I stood in this foyer for a long time. My nervousness built with each passing minute. There was no invitation to sit down, wait in the library, or to partake of tea and cake. Eventually the Snelling's tall, oldest daughter, who took us six boys for an occasional automobile excursion, swept down the broad, curving main inner stairway, strode magisterially across the hallway's marble floor, and halted before me. I believe she'd been delegated much of the estate's administration in the absence of both her father and an Army-serving brother, plus the reported poor health of her mother.

Dressed in a Harris Tweed brown skirt, a mustard sweater, and a matching bandanna around her long neck, she looked like someone on the cover of an English country-living magazine. From her towering height she fixed me with her scrunched-up eyes. Now I knew why they needed a house with such high ceilings. Studies have ascertained that there is a tendency in Britain for aristocrats and the monied-class to be tall; blue-collar workers tend to be short. There could be no doubt to which social sub-groups we both belonged. With her lips pressed tightly together, and nostrils slightly extended, she also looked angry.

"Boy, explain why you find it necessary to agitate our cows?" she asked from her lofty vantagepoint in best Oxford accent.

I don't think I'd ever heard the word "agitate" before, but somehow I seemed to know its meaning. Try as I might, I could think of no plausible explanation for my mindless action. As I struggled hard to think of something to say I believe I forgot her question. But part of a truthful answer would have included the sense of a great new power I derived after discovering I could dictate cow behavior. But it had proved a fleeting satisfaction. More recent episodes were driven by pure mischieviousness. Suddenly various parts of my body seemed to need a good scratching, and I responded vigorously in the pressure of the moment. I remained nervously itchy and utterly speechless. Several eternities came and went.

"Boy, I'm still waiting for your answer. Your conduct is appalling. There's a war on, and I'm a busy person."

You don't have to tell me there's a war on, shot through my mind. That's why I'm sleeping in your stables. It occurred to me that she wouldn't treat her horse like this. But I wasn't sure whether this line of reasoning would answer her basic question, which remained unanswered and, I sensed, unanswerable. Shifting my weight from one foot to the other, and tugging on my shirt collar, also failed to produce an answer. Her fierce gaze never left my face, which I diverted, to the lofty ceiling, wide floor, tall wall, and heavy door. An unnatural silence engulfed me.

"Oh, you stupid little frog!" she at last exploded between clenched teeth. "Don't you know causing cows to run curdles their milk? Right now every drop of milk is needed for the war effort. Your conduct is tantamount to criminality."

By throwing more long words at me she could have been talking in a Ugrian dialect. Despite the enormous gulf that separated us in verbal understanding, I felt the heat of her irritation. During our memorable tête-à-tête I wish I could report my mind finally came up with some scintillating response to her ostensibly simple question. Sir Snelling's disciplined daughter would surely have seen my point of view had I said: "Madam, I have to chase cows, like Mallory and Irvine had to climb mountains, because they are there." Instead, I remained dumbstruck. She sentenced me to a permanent ban from her auto excursions. She further warned me if I misbehaved again there would be even more dire consequences for me. She opened the solid-oak door and banished me. I went out passing well below her outstretched arm holding it. The door slammed behind me.

After I descended the steps and started on the walk back to my stable residence, I turned with the intention of sticking out my tongue, my way to ensure I got the final word in the uneven exchange. But she stood at the tall front window watching me, eyes still scrunched up, probably weighing whether her family would lose face if they kicked my butt back to London where, hopefully, a German bomb might rid Britain of this milk-curdling pest. My first one-on-one encounter with a member of the British aristocracy hadn't gone well.

Only years later did I realize how privileged the motoring excursions were because gasoline for pleasure driving was banned during the war—unless you were the child of a most senior official in the ministry office for energy. Then, even more years later, I was told that cow's milk doesn't sour if the udder is swung a little boisterously during a bout of cardiovascular exercise. So Miss High & Mighty wasn't always right, even if she did live in a big house. I'd sure have something to say now if I could relive that one-sided exchange.

When school convened the London evacuees weren't amalgamated into the village school. Area authorities probably feared we carried some contagious big-city disease that might be contracted by their own country-innocent, rosy-cheeked youngsters, much as invading armies have brought illness to pristine natives throughout history. At the very least they wanted to shield their own from Cockney manners, morals and speech patterns.

The village's small community hall became our school. All forms (grades) were lumped together in the one room. Pupils five years old were rubbing shoulders with fourteen year olds, although each form was assigned its own long table. My guess now is that we numbered about 150 students. Not a propitious environment for the transmission of erudition.

A desperate national government, its fiscal outlays on the war now at stratospheric levels, placed the whole burden of educational support to London evacuees on the receiving local rural councils to finance from their own resources. They had no say in whom they had to accept into their quiet communities (5). These unfunded demands on local councils must have severely increased the strain on already tight budgets. One can only conjecture the bitter taste this left with many conservative local officials. For them to refuse, however, would suggest unpatriotic tendencies. Meanwhile, the big cities suffered the bombing which resulted in many huge expenses for infrastructure and building repairs, extra fire and police protection. The London school children were squeezed in the middle of this bureaucratic power play. For them it manifested itself in teacher inadequacies and textbook and school supplies shortages. The miserable textbooks used at our London school were suddenly desirable teaching tools compared to those now in use.

Younger male teachers had generally already been called to military service. A small group of female and elderly male teachers brought out of retirement was in charge of our so-called intellectual development. Our teachers must have been discouraged by such unfavorable conditions to say nothing of the alien collection of somehow deeply cynical youngsters seated at the long tables before them. Just the noise level from so many children in one room must have been daunting. We didn't inspire them; they didn't inspire us. The tired, somnolent male teachers no doubt resented being dragged from a well-earned, restful retirement to work with this scruffy horde of children of the underclass. They were probably paid a pittance for their time, and I can't but help feel their efforts reflected this.

When all teachers occasionally absented themselves from the hall, apple fights would erupt. The boys were always the perpetrators. London kids instinctively respected private property rights far less than their country counterparts. Area orchards were constantly plundered, and our pockets nearly always held ready ammunition. Normally these fights flared up at the tables of the older students, but rapidly spread to the entire assembly. Apples whizzed in a withering crossfire just over the heads of the seated students. Participants imagined the thrown fruit was an artillery shell aimed at the evil Adolf Hitler. An apple thrown might have been an imaginary blow to the enemy, but it was certainly a real destructive blow to learning. But that is only a hindsight comment; I chucked apples with the others, and surely was as undisciplined as most.

When a returning teacher appeared at the door, there was a frenzied scramble to regain seats and not be the unlucky one or two caught, arm raised, projectile in clear sight. Swift punishment, comprising one or two whacks with a short bamboo cane on each reluctantly outstretched hand, soon became a tradition of this temporary school's preferred solution to these internecine outbreaks. Then those apprehended, with their pained appendages, had to pick up the scattered bruised and splattered apples and put them outside. Reserve ammunition in pockets were surrendered and placed on a classroom table. I now suspect that our teachers, or their wives, baked a lot of apple pies during that time. Since this fruit had mostly been stolen from nearby orchards, surely this made the teachers guilty of receiving stolen goods? Yet they always acted so righteous!

In such circumstances only the most determined students learned. Unfortunately, I was not in that enlightened group. My own feeble desire to learn soon went out the window with my daydreams about roaming what then seemed to me the wide spaces of the English countryside. On the credit side, perhaps it was at this time that my lifelong enjoyment of being in the open was born. Does this prove that there really is a silver lining to every cloud? Although my chances for a decent education were always meager given my social circumstances at birth, I've long felt this wartime disruption, and the implementation of a national survival plan for school children, sealed my fate. I, and, of course, hundreds of thousands of others. Notwithstanding, matters must be kept in perspective. At about the time these events were happening to me, I had a 19-year old cousin who was laying down his life with the British Expeditionary Force during the German blitzkrieg in France. The war's far-reaching impact hurt my education chances; for my cousin, it snubbed out his young life.

While London suffered the grim reality of savage nightly bombing, my recollection of that time contains many pleasant memories. It is of an old world time and slow pace of an agricultural community and the gentleness of English villages. Instead of the endless ocean of cement that is the prospect of East London residents, I recall fields of tall-stalked, ripening barley and wheat, gently rustling in late summer afternoon breezes. The narrow lanes, walled by high hedgerows, carried virtually no traffic. A brash disheveled London kid could walk in the lane without the fear of vehicles, perhaps eating a scrumped apple or two. The surrounding scene comprised a checkerboard of large green pastures bordered with rock dry walls. An occasional iron-rung cattle gate, its evenly spaced cross members so inviting to that youngster to climb over and enter a vast vibrant, airy, wholesome universe such as his young eyes hadn't encountered before. Sometimes such fields contained a solitary oak tree with a girth and limbs so massive it defied attempts to mount into its canopy. The branches spread over a wide circle and generously rained huge acorns much loved by the local pigs. I suppose these lonely trees were remnants of the forests that once covered England before being felled to become the man-of-war sailing ships at the earliest stages of the British Empire.

Yet it was not all happiness at our stable accommodation. I recollect hunger in the early days there. Tramping through the surrounding countryside made for a healthy appetite. But it wasn't just the exercise that gave six boys gnawing hunger pains. Something else was amiss. Then the woman from East London, supposedly there to care for us, suddenly left. Although I know none of the details, it seemed she was not feeding us even to the extent of the small monetary benefit and food rationing allowed. She was sticking to a portion of the money and getting her own caloric needs satisfied at the local pub. I don't remember her name, nor do I know her fate. However, in later years I've thought she must have been especially mean-spirited.

She would have received some payment for her services, no matter how meager. She and her daughter, as did we boys, enjoyed the possible life-preserving privilege of living well clear of the nightmarish London bombing. She was from the same disadvantaged social class as her charges. Yet she chose to cheat six innocents whose small world had been stood on its head. She belongs to that category of people so aptly described by George Bernard Shaw—"the undeserving poor."

Fortunately, another lady soon appeared to provide for us. Mrs. Price, a kind person, was the stereotypical English Mom. Always attired in a floral apron, she seemed to have a brown ceramic teapot permanently welded in one hand. She was a good den mother to her six brats. Her duties were always executed with a smile. This good lady stayed with us until the bombing ceased and we returned to our London homes in mid 1941. Not all WWII heroes wore military uniform; some wore floral aprons.

One ritual that remains with me from my days at the Gloucestershire estate is the weekly bath, or at any rate one particular session. Two large Victorian cast-iron tubs, separated by a rough wood plank partition, had been installed in one room along our corridor above the stables. Because none of the workers' cottages had baths, their occupants used one of the tubs in our stables according to a schedule. Occasionally when I performed my quick weekly ablutions, I could hear the voices of two of the Land Army women having theirs on the other side of that partition. When this occurred, for reasons I couldn't explain then, my imagination went into high gear conjuring up pictures of those hard-grafting ladies, minus their natty uniforms. In truth, my vision of their bodies was hazy. It would be super if I could resolve this uncertainty once and for all.

I imagined hoisting myself to the top of the partition and poking my nose just above to gaze down ecstatically at all that feminine, if muscled, pulchritude. But I was much too stunted to reach the partition top even standing on the tub rim. Furthermore, no opportunity ever presented itself to turn my fantasies into a real sighting of these wet damsels. We boys were scheduled one right after the other. As soon as I had dried and dressed myself and pulled the plug for the dirty water to gurgle away, the housekeeper or next boy was banging on the door.

In the spring of 1941, perhaps to get a break from the night time air raids on London, Mom arranged to visit the estate for a two week stay, bringing my three-year old brother with her, and renting a spare room in the head cowman's cottage. Dad and Vera remained in London.

I still have a memory of how on nice days, after I arrived back from the community hall make-shift school, Mom and I, with Roy in a push-cart, walking to the village where she'd buy me a candy bar and a Tizer, an English soda. It was like being on a real holiday.

Apparently even Moms get dirty, and while at the estate mine had to squeeze a quick dip into the busy bath schedule at the stables. Because hot water usage was carefully controlled, and Mom's ablutions would be extra to usual needs, we were required to use my water allocation between us. We were also programmed for a time different from that of the other five boys. When our wash afternoon arrived, Mom had her bath, didn't pull the plug, leaving the water for me, and then rousted me out of the rumpus room where I'd been watching Roy. As soon as I walked into the cubicle, I could hear the sweet voices of a couple of the Land Army ladies splashing just on the other side of the partition. My opportunity was upon me! The coast was clear with no one scheduled right after me!

Drawing the rusty nail from my trouser pocket that I'd kept especially for this moment, I went right to work to remove a plank knot at a height perfect for my viewing pleasure. My nine-year old hormones pounded strongly in my head with a choral accompaniment in the belly. I worked ardently to dislodge the pesky knot that resisted my passionate efforts. Of course, it was necessary to work as silently as possible because of the naked nymphs on the other side of that pesky barrier. I only needed to weaken the wood around the knot, push the nail through, and lever the knot out quietly to fall in my hand. A peephole into paradise! I contemplated I could replace the knot so no one would notice and I'd be able to indulge my desires on future bathing details. Oh the excitement of immorality! After perhaps 10 minutes of fevered scratching and gouging I felt my attack was about to penetrate enemy defenses. What tales I'd be able to tell the other innocent boys once my eyes had feasted on the wonders of womanhood! How this achievement would elevate me in the opinion of the older boys. Perhaps they'd even let me accompany their gang of three. Just then the cubicle door opened and Mom stepped in. She'd forgotten something, and I'd forgotten to lock it.

"What ARE you doing?"

"Nothing."

"What's that nail for then?"

" Oh... er,... er,... jus' carving me name."

Mum closed the space between us in a flash. She cuffed me on one side of my head with an open right hand and then, faster than a bantamweight boxer, swung her left to deliver another.

"One's for what you were doing, and one's for lying to me, you naughty boy!"

It amazed me how fast Mom assessed the situation. I couldn't think of alternate excuses, certainly no viable ones. So I just gave another of my struck-dumb silent performances.

"You get in that water fast, and be out of here in five minutes, washed and dressed. Leave the door unlocked. Don't stand there, get going! I'll be back to check on you."

She picked up the costume necklace she'd forgotten on the windowsill. I hadn't spotted it in my heat to drill through the partition. For all my eager efforts, I still had virgin eyeballs. But far worse, the ladies next door would have heard the exchange. They knew which boy had his mother at the estate. They'd know my identity and that I'd been doing something improper. I plunged into excruciating embarrassment and my inflamed hormones deflated faster than a spooked stock market.

Shortly after this ignominious bathroom defeat, the intensive nightly bombing of Britain abruptly ended in mid May 1941. The previous nine, nerve-shattering months cruelly tested the resilience of urban populations. While London received the heaviest onslaught, 15 other cities were subject to major bombing attacks (7). When the all-clear siren sounded after the 16 May air raid, none of the fatigued firemen, policemen, anti-aircraft gun crews, air-raid protection wardens, or the pulverized civilian population in general, knew this was the last night raid, at least for now.

Although Hitler's brutal air onslaught failed to terrorize the British civilian population into demanding their government surrender, 20,000 Londoners died under the rain of bombs from the dark skies over their storied metropolis (8). Many of those killed lived in the small, mean, back-to-back row houses close to the docks in the East End. They were innocent victims of a war whose power-politics origins were well beyond their cognizance. Hitler withdrew a major portion of his air forces from the western front to move them east to support his strike at Russia, which came the night of 22 June 1941. Along a 1,500-kilometer front, from the Baltic to the Black Sea, 150 German divisions, with about three million men, the most powerful invasion force in human history, attacked territories occupied by the Soviets (9).

Sometime in the summer of 1941 our school evacuees left the crowded community hall, Ampney Crucis, and returned to the Victorian brick building of Salisbury Junior School in Manor Park. No doubt the gentle villagers were gleefully kicking their heels. They could certainly expect to harvest more of their apple crop that fall and their community hall could be put to more traditional uses than as an education center for an unwashed East End tribe. I was now nearly nine and a half. Roaming, climbing trees, and avoiding responsibility, were my trademarks. Being popular with a selection of school chums was also important. Studying or reading was beyond my ken. The die was cast.

One could debate the altruism of Sir Wilfred Snelling's wartime gesture. While he did not accept any London children into his personal residence, he paid for the renovation and beds that allowed six east London boys to inhabit his grooms' vacated accommodation above empty stables. He proffered a helping hand, if not an embrace. In 1979 I went with my own family, and Mom and Dad, on a visit to the area. The big house had been turned into apartments and could be rented for vacations. The stables were now part of another property behind a chain link fence separating the two. What profound transformations the war wrought to so many lives from so many and diverse backgrounds!

Children on evacuation train.

At the evacuation billet at the Waterton Estate in late summer 1940. Mrs. Price with omnipresent teapot to hand and her six displaced London boys (me in front). Chimneys of "big house" can be seen in background above stonewall.

CHAPTER 5

The skies over London were mercifully quiet now after the near year-long bombing onslaught. This relief from tension, and sleeping through the night, equaled pure joy for my parents and sister who had stayed in the city during the entire siege. I saw little evidence of the blitz in my immediate area. On my walk to school I passed a bicycle sales and service store heavily damaged by a stray bomb. Its two boarded front windows gave it the appearance of a blind man. Soon settled in at home, the pleasure of eating my own mother's cooking again represented Nirvana. Mrs. Price had been a wonderful den mother, but now I had privileges not available in the stable foster home. Extra sugar on cereal and extra jam on bread even though both items were rationed. At the foster home table, if one got a bit more, it deprived other boys. Now I deprived only family members, and that free of guilt.

My sister and brother were six years older and younger respectively than I was. My sense is our childhood was remarkably detached from one and another. I don't recall much sibling rivalry. Even so, not too long after returning to my normal surroundings, and possibly motivated by an unrecognized need to reassert my "oldest boy" domestic status, I sold the family cat to my gullible younger brother for three pence (pennies). This clever ruse unraveled when my parents found out and made me refund his money.

Back in the bosom of the family, it's an appropriate spot to give credit to my mother's cooking from the perspective of current knowledge of what constitutes a healthy diet. Unlike many English working class families, we did not eat much fried food. Mom mainly boiled potatoes and steamed vegetables. In those days, fish was more affordable than meat, and we normally had a piscatory entree twice weekly, almost always boiled or grilled. I'm not sure if Mom knew what constituted healthy eating, but I'll give her the benefit of the doubt and count our family fortunate that she made that extra effort. If our meals were unadorned, they were healthy according to current wisdom.

Because of the considerable distance to the state elementary school when Vera started, Mom succeeded in enrolling her in a closer Catholic school taught by nuns. My sister tells of an incident illuminating how relatively well our family dined. On her way back to her Catholic school from lunch at home, Vera fell in step with one of her teachers. Probably making suitable teacher/pupil conversation, Miss O'Brien asked what was on that day's menu for Vera?

"A lamb chop, peas, and potatoes, Miss, followed by cherry pie."

"Don't you give me your make-believe, young lady," snapped the teacher in disbelief, who had probably settled for a midday cheese roll. Both parties finished the journey in a hurt silence. Perhaps resentful of a non-Catholic in the school, and hoping to catch Vera in a lie, Miss O'Brien actually sent someone to our house the next day to check on the veracity of Vera's claim. Vera had told the truth.

Only as an adult did I learn of events involving my sister that show our loving parents had their quota of shortcomings. Vera proved a diligent student and achieved good grades. In 1937 she passed the dreaded, life impacting 11-plus examination, which both Roy and I later failed. Vera should have moved to a Catholic grammar school, which groomed pupils for more academic pursuits. But the nearest one didn't have space for a non-Catholic pupil. Mom and Dad were advised to apply to a county (state) grammar school to which she was entitled having passed the fork-in-the-road test. Our parents failed to act and Vera lost her opportunity.

Vera stayed at the Catholic school and continued to do well. But at age 14, in 1940, she could no longer remain there. The headmistress considered my sister worthy of further education and that concerned educator said she could get Vera into a teacher's training college. When approached, however, Mom and Dad declined to let Vera continue at school beyond 14. Vera went to work in a nearby factory, producing washing-up liquid and scouring powder, where she packed filled bottles into shipping boxes. After a few years of performing such boring work, Vera decided she would like to enter nurse training. The need for nurses was then especially urgent. But it meant Vera would have to live at a training hospital. Again, our parents wouldn't let her go. Mom said she couldn't handle Roy and I with Dad's imminent military call-up.

Their decisions not allowing Vera to attend teacher or nurse training were made under the pressure of wartime when the future would have been especially uncertain. Even so, in retrospect, they seem exceedingly shortsighted and rather self-centered decisions barring a child from a chance to move up in society. They essentially stunted her educational progress. Later I resented my parents' record over what I perceived as their failure to help Vera who'd demonstrated a capability for something more.

My parents were, however, most loving toward their children. Their attitude reflected a measure of the prevailing working class attitude that one accepted the status to which born.. Over generations, the rigid English class lines appear to have hoodwinked them into believing it unwise to challenge the system. Perhaps Victorian thinking that a girl didn't need an education also played a part. Their views, of course, reflected their own deficient education. I came to feel this mentality was promoted not only by the political/social system; the church quietly endorsed it. I make that statement because of a popular hymn we sang often in school: "All Things Bright and Beautiful," written by Cecil Frances Alexander (1818-1895). Verse #3 reads:

The rich man in his castle
The poor man at the gate
God made them high or lowly
And ordered their estate

This verse cajoled us to accept the accident of birth when deposited on the wrong side of the tracks. It fitted right in with the propaganda of the Monarch's picture in every schoolroom and the red-splotched world maps hanging in school corridors.

In my teens, I came to interpret Mrs. Alexander's words as pure brainwash. Aspirations by lower social orders to achieve a better life were discouraged. We should be content.. The hymn's words certainly pressed my button. A deep, heated resentment formed and this passion stayed with me for years. Current hymnals drop that obsequious verse because of political incorrectness. Even Britain is capable of change!

One thought arousing my adult curiosity is my paucity of memories from my middle school. Perhaps it's because of the tumult of war crowding school memories off the recall screen. Yet because the educational years are such a growing part of our lives, it bothers me the little I remember tends to be negative.

At our co-ed school, all students were gathered together at the start of the day for a prayer said by the headmaster and then to sing one or two hymns led by the music teacher. The rest of the day is almost a blank. We often sang the hymn "For Those in Peril on the Sea" presumably as a gesture of recognition of Britain's proud maritime heritage. The country had long relied on food and raw materials from overseas carried to British ports by many merchant ships. In the early part of the war, German submarines were devastatingly effective in sinking large numbers of these vessels, especially those coming from North America. Government wall posters exhorted the population to give thought to our brave British merchant seamen. Those voyages were indeed perilous. Yet our earnest prayers and not too melodic singing failed to help. By the time the war ended, 35,000 of these brave sailors without uniforms had died (1).

If I achieved any academic progress during this time, it is gone from memory. One school incident, however, remains vivid 65 years later. Boots were common footwear for boys back then. My father implanted round metal studs along the outer rim of the sole to extend its life. I sounded a bit like a British regimental guardsman walking on a parade ground. On the school's imitation marble corridor floors, they were as slick as steel blades on ice. I could slide 15 to 20 feet on that surface with a short run. One day, on my way back to the classroom from playground recess, I launched into one of my by-now graceful, arms outstretched glides, which would take me past an intersecting corridor. One last little bit of fun before sitting again, as I then viewed school, in a boring class.

As self-impelled momentum carried me blissfully forward, my homeroom teacher, the unmarried Miss Davenport, suddenly emerged around the corner bearing a pile of exercise books at chest height. An open container of ink to replenish classroom supplies sat on top of the stack. We still used pens dipped into inkpots located in the ledge of our desks with a sloped writing platform.

My graceful slide ended the instant my head collided with the books. The kinetic energy released by the impact of the two opposing forces launched the ink container into space. Miss Davenport reared backwards, no doubt to avoid her wartime, hard-to-come-by dress being re-dyed a blue-black ink color. The good, long-suffering lady lost her balance, and fell inelegantly on her derriere. Ink, I remember, was almost as widely dispersed as crude oil from the Exxon Valdez in Alaska's Prince William Sound.

Sometime after I had wiped up the lakes of ink with rags from the janitor's cupboard, I stood in front of the entire class in my now modern-art shirt and short pants. Boys until about age 13 wore short pants in those days. The still highly agitated Miss Davenport lectured me on the shortcomings of my character. She didn't seem to give any credence to the irresistible attraction between hob-nailed boots and imitation marble floors. Scholars can be effusive about the fairness of the British legal system, but I don't recall being invited to offer any words in my defense. While the nation was hourly spending all the national wealth defending democracy, I felt there was precious little of it in my classroom that particular afternoon.

Although all pupils knew she didn't hit as hard as the male teachers, I still watched in a state of profound unhappiness as she walked to the storage closet to retrieve the meter-long, thin bamboo cane with which she would mete out my punishment. Up to this moment, I saw myself as something of a hero. Knocking down a teacher is worthy of a good ration of notoriety. All eyes were riveted on me and that's enough to turn a boy's head, especially a short one. But six cane strokes, even female ones, three alternately on each hand, quickly deflated my hubris.

Another humiliating incident, but somehow more scary, took place about the same time. With much military activity going on in the length and breadth of the country, it awoke in me a boy's natural militaristic instinct. Some of Hitler's most successful programs to arouse unquestioning loyalty were directed at young people. Film of that era's Hitler Youth members eagerly parading through towns, behind flags and marching bands beating out martial music, provided a lesson in clever child manipulation. I yearned to wear a uniform like all the military personnel nowadays loose on London streets. Boy Scouts was viewed as too goody-goody in my neighborhood. The less known Boys' Brigade represented a group into which I might better fit. Born in the slums of Glasgow, Scotland, around the beginning of the 20th century, the Boys' Brigade charter offered healthy diversion from the general poverty of boys' working-class families. It is a uniformed youth organization for boys (2). Each group is part of a local church, offering a variety of progressive programs based on adventure and community. It is a Christian organization providing religious education and support through a range of church activities. All very wholesome.

In 1941, the East Ham chapter I joined was rather meager. It met one evening a week in a local church hall. Needless to say, I don't remember the denomination. The program was of elementary floor gymnastics and tumbling on some beat-up floor pads. This was passable, but wearing the required uniform in public interested me far more. I pestered Mom to let me join. She was probably glad to get me out of the house so eventually paid the membership fee and the cost of the uniform, which I don't recall. It consisted of a navy blue pillbox hat encircled by two thin white stripes. A black plastic chinstrap let a show-off wearer tilt it to one side at a racy angle. A white plastic strap over the right shoulder connected to a wide belt, similar to the design of the British Army officer's Sam Browne leather harness supporting a standard long-barreled revolver. We boys, of course, didn't have weapons. But we had vivid imaginations. I liked to wear the Brigade uniform for my weekly walk to and from the church hall. While a London child could still get killed by the occasional German air raid, safety on the streets otherwise was not a problem. But dangers to children lurked in unexpected places.

On the few Sunday mornings we paraded along East Ham side streets, I was bursting with pride. Surely I was right up there with the heroes of the Battle of Britain? Surely every 9-year-old girl who saw me fell in love? Hopefully, a few older ones even. Then my brief, happy time in the Brigade shattered, not from a German bomb, but again from twisted human nature.

Following an evening's gymnastics, the adult male leader told another small boy and me we should remain after the others departed because he needed more details about us for his records. At the end of the session, the leader escorted the other boys to the front door and, I suspect, locked it. No escape and no one could interrupt.

Although I have no recollection of a face, he must have been in his forties, or he'd probably been in the military. He led us to a rear office, and had us sit on a bench. The leader picked up a register, which I recognized as being where member's names and addresses were recorded. He moved the office chair to sit down close in front of us.

The man ran a finger along the line when he found our names in the register. He frowned, and looked up shaking his head as if in doubt. His gestures indicated a problem existed. Because we were small, he needed to ensure we were physically strong enough to be Boys' Brigade members.

Would we stand on the bench and lower our trousers and underwear? He could then determine our fitness. We both complied.

My memory is he never touched us. He studied our genitals, however, with considerable interest and what seemed like a long time. I never told anyone of this first incident in my life of child exploitation. Although I knew I didn't like what happened, my shyness and embarrassment were powerful. And I didn't understand. Mom couldn't comprehend why my interest in the Boys' Brigade fizzled so suddenly. I had pestered her relentlessly to buy me the uniform so I could join. Now I wouldn't go to group meetings. She probably attributed it to my fickleness.

One afternoon in fall 1941, I played after school on the edge of the common in a contractor's abandoned sand pile. Dad had told me two houses along the road sustained hits by phosphorous bombs while I was evacuated. When German bombs damaged private property, the local council assessed the impairment and contracted repairs.

A boy I didn't recognize as local, who looked a few years older than my nine and three quarters, limped along on the sidewalk carrying a portable, but bulky, phonograph. With his lurching gait, he appeared to be having difficulty with his load. Rather uncharacteristically for my egocentric self, I shouted an offer of help. Edward Wentworth accepted. Thus a long, and at times, stormy, friendship was struck. I'm looking back as I write this with a perspective of 65 years. He proved to be probably the most influential person in my life.

Known to all as "Eddie," he was good looking, with even features and naturally wavy brown hair. He dressed neatly. There was an adult air about him uncommon in east London boys of comparable age. He didn't speak with the Cockney accent normal for his east London birthright and Eddie was well beyond playing in sand piles.

If a reader, I might have thought of Byron, the English lame, romantic poet. But since I never cracked a book outside of school —and inside as infrequently as possible —it is likely I thought only about a tip he might offer for my services. As we walked along, I learned that Eddie's family had moved to our road while I was evacuated. His father, a lifelong stevedore, was exempt from military service. German bombs destroyed their former Canning Town home, adjacent to the dockyards on the River Thames, late in 1940. The docks were London's most heavily bombed area (3). He told me he was 12 years old and already at the secondary elementary school in Forest Gate to which I would later transfer. Although my understanding of such matters was primitive, I instinctively felt he was brighter and worldlier than the average boy in my circle of friends. He was not working class dumb. His general confidence in himself was impressive to this boy full of painful self-doubts and inferiority feelings.

I don't remember if it was during our first meeting or later that he told me he'd passed the life-important, 11-plus-school examination. Then, because a friend bad-mouthed the grammar school experience, Eddie decided against transferring and continued at the secondary elementary (vocational) school. To this day, I don't know if Eddie spoke the truth in this claim about conquering the 11-plus. Of course, if he had, his decision not to go to grammar school was highly questionable. He had no interest in any vocational skills, so the academic side would have been a natural. During the course of the war years, he displayed an entrepreneurial talent that, backed by more education, could possibly have led him to great achievements.

In time I learned Eddie contracted poliomyelitis as a baby in the early 1930s when the disease was rampant. This monstrous viral infection had affected the alignment of his spine and had somewhat withered the muscle and bone in his right leg, causing a structural deformity that resulted in the limp.

Our friendship grew. Our age difference didn't seem to bother him, and I guess it made me, the urban bumpkin, feel more sophisticated to have a friend with a measure of poise compared with average locals. We went together to the movies or to see our nearest professional soccer team, West Ham United. We took walks across the common to a park located in Wanstead, the fancier area. Unlike so many English boys, Eddie didn't seem to be plagued by shyness.

Although physically handicapped, he took part in the sports I played. And he always participated in these games on an equal basis, expecting no special consideration. He mostly elected to be a goalkeeper when we played our Sunday soccer, a position not requiring so much running. When the summer came, Eddie played a far better game of cricket than I did, both as a batsman and bowler. I secretly feared the game's hardball. He didn't.

As years went by, I slowly discerned that Eddie had a need to be the dominant one in our friendship. My own tendency to childishness, over-sensitivity and an emotional low flash point led to quite a few strong arguments between us. In fact, our friendship occasionally turned sour. In my experience, he also liked to paint a most favorable picture of himself. I found this particular characteristic most irksome as I got to know him more. Only many years later, after much reading and a few college courses in psychology, did I come to believe Eddie's polio had left him more than physically scarred. I suspected his need to dominate might be traced back to feelings of his own inadequacy stemming from his handicap.

With my by now well-established dislike for school, I began to develop a great liking for soccer, the British working-class male passion. With the public common across from our house there was a ready, if egregiously ungroomed, playing field for neighborhood boys. I never did own a football, only a pair of the old-style hard-toe soccer boots. Some one from a better-off family owned a ball. We'd select two captains, and they'd pick their team members in turn based on their assessment of each boy's skill. We'd agree among ourselves as to the playing field's boundaries, drop four coats on the ground for goal posts, and play our hearts out: after school, during the summer, and on weekends year round.

Even my love for tree climbing soon took second place to soccer. Some of us were so devoted to the sport we kicked tennis balls to each other as we walked along the roads leading to and from school, morning, lunchtime, and afternoon. The four daily journeys of half a mile went too quickly; the tedious classroom hours too slowly. My values were sadly confused. In those days, the roads were mercifully free of automobiles. Kicking such small spheres helps to develop ball control. The canyons of identical, drab houses through which we passed faded from consciousness as we kicked, dribbled or headed the ball and mystically transformed into stars of the two best teams at the annual cup final played in the national stadium.

CHAPTER 6

In mid June 1942, at age 39 and six months, my father received call-up papers for the army. In just six more months he would have avoided the draft. It cut off at age 40. Men beyond that age, up to 60 years, served in local units of a national home guard. The evening before he went to war is still a vivid memory. Mom prepared a special dinner. Afterwards, a few neighbors came in to say goodbye. I thought it all rather exciting, but my mother and sister were tearful. Later we settled in our small sitting room near the fire-less open grate. Normally Mom and Dad sat in the two small armchairs opposite each other on both sides of the hearth. This night one chair stayed unoccupied because Mom sat on his lap. They talked quietly to each other, and I saw a few tears run down his face; the first time I'd seen my undemonstrative father cry. When I got up the next morning, he'd already gone. An aunt was on duty to watch Roy and I. With your indulgence, I devote some space to Dad's war service because I failed to honor his record during his time here, and it's one of several regrets I now carry.

Dad hadn't wanted anyone to go to the train station with him, possibly because he knew he'd be unable to control his emotions; embarrassing to this shy man. However, soon after he'd left the house, Mom and Vera followed to meet up at Waterloo station before he boarded the train to his Army induction center for two month's boot camp near Bournemouth on the south coast.

In researching material for this book, I found there were many induction and other training camps established early in the war along the south coast. Military planners presumably calculated that if a German invasion came it would likely be at an English Channel point. Any hope of throwing the powerful Germans back into the sea would take all the Army's available manpower, even green soldiers still undergoing basic training.

It seemed to me that I'd only recently adjusted to being back at home with the family, and now we all faced the departure of its head for an unknown period; another emotional upheaval. Dad's subsequent four-year absence from the home denied me the influence of a good father during my formative years, 10 through 14, a crucial developmental stage. Removal of the father from a family is today recognized as a serious handicap to the children, especially if they are young. My sister was 16, my brother four, and I was ten years. For me it was particularly unfortunate. My willful nature came seasoned with distinctly selfish tendencies. Although Dad was not a big disciplinarian, he engendered more respect from me than did Mom. With him gone, I was able to test the behavior boundaries almost as I pleased. For my essentially self-centered nature, this occurrence represented one more ill boding development.

Dad's years as a taxi driver made him a natural for a driver in the Royal Army Service Corps, roughly equivalent to the U.S. Army's former Quartermaster. After boot camp, his first specialty training assignment sent him to the newly forming 20th Tank Transporter Company at Walton-on-Thames, Surrey, southwest of London. He received instruction as a driver of the large tank-transporting "T" tractor, built by Chicago-based Diamond Motor Company, with drive power to all axles. Diamond "Ts" are claimed to be the best-known American vehicles of WWII. Dad drove the model #980 hauling a Rogers's 45-ton, 12-wheel trailer, capable of carrying British Churchill, Valentine and Stuart tanks. No vehicles of this capacity and dimension were then built in the U.K. These tank transporters remained in use in the British Army into the 1970s (1).

During August and September 1942, while building to its authorized strength, the 20th TTC conducted driver and arms training. The results of the company's familiarization with arms is recorded in the unit commander's daily log as "very poor," but largely attributed to inclement weather and "bad" rifles (2). The company also went on tactical field exercises at the Army's large training area on Salisbury Plain in Dorsetshire. A detachment was detailed to attack using blank ammunition and thunder flashes together with dummy hand-grenades. The exercise conclusion report stated the company moved into location slowly and the defense posts were sited too far out to retain contact with headquarters (3). The 20th TTC didn't appear a candidate for the coveted description of a "crack company."

Dad came home for a few days leave shortly after reporting to the 20th TTC. During the war, military personnel who were issued a weapon had to carry it at all times, although without ammunition when not on duty. As is often the case with boys, I don't recall how glad I was to see him, but I do vividly remember how I loved handling his Army standard Enfield rifle with its canvas sling. He let me walk around the house carrying the wooden-stock, bolt-action rifle, which weighed about 10 lbs. I'd work the bolt mechanism and squeeze the trigger time and again. Somewhere I'd learned the German word "achtung," or attention, and marched in and out of rooms calling "achtung, achtung, achtung," blazing away at imaginary foes. It didn't help the war effort, and probably drove the adult family members crazy.

In November, the company received notification that it had to prepare for overseas. No destination was indicated. All drivers were given additional training in firing revolvers, rifles and Thompson sub-machine carbines. Fortunately, they achieved improved results over their earlier efforts. During December the men were given medical inspections, inoculations and vaccinations. By the time they were ordered to perform desertization of their tractors, they had a pretty good idea of their likely destination: North Africa.

Dad came home a second time for 11 days' embarkation leave early in January 1943. I again enjoyed this time with Dad's rifle still shooting imaginary Germans. And then he went. Four years passed before we saw each other again. I didn't realize just how critical Dad's absence would be in my life.

Unfortunately, I have no clue as to our family finances during the war years. Some of Dad's Army pay automatically transmitted to Mom through the British Post Office, which was, and still is, involved in government-to-people payments and other financial matters far more than its American counterpart. I believe that when Mom found herself alone with three children to raise, it taxed her to the fullest. Undoubtedly, I represented a large percentage of that tax. Vera, now aged 15, was required to be at least a partial surrogate mother. This organizational arrangement would have worked on my strong sense of territoriality. I can hear myself now shouting at Vera, "you can't tell me what to do—you're not my mother!" How unjust for my innocent sister whose own education was not only curtailed by the war, but whose adolescence was, in a very real sense, withered. Again, wars exact a toll far beyond the death and maiming on the battlefield.

After returning to his unit from embarkation leave, Dad then, so typical with the military, cooled his heels until boarding His Majesty's Transport P41 two months later. This nameless military cargo ship left Grenock, a port just west of Glasgow on the River Clyde, on 14 March. It joined a convoy code numbered KMF 11, just off the coast of Scotland. The "F" in the designation meant it was a fast convoy; no ship stopped to aid a fellow vessel in any circumstance (4). The convoy sailed in a wide northwesterly arc into the Atlantic Ocean before turning southeast toward the Straits of Gibraltar. At one time during the journey, the convoy sailed closer to North America than to Europe. This extensive detour was to avoid German submarines, operating from several French west coast ports, which stalked Allied ships transiting the Bay of Biscay.

Despite this evasive tactic, Dad's convoy came under aerial attack on the moon-bright night 22/23 March in the Mediterranean Sea when only 60 miles from its destination, Algiers. At 2:45 a.m. on 23 March, an aerial torpedo dropped by a German or Italian aircraft, based on Sardinia or Sicily, holed HMT P41 (5). The transport flooded quickly through its torn side below the waterline. The dreaded order to abandon ship repeatedly boomed from loudspeakers and riveted an unquestioning focus amid fearful uncertainty among its military passengers..

Available lifeboats were insufficient to hold all the men. Non-swimmers, of which there were many, received preference. One can only imagine the fear gripping the non-swimmers, standing on P41's top deck, the moon-glistening sea stretching away all around them, as they awaited assignment to rapidly decreasing lifeboat spaces. A watery death could be just minutes away. What thoughts raced through their minds? Bittersweet feelings for family at home no doubt filled their hearts. Probably tsunamis of regret swept them as they thought of actions undone and things unsaid. Such thoughts flashed in their consciences like high-tower warning strobes at night. And the unanswerable question: why must I die in a war not of my making? Each individual must have been emotionally full and empty at the same time. Yet military discipline endured. The official record reports there was, in fact, no panic among the soldiers. Fortunately, Dad had learned to swim as a boy when his family briefly lived near the sea. Those who declared themselves swimmers slid down ropes dangled over the side and into the water. Many sustained cuts and blisters from the coarse rope. They had been told to swim clear of the ship because of vortex created when it disappeared below the surface. To lessen the grim outlook for those going over the side, the comforting word passed around that Royal Navy escort vessels would search for survivors as the convoy moved on.

Dad swam to a multi-person raft bobbing on the choppy surface perhaps 150 yards away. Through the moderate waves he could see the outlines of a few other soldiers already occupying the raft. When he reached it, the others dragged him out of the sea. He slithered to the center of the flat raft panting hard and lay there gulping air for minutes like a large fish landed on a yacht . Soon he was handed a paddle and the wet soldiers propelled the raft until they were clear of the sinking transport's whirlpool (6).

The sea/air battle continued spasmodically. Ships sailed without navigation lights to conceal their positions, but occasional barrel flashes revealed the locations of British Navy escort cruisers and destroyers. In time, the enemy planes flew away, probably because of fuel limitations, and a silence of disbelief fell on the men aboard the life raft. They were again left to their own thoughts and the brutal reality of war.

After about an hour, a British destroyer picked them up in its searchlights sweeping the sea surface and acknowledged their presence on its klaxon. Dad said it was the sweetest machine sound he'd ever heard. I remember him giving credit to the escorting destroyers that zipped about rescuing survivors even before the attack was over. At the end of this long, sleepless night, one officer was lost, ironically with the surname Davies. Only three other ranks were never accounted for. Fortunately, the sinking occurred in a calm Mediterranean and not the colder, and normally rougher, Atlantic at that time of the year.

All survivors from HMT P41 landed at Algiers, their original destination. They had lost their clothing and footwear plus the few personal belongings they carried aboard the transport. Most, including Dad, had lost treasured family photos. From the dock they marched to a checkpoint at L'Orient and then were bussed to L'Arba reception camp, a few miles east of Algiers on the main coast road. A former wine distillery improvised as their camp for the night. Here the men gulped their first food in 26 hours (7). The officers occupied the former owner's house. Other ranks slept in the buildings with empty cement wine vats. Dad told me he and a few others searched the premises for forgotten wine caches, but without luck. Disappointed and damp, they wrapped themselves in blankets and bedded down on the stone floor.

Yet personnel of the 20th TTC weren't given much time to baby their bruises or ponder survival from their rude immersion in the sea. Within 48 hours of arriving, the company was hauling ammunition and drums of gasoline as far forward as the Kasserine pass, in Tunisia, close to the Allied front line. Soon Dad drove his transporter loaded with its first tank to a forward base. He once mentioned how tank surfaces became so hot under the African sun, he'd fry eggs on a flat section, after wiping it clean with a gasoline-soaked rag, of course!

I found a specific reference to Dad, Driver F. J. Davies, Army #10706616. Major Etterley, their company commander since its inception in England, had included him in a weekly personnel status report requesting that he be returned to duty as soon as he could be released from confinement to the No.5 General Hospital. It would be good to think the commander had singled out Dad for particular mention because of service above and beyond. However, he was, in fact, but one of 27 drivers on the list confined because of digestive tract problems, fairly frequent among British soldiers, as their water sources weren't always sanitary.

In my inexpert tracking of official materials on Dad's wartime efforts, I came upon "The Story of the Royal Army Service Corps 1939-45," the official history published by the RASC Institution in 1955. It includes a number of personal narratives. One, entitled "I drove a desert Dinosaur," is an account by a tank transporter driver in North Africa. The author, R.A. Richardson, observes in his humorous musings that "... the Army seemed to believe in the principle that the larger the vehicle, the smaller the driver." He surely had my Dad in mind when he wrote those poignant words. My father's official military record shows him as standing 63 ¾ inches, and weighing 119 lbs. British Army vehicles and loads didn't come any bigger than he drove and, it seems, men didn't come much smaller.

Roy (4) and me (10) in 1942. Picture made to replace that which Dad lost when his transport ship was sunk by enemy torpedo.

Dad in Army somewhere in North Africa (1943) dressed in the unflattering uniform issued to British enlisted personnel.

CHAPTER 7

By fall, 1942, following America's entry into the war the previous December, the U.S. Army Air Force had taken occupancy of many hastily built, east-coast airfields in Britain. Most offered only grass runways. The RAF and the USAAF were working 24-hour days to increase the size and frequency of combined raids on Germany. These efforts were facilitated because Hitler's piercing, brown, reptilian eyes now focused on the USSR. Despite Hitler's over-reaching plans in the east, he continued to order his squadrons remaining in France to mount occasional night raids on Britain, with London the primary target. Thus the civilian population knew first-hand the battle had diminished, but not yet ended.

Although I missed the fearful 1940/41 fall and winter blitz of London, now these intermittent raids still involved the misery of dragging ourselves out of a sound sleep in a warm bed to grope down to the cold, damp shelter at the bottom of the garden; for me, the deepest agony. The shrill wailing of the public air raid siren, splintering the night calm as it warned of approaching enemy aircraft, didn't stir me. I'd wake only when Mom, seated on the side of the bed, shook me vigorously by the shoulder. My whole mind and body resisted arousal and I generally refused to budge. As I slowly absorbed Mom's urgent pleas, I offered dumb comments about preferring to die from Hitler's bombs than going to the doghouse. This must have been painfully trying for Mom. No mother wants to disturb her child's sleep, but the risk of injury, even death, loomed larger in an upstairs room of a house with a heavy slate tile roof, versus the air-raid shelter.

A new feature of sleep disturbance now also came from our own defending forces. An anti-aircraft artillery battery had been established on the common, about a mile from our house. When the German planes came within its air sector, its Bofors Mark One 3.7- and 4.5-inch guns, made in Sweden, would open up and shatter neighborhood nerves. These reverberations only frazzled my poor mother even more.

In time, Mom found it necessary to work outside the home at a part-time job while Roy and I were in school.. She found employment at a small candy manufacturer. This was highly desirable work because she sometimes brought home samples, probably heisted. She also worked as a waitress at a local café on some evenings. Vera, who had been working since 1940, was required to watch Roy and myself on those evenings. Again, this deprived Vera of some of her free time. It is small wonder that war brings so much change to the civil side of society. With the father gone and the mother having to assume total responsibility for the family, including working outside the home, everyday life is hugely disrupted. In our home, this situation provided me with a great deal of freedom, far more than good for healthy development.

To while away a day during summer vacation 1943, a friend and I caught a bus for the 15-mile trip to Woolwich, a manufacturing area, to ride a free public ferry across the River Thames. Of course, we weren't content just to enjoy the 15-minute cruise, but clambered down the dirty, mud embankment to gambol in what must have been an almost toxic playground. The River Thames, England's longest, served as London's sewer main since the city began. By the early 19th century raw sewage from two million people arrived via tributary streams and creeks at the watercourse. Cholera broke out in 1848. Toward the end of that century, a series of sewers were built to divert human waste from the river to holding tanks from where sludge vessels carried it downstream for dumping in the North Sea. Yet the River Thames, especially to the east of London, remained heavily polluted until the last quarter of the 20th century. In 1943 the waterway was still disease-laden.

Within days I came down with scarlet fever, with symptoms of vomiting, sore throat, scarlet rash, high fever, and chills. At the time, this acutely contagious disease required quarantine. I was taken by ambulance to the nearest qualified hospital at Chingford, Essex, about 50 miles north of our home. Apparently I was one sick boy for a week and kept isolated. Then I had to remain for observation, but shifted to a small ward that housed a few other children.

Because my later life passion for reading had not then taken hold of me, I recall how slowly the time seemed to pass: an agony to an impatient, nervous person like me. Compensation that helped ease the boredom were the several nurses from Ireland and, after I was over the worst phase of the fever, I succumbed to my first ever attack of puppy love. My favorite nurse was from County Mayo, on the West Coast of Ireland. I don't recall her as a fantastic looker, but she had a gentle sweetness so attractive to me. Her cottage home was in the west of County Mayo, she told me; close enough to see the Atlantic Ocean. I looked forward to the time this nurse came on duty. In my own peculiarly intense emotional way of pining, my imagination conjured up idealized views of the nurse's rustic home. For a boy who usually thought mostly of soccer, she occupied my thoughts a lot.

Miss Mayo, as I called her, became my personal Florence Nightingale, and I, the wounded war hero. I hadn't contracted scarlet fever from playing in a polluted river; I'd sustained severe wounds while single-handedly fighting the brilliant, proud German General Rommel, the "Desert Fox." Death nipped at my heels, and Miss Mayo labored endlessly to save my life, so I could save Britain. She loved me deeply, but was too shy to speak of it, or show it.

Meanwhile, in the real world, by mid 1943 the tides of war had turned against Germany, actually without the slightest help from me. The Russians had halted the massive assault on their empire and went on the offensive. Allied forces had won the seesaw battle in North Africa, and were about to invade Italy. Although U-boats still inflicted losses on merchant shipping in the Atlantic, Allied counter measures became more effective. Allied air forces were smashing Germany's industrial capacity with raids sometimes composed of one thousand bombers. Even so, the remnants of the Luftwaffe still in France mounted an occasional raid on Britain. These gestures were no doubt put on for propaganda, rather than military, purposes. During my time at the hospital, there were several night air raids. This hospital had large picture windows crisscrossed with masking tape to stop flying glass if blown in. But there was still enough uncovered pane to see the flashes from the guns of a nearby anti-aircraft battery. Sometimes, in this new setting, the noise of the guns and air raid sirens woke me. A night nurse would circulate through the darkened wards, navigating by flashlight, checking on the young patients. I would lie in the warm bed, bursting with the hope it would be Miss Mayo, the intensity of my feeling quite overwhelming.

When it was my lucky night with her on duty, the air raid became unimportant. Important was she'd eventually be at my bedside talking to me reassuringly in her soft Irish brogue. These emotional moments thrilled in a new, different way. Life had somehow changed. My feelings for Miss Mayo put me in a floating state of being. She ennobled me and I would have laid down my life for her. Yet such is male fickleness, at the very first opportunity my flesh was weak and I was unfaithful.

Although nature might have chosen this particular time to infuse some early hormonal changes into my unsuspecting body, I still was an inmate of a hospital for children, and the wards were mixed sex. Other children on our ward came and went, but I seemed to be there for the rest of eternity. Eventually it came to pass that the only other occupant in my ward was a girl, about my age. During one of those long, tedious afternoons, sex floated into the ward, unexpected, not understood, uninvited, but not rejected. We lay in our beds, she on one side of the ward, me on the other, staring idly at the ceiling, likely she just as bored as me. She couldn't have been a reader either. Ungentlemanly though this claim may sound, I honestly believe I was far too shy to be the initiator of what followed. She gets all the credit.

"I'll show you mine if you show me yours."

"Show you what?"

"What you've got between your legs."

"I don't have anything between my legs."

"You know, silly, your pee-pee."

"Oh."

For all my shyness, I have to report my curiosity was stronger. Casting aside all modesty, we both, on our knees, waddled ungainly like a pair of fattened geese to the end of our beds, raised our unisex flannel nightshirts, and thrust our pelvises forward. Across the space between the beds, we both stared, dumbstruck and doubtful, at each other's weird anatomy. This inspection was conducted in a total silence. I'm not sure if I was stunned or just lacked articulation. For purposes of historical accuracy, I must reveal that I don't recall if I was in a state of excitement at the time.

Probably because our arms were getting tired, we eventually dropped the front of our hospital-issue nightshirts, wiggled back along the bed, pulled the covers up, and continued to silently survey the reclining, strangely-constructed person in the bed across the ward.

At long last her lone, descriptive comment was "it looks like a thumb without a thumbnail." Unfortunately, I was not so inventive or imaginative, and remained silent and awestruck. Ever since I've wondered if her remark was innocuous or a scathing put-down. My sex life had gotten off to a shaky start. I left the hospital a couple of days later.

Mom didn't know about her son's obvious entrapment in this public exposure incident, remarking shortly after I arrived home that she felt my stay in the isolation hospital somehow changed me. For years she maintained I never really settled down after my time at that institution.

When it rains, it pours. Life socked me with another major disillusionment at about this time. For many months I'd been awaiting in tingling anticipation the arrival of a package from Dad. In a long-ago letter he said he'd mailed a box of pomegranates from North Africa. We didn't know this tropical fruit. My mind conjured up visions of something exotic, even magical, on its way to our East London house from a hot, far-off continent. But the box of this enchanted fruit had a low mail priority from the desert war zone. Yet, despite the nine months that elapsed before the fruit arrived, my boyish expectation remained intense.

Mom used a screwdriver to pry off the box slats and then peeled back the flaps of the by-now mangy-looking cardboard container inside. She lifted out a couple of the bone-dry, crimson pomegranates. The fruit has a hard rind, and thus now had the feel of a small, hairless coconut. It easily resisted Mom's efforts with a peeling knife, and she resorted to a hammer to drive in a heavier-bladed knife. Inside, the pulp was dehydrated and bitter, and its many seeds, pebble hard. This long-awaited fruit, which had tormented my patience for nearly a year, was thrown in the rubbish bin (trash can).

It must have been in the late fall 1943, during one of the sporadic night air raids, when the glass in several of our front windows on both storys was blown out by a bomb dropped on the common. The German crew possibly targeted the nearby anti-aircraft gun emplacement. Our house was one of half a dozen so damaged. Because it was already cold, Mum and Vera tacked up some thin vinyl, known as American cloth, and reported the damage to the local council office handling such claims.

After a few weeks, three or four workmen appeared. They progressed along the road working at a government pace installing missing windowpanes. Ours was the last on their list, and I arrived home from playing soccer after school just about the time they'd finished and loaded the council van for the night. I went into the rooms where the new window glass had been installed to make my necessary inspection. In one I found a neat little glasscutter they'd forgotten. A mindless compulsion took charge. I just had to try my etching ability on the brand new panes.

My first stroke was short and tentative. Each succeeding one grew in length and confidence. Before Mom caught me, I'd performed my artistry on at least half of the replaced windows. She exploded almost as loudly as the bomb that did the original damage. Right off, she categorized me as an idiot. Why had I done such a terrible thing? Couldn't I see the consequences? The Council wouldn't replace these panes a second time, or they'd charge an exorbitant fee. Winter would soon be here and the glass, now vulnerable, would break at the first strong wind. Didn't I know glass, like most things in wartime Britain, was hard to come by?

Now, at 11 and a half, a show of muteness this time didn't seem an effective defense. I admitted it had been but a fleeting thrill as I carved my little lines on the new glass. I'd soon tired of the pastime, but continued anyway. Mom paused, a quizzical look on her face, as she analyzed the content of my confession. Perhaps finding my explanation more imbecilic than the action itself, Mom lunged at me with ferocious intent. But by now I could mostly dodge her blows, or used my arms as protection and she soon hurt her own hands. The attack ended. I didn't know then, or now, if it was pure cussedness or plain dumbness that motivated me. Probably both.

But this little saga had a sort of happy ending. The next day, the workmen returned seeking that very glasscutter. Mom sweet-talked them into replacing the hacked-on panes. After describing me to them, she said later, they took pity on her. When I look back on my wartime misbehavior, I can't help feeling I played a role, albeit unwittingly, that could be construed as providing aid and comfort to the enemy. I bet Adolf Hitler didn't even know he had a little friend in East London.

North America now supplied a large portion of Britain's essential needs. Despite the merchant ship losses inflicted in the Atlantic, the productive capacity and generosity of the USA and Canada was so great that Britain never really faced starvation. In our home we ate many meals of American powdered egg prepared by Mom in several ways. It came in a squat, rectangle, khaki-colored, cardboard box, with the American bald eagle national symbol as the background to the contents printed over it.

Down one side, in bold letters and digits, was the government contract number. We also drank lots of powdered milk, reconstituted with water, by the glass, over cereal, and in our beloved tea. But what I deemed life essential items—chocolate, sweets (candies), and jam (jelly)—were scarce. I'm pretty sure such luxuries were available, just not in local family shops of the East End.

About 40 years later a British government report flabbergasted me when it declared with conviction that the British people were healthier during the WWII than today. Presumably, people received their basic caloric requirements but no excess. Today, the junk food availability practically matches that of America.

The Ministry of Information kept the nation well reminded through wall posters about the "marvelous men of the merchant marine." Justifiably so. These true heroes sailed all the oceans, but most frequently the cold, gray, North Atlantic, bringing desperately needed food and war materials. For once, a message that sank into the consciousness of all adults and many children down to a young age. We knew the merchant mariners were the nation's lifeline, and faced some of the worst dangers.

Certainly, Eddie got the message. During this period, he displayed considerable entrepreneurial talent when he organized a paid-admission amateur variety show. The profits, although modest, were donated to the Merchant Marine Comfort Association, which had a main office and recreational club in Central London. Although not of the faith, Eddie obtained permission to use a community hall, accommodating about a hundred people, at the local Catholic Church. This was the closest suitable facility with a stage to where we lived. Eddie and I rang doorbells and advertised in the immediate neighborhood with handmade posters at key points.

On the big evening there were four acts: two before an interval; two after. During the interval, everyone was given a cup of tea and one biscuit (cookie.) The tea and biscuits were gathered from family members who donated their precious rations to the cause. The church's stock of canteen-type, heavy-duty plates, cups and saucers were called into service. He also organized a raffle, whose prize I don't recall. But the drawing was to be made after the show; a wrinkle to keep the audience in their seats until the bitter end.

The show opened with three girls Eddie knew who had attended dancing school. This trio, dressed up in sailor-boy suits and pillbox hats, sang and tap-danced several songs, with each girl performing a solo act between the combined numbers. In reverse of accepted vaudeville practice, Eddie began with the most polished performers in the hopes people would stay on in anticipation of even better entertainment. The same phonograph I helped carry on the first day I met Eddie supplied the music for the girls' performance.

Next, Eddie and I put on a skit in which he was the straight man and I the clown. The curtain lifts on Eddie, a harassed, no-nonsense military recruiting officer sitting at a desk (stage center) talking on a telephone (a play one) with the Air Ministry about why his weekly report is late. In deferential tones he promises to make the report his very next task. The stage goes quiet as Eddie bends over his desk filling in the form.

Suddenly, an outer door opens noisily, loud footsteps approach along a corridor, the on-comer falls over a trashcan, and then the inner door opens with a crash. I enter (stage left), the village idiot, shod in way-too-large boots, loudly declaiming my eagerness to join the fight against the hated Hitler and demanding my very own Spitfire (Britain's WWII successful fighter aircraft). Eddie, in cultivated tones and a few "my good fellows," tries earnestly to reason with me as to why the ministry can't give me my own plane. He indicates I might more suit a kitchen job at a remote outpost, with an emphasis on its remoteness.

I get ever more demanding and hysterical, jumping around his desk, until I stumble out of the oversize boots, fall down, bringing Eddie and his table with me. I'm not quite sure how it ended, but it produced a few laughs. My small size and the large boots were a sure bet.

After the interval, Eddie, who had a passable voice, imitated a 1940s crooner for three or four songs. This stretched it a little, but we had to fill up at least 30 more minutes. I inflicted the last act on our patient audience. I came on, decked out in a workingman's old clothing and flat cap, to sing a song Eddie said one of his grandfathers created. East Londoners and probably no one else would understand the song, which used a lot of Cockney slang. Fortunately, singing ability is not required for this number, and the lyrics are mindless. Again, about all that can be said of my unmusical effort is that it produced a few laughs.

To watch this unpolished show, Eddie charged one-shilling admission. All told, the event raised £5 sterling from admissions and the same amount from the raffle collection. £10, while not a princely sum, equated to four weeks of the average wage of the day. Eddie donated it to the Merchant Marine Comfort Association, a type of welfare activity for the civilian sailors. We went to its main office in Central London to give them the bundle of 10 one-pound notes we had carried on the bus rather nervously. In return, the MMCA permitted us to spend the afternoon in the recreation wing of its facility where we played billiards along side some of the heroic mariners. I guess our chests were bursting with pride. Completely his initiative, this was a remarkable display of enterprise on Eddie's part. There could not have been many boys in all London with so much drive. Eddie's gumption and get-up-and-go were, I believe, special.

Since returning to London, I'd sensed in a boyish way the country's normal tranquil air had mutated to a supercharged expectancy: live for today, for tomorrow we die. Without really understanding this change, it accommodated my own situation to a tee. Although now returned to my normal setting, my life was anything but normal. My year-plus in Gloucestershire had allowed wild, irresponsible tendencies inherent in me to take over. I didn't need any bait. I entered the trap of idleness and disinterest all too eagerly.

In a home where learning was not emphasized, and at a poorly equipped, antiquated school where even some of the wartime teachers were reluctant participants in the instruction process, my slim chances of becoming a decent student evaporated. A rather exaggerated indifference to education became a marked trait for the remaining years of my brief formal schooling. I accept that my opinion of the British educational system of my time is prejudiced. But Professor Arthur Marwick, University of Edinburgh, wrote in his 1968 book *Britain in the Century of Total War*: "... an educational system based on an inequitable competitiveness created an iniquitous segregation between those children designed to acquire useful knowledge and skills, and those to be cast aside at age 15." (1) In my case, it would be at age 14.

Another of Eddie's initiatives introduced us to the horizon-broadening adventure of riding the world-recognized red, double-decker London buses. On weekends, the London Public Transport Board offered six-penny, ride-all-day tickets that let us explore some of the many different routes within metropolitan London. As an example, we'd ride to central

London and, from there, board a bus with a route that took it to the outer edge of the city's western or northern suburbs. These explorations were infrequent because six-pence represented a sizeable sum. But when I could afford it, I saw that other suburbs offered more graceful living than my own. The houses weren't all attached to each other. They had neat, if small, front gardens and bigger versions at the rear. They had space on both sides separating them from their neighbors. Each time we passed through central London, I also became aware of the huge numbers of foreign military personnel in the city. One saw uniforms from the United States, many continental nations under German control, and virtually every nation within the British Commonwealth. Their hats, in particular, were varied and colorful, and their regimental badges so pridefully macho.

This was, I believe, when I first fantasized about foreign countries, despite my skimpy knowledge of geography. An ill-focused yearning about international destinations lodged in me. I thought wistfully of these places while, at the same time, retaining a sentimental attachment to home: all very confusing.

A life-molding event arrived for me in 1943. Now 11 years old I, in common with same aged children attending state schools, sat the education test that determined whether one was channeled into a more academic program or dumped into a school where vocational skills were, theoretically, taught. Unlike my sister, I failed that fateful examination. This meant my last three years of formal schooling were at a facility disbursing a minimal level of instruction in anything. Of course, at that time I wasn't concerned over this failure because I simply had no concept of its significance. Further, the adults in my world seemingly had no better understanding of the importance of this "Y" in the road of life than I did myself.

Thus, when school resumed after the summer recess, I transferred from Salisbury Junior co-educational school to the all-male Sandringham Secondary modern school. The reality of these so-called vocational schools meant the average student emerged virtually useless. Reading, writing and arithmetic skills achieved were abysmal. The facility was not equipped to teach any trades except perhaps a little carpentry. After three years that was all I came away with. Inadequate skills for a 14-year-old to bring to the labor market

At a distance of about 2 miles from our house, I walked to the new school and back each morning and afternoon. It was too far to go home for lunch. This meant Mom's tasty, individually prepared lunches had to be given up for the midday offerings of the student cafeteria where mass-produced meals were mostly bland, sometimes unappetizing.

An interesting but rueful bit of information I learned much later is that the British government, in 1939, had decided to raise the school leaving age to 15 years. It was officially scheduled for implementation on 3 September 1939. That just happened to be the day Britain and France declared war on Germany. This educational reform was put on ice because of the war. Tens of thousands of children, myself included, lost out on an extra year of schooling.

In time I developed a strong, if rather impractical, resentment against the British educational system which, I felt, had short-changed me. The children of the bigger cities, evacuated two or three times, had their schooling so disrupted they stood little chance of passing the critical 11-plus test. It seemed that simple fairness required the authorities to make some kind of special arrangement to assist my generation to make up the serious gaps in our education. Of course, the war had sucked dry British resources and evacuees were destined to live with their seriously atrophied education.

Ironically, and with the benefit of much hindsight, it seems just keeping children in school extra time does not necessarily achieve much. Since WWII, Britain has twice raised the state secondary school leaving age. Children now leave at 16. Yet many of these school-leavers emerge no better educated than those generations that left at 13 and 14. In America, keeping youths in school until 18 certainly appears to do nothing for those unmotivated.

Probably in some kind of perverse effort to show the world I didn't care I'd missed the education train, at 11½ years I acquired my first girl friend, Amy Nichols, aged 12 ½, one of the performers from the song and dance trio in Eddie's amateur variety show. Amy, too, had failed the 11-plus examination and was now in an all-girl modern secondary school where, theoretically, she learned the basics plus a little smattering of home economics. In reality, Amy no doubt learned as little as I in my all-male vocational school. At least with this infatuation, there was not so great an age difference as with the Irish nurse. My amour was, regrettably, two inches taller than I was but I took our puppy love as wondrously as kids do. Just being with her was like Christmas. Eddie liked Donna Moledina, the smallest, darkest, and most flamboyant, girl of the trio. Supposedly her family could be traced back to Iberian origins. Amy, my choice, was probably the most plebeian of the three. The third girl, Shirley Lockman, arguably the classiest and no doubt most intelligent, didn't have a male admirer and didn't seem to want one. Unfortunately, she always tagged along and, like a chaperon, reined in her friends.

We met as a group some summer evenings. Mostly we had no money, and just walked the streets window-shopping in Manor Park's "downtown." On the rare occasion a few coins jingled in our pockets, we'd take a bus or walk the mile and half to a milk bar on East Ham High Street. Gathered round a small circular table mounted on a pedestal, we each strained to be the wittiest of the group as we sucked on milkshakes that were an anemic substitute for those we saw made and served at soda fountains in American movies. Usually I'd be the first one to finish the drink because I always wanted to get to the next phase of evening's proceedings that happened on the street where these dancing divas lived. Good things awaited me under a covered stairway leading to the emergency backdoor of a community social center at the end of their street of menial row houses.

We'd first sit on the lower steps where an overhead entrance light illuminated the group and we'd continue with our idle chatter that had occupied us at the milk bar. Halfway up, the flight turned a corner, and a shadowy dimness prevailed. It wasn't too long before I urged my chorus girl to climb the steps. Once there, the serious petting began. But Shirley Lockman, the annoying, self-appointed chaperon, would remain on the bottom steps and continue a running conversation with her two friends. Their protectress played her role effectively. It only occurred to me later that this routine probably was part of the trio's secret plan to keep Eddie and me in check.

Amy and I did get to be alone, however, on some Saturdays when we went to a local cinema featuring morning American cowboy serials for kids. Riding on the bus to the theater, and lining up with her until the show started, was the highlight of my week. With Amy as my older and taller sweetheart, I believed I'd achieved a type of precocious manhood. Inside the darkened auditorium I enjoyed the magic of her kisses. But the passage of time cruelly taught me this thrill doesn't last, and my budding hormonal chemistry pushed me to seek a fuller destiny. Eventually my persistent pestering gained me the privilege of touching her rudimentary breasts through her clothing. They were so rudimentary, however, and her clothing so thick, that this, too, quickly lost its initial exhilaration.

One Saturday morning, in the movie's especially action-packed, penultimate episode, the good guys were on the verge of suffering a humiliating wipeout. American justice, or at least the Hollywood version, was at risk of being snuffed out in the rocky, dusty Wild West. The audience of excited children was on the edge of their seats, hoarse from cheering the white- and booing the black-hatters. The high tide of roiling emotion that swamped the local movie fleapit must have swept Amy up and carried her along. She wanted to contribute something. With her mouth against my ear, I received the startling information that I was cleared to insert a hand inside her dress at neckline. She imposed one restriction: my hand must remain in the center and not stray east or west.

Without considering how I was limiting my development as a complete male, I hastily agreed to her terms. With the steely determination and high anticipation of the weekend amateur spelunker, I started down. It proved a difficult gymnastic maneuver to execute while trying to maintain the inconspicuous appearance of the normal child movie viewer. I discovered that her family's position on the social scale meant she wore only clothing several sizes too small constricting access even to my slim arm. While I struggled, she just sat there watching the silver screen as though not involved in our own little melodrama. Her detachment seemed inappropriate at this tingling, first-in-a-lifetime event. To gain access, I finally found it necessary to half standup and turn sideways to wiggle my hand down to the promised land. At the same time, I kept my head in the direction of the screen to avoid missing the not-quite-Oscar-level goings-on. A less-than-graceful posture.

My explorations attracted the attention of nearby kids. A snide remark or two echoed around us. They couldn't have appreciated the purity of my relationship with Amy. I sensed she was becoming uneasy. Fearing the greatest moment in my life might end almost before it began, I impetuously let my hand dart sideways to touch one of the tiny, forbidden nipples. She let out a squeal, which was taken up by what I estimated to be a majority of the boys in our section of the packed theater, and grabbed my forearm to drag my groping digits to the surface.

The film ended with the good guys trapped in a gulch about to be flooded by the bad guys dislodging boulders from the high wall of a valley reservoir. At least they were in a valley; I never found hers. We had to return the next Saturday morning to find out which side won. But I was never again allowed to roam in that territory soon to erupt with wonderful protuberances, and shortly after she dropped me.

CHAPTER 8

In July 1943, the Allied Forces invaded Sicily and, in early September, landed on the Italian mainland. My father participated in support of these major military actions. A defiant, increasingly irrational Hitler, from the safety of his Berlin underground bunker, continued to order his token western-based air squadrons on intermittent nocturnal bombing raids on London. One night the air raid siren sounded in our immediate area.

Mom aroused Vera, came into my room to shake me awake, and picked up Roy, who still slept in my room. She wrapped him in a blanket and headed out the door on her way to the garden doghouse. As she went out, she shouted at me to come to the shelter immediately. I turned over and went back to sleep. How long Mom waited for me I don't know, but she eventually returned to shake me again. She went through her patient pleading ritual once more, and I repeated my practiced objections that I'd take my chances with the Luftwaffe rather than get out of bed.

My words represented a childish display of dumb obstinacy. I'm certain I wouldn't have traded my life for a few more minutes in that warm bed, no matter how cozy. But defiantly I lifted the pillow and thrust my head under it, clinging to the sides in case Mom tried to pull it off. She didn't. She left the room, and I probably smirked to myself that I'd won this little battle with Mom. I had not. On her way back to the shelter, she encountered our neighbor, Mr. Trent, in his garden en route to his safety hole. She asked for his assistance to roust me out of bed. Although endangering himself by not going straight to his shelter, I suspect he gladly complied with Mom's request. Over the years I hadn't endeared myself to the plain-talking, no-nonsense Mr. Trent whose life passion was his back garden.

Several times when he and his wife were out, I stole into that small, sacred domain to sample a few of his ripe, plump gooseberries. The man must have been a genius because he instinctively knew who had performed these outrages. This pumped-up Sherlock Holmes saw my footprints in his gooseberry patch. With all the aplomb of a district attorney, and in front of my mother, he accused me of these back-yard border violations. I, of course, denied all knowledge, feigning a deep hurt. Thus, he must have salivated when he stepped into our garden through a neighbor-friendly gap in the fence, came into our house, and mounted the stairs to the bedroom where I slept.

The strong, bony hand that grabbed my shoulder practically lifted me off the bed. Somehow my resistance, so invincible against my mother's imploring, melted at Mr. Trent's gruff exhortations. I knew deep down his motivation wasn't my bodily safety. I leapt out of bed, tugged overcoat and shoes on, and bolted for the shelter. He followed me through the dark garden, with the aid of a flashlight, to finish his lecture. According to him, my usefulness on earth was questioned because I gave my mother so much trouble. Her life was difficult enough with the war and three children to care for alone. He asserted I represented triple the trouble of Roy, my goodie-two-shoes brother.

He must have then strode triumphantly through the opening in the fence and went to his own shelter to await the all-clear siren. I sat on a bunk in our doghouse, wrapped in a blanket, mad at Hitler, mad at Mom, mad at the neighbor, but especially mad at Roy. Why couldn't Roy dispense some trouble as well? Why did I have to do it all?

The new school I now attended bore the impressive name "Sandringham." This customary Victorian-era, multi-story prison-like building, however, had nothing in common with the ornate Tudor-style Sandringham House, the Royals' grand residence on a large estate in Norfolk, and designated as their summer residence. My recollection of the learning imparted at the new school is almost as non-existent as at the previous middle school. Yet one incident remains vivid. Most of the lunch meals were basic and unimaginative, although wholesome. Occasionally, however, the "item du jour" was tapioca, which resembled frog-spawn, something that some boys gagged on. On a day this loathsome food was served, instead of wolfing it down to spend as much of the one-and-half-hour break in the playground as possible, a few boys ate most reluctantly and time dragged on. The elderly male teacher on lunch duty was delayed for his own break-room lunch, cigarette or pipe, and the daily newspaper. Anger mounted on both sides.

Finally, five or six boys remained, me included, dawdling over the repugnant, gooey dollop on our plates. The teacher, now patrolling the aisles like a prison guard, warned us that we needed to "eat up this good food." Each time the admonition came, we reluctantly shoveled in another mouthful and then reverted to pushing the now cold slime from one side of the plate to the other after he passed by. I suspected tapioca wasn't the teacher's noontime fare.

"Sir, I don't want to eat any more. It makes me feel sick," one boy complained as the teacher reached his table, reversing the famous grievance in Charles Dickens' *Oliver Twist.* The teacher stopped abruptly and turned, glowering fiercely at the lamenting boy.

"There's a war on, boy! Food is scarce. You *will* finish it all," was the snarling reply. Ominously, the teacher sat on the bench next to the protester. All our eyes were now riveted on the table and plate at the center of the confrontation. The isolated boy took a mouthful and masticated for the longest time before swallowing.

"Sir, I just can't eat more. It'll make me sick," he repeated, defiantly pushing the plate to the center of the bench table.

"Disobedient ingrate! You will eat it all," the teacher bellowed as he turned to the boy and, using alternate hands, he slapped him hard on both sides of his head, and then delivered two closed-fist heavy punches the boy's nearest shoulder. On the second blow the dissenter slid several places along the seat and leaned his head forward to rest on the table, audibly spluttering as he tried to stifle his sobbing.

An electric atmosphere now pervaded the room. Used to being hit with the open hand, especially by the male teachers, these punches took physical punishment to a different plane. It both shocked and scared me. I also wanted to protest the food, but kept a cowardly silence. I had a deep-seated although vague feeling the school had no right to force us to eat what was repulsive to us. Unfortunately, the civil rights of British working-class schoolchildren were still somewhat theoretical at that time. Whoever had right on their side, the teacher won. We all finished the tapioca. But I had great admiration for that brave boy whose courage to say what he felt put the rest of us to shame. It is sadly ironic to reflect that today students are no longer scared of teachers. Society has come to almost accept the reverse.

Another aspect of the educational system of which I was a product has long perplexed me. Separating the sexes at the onset of puberty tends to generate a strong shyness among the genders. This has helped produce a culture where boys and girls are rarely friends. I suspect this helps promote the perception among some teen boys that girls are mere sex objects. An early observation of mine in America, where the sexes are not separated in state schools during the educational years, was that boys and girls are far more at ease in each other's company than in Britain. There is noticeably less shyness in children. Yet such separation often is better from academic aspects. Another imponderable of human nature.

Perhaps this touches upon another comparison that intrigued me between Britons and Americans, especially in my first decades in America. I early read of a perceived difference between the two peoples, famously said to be separated by their common language. Americans were characterized as optimists; Britons as pessimists. In broad, general terms, I felt this to be true. If valid, was this related to the two education systems? Or was it more the outcome of a frontier land with room to move and grow versus the Brits on their tight little island where some 400 families have owned much of the land for hundreds of years? I'm still pondering this one.

Meanwhile, in early 1944, the war moved closer to our house. It came, in fact, immediately opposite us on the common. One day, a fleet of Army trucks drove on to the open land and British soldiers unloaded several hundred rolls of barbed wire. This they stretched to enclose an area that to my mind looked enormous, outrageously encompassing our sacred soccer field. Days later neat rows of large khaki teepee tents sprouted like forest toadstools. Young, boisterous Canadian soldiers soon occupied them all. We who lived opposite the common in sight of these boyish Canadians observed them with interest exercising and relaxing around the tents behind their barbed wire stockade.

They spent a lot of time throwing balls at each other which they caught with one hand enclosed in what looked like a an oversized boxing glove with fingers. I didn't know the national game of North America, but from my side of the barbed wire, it didn't look as thrilling as blasting a ball with one's feet.

The presence of these well-paid young men noticeably impacted our community, some of it appreciated by the locals, and some not. At the nearby "Golden Fleece" public house, situated only about 100 yards from our house, their relative wealth soon exacerbated the problem of limited supplies of beer and spirits. Those locals who regularly frequented the establishment moaned among themselves when the various types of liquid happiness quickly sold out. Among the area's single women, these soldiers were a refreshing source of fun in blacked-out, scarcity-ridden London.

The big picture, however, escaped the understanding of us local boys, who mostly saw things starkly in terms of the game of soccer. We were mad that our soccer pitch was now in the middle of their encampment and had to move to an area nearly at the eastern edge of the common. Some of the land there had been turned into victory vegetable gardens rented out by the local council to private individuals. The national government had a program encouraging people to grow food to help win the war. Our half-day-long Sunday soccer games often saw the ball ballooning over the waist-high wire and wooden stave fencing right on to someone's victory garden. If that individual happened to be working the allotment, a shouting match ensued. The patriotic vegetable growers, mostly elderly men, would threaten to puncture our ball with their gardening forks. We, smart alecks, would retort we're on public land and could play football in perpetuity. Our language wouldn't have been so formal, of course.

We had no choice and soon became accustomed to seeing the Canadian soldiers in their bivouac, or walking to and from the station to catch trains to Central London. Then, in mid-April 1944, they were confined to camp. If they knew why they were restricted, we certainly didn't. But it inaugurated an interesting time for us neighborhood kids. In the afternoons, when they had finished their daily routines and we arrived home from school, quite a few soldiers congregated inside the barbed wire fence each armed with a metal bucket and broom. But this was no clean-up squad. The buckets, hung on the end of the brooms, contained English money and were passed through the rolled-wire fence. We took the buckets to the nearby "Golden Fleece" to get them filled with beer while the rationed supply lasted. The local beer swillers weren't happy, but we kids were on to a good thing. We struggled back to the fence with the sloshing meads foaming, moving slowly because of a bucket's weight and to avoid spillage. The young troops would use their brooms and muscles to maneuver the smelly brown liquid through the wire stockade. They tipped us generously, and we enjoyed a brief, rare prosperity.

Then, toward the end of May, they were prohibited from having us eager, unkempt barmaids in short pants, make these beer runs. So these Canadians dreamed up a new game to help pass the lengthening light evenings. They came to the perimeter fence and threw English coins through the wire to watch us local girls and boys scramble and squabble like hungry hyenas picking up their scattered loose change. The bigger kids got the lion's share, and all endured a few trodden-on hands in the melee. My treasure wound up at the candy store. The soldiers knew they had no further need of their money.

One morning, at the end of that month, I came out of my house to find the camp deserted.. As we learned later, the troops departed overnight for the English south coast in preparation for the D-Day invasion of Normandy. Planned for the early hours of 5 June, bad weather in the English Channel forced a torturous 24-hour delay. We local kids felt abandoned by the Canadians. We had to entertain ourselves again, and without financial rewards.

At dawn on 6 June more than 6,800 vessels, large and small appeared off the Normandy coast. The Canadians stormed ashore at Courseulles-sur-Mer to form a beachhead designated as "Juno," one of the six Allied landing sites of the biggest military sea-borne invasion in all history (1). Many of these young men, who had ordered their beer by the bucketful, and who rained coins on us kids for fun, never survived to have kids of their own.

The hard-fought, successful Allied invasion of France sent a wave of high hope sweeping through the British people. At last Hitler had been dealt a real bloody nose. But our national jubilation was short-lived, as the fight wasn't over for the German nation. One week after D-Day, Hitler came out of his corner swinging. On 13 June 1944 he directed the first V-1 flying bomb, the Vergeltungswaffe Eins (Vengeance Weapon 1), against London (2).

German scientists and engineers had secretly designed and tested, and thousands of slave laborers now built, a new class of weapon. The pilotless drone was launched across the North Sea from sites on the coast of Holland with one thousand kilograms (1.1 tons) of high explosive packed in its nose. It had a range of about 150 miles, flying at 360 mph at an altitude of about six thousand feet. The drone's primitive magnetic compass and mechanical clock made it highly erratic, but London's 874 square miles provided a large bull's-eye (3). Its pulsejet engine was loud, and it became known among ordinary people as the "buzz bomb" or "doodlebug" because of this distinctive sound and rather plodding pace. When the pre-set timer stopped its engine, it was eerily quiet, but you knew to take cover as the projectile at that moment plummeted towards earth. They succeeded in wreaking great, if imprecise, damage. Some 3,500 V-1s reached the London area and took the souls of another 6,184 people and injured 42,146 more (4).

On one clear night I stayed out late with my girl friend even though the air-raid siren had sounded. As I walked home, I witnessed several of the stub-winged cylinders droning overhead to their random targets with orange/yellow jet trails lighting the sky. Regardless of danger, I found it thrilling. When I reached home, I encountered an especially angry mother. Rather than going to the garden shelter, Mom had remained in the house knowing I had no door key. I'm sure I didn't recognize my mother's good deed.

Meanwhile, the introduction of this revolutionary weapon concerned and galvanized the British government to organize yet another evacuation of London children. This program went much faster and smoother because of the experience gained during the 1940/41 London Blitz. My brother, Roy, now six and in school, and I were swept up and shipped out. Devon, in the southwest of England, became our destination for this war-induced separation (the third for me.) Mom accompanied us on this evacuation. Torquay had been selected as the town on which the children from our district schools were dumped. In mid July 1944 we traveled there by train. Because of its larger size, an invasion of kids from the lower classes into Torquay did not carry the same impact as in the Gloucestershire village.

Torquay, a more refined seaside resort and retirement spot, sits on a promontory forming the southern end of Babbacombe Bay, on the English Channel. It was not our fate, however, to be assigned to a comfortable family or well-heeled pensioners. We wound up billeted with a semi-rural, older couple eking out a frugal living from a minimal smallholding in Barton, a community then on Torquay's outskirts. They reared half a dozen pigs, raised many more chickens, and grew some vegetables, all on about a half-acre plot. No doubt the couple volunteered to board evacuees solely to supplement their subsistence-level earnings with the government allowance. Their home was already small for them and a rather sullen girl, aged 16 or 17, with ginger hair, who occupied a second bedroom. I didn't know her familial relationship to the couple, but she didn't appear to be their natural daughter.

Roy and I were assigned to a tiny, sloped-ceiling garret wedged under the roof that looked like a hasty, self-made plywood addition that just met the requirement of a separate room to qualify for the allowance under the evacuee program. Mom stayed a few days with us, sharing the bed in our cubbyhole, while we settled into the house and routine of our new, money-grubbing guardians. School was out for the summer, so we didn't have to worry about that for another month and a half.

On Mom's last day, she took Roy and I to Torquay's fashionable sea front where, although none of us could swim, we enjoyed a sunny summer day on the beach. I can still recall building sandcastles, climbing on rocks, and seeing trapped salt-water pools when the tide went out. Our happiness on that day was conditioned by the dreaded knowledge that on the next day, Mom had to return to London.

A brief distraction from my feelings of foreboding occurred as the three of us walked along the town's sea front esplanade to the stop where we caught a return bus to Barton. A large number of American sailors were stationed around Torquay. That afternoon we encountered two young ones, both highly intoxicated, as they staggered along the sidewalk on the other side. They had their arms around each other's shoulders as mutual support and, perhaps, a gesture of the bonding achieved while reaching their advanced state of inebriation. After every few steps one or the other would sink to his knees, pitch forward and dislodge his pillbox style cloth hat that rolled in a circle on its side before stopping upright. The bulging contents of the jumper breast pockets of their white uniforms spilt prodigally onto the sidewalk. Even packs of cigarettes, tucked neatly in rolled up sleeves, were abruptly jettisoned. The still standing buddy would unsteadily sink forward onto his hands and knees, as if about to pray to Allah, to join the other rummaging around on the sidewalk, cursing colorfully, picking up cigarette packs, lighters, combs, keys and coins and other items. With possessions now reloaded into the breast pocket, they'd manage to stand-up and set off again. Roy and I watched from across the street in stunned awe at our very first sighting of drunken men. Eventually Mum said that men were silly, and we needed to hurry for the bus to our new accommodation.

Next morning my heart broke. I started crying the moment I woke and instantly remembered Mom's departure. My balling continued nonstop. The woman of the house, whose name I don't remember, complained that, at age 12, I should be ashamed of acting like a baby. Roy, six years my junior, was not nearly as tearful. Mom told the woman that it was just the way I was—a not very insightful comment in retrospect.

After Mom left the house to get the bus to Torquay's train station, I continued crying up a storm. Either the women sent me outside or I chose to go, because I can remember sitting on the street curb sobbing loudly, telling Roy he shouldn't do the same! Slowly my distress subsided, but it was well toward evening. I choose to believe now my excessive tearfulness was an early manifestation that my emotional health was already out of kilter.

Our austere quarters were constantly pervaded by the unpleasant smell of pigswill cooking in large metal kettles on two gas rings right outside the kitchen window. Each morning the elderly smallholder walked the blue-collar neighborhood streets collecting food waste in two trashcans mounted on a homemade handcart. A few mornings, while school had not convened, he said I should accompany him. It doesn't take much imagination to visualize the pitiful food refuse thrown out by ordinary people during wartime. I even felt it insulted the pigs. But my guardian always told me to get everything by scraping out the resident's old buckets placed on the street curb as far from the house as possible.

The couple proved strict, at least for my self-indulgent taste. Roy and I had to make our own beds, hang up our clothes, and clear off the table after we ate. This lifestyle was so contrary to how we lived at home. My undisciplined self resented these practices which were, in reality, not all that stringent. They discouraged talking at the meal table, so we mostly ate in an oppressive silence. Yet the old man on occasion chose the meal table to castigate the red-haired girl for some perceived failure in her performance of one or other of several household chores assigned to her, including all the washing up.

At the time, Torquay crawled with military personnel from all three services and many countries. As a teenager she was no doubt itching to date a few of them. He knew this and railed against it. She usually chose not to respond and, dejectedly, continued eating her food. One time, however, she must have gone out secretly with a military man, and our guardian found out. He screamed at her that he forbid this behavior. This time she was brave enough to scream back. She told him that once she reached 18 he would have no more control over her and she'd do as she wanted. He jumped to his feet, knocking his chair over, and stormed out the room into his yard, perhaps to abuse the pigs or the chickens. Roy and I cowered, exchanging fearful glances, glad we were not involved in this noisy altercation.

After just a few weeks in Torquay I was convinced my fate was eternal unhappiness. Compared with the easy-going ways of home, this severe, tense household represented utter misery. I began writing frequent, cryptic, misspelled, and ungrammatical pleas to Mom. *Yore sons despirit and unhapy; let us come home imidliatly. Pigs nicer than gardeuns.* No doubt I exaggerated my sadness because I do have pleasant memories of the area countryside we explored before the summer vacation ended on 1st September.

An abandoned quarry not too far from our Barton billet made for a marvelous playground. It contained a large disused limekiln in which we could take refuge when it rained. If there was a safety fence around the quarry I don't remember, but we were never barred from gaining access. In my boy's mind I recall the quarry as dug to a tremendous depth. A brief return visit in 1998 showed the depth to be 75 to 100 feet only. In England's tight little island, neat houses now crowd the quarry floor and climb a short way up terraced sides.

There's no doubt we earthy London kids failed to appreciate the natural attractions of our new evacuee site that provided us another hiding place from Adolph Hitler. We were now lowering the quality of genteel life in Torquay with its Riviera-like climate. Its elegant streets rose from Babbacombe Bay waterside on terraces of fuchsias, mimosas and flowering palms. Indeed, the county of Devon exuded a charmed wholesomeness from its lush rolling uplands where sheep flecked verdant fields to the tradition of cream and jam scones at high tea, regrettably much curtailed by the war. We were, however, indifferent to county hallmarks.

During our brief stay in Barton, as we walked along lanes and through fields exploring the area, we discovered a new and exciting pastime: smoking. Some local kids showed us how to make pipes from nature. For the bowl we hollowed out a large acorn from an oak tree.

The pipe stem came from Cow's Parsley, a widely growing hedgerow weed whose stalk had a hard casing, pulpy interior, and small center hole extending its length. Inserting a five-inch piece of the weed into an aperture made at the base of the acorn produced an efficient smoking device. None of us, of course, had money for tobacco, but the large numbers of American military in the area solved that problem. We didn't have much luck begging cigarettes from them. They said we looked too young. So we relied on their generous discards. We discovered that the wealthy Americans threw their cigarettes down in the street when only half-smoked. The Brits smoked theirs until lips burned.

We searched street gutters for the wasteful American leavings. These were broken open and we used the loose tobacco in our native pipes. Then, behind hedgerows in secluded fields or up among concealing tree branches, we'd light our pipes like little old men with the seriousness of an American Indian calumet ceremony. I don't remember what we discussed during these pow-wows, marked by coughing fits, but almost certainly conversations excluded schoolwork, scripture, and wholesome citizenry.

My syntactically flawed pleas about my universe of unhappiness, mailed regularly to Mom on postcards, eventually worked. She let us return to London even though the new bombing emergency still existed. The county authorities discouraged return of children until sanctioned by the national government. It must, therefore, have been a difficult decision for Mom, and she would have had to pay our fares. But Roy and I returned to London, I believe in late August 1944.

That summer had seen the Allies pushing the Germans back on the western front, and the Russians doing the same in the east. Within days of Roy and I arriving back at our London home, Hitler produced still another trick from his sleeve. On 8 September, he introduced the V-2 guided missile into the arsenal of man's evil devices. Shaped like a giant artillery shell, the 46' long V-2 packed more than a ton of explosives. Launched straight up it zoomed to a height of about 60 miles. Its automatic pilot guidance system shut-off at a pre-set time causing the missile to dive onto the target. At peak speed, the missile traveled three times the speed of the V-1, or 932mph. Faster than the speed of sound, people could not hear it. Only a massive explosion announced its deadly arrival (4). Hitler's ultimate terror weapon penetrated to a deeper level of fear in Londoners who were, by now, traumatized after five years of war.

The V-2 had one great tactical advantage over the V-1, which required a fixed elevated track to launch. The V-2 could be shot from virtually any solid, flat space. The firing crews, in fact, moved the projection pads frequently to avoid detection by Allied bombers who by now dominated the skies over Germany and its occupied areas. Germany's first V-2s aimed at London were fired from the Ardennes, the heavily wooded, elevated plateau of northeastern France, that slops over into Belgium and Luxembourg. Within four months it was to be the scene of the Battle of the Bulge, some of the bitterest WWII fighting on the European Continent. The weapon had come late in the war, and this most advanced invention of WWII was prohibitively expensive. They then required large amounts of alcohol and liquid oxygen to propel them on their deadly mission (4).

Mom worried our return more or less coincided with the V-2's arrival in our capital. She would never have agreed to my request had she known the true nature of this new weapon falling on London. But no one of the Allies, high or low, knew the fearsome nature and destructive power of this weapon. On 12 October 1944, Hitler ordered that the V-2 campaign be concentrated on Britain and Belgium. During the following six months, more than a thousand V-2s struck Britain, over half in London, and nearly two thousand in Belgium. There was no effective defense against the V-2. Had this weapon been available to Hitler in the first two years of the war when Britain stood alone, there could have been a groundswell of fear among British people that they might well have demanded the country surrender, something not attained by heavy bombing from manned aircraft.

Then war's destructive hand came as close to our home as anything so far. On a cold day in January 1945, Roy went to a friend's house on a nearby street, about a three-minute walk away, to play indoors. The house sat across the road from the London Cooperative Society's milk bottling plant enclosed by that grim 8' high brick security wall, topped by broken glass. During the morning a V-2 fell perhaps 25 yards inside the bottling plant compound across from the house where Roy played. The security wall absorbed the main force of the explosion. Even so, the fronts of several houses in that section collapsed. Fortunately, Roy and his friend were in the rear. The only injury to any of the occupants was a three-inch cut on Roy's forehead from flying debris. Mom's compassion in allowing us to come home could have had a tragic outcome: I, as usual, the little instigator.

The V-2 rocket was the last punch Hitler threw at Britain in the war, and the last individual V-2 fired at England, two days after my 13th birthday, fell on 29 March. The air raids ended. Mom and us three children weren't physically maimed, save for Roy's recent head abrasion. Dad, despite the sinking of his troop ship, also hadn't been injured. Our family had survived. Yet as a family we had sustained a degree of psychological trauma. Whether it was more profound on the adults or the children would be for an expert to say.

By then all indications were that each day the Allies moved closer to delivering the coup de grace to a Germany fast caving in on both fronts. A griping account of the last days of Germany's Third Reich is in the memoir *Inside the Third Reich* by Albert Speer, Hitler's Armaments Minister (5).

CHAPTER 9

When American teens finish high school, their right of passage is elaborately celebrated. Nothing commemorated our transfer into the world of work. In fact, I have no recollection of exchanging farewells with any teachers, not even the soccer coach with whom I'd had cordial relations. One day I was an object on the state education conveyor belt for working-class children, the next I stood on the threshold of working life. It is a singularly mean-spirited education system that doesn't observe this significant right-of-passage. Having been a heedless student, of course, I now confronted the cold shower, make-a-living world. Yet I really had nothing to offer prospective employers. My reading level was modest, to be gentle on myself. I had never gone beyond fractions and percentages in arithmetic. Since age eleven I'd attended a supposedly vocational school. In reality, it had been equipped with nothing but a few carpentry benches and a tiny selection of ancient tools. My exposure to carpentry had been so limited as to be virtually useless, although the subject did have some appeal. I liked working with wood on the bench in our cellar whenever a piece of scrap fell into my hands. Essentially, however, at age 14, I had no clue as to how I could or should spend my working life.

Remarkably, this pitiful state wasn't exceptional among my fellow elementary-school leavers in war-shadowed 1946. Only a few were headed for apprenticeships, arranged by fathers who were themselves skilled tradesmen. Many would become laborers on "the buildings" as construction work was called. Such unskilled jobs paid the most to beginning manual workers. Contractors were just getting started on many repair or new construction projects in Britain's bomb-damaged cities. Shoveling rubble into buckets on a construction site, however, did not appeal to me, but I'm unclear why. Getting dirty never bothered me. I was truly ignorant of what my options were. With Dad still overseas, Mom found my first job, just around the corner from our house, only a four-minute walk. The London Cooperative Society (LCS), a member-rebate early supermarket-cum-department store chain, was my first employer. Its facilities stood behind that now re-built brick wall that possibly saved Roy's life when the V-2 fell inside some 15 months earlier.

It offered its East London customers the service of mattress restoration. In those days people didn't automatically throw out old or dirty mattresses. The LCS removed and laundered the cover, and the filling, normally made of clump-prone cotton felt or curled horsehair, passed between spiked rollers that milled the material smooth. My vital job in this grungy process was where it began. Armed with a seam ripper, I unpicked one end of a cover, plunged an arm inside to start extracting the mostly lumpy innards onto a light workbench. John Parsons, a boy who'd done this job before, spent a few hours showing me the ropes. Now sixteen, he'd been promoted to work in the more exciting shipping department. He had started at the plant in 1944 while war still raged. We became friendly during the morning and afternoon tea breaks.

John filled me in about my first employer. In addition to the mattress factory, the LCS included a large milk bottling plant already mentioned. Shoe and upholstery repair—both big business in those days—occupied other decaying brick buildings. The parking lot for the sizeable fleet of milk home-delivery vehicles, and the garage that maintained them, claimed the biggest area. But not all of John's tales concerned facts and figures of LCS services.

He related that, because of the shortage of men during the war, a mixed-gender staff worked nights at the milk plant. Alongside the clinking bottles being filled as they traveled along belts, a few war-induced romances bloomed in those uncertain times. But the pervading slightly sour smell, and the lowered temperature maintained in the premises, tended to discourage ardor. So these urgent couples took to sneaking into the mattress restoration facility to temporarily occupy customer property for the release of their war-induced tensions. An interesting variation of traditional British tea breaks! His supervisor assigned him the job of walking among the mattress piles when the day shift started to pick-up the evidence of this nocturnal lovemaking. Proof that humans devise clever ways to relieve the pressures of war. When the LCS business operations returned to what passed for normality with the advent of world peace, the practice of unauthorized nocturnal use of customer property had stopped by the time I arrived.

John telling me about this unusual aspect of industrial relations led us into the whole and, for me, still mysterious, field of human sexuality. He seemed to know everything relating to this exciting topic. This was a subject in which I was intensely interested because the urgent, merciless male sex drive had now kicked in the front door and taken possession of me. I listened in stunned awe as he revealed for me the wonderful world of women. He'd achieved a self-taught mastery in the mechanics of self-release, which threw open the gates of paradise. But "I digress as a man with a grievance always does," to quote George Bernard Shaw.

After emptying a bed cover of its contents, which sometimes proved as difficult to emerge into this world as turtle hatchlings on a remote beach, I then broomed the mess into a large canvas bag rigged on a trolley. I wheeled it to another unenthusiastic worker who fed it into the milling rollers. Then back to the bench to re-start the process. Within days this dreary work brought me to the realization school hadn't been so dull after all. The work wasn't dirty, but extremely dusty. Nobody wore protective masks. The collective malodorous smell of the mattress covers, which nightly had supported so many unwashed east London bodies, offended my nostrils. A stale mustiness permeated my area of the factory.

After the first week I disliked it so much, I determined to quit. I complained about the dust, and probably exaggerated it, to Mom. She agreed it could present a danger in time and did not object to me leaving so soon. Even though my first job was brief, later I realized I gained a few bits of life experience at the mattress-restoration game.

Once as I pulled the stuffing from the corner of a mattress, a rather dingy pearl necklace dropped onto the bench. Someone had hidden her prize jewelry piece, probably the only one owned, inside the mattress. Whether it had any value I didn't know. Fifty percent of me said stick it in my pocket; 50% suffered from a youthful conscience. So I proudly carried it to the supervisor who didn't even commend my honesty. He casually tossed it on the edge of his worktable and, without looking at me, mumbled it would be returned to the customer. His demeanor, however, made me suspect he was not too burdened with a youthful conscience.

Further arousing my suspicions, during the next few days, he seemed to avoid my work area. My early natural cynicism started to tell me that the necklace now graced his wife's neck when it should have been around my mom's. Eventually I found the courage to go to his small office to ask him if the necklace had found its way back to the customer. He surveyed me with palpable disdain and exploded.

"'Oo the fucking 'ell you fink you are? You 'oose only been 'ere not a munf! Don't you be telling me 'ow to do me job! I been 'ere 12 years and don't forgit it! Get back to your bench and stay there, you bleedin' little runt!"

Suddenly he noticed that so far he hadn't really answered my original question.

"I turned that bit of junk over to the plant manager and 'ee made sure it got back to the customer. Now fuck orf!"

Totally unsatisfied I returned to my work area, now convinced the necklace was a string of rare, large cultured pearls from the fabled Japan Sea oyster beds. But I couldn't decide if they were around the neck of the wife of that dubious supervisor or the higher plant manager whom I'd only seen once. Nothing else happened about my find, and I'll go to my grave believing a reunion between necklace and customer never took place. This little incident, I firmly believe, taught me something of the ways of human nature; the learning was just as real as that derived from a social science course in human behavior. I just had to find an alternate occupation because, at the time, I faced a working life of 51 years.

One of the boys I knew at school and with whom I still played Sunday soccer told me about his job. His company made linotype print blocks (a metal mold on wood backing) of advertisements for publication in newspapers and magazines. As a messenger in its sales office, located in a fashionable part of Central London, he delivered these blocks to newspapers and magazine publishing houses. My friend's job required riding buses around London. Since that's what Eddie and I did some Saturdays at our own expense, I thought being such a messenger could be a pleasant enough occupation. Working in an office instead of a factory appealed to my latent, if subconscious, snobbishness. I applied and began one week later. The economy had started to gather momentum some nine months after hostilities ended, and jobs were plentiful.

I went as long as three weeks before I disliked my second job. Each day the shipping office made up a route and the four messenger boys left with a full shoulder bag of advertising blocks. It took until mid afternoon to deliver a bag's contents. The job brought me out of a blue-collar environment and into the white-collar world. I soon gleaned the people with the good jobs sat behind desks looking important. This messenger position also contributed to my sex education, although in a quite different way than at the mattress factory.

Normally, I lugged my bag of printing blocks to the top deck of the bus to a window seat to watch the passing scene on London's busy streets. I'd become something of a people watcher, with a penchant for pretty girls. Unbeknown to me, while I scanned for these tantalizing creatures, occasionally a man watched me with perhaps a longing roughly equivalent to, but somehow quite different from, mine. Several times men came and sat next to me, closer than the bench seat dimensions necessitated. They casually folded their arms so that a hand rested lightly on my thigh.

The first time it happened I froze in fear and confusion. Perhaps the man wasn't aware of his hand's position? But every so often it started to inch upward and I knew he had full knowledge of his paw's whereabouts. Thus I became aware that, while all my new and bothersome desires were for the opposite sex, a few men felt similarly but for the same sex. I'd get up, politely ask the man to excuse me, and went down to the lower deck. The big world contained a few unpleasant surprises for an untutored youth. Any enjoyment in riding London buses soon faded. For some reason my lack of self-acceptance kept me agitated about the lowly positions I'd found so far. I didn't know what motivated this unhappiness, but its insistence couldn't be ignored.

During my six weeks as a messenger boy, Dad arrived home in early June 1946. The war had been over more than a year. He'd been in the Army for 48 months, of which 40 were continuously overseas. I'd gone from 10 to 14 years of age and developed into a difficult teenager with rebellious tendencies, inwardly tormented, and unknowingly self-destructive. For some time I'd harbored mixed feelings about Dad's return. Now it had happened, I selfishly resented that my self-indulgent, do-as-I-please days, were over. In truth, Dad was the opposite of a disciplinarian. But shortly after his return he had occasion to punish me.

For a while I'd been associating with a neighborhood youth, other than Eddie, a couple of years older than I. We spent one morning filching chocolate bars from local tobacco kiosks. How Dad found out, I don't remember, and he quickly confronted me in our living room. Asked if I'd been stealing, I dumbly and unconvincingly denied it. Dad delivered one swift, heavy slap to my face, threatening far worse if I continued such activity. This was the only time I ever recall Dad physically chastising me. I know now that the incident would have been far more painful for Dad than me. Perhaps his arrival home was most timely because I might, as a cocksure, willful teen, graduated from chocolate bars to more valuable merchandise.

I indulged my resentment at his return for some months while giving no thought to how difficult this transition must have been for him. His essentially quiet, undemanding ways were no doubt tested heavily by a return to head of household status. Readjustments undoubtedly necessary for all of us, but no doubt the biggest by Dad and Mom. I do recall that, like so many returning servicemen, he didn't talk much about his war experiences. Some of his reticence likely stemmed from his personal modesty, but I suspect I displayed little interest. How could one's own father be a war hero? An unbelievable level of selfishness in this unthinking youth.

A revealing story he told us, however, did fix in my mind. In the fall 1945, now in Berlin, he transferred from long hauling tanks to the 743rd Tipper Company with the mission of transporting supplies within the devastated city. He made daily runs carrying coal from rail sidings to various former German barracks now commandeered for quartering British troops. The winter of 1945/6 proved particularly harsh in Europe and the tippers delivered extra fuel. Dad made a practice of leaving open his tailgate to let modest amounts of coal fall out when he accelerated or turned corners. Quickly, the hungry, cold Berliners out scavenging the streets pounced on the precious black nuggets to carry them appreciatively to their bomb-damaged, cold apartments. This small act, contravening military regulations, was Dad's personal gesture of humanity to a former enemy, now down and out. It surely demonstrated Dad's basic decency. It took me years to understand.

One other recollection I have of my relations with Dad shortly after his return comes with less pleasant emotions. Dad quickly returned to his former London cab driver occupation. We met at the dinner table one evening and I held the floor loudly proclaiming my unhappiness for a job not meeting my image needs. Dad suggested the life of a postman for my consideration. He saw its upside as steady work, modest but regular pay, a company bicycle, and a day spent mostly out of sight of petty bosses. And it came with a uniform and cap. His recommendation came from true working-class logic, sincerity and goodwill. I was appalled! In those days, postmen on bikes delivered mail in most areas, one pant leg encased in a cycle clip. A momentary vision occurred of spending my next 50 years peddling a company bike through streets of East London with a sack of mail on my shoulder. The seat of a postman's pants was always worn and shiny from the constant contact with the bike's saddle. I saw this as a metaphor for my brain at the end of a lifetime of such dull work. My false, fierce pride was hurt. Because I was still uncertain of myself around Dad, I bottled my outraged sense of infra dignitatem.

Although in reality I had nothing to offer the work world, other than perhaps a strong back, somehow I had become fixated on the need for a job that would do justice to the inner image I had of myself. I needed to do something that would bring admiration from others. After dinner I went to the bottom of the garden where bushes hid me. There, my unhappiness, frustration, and rage bubbled over and I indulged myself liberally in a crying jag. At 14, I felt strong dissatisfaction with a social status that most boys I knew seemed to accept with equanimity. My feelings denied me that self-assurance.

One day my delivery route took me to Fleet Street, the small historic road where, since the early 1800s, London newspapers had established themselves. In addition to national publications, as the years went by many provincial newspapers opened offices in the capital along this street or in the immediate area. Now it represented the heart of Britain's newspaper industry. At the time, per capita newspaper readership was higher in Britain than any other country. This figure covers all newspapers that ranged from the august *Times*, the literate Sunday *Observer*, or the intellectual, liberal *Guardian*, to the numerous sewer-smelly tabloids that pandered to the vast British under-class. This broad social element encompassed those who received a second-rate education and, from lack of motivation, never attempted to emerge from their own mental fog. A newspaper for them had only to feed their stunted mental horizons of scandal, sports, especially soccer, horse and dog racing, and a daily blow-up picture of a set of young boobs.

That day's deliveries included a print block for the *Birmingham Mail and Post.* These morning and evening newspapers served Britain's second largest city, then with a metropolitan population of about 2.5 million.

A hand-written sign on the front counter read "Editorial Boy Wanted." Although clueless as to what such a position entailed, the title had a better ring to it than "messenger boy." I applied and was accepted at the weekly salary of £2 and ten shillings sterling, equivalent at the then exchange rate of around $10. Because applicants were scarce, the newspaper agreed to hold the position open for a week. I needed to give the advertising agency that much notice before starting my third job. I'd been at work for about four months only.

At the newspaper my work site was the second-floor small newsroom that didn't have the frenzied drama of newsrooms often portrayed in movies. At one end were the side-by-side desks for two sub-editors. They reviewed the incoming copy received from Reuters, Associated Press, United Press International and other domestic and foreign news agencies, via a bank of teleprinters standing back-to-back in the center of the room. At the other end, the editorial switchboard stood bulkily against a wall, answered by the editorial boys. Next to it on an ornate wood pedestal, like a monument to the 1920s, sat a glass-bubble telegraphic ticker machine that regurgitated half-inch wide paper tape. Intermittently it sprang noisily to life jerkily printing prices of securities traded that day on London's Stock Market.

A worktable with two wooden chairs, where the two editorial boys sat, occupied the third wall at this end of the room. Of course, we weren't supposed to do much sitting, as our tasks were many and required us to be mostly on our feet. It proved to be that only for a few hours each day were we both in the office together. As soon as the clack-clack-clack of the teleprinters stopped, we had to tear off the completed story and put it in front of either sub-editor. If they deemed the item worthy of sending to the Birmingham office, they performed some cosmetic editing and threw the copy in an out-box for an editorial boy to stuff into a pneumatic tube which whooshed it to the top floor of the five-story building. There, teletype operators re-typed the revised material to electrically transmit it to the head office. Items of no interest were literally skewered by the copy editors on a wood-based spike, which we cleared several times a day.

The floors between the second and the fifth contained the individual offices of the London editor, a general reporter, and those specialist correspondents whose beats covered national politics, the financial scene, and one devoted to industrial and labor union matters. The only female correspondent encompassed the catchall category of "lifestyle," including juicy morsels of the capital's social world, personalities, and women's affairs.

Each day required a trip to the financial district to pick-up an article on stock market activity written by a broker under contract with the newspaper. As the junior of the two boys, it usually fell to me. From the business department cashier I collected the money to cover the round trip bus fare, which I believe came to six pence. It was about three miles to the broker's office, and traffic in the narrow streets of the financial district often snarled. I learned some back road short cuts and, by running most of the way, I could be back in the office with the copy more or less as fast as riding a bus. I supplemented my modest salary that way most any day it wasn't raining which, given London's weather, meant I didn't get rich through that little scam.

The other editorial boy was nearly eighteen, tall, handsome, and sported a moustache. He dressed well and could have been taken for one of the reporters, and would soon be called up for national (selective) service. While our responsibilities were mundane, there was an excitement to the atmosphere in which we worked. News clacked its way into the office from around the world. Datelines from countries and capitals I'd never heard of before now became familiar. I liked learning the world locations of Vladivostok, Zanzibar and Patagonia. Perhaps indicative of an incipient affinity for geography, this work aspect stirred memories of standing in school class rooms studying red-splotched wall maps of the world.

The correspondents stopped by the newsroom to discuss all kinds of matters with the sub-editors. I marveled at their wide knowledge and eloquence. Awe struck, I stood slack-jawed among educated people for the first time. This sleeping teenager had awoken in a new universe.

Another of our duties required delivery of a copy of each day's two Birmingham newspapers to the correspondents. The senior boy chose to deliver to the London editor and the lady journalist. I delivered to the rest, including the clever general correspondent, Trevor Bennington, who tended to be lackadaisical about his appearance. The affable Mr. Bennington carried quite a paunch, apparently attributable to a partiality for a beer or three on his way home after a hard day. His suits often looked like they came from the time when the general correspondent was a slim cub reporter. Now his pants and waistcoats appeared on the verge of bursting from encasing too much mature reporter. Sooty splotches festooned his waistcoat and jacket from his heavy cigarette smoking. He rarely bothered to tap the ash into a tray. Rather, it broke off to sweep down his front, like snow in a mountain avalanche, lodging in garment wrinkles it encountered en route to his typewriter keyboard. The good man also had the whimsical habit of investigating in his nostrils as he intently reviewed the story he'd just banged out on his manual machine with two fingers. All this appalled the senior boy.

After a few weeks, as I fixed the latest issue to the cane pole file on his sloped reading desk, Mr. Bennington began to talk to me about my future. He knew I was just another of the countless uneducated London youths filling dead-end jobs who would continue in such work until old age. He advised me, if interested in a career in journalism, I would have to do a great deal of educational catch-up. He represented the first educated person to take a serious interest in my life. My father hadn't been around to give me advice and no teacher ever spoke to me about the long years that lay ahead. Perhaps I wouldn't have listened to my father or a teacher, but I listened to Mr. Bennington.

Undoubtedly, however, the most profound difference in my life occurred when I acquired the habit of reading after Mr. Bennington powerfully extolled its virtues. It was as if a switch in my head suddenly turned on, and my mind came alive like a parched desert renews itself with the arrival of spring rains. I obtained my first library card, and brought home a volume. Regretfully I don't recall its title or author, but from being a person who never looked inside a book, almost overnight I became addicted to the printed word. It surprised the heck out of me, but it probably surprised my family even more. Without knowing, I'd entered a new cosmos—the realm of "heightened consciousness," a phrase from Alan Sillitoe, a contemporary British writer, also from humble beginnings.

A copy of each of London's quality newspapers was available for the editorial staff to read. Although it was not intended by management that this include the editorial boys, I began to read them. Once when sent across town to pick up a document from a political party office, I took *The Times* to read on the bus. One of the sub-editors wanted it while I was out. I received a stern lecture when I returned as I drew the crumpled copy from my raincoat pocket. Because it was my job to dispose of these newspapers when they were a few days old, I would rip out features and opinion pages I'd not had a chance to read and absorb them during my daily commute which involved more than a hour by steam train and bus.

The startling revelation that I was so different from these educated newspaper people delivered a profound shock to my consciousness, perhaps on a par with the announcement one has limited time left on earth. While my heart didn't stop, this brutal awakening inflicted pain on my soul. For me it perfectly illustrated Benjamin Disraeli's statement that a greater difference existed between educated Englishmen and working class Englishmen than between Englishmen and Chinamen.

Mr. Bennington continued to talk to me from time to time about how I was going to spend my working life. There were plenty of menial jobs in the press world, but I'd come to aspire to something better. I found the newspaper industry exciting and by now a vague hope of becoming a journalist had formed in me. If I wanted a more fulfilling life, he advised through a cloud of cigarette smoke, that I needed to achieve a face-lift of the brain in quick order. This meant immediately buckling down to serious study, a revolutionary concept for me.

I relished these pep talks like a dog craves attention. When assignments kept Mr. Bennington gone for days at a time, I missed his support. To have someone interested in me and my future was new and uplifting. Most importantly, his concern was genuine. There were never any incidents of the hand-on-thigh type. Thanks to him, from being a person without objectives, I transformed almost magically to someone mission-focused.

Unfortunately, my nature tends to impatience. The prospect of the years required to accomplish anything via the night-school route promised to be too far into the future. My circumstances and character had essentially wasted my years 5 through 14. This gave rise to the idea of returning full-time to school. Education in Britain is administered by counties (equivalent to states in the U.S.) that delegate this responsibility to lower borough, urban and rural councils. When I approached the East Ham Borough Council about going back to the secondary modern school I'd so recently left, I ran into a brick wall. I kept hearing the ingrained British mantra: "it's never been done before." Because I'd failed the 11-plus examination, the academic-leaning grammar school path to higher education was closed to me. The grammar school provided what is essentially a liberal arts exposure. My local education authority suggested that a technical school was perhaps the only possibility. Someone else could deal with this boy who'd become serious about education—many years too late.

Mr. Bennington said I needed to study a range of subjects, with a heavy dose of English. Perhaps unique in the world, British journalists were usually competent stenographers in those days. Tape recorders had yet to appear. Grammar school, and sometimes the university, was the usual source of journalists. Technical schools catered to boys who were mostly already in trade apprentice programs and those headed for engineering careers through either full- or part-time study. It didn't sound promising, but I did get an interview with an advisor at the nearest technical school, and Dad came with me.

At the meeting it soon became apparent that what I was looking for could not be found at this institution. My requirement and the local state school system could not be melded. My particular situation could possibly have been fitted into a private school, but financing it would have been too big a burden on my parents. I never raised this idea. The fateful meeting on that long-ago day did not last long. Almost certainly I didn't make a good case in explaining to the advisor what exactly I wanted, perhaps because it wasn't really clear to me. Dad didn't say much, but several times he uttered the phrase "I'm only a working-class man." These words revealed for me that Dad had been conditioned by his lower social background and could not envision beyond its restrictions. I left the meeting angry and frustrated, believing Dad's concern revolved around costs had my idea worked out. Even the councilor commented that I deserved credit for wanting to attempt to remedy my lack of learning.

On further reflection, I don't believe Dad would have stopped me going back to school if it had been possible. While a prisoner of the British working-class mentality, he was basically a loving and generous man. He'd probably never heard Robert Browning's exhortation in his poem "Andrea del Salto" that "…a man's reach should exceed his grasp, or what's a Heaven for?"

In September 1946, I went one evening straight from work to enroll in night courses in English composition and grammar, shorthand theory, and typing, offered free by the local council. It required attending four nights each week at a local county secondary school. I speedily completed the County application form eager to get home for dinner. Then a distressing nervousness swept over me. Embarrassed, I glanced at the other applicants, bent over the application form, worrying they might somehow know my sudden difficulty. The form required spelling middle names. I froze in shock when I realized I didn't know how to spell my own middle name. Did the "v" or the "o" follow the "I" in "Ivor?" I tried it both ways on a piece of scrap paper. Even so, when I handed in the form I wasn't certain I'd spelled it correctly. There was, indeed, much catching up to do!

CHAPTER 10

The winter of 1946/7 brought power shortages that plagued our lives. Daily two million people used London's electric underground (subway) system to reach work. On some days chaos reigned. Britons, however, tended to be too polite to complain publicly, at least back then. They stoically tolerated a level of service that would cause the spilling of blood in America. The Labor Party had already brought the railroads under government ownership. One of the improvements the new owners undertook included electrification of the aboveground steam trains connecting London and its eastern suburbs, my own route to the newspaper. The weather, combined with the construction, sometimes caused horrific delays.

But I had now joined the ranks of the reading public. I happily inhabited a private world, somewhat immune to the delays and crowded conditions of my rejuvenating, socializing country. For the first time my life had a discipline and purpose. I was going to night school four evenings each week, performing homework on two others. Every other Saturday I worked, but evenings were allotted to entertainment. Sunday daylight hours involved physical activity: morning soccer and afternoon bicycling. Without realizing it, I was embarked on a personal transformation that was to bring both pleasure and pain.

During those bitter winter months, the only heated area of our house was the living room with its small, open coal fire. But in that sanctuary in the evenings my parents talked and listened to the radio. I needed quiet to study because of my easy distraction. Thus I worked at a small table in my bedroom, fingers often stiff with cold. I remember putting on up to four pullovers (sweaters) and wrapping myself in a bathrobe that Mom made for me from a blanket. Despite these adverse conditions, in all modesty, my dedication was such I doggedly persevered.

Eddie Wentworth had also finished school at 14 and changed jobs a few times quickly thereafter, but now seemed settled in a clerical position with an insurance company in the city. He attended night school twice a week, studying English and business arithmetic. He had also become involved in the youth-equivalent of the local council, intended to educate young people in the ways of regional government. Because of this interest, he planned to attend a 7-day youth festival in July 1947 in Prague, Czechoslovakia (now the Czech Republic). Arranged by the World Federation of Democratic Youth, its stated intention to show European youth different peoples could live in peace after all the divisiveness, destruction and death of World War II. When Eddie asked if I'd like to go with him, I immediately joined the Youth Council to qualify.

Organizers levied a nominal charge of £5 sterling to help defray lodging and food costs. The train and ferry fare from London via Paris to Prague amounted to £15, a more formidable expense at the time. I would require external funding so I raised the issue at home. Dad said I was, at 15, too young to be alone on the European continent. I asked Eddie, now nearly 18, to plead my case with my father. His confidence and facility with words soon convinced Dad his oldest son wouldn't be in danger on the Continent. Dad knew how disappointed I'd been the year before when it proved impossible for me to go back to school. Maybe he didn't want to be the spoiler of my latest aspiration. As it turned out, however, Dad's opinion was validated.

Once again, Eddie employed his talents as an entrepreneur and organized a public dance on behalf of the East Ham Youth Council. Most of the profits went to the Council, but some were used to help partially pay our lodging, food and transportation. Impatient for weeks to go on my first trip overseas, when departure day arrived we were delayed about five hours at the Dover ferry when its propeller snagged a cable, which required a diver to untangle. We arrived so late in Paris, the specially chartered train, scheduled to leave from the Gare de l'est station, had been delayed for 24 hours. This unplanned night in Paris exacerbated our tight money situation. To conserve cash, we carried our baggage the 30-minute walk between the north and east stations through streets only three years before liberated from German occupation. A nearby small, basic hotel, jammed like an afterthought between two larger properties, provided us beds for the night. Afraid to venture far, we strolled in the St. Martin canal area and ate in a cheap restaurant whose interior had, I suspected, become permanently fogged by a loyal, long-term clientele addicted to Gauloises, the French working-man's cigarette.

Next day around noon we boarded the train that filled with eager, young people, mainly college students from France, Spain, Holland, Belgium, Denmark, and our own country, plus, I believe, a few others. The carriages were old, with wooden bench seats. We finally departed at 2 p.m. and were supposed to arrive the same time next day. It is approximately 600 miles from Paris to Prague. This meant we'd travel at the painful average of 25 miles per hour. We made quite good time in reaching the German border. Once inside the defeated nation, our speed slowed to a pace not even equivalent to that scheduled. The snail-like progress might have been because of damaged track. However, we must also have had a low priority, as we stopped often to allow freight trains to pass, and these halts sometimes lasted an hour.

The wooden seats became torture racks. The continental sun beat down from a cloudless sky. Sweating youths tied open the doors to let more air into the oven-hot carriages. During lengthy stops, they started jumping down to gather hay by the armload from adjacent fields for softer seating and bedding on compartment floors. The frequency of these stops caused some boys to grow bolder in how far they strayed. Mostly the train would move off slowly and the roamers could run back to climb aboard as it shuddered and strained to gather steam. Perhaps the engineer became distressed at the state of his train with its carriage doors tied back and straw protruding from the openings. At the next halt, after a short stop, the train emitted a whistle and accelerated with a cheetah-like velocity we'd not so far experienced. Everybody off the train scrambled to clamber on board. I looked out of my carriage window and saw two French students in the middle of the track waving their arms with Gallic agitation. I don't know if they ever reached Prague.

Our slow train took us through the major cities of Metz, Mannheim, Nuernberg, Plzen and, finally, Prague. As we passed through the German cities we could see bomb damage near the tracks, including lots of destroyed hoppers, carriages, and engines. In the countryside, we noticed most field workers were women, headscarves tied under the chin, and saw only a sprinkling of ancient males.

The train halted at Nuernberg, the last major German city on our route, at 5 a.m. Dawn hadn't yet arrived. The darkness prevented us from seeing much beyond the closest platforms where only a few overhead lights worked. Platform roof struts that once supported canopies were broken and bent like trees damaged in a hurricane. We could see the bottom layer or two of wall bricks where once stood waiting rooms or bistros. The rubble had been cleared, but the remaining layers of bricks spoke eloquently of past human construction destroyed in seconds. The havoc and horror that Hitler's psychopathology had produced for the German people were encompassed in this stark, eerie scene. We didn't see a soul except for a lone African-American soldier on a nearby platform, languidly smoking a cigarette, his black skin shining in the circle of yellow cast down by the lighted lamp post against which he leaned. Nothing we'd seen from the train thus far portrayed the state of a defeated Germany as did this pre-dawn scene.

The now-famous war crimes trials of Nazi civilian leaders and some high-ranking military were under way in this city at the time. They were held in Nuernberg because the once boastful city had been a National Socialist Party (Nazi) stronghold. The party held its congresses and mass party rallies here. The Nazi manifesto outlining its broad plans, while not revealing the hideous details, was signed in this city. I could never have conceived that, as I gazed at the somber picture at its train station, much later it would be among the numerous residences to which my life wanderings would take me.

When we arrived at Prague's central rail station, we discovered this medieval metropolis was spared the war damage that had befallen so many European cities. Because it is an historic city, rich in culture and great architecture, both the Allied and Axis forces mercifully refrained from the destruction wreaked freely elsewhere. We were billeted in the spartan residence halls of a college, with two-tier bunk beds sleeping six males to a room, near the National Museum at the upper end of Wenceslas Square. In front of the museum stood the imposing, green-patina bronze statue of Wenceslas, an early ruling Duke of Bohemia, the patron saint of that principality. He is a cherished historic figure and now a symbol of Czech life.

The principal East Ham Youth Council delegate, a woman in her mid 20s, represented our organization at most events. Our companion did give a talk on the goals of the Youth Council. Eddie and I didn't open our mouths, and I believe she was happy with this arrangement. We attended some of the functions hosted by the youth of different nations, such as athletic displays, folk dancing, plays, and music. We discovered that some of the participating groups were really there to promote communism as much as a peaceful world.

On our last day in Prague, Eddie and I were strolling the promenade on the bank of the Moldau River that bisects the city. Two Czech street photographers, who spoke passable English, sought to take our photo. We declined, but the two, who appeared to be around thirty, engaged us in conversation anyway. That should have put us on alert. They asked all of the right questions about where we were from and how we liked their country. They told us they greatly admired the British people because we withstood the German bombing during the recent war. Further, the Czechoslovakian National Government in exile was based in London and thousands of their military personnel found refuge in, and fought for, Britain.

They just happened to live close by. Would we like to join them for a glass of wine to affirm the close ties between our two nations? Back then the wine didn't especially pull us, but they also mentioned bread, cheese and sausage. Since the primary purpose of the festival was human understanding and tolerance, by accepting we'd be fulfilling our goodwill ambassadorships. Furthermore, their snacks would be free. Eddie and I shared one trait in particular: careful conservation of capital.

Once in their flat, they produced several containers of what was, I now guess, especially cheap wine. This was liberally poured into large glasses to toast the friendship between our two nations. I certainly wanted to perform my duty in a manly way, and guzzled the stuff each time one of them smilingly refilled. They seemed to have forgotten their promises of solid food. This was only my second exposure to wine, and on an empty stomach, it wasn't too long before I began to see life through a comedic haze. My extremities began to feel strangely puffy and tingly. My tongue felt swollen. Our two hosts undoubtedly were watching for such symptoms. They invited me to stretch out on the couch. I did so, remembering to remove shoes. After a few minutes, one came and sat on the edge of the couch and leaned forward.

"How is our little britsky pritel (British friend)?" his smiling face now close to mine. His right hand pushed my hair away from my forehead; he rested his left hand casually on my thigh.

"Anglicky pritel (English boy)! You're not used to our good Czech vino." His hand moved slowly but noticeably across my thigh to rest on my crotch. I tensed and tried to sit upright. But now his right hand on my shoulder held me down. At last it dawned on me we were in the apartment of men who wanted something more than cementing the bonds of friendship. The shock seemingly sobered me instantly. This ever-so-friendly Czech suggested I might like to recline on his bed, and even spend the night. I'd be fully recovered by the morning, he told me in an oozing, concerned way. But I was now fully alert and alarmed. I pushed his hand aside, pulled up my knees, pivoted to place my feet on the floor, and bolted upright.

Eddie had witnessed this couch drama as he stood talking to the other photographer. He quickly came up with an excuse for us to leave right away.

"We can't stay. We're meeting all our delegates for a farewell dinner at eight. We're already late. Our group leader will be looking for us and we'll be in trouble if we don't show. It's a mandatory dinner for the British delegation."

Meanwhile I hurriedly put on my shoes. Fumbling with the laces, I was glad Eddie dreamed up this long list of the reasons why we just had to leave immediately. The solicitous photographer's attention turned to Eddie who made it sound as though we were the festival's most important British delegates, apparently convincing these two street bandits. They didn't put up any objections, and never pressed one for the road. We fled the scene with the unbridled joy of animals released back into the wild, but certainly with less dignity. There is no doubt Eddie saved my honor that night. Me, the eternal innocent abroad!

Seven months later, in February 1948, Czech communists seized power through a Moscow-directed coup d'etat just ahead of scheduled national elections. The iron curtain, stretching from the Baltic to the Black Sea, slammed shut. The prophetic words of warning of Winston Churchill at Fulton, Missouri, in 1946, had now come to pass. Some historians mark the Czech coup as the beginning of the cold war. No one could have predicted that the iron curtain would remain closed for the next 41 years.

CHAPTER 11

Although only recently returned from Czechoslovakia, Eddie proposed we add two days to an upcoming weekend and cycle to visit the family with whom he'd been billeted during his summer 1944 evacuation from the revenge weapons bombardment. They lived in Wells, Somerset, about a 160-mile one-way ride. This idea smacked of over confidence. Neither of us owned modern bikes and we weren't strong cyclists. In fact, when I mentioned this proposed escapade at home, Dad, concerned for our safety, expressed reservations about us undertaking a 320-mile bicycle odyssey involving twice transiting the large area of London. .

I smugly pointed out I'd recently returned safely from Eastern Europe. Of course, I'd never informed my parents how close I came to becoming a pederastic victim of the Prague street photographers. Then Dad made a comment cutting close to the truth. "You shouldn't be so cocky, son," he said thoughtfully and pointedly, "I doubt you'd be anything like so adventurous but for Eddie. Your restlessness and attraction for places other than home isn't really you."

Dad's insight and apparent understanding of my make-up and relationship with Eddie surprised me. Increasingly I thought I had the monopoly on brains in our house, no doubt, I blustered a defensive retort. But my father had honed in on something of which I was vaguely and uneasily aware. In our pack, Eddie was unquestionably the Alpha male. I resisted only when I lost my temper. I had no understanding of human psychology and never thought of the possibility of sub-conscious needs motivating either Eddie or myself. Unquestionably, he was smarter. He possessed a maturity and social polish well ahead of mine. Undoubtedly, I went places and had experiences with Eddie that was unlikely with any of the other youth I knew. Dad agreed, however reluctantly, to this four-day jaunt. He probably now saw me as too headstrong to listen to his judgment. He might have seen it as a losing battle, preferring to expend his energy more productively. In fact, I believe I never again sought his agreement for any other undertaking. In unacknowledged deference to Dad's caution, we took an extra day off and left from our homes immediately after work on Wednesday to cross London that evening to have all of Thursday to reach Wells.

Heading westward to Central London, we cycled on the A-12 (arterial) road that throbbed with the commercial activity of daily life. The heaviest rush-hour traffic, however, headed east on the opposite side. Yet, even though the automobile age for the common man was still 15 years in the future, traffic density required riding single-file. We shared the road mostly with London's symbols: the ubiquitous double-decker, red busses and boxy, black taxis.

Once through the city, we headed out of town on the old Great West Road. It was still high summer and at London's latitude an anemic daylight hung on until around 10 p.m. By that time we reached Slough, Berkshire. We were in a built-up area, with small workshops or factories fronting on this main road. We shortly spotted one, somewhat back from the road, with a watchman perched on a hard-back chair leaning on two legs against the front door. He smoked a pipe and looked at peace with the world, as pipe smokers tend to do. I didn't have the courage, but Eddie turned into the driveway and asked him if we could make camp on a small patch of grass near the building.

The kindly guard gave permission on the understanding we'd leave early and leave no trash. He let us pitch Eddie's small tent only a few feet from the front door. Possibly he welcomed company. It was now almost dark and a wall light over the door helped illuminate our site. We spread a plastic ground sheet, crawled under blankets that had performed war service in the garden bomb shelters, to sleep in our street clothes.

"I'm going in myself now," he soon called in a friendly voice. "Bang on the door when you leave in the morning. I'll be just inside. Don't forget, boys, make no mess."

We heard him throw a front door bolt and the outside light went off. Eddie and I fell asleep to the sound of an occasional car or truck passing on the Great West Road. Fatigue insured a good night's sleep.

My watch showed nearly 8 a.m. when we stirred ourselves to sit up to eat a jam roll and drink now-cold tea from a thermos. We struck camp quickly intending to make a fast start to a long day. The thought we still had around 120 miles to ride was foremost. We hoped to maintain the ambitious speed of 15 miles an hour, which would put us there in about eight hours. More likely, it'd take ten. As we banged on the front door to summon the guard, through a small window we could see him inside dozing on the same chair leaning in the same position. His pipe, now apparently extinguished, still hung between his teeth. His eyes opened, he blinked a couple of times, pitched the chair forward, and came to unlock the door. He removed the pipe to say we could use the lobby restroom.

"Where you boys headed?" he asked us when we came out, now a little more refreshed. .

"We're going to Somerset. Wells, to be exact," Eddie offered.

"Bloody hell," he exclaimed, "that's a far bit for those old junkers you're pedaling." He returned the pipe to his mouth and it rocked up and down a few times as he stood pondering.

"As I sees it, even if yer bikes hold up, I kinda doubt you two will." He laughed a loud belly laugh.

"Tell you what, boys, we got an empty truck going to Bristol in about half an hour. I reckon the driver wouldn't mind you going along."

This good fortune would get us to Wells by noon on Thursday. We could spend Friday in Wells and give ourselves the whole weekend to return. We'd have done it, despite Dad's doubts. About an hour later the truck arrived, with a driver and his assistant in the cab. He agreed to take us if we rode on the truck's open flatbed. Eddie climbed on board, and I handed up the bikes. We braced ourselves against the truck bed headboard, holding on with one hand, while the other gripped our bikes to stop them sliding off from the vehicle's forward motion. While it was windy and uncomfortable, this mode of travel sure beat pumping the pedals. And we needn't ever tell anyone we got a lift for more than half the distance!

We actually cycled about 20 miles that day, from Bristol to Wells, rather than the expected 120 miles. Around 4 p.m. we located Eddie's brief wartime home on a lane at the edge of town. The cottage hid from the road behind a barrier of overgrown wax-leaf bushes. The tiny grass area in the front garden had surrendered to invading weeds. Eddie's hosts appeared typically English in their passion for privacy, but without the usual accompanying passion for gardening. All external evidence made it a safe bet that its occupants offered accommodation to the evacuee Eddie for the government allowance he represented more than for altruistic motives.

A short, bald man in a grungy cardigan, stretched mercilessly by the corpulent body of its owner, opened the door after our third knock. His ancient corduroy trousers bagged at the knees, resembling the bulbous joints of a cast-iron rain downspout. After a few years as a young man with the British Army in India, his heaviness reflected many evenings at the local pub and many years as one of the town's butchers, now retired. Mr. Jenkins stared at us through thick lenses, his face registering a distinct displeasure. Probably our unexpected arrival came low on his preference list for the passing of a quiet afternoon. Even smooth-talking Eddie had trouble convincing this solid citizen that the young man on his doorstep, only three years before, had been a member of this household. We hadn't called ahead because working people didn't have house telephones back then. The situation resolved only when Mrs. Jenkins, clad in a cotton dress covered by a floral apron, feet in bedroom slippers, rose in a flurry of embarrassment from a straight back chair and came to the front door. Small and fragile as an English sparrow, she dropped the sock she'd been darning into an open wicker basket. I suspected she recognized Eddie immediately, but stayed quiet in fear of embarrassing her vacuous, bumbling husband. Only then were we invited into the postage stamp-sized parlor of their residence.

The man settled himself into an overstuffed armchair, moving the newspaper he'd been reading to an end table. Mrs. Jenkins sat back on her chair and resumed sock repair: a good wife is never idle. We sat on a wood bench under the room's only window. After a brief exchange of pleasantries between the four of us, Mr. Jenkins launched eagerly into regaling his years in India. It appeared, contrary to history books, the diverse millions of the Indian sub-continent, crown jewel of the Imperial British Empire, had been single-handedly controlled by one Corporal Jenkins. This man loved an audience, even two teenage boys. We feigned interest not so much because of the riveting content of his dissertation, but at the prospect of a free meal.

Eddie later told me he'd heard all these windy anecdotes several times during the five months he stayed there in 1944. Meanwhile, as her husband grew retrospectively grander and more vital to the power of the Raj, Mrs. Jenkins never interrupted this obvious household master. In the midst of his apparently heroic involvement in a mounted patrol in the Punjab city of Amritsar, he suddenly turned to his wife and declaimed "...it's time for you to prepare our tea." It appeared his imagination had transported him back 40 years and he issued orders imperiously to an Indian servant of the untouchable class. Mrs. Jenkins rose instantly, whispering "yes, dear," and, like an obedient Helot, padded to the kitchen.

After a tiresomely long 15 minutes, during which he prattled on, she returned to invite us to the poky kitchen's poky rectangular dining table. Mr. Jenkins sat at what had to be the head position, with Eddie and I on the sides, and Mrs. Jenkins at the foot. She had cut and buttered a plate of white bread, another plate contained thin slices of cheese. A dish of unpretentious cookies sat in the center. She busied herself at the sink filling a teapot with boiling water from a tin kettle.

The bread and butter plate rested immediately in front of Mr. Jenkins. He reached with a pudgy hand and put four or five slices on his plate, before passing it to us. Patrolling vast, hot India brings out the appetite in a man! Then I saw him grimace toward the cheese plate, which sat nearer her end of the table. He could've reached it easily by raising his fat backside off the chair. Instead he barked, "can I have my cheese?"

"Dear, it's on the table," Mrs. Jenkins called gently, now straining tea into cups.

"*That I KNOW*, dear, but I'm *HERE* and the cheese is *THERE*!"

Gentle, compliant Mrs. Jenkins put down the tea pot, again padded across the kitchen, lifted the cheese plate and moved it horizontally not more than 2.5 feet to place it next to his lordship's generous helping of the staff of life. I have never forgotten this exchange. In later years when I've heard women complain that marriage turns them into slaves, I think back to that tea time episode. They have a strong case!

In the fall 1947, I completed my first year of council-operated, free night classes. My progress in typing, a rather mechanical process, was satisfactory. In English I enjoyed writing assignments, but had only modest success keeping the rules of grammar straight in my brain. Shorthand's complexity was also proving difficult to conquer. Pitman's shorthand is a phonetic system, invented by Isaac Pitman in Britain in the 1830s, based on the sounds of speech and the science of phonetics. Symbols represent consonants and vowels as spoken, and shading differentiates many symbols. A page of properly executed Pitman shorthand looks neat, almost as elegant as Chinese calligraphy, and for a while I might just as well been trying to master that Oriental tongue. The private Pitman School, with its main teaching facility in Central London, had a branch in Forest Gate. I thought I'd make better progress there and signed up to continue studying the same three subjects, but now paying my own school fees.

The Daily Telegraph, a London conservative newspaper, serialized segments of Winston Churchill's new multi-volume history "The Second World War" during 1948. I was reading them and cutting out each article when possible from the free office copy. This was the first of Churchill's writing I'd read. It impressed me immensely. One day I was sent to Churchill's London home to collect an advance copy of a speech he would make the next weekend in Birmingham. His 29 Hyde Park Gate house off fashionable Kensington Road, on the south side of Hyde Park, stood just a few blocks from the Royal Albert Hall.

Although he and his Conservative Party had been abruptly turned out of office in the fall 1945 election, as the leader of that party he now sat on the opposing bench in Parliament. He was, without doubt, the nation's most famous figure, commanding respect worldwide as a statesman.

The London Editor himself assigned this errand and his commissions were of special importance. I received strict orders not to go to the main door of Churchill's residence. Like tradesmen, my dealings with the great man had to be conducted only at the entrance designated for the serving classes. Regardless, on the bus en route, I indulged visions of being invited inside, offered tea and cake, and the great man eager to hear my take on the world war fracas the nation had been through recently.

I located the Churchill home on a quiet cul-de-sac. It was not as imposing as I'd expected. The central portion of the regular brick, four-story structure was crowned by a gable roof ornamented with prominent exposed end-roof trusses. The heavy, main front door—the one on which I was forbidden to knock—was encased in a box-like brick porch which presumably offered sufficient security in what seems now gentler, innocent days.

I expected my second-class-person entrance to be at the rear. When I went around there, however, the garden was enclosed with a high brick wall. Again I came to the front and then noticed my entrance was below street level, just like in the "Upstairs/Downstairs" television series of recent years. A heavy iron railing along the entire front of the property ended on one side with a gate to stairs leading to the servants' quarters. These dozen steps I descended to reach the tradesmen's door one story below the main entrance. I patted down my hair, buttoned my jacket, straightened the collar on my tie less shirt, pressed the bell, and stood poised to step adroitly across the hallowed threshold.

Apparently the Churchillian staff didn't drop everything because I was pressing their tradesmen's bell. Some minutes passed. The paneled, black-painted, heavy wooden door remained firmly shut in my face. I rang again. Still minutes passed before it opened inchmeal. A uniformed houseman looked me up and down with an expression suggesting he didn't really approve what was standing on the doormat. I explained the reason for my presence and, to my eternal consternation, instead of being invited in, I was told to remain outside while this liveried doorman contacted a press secretary. This wasn't at all how it should be happening. For a while I waited dejectedly, my sense of rejection aroused. Then I spotted dozens of empty colored bottles in crates stacked along the sunken walkway below the property's front railings.

Curiosity aroused, I stepped over and lifted a few of the colored, elegant bottles to study their ornate labels. They were exclusively containers of products of France—wine, liqueurs, cognac and champagne. I really didn't know what these alcoholic drinks were. I'd never seen such grand bottles and artistic labels, let alone savored such contents.

Then I remembered I'd been left waiting outside. Without even a cup of tea. Churchill was in there drinking glass after glass of this expensive stuff. I immediately concluded the old lion had deserved to be kicked out of office just because of the way he treated hard-working editorial boys. My feelings of insult fueled my prejudices about the privileged wealthy and the downtrodden poor. These thoughts allowed me to see I'd stumbled on hard evidence Churchill was really anti-Empire; he didn't support the striving vineyards of our far-flung Commonwealth. Winemaking was a burgeoning cottage industry at least in South Africa, Australia, and New Zealand. I knew this for certain because my working-class family (now in my mind the archetypal representatives of the downtrodden masses) at some Sunday lunches drank a six-shilling bottle of wine from one of these dominions. The high-and-mighty Churchill, on the other hand, guzzled only over-priced Froggy beverages with unpronounceable names. I could pull off a scoop and expose to the world the wartime leader's disloyal, and apparently excessive, drinking habits. Perhaps I could break into journalism without having to know shorthand and English!

The door opening arrested my wild ruminations. The same jumped-up flunky delivered yet another blow to my now shattered ego. He was too important to step outside. He beckoned me with an authoritative, crooked finger. He uttered no word. I walked back to him to be handed a large manila envelope, sealed with red wax to make sure I couldn't steal an early glance at the statesman's impending profound words. The gulf between Churchill and me was wide indeed!

The Labor Party under Prime Minister Clement Atlee, now in its third year in power, pushed ahead with its socialist agenda. In 1948, it introduced the National Health Service, the cornerstone of massive social reforms, which offered all citizens government-funded medical service more or less across the health spectrum. It basically provided cradle-to-grave health security. The first year's operation was funded with £400 million sterling. The very next year had to be budgeted at £800 million. These two figures have stayed with me ever since. People so abused the system its costs doubled in one year!

Back then I essentially believed socialism the best system to govern a country. The NHS experience showed me first-hand the effect of government free offers. Many people who take shameless advantage do not respect such handouts. Doctors' waiting rooms suddenly overflowed with people with minor aches and pains who wouldn't have been there had they faced a charge. They ordered three sets of spectacles and false teeth when before they had one or none at all. Doctors were overworked. Many left Britain to practice their skills in Commonwealth countries or the USA. This human trait crosses all geographic borders. Many years later I read a letter from a U.S. military doctor who complained that some people in the service go to the emergency room of the installation hospital when they have a headache because they can get free aspirins rather than buy them at the base exchange store.

My by-now established addiction to reading put me in hot water again at work. For one errand on a bus, I grabbed *The Times*. Unfortunately, during my absence, the London Editor called for the same newspaper.

When I returned, the sub-editor noted for his kiss-up and kick-down management style, relished the chance to read me the riot act:

"You know, boy, this newspaper can't fulfill its responsibilities to the citizens of Birmingham if a mere office boy makes off with the country's principal daily. There are other papers (here he was alluding to the tabloids) more suitable for you. The most junior cannot disrupt the most senior staff member. You delayed the London Editor from preparing his daily report to the Head Office. We had to send the other boy out to buy another *Times*."

The next time I was in trouble, the water was both hotter and deeper. Some London publishers sent pre-release copies of their books to the bigger provincial newspapers for review. The editorial boy's role in this process was merely to package the books once weekly and send them to the Birmingham Office where book reviews were written.

Continuously immersed in my own reading program of British and foreign popular classics, only rarely did a new book intrigue me enough to delay its onward journey to the Head Office. But an exception came in 1948 with *Crusade in Europe*, General Dwight Eisenhower's account of leading Allied Forces to victory in his role as Supreme Commander. I thought I could finish its 559 pages in two or three days. My estimate proved wackier than the NHS annual budget. Reviews of the book started to appear in other newspapers. Soon the Birmingham review editor wanted to know the whereabouts of our copy of this important book. Just then it resided, half read, on my bedroom nightstand! In truth, I thought my bosses should admire me for wanting to read such a work. But it transpired my eagerness to get educated didn't rank with their annoyance at getting left behind by the competition. I confessed my crime and received another humiliating but justified tongue-lashing from the same pompous sub-editor.

"You know, sonny, you alone are causing this great media organization serious problems. Taking a newspaper off the premises is one thing, but carrying off an important book is unforgivable. How do we know you even planned returning it?"

"This newspaper's been made to appear incompetent. We're weeks behind other leading provincial dailies in bringing General Eisenhower's chronicle to the attention of our readers. This is a grievous embarrassment for us and a bad infraction on your part." In earlier times I'd have been out the door. But in post-war Fleet Street the general labor shortage meant office boys could get away with a few mistakes because we were hard to replace.

Nearly sixty years later, I've still not finished Eisenhower's book. He was the President when I arrived in the USA in 1955, but somehow he never inspired me in that role. Perhaps if I had finished his book, my opinion of him would have been better.

During our next talk, Trevor Bennington, my mentor, also admonished me for taking Eisenhower's book. Because I cared what he thought of me, I resolved not to borrow review copies again. It was on this occasion that he also revealed he thought Britain's prospects appeared bleak following the gigantic expenditures and efforts necessary in the war, and said he was thinking about emigrating. He asked me not to repeat this to anyone, which made me feel special that he'd confided in me. Then he said that, as a young man, I should also give thought to leaving Britain. That idea scared me. It seemed such a huge step. It would be another six years before I made the leap into the unknown.

CHAPTER 12

Although jobs were plentiful, life in post-war Britain remained restrictive and bland. Food rationing remained in effect. Housing shortages made for serious social difficulties. Consumer durable goods were scarce. People waited up to two years for installation of a telephone. Peace hadn't yet brought the "bright, sunny uplands" of which Mr. Churchill spoke during the dark days of war. As throughout history, such colorless daily living drove bolder people to seek a better life overseas. Citing this bleakness of British life, Mr. Bennington announced his emigration to Australia. Although I had expected it, when he departed it saddened me. This person had become a mentor whose advice and encouragement I cherished. His going meant I was deprived of this support, a blow to my ever-wavering self-confidence.

I've sometimes wondered if Mr. Bennington hadn't disappeared, perhaps with his guidance I might have found my way from copy boy to cub reporter. To become a journalist, from my disadvantaged starting point, I would have needed to join a small, local newspaper as a cub reporter. The minuscule wages such beginners earned represented a deterrent. In fact, some small newspapers even required youths straight out of grammar school to work without pay in exchange for the opportunity to learn the business, a custom for many trade crafts going back to the Middle Ages. I gave my parents a modest sum for my board, and paid all my other expenses. Earning less than my current wage didn't seem an option. Fallacious thinking. While I had by now achieved a reasonable proficiency in shorthand and typing, I was still way behind in English grammar and writing fluency. As events turned out, I didn't keep my eye on my hoped-for career, and soon drifted off course.

Mr. Bennington talked only once more to me before he decamped. He again urged me to also think of leaving the country. By this time I had given it thought and the contemplation terrified me.

"I'm far too sentimental to ever leave England and my family," I told him. He scoffed at my attitude. I immediately felt wounded by his derision. I wanted and needed this man's approval. But life is nothing if not ironic. He eventually returned to remain forever in England. I left, and after one false start, stayed away for the rest of my life.

In common with many European countries in the second half of the 1940s, bicycling was a mass activity in Britain, both as basic transportation and for recreation. On weekends one sometimes saw 100-member cycling clubs streaming along like a swarm of sparrows swirling in for a landing. I, too, had become a keen recreational cyclist. With a few friends, we made excursions into the country on Sundays after soccer. Normally we cycled beyond the urban eastern edge of London and into rural Essex County.

I purchased a second-hand bicycle with a lighter frame than my old model. I retrofitted tapered, curved front forks and drop handlebars, and then had it spray painted British racing green, all for a total cost of about £10 sterling. A new racing bike with derailleur gear was double that and too pricey for me.

One long holiday weekend trip took Eddie and me to the Isle of Wight where we enjoyed two glorious days touring the island. On the return journey we decided to follow the coast east to Beachy Head that, at 530 feet, provides a panoramic view over the English Channel. This route took us up over the rolling, verdant downs of Sussex. As we spun across the grassy undulating landscape, on our left were vistas of the broad, fertile weald dotted with timeless villages. On our right were the white, curving chalk cliffs, the main topographic feature of the English coastline nearest to France. This wonderful exposure to nature at its best must have overwhelmed our better senses. We decided to spend the last night in the open sleeping on Beachy Head. But the weather turned inclement: wind picked up, and rain started and steadily increased. We decided to cycle back to London through the night.

The precipitation became heavy, and neither of us had adequate rain wear. Riding in these conditions drove the moisture through clothing to the skin. We rode all night and by the time I reached home in the morning I felt lousy and spent the next two days off work with a heavy cold. I still remember the book that occupied me when not sleeping. John Buchan's 1916 novel "*Greenmantle*," an adventure where an ordinary Englishman does battle with a 6'5" German brute in exotic locations in the Middle East in the years of the Great War. It was a thrilling yarn that sucked me in and kept me enthralled. Reading Mr. Buchan's self-assured, if somewhat stiff, prose provided two days of intense pleasure.

While I was making a genuine effort to read books of literary quality, at that time I had a decided penchant for adventure books. I eagerly lapped up those of H. Rider Haggard, H.E. Bates and John Buchan. I also immensely enjoyed first-hand travel accounts of journeys to far-off places. During my commute to work, there was always an inner tussle over whether to read a book on history, English grammar, shorthand theory, or something that was pure pleasure. Far too often my hedonistic tendency won.

These larger-than-life stories, I now feel, served to increase my already active discontent. My existence was so tame compared to that of the protagonists in these exciting books. I didn't have my feet anchored firmly to the ground by virtue of education or experience. What I was doing to myself wasn't any better than youths who see too many movies. Years later I read James Boswell who reported that Samuel Johnson, as a boy, had a fondness for reading romances of chivalry. The learned doctor later attributed to these "extravagant fictions" that unsettled turn of mind that prevented him ever fixing in any profession.

Whether it was in the head, heart or gut I couldn't be sure, but formless aspirations to become a writer were starting to inhabit my being. I was thrilled by the different worlds one could experience between the covers of a book. There was something exquisite, even otherworldly, in the deep pleasure derived from communing with another human through the printed page. About this time I fell into the trap Goethe warned us about when he wrote "men are so constituted that everyone undertakes what he sees another successful in, whether he has aptitude for it or not." Self-doubts were never far away for me. Was I capable of defying the tenets of the English hymn that exhorted us to stay at the station in life to which born? While I rejected this thinking out of hand, uncertainty closely stalked me. I battled with myself. Then a small victory came along.

The Christmas 1948 issue of *Students' Miscellany*, a literary magazine published annually by Pitman College, contained a short short story of mine. It was the only item selected from students attending the Forest Gate branch in East London. It represented a toenail curling thrill, and so sweet. The boy who once wasn't sure of the spelling of his own middle name had become a published author!

Although it was more fun to make trips with friends, about now I started to make solo voyages. I found that I didn't mind my own company, or at least could tolerate being on my own. This was something new because, as a boy, I always preferred to be part of a group. Was this maturity or withdrawal? Whatever, it dawned on me that being alone offered more chances to observe and absorb the natural surroundings.

England has more than its share of cloudy days, but when the sun did shine a sense of joyful wonder engulfed me as I moved along those quiet country roads, bordered by high hedgerows, under a sky ornamented with thick, fleecy clouds drifting leisurely across an infinite, blue background. In those years automobile traffic was light and thinned until virtually non-existent the farther from London one rode. I relished the thrill of rolling at a good clip, feeling as one with the bicycle, with the wind slapping the face. To leave the city's endlessly identical streets of mean row houses, with their ugly slate roofs, and come into a vibrant rural landscape provided an intense personal elation.

Of various solo cycling trips I undertook during this period, the most bittersweet were two visits to Cambridge, the enchanting university town. This medieval community, resting happily on both banks of the River Cam, required a 60-mile ride north of my home. For these weekend jaunts, I made it a Saturday ride there and returned on Sunday, spending the night at a youth hostel close by the train station. Both weekends were blessed with sunny, warm weather.

I set out around eight in the morning. Mom packed a two-day supply of sandwiches and cakes, which I carried in a saddlebag. I followed a series of what would now be classified as secondary roads and the light traffic made it a cyclist's heaven. This route led through peaceful villages and unhurried small towns with names of Great Parndon, Sawbridgeworth, Bishop's Stortford, and Saffron Walden. Their Saturday afternoon life beat as slowly as the heart of a hibernating bear as, like a shadow, I passed silently through them.

I discovered the center of Cambridge is a jumble of venerable colleges and much more recent development. It is very compact, with the principal points of interest contained within less than two square miles. This mixture is personified along King's Parade, the delightful main thoroughfare. Imposing colleges on one side contrasted with private houses and small shops on the other.

Many of the stately, pinnacled colleges back up to the river Cam. They have wide, close-cropped lawns sweeping down to the slow-flowing river, dotted with graceful willow trees. Flat-bottomed, square-ended punts move lazily along, propelled from the rear deck by a student earning some money by pushing a long pole into the riverbed. Passengers are groups of relaxing classmates or eager tourists absorbing the sights.

One great charm of the place is the students, dressed in gowns and mortarboards, pedaling around town on rusty, aging bicycles. Each student owns such a post-obsolescence machine that is handed on at graduation to a student of the next wave. Pupils come and go, but these ancient push-pedal bikes stay on seemingly forever. The atmosphere of quiet but intense scholarship is extremely attractive. I mingled close to, and yet so far from, the undergraduates thronging the historic lanes and alleyways. I believe I sensed their intelligence and strength of character. It seemed a palpable self-assurance emanated from them, which, I surmised, came with acquisition of knowledge in those august institutions. This spirited enclave seemed somehow free of the normal banality of life.

Oxford and Cambridge in those days were Britain's two foremost universities. Being a graduate of either carried a prestige that no other university could bestow. Cambridge's Peterhouse College accepted its first students in 1284, just 20 years after the first Oxford college opened. Cambridge University, I also learned, comprises 35 separate, semi-autonomous colleges. They provide informal teaching to undergraduates, singly or in small groups, and handle the logistics of room and board. The university's total student body of about 15,000 gave each college an average of less than 500 students (1). In the early evening, after an inexpensive student meal, I headed back to the hostel to read for a while in the community room and then turn in. A 60-mile bike ride is an antidote for insomnia.

Sundays provided another enjoyable part of the excursion. I went to the river-edge grassy area behind the Fitzwilliam Museum. It was not as busy as the banks behind the colleges, and some students came here probably because of its greater seclusion. They usually came alone with a towel and books to stretch out and indulge in a concentrated reading session. I did the same. While they were no doubt reading some tome on philosophy, history, sociology, political theory, or may be even a science, my nose was buried in my current novel. Hopefully, it would at least be a book that would qualify as literature. They were remarkably peaceful gatherings. There were no radios disturbing the quiet and certainly no beer or soda cans popping. A collection of young males, exclusively back then, with focused minds. There were moments when I would have liked to strike up a conversation with one of them. Shyness, and my sense we were worlds apart, stopped me from ever making an attempt. And none ever talked to me. Such fierce British reserve.

I felt a deep yearning to be a part of that student body. The ache in my heart was real. Although being there caused pain, I was drawn to that hallowed place of learning. Night classes could never compete with Cambridge University. My genuine but unrealistic desire to be a part of that special world was motivated by an unhealthy measure of envy and self-pity. I didn't then understand this.

Lingering at this magical spot as long as I dared, around two o'clock I forced myself to begin the return journey that required six or seven hours of riding. A return journey to my world of copy boy and catch-up night school.

River Cam, Cambridge, England. Students on river bank (photo date unknown). This setting stirred my young soul.

CHAPTER 13

During the summer of 1949 I made up my mind to leave the newspaper. While I enjoyed the "center-of-it" atmosphere, after three years I felt I'd torn off teletype copy enough to stretch around the globe. At least by now I could offer shorthand and typing as marketable skills, although macho conceit made me a reluctant candidate for a secretarial position. In reality, male stenographers were disappearing from the labor market.

As a shorthand writer, one line of work was court reporter, expected to be able to write at about 180 words a minute. I'd never passed any shorthand speed test above 100 wpm; the gulf seemed uncrossable. I felt I didn't have the necessary brain-hand dexterity to attain that kind of speed to accurately capture the spoken word consistently for lengthy periods. Furthermore, about the time I learned this arcane skill, the stenotype machine became available. This 21-key shorthand typewriter could record speech with more facility than hand-written shorthand. I'd spent approaching three years learning a skill about to become obsolete. In retrospect, it's a wonder I persisted with shorthand. Normally the only male student in the room, except for the instructor, shyness drove me doggedly to a seat in the back row. Maybe once a year another male student would appear, come for a few sessions and then disappear, never to be seen again. I showed up with the regularity of the dawn.

The English class I attended had no more than ten students, taught by a diminutive Austrian-Jewish refugee from Nazism, who spoke English with a moderate accent. She had been living in London since the late 1930s. While I saw her then as someone elderly, she was almost certainly less than my own age now. Unlike a few teachers I've encountered, she devoted the class hour strictly to the course subject. Never would she steal time for personal trivia or self-glorifying anecdotes. But on one occasion she told us that, on a foggy night en route to her home in north London, she was mugged while walking alone from the train station.

Two male teenagers confronted her, demanding money. When she refused, they pushed her hard against a brick wall and she fell. They snatched her handbag and fled. She sustained a shoulder dislocation, a sprained wrist, and a great shock. She said she would have expected this from the Nazis, but it saddened her that it happened in a country where people were known for courtesy. This little lady was living proof for me that Hitler drove out the best and brightest of his nation's citizens. Not too long after my short story appeared in the college annual publication, this same teacher boosted my self-esteem by confiding to me she thought I possessed a "divine spark."

I didn't really understand what the phrase meant. At home I looked up "divine" in the dictionary. When I saw that it related to, or characterized God, I was both delighted and dumbfounded. I wondered what the Austrian lady would think of my lustful daydreaming about some of the girls attending Pitman College evening classes? Whatever it meant, however, I decided it sounded like a huge compliment. Praise from someone with her qualities was praise indeed. Her words fed my ego and helped further fuel my fuzzy aspiration to be a writer.

Four years had passed since the end of WWII and an austere daily life continued for Londoners. The relentless global conflict in Europe had devastated the participating states, many physically and all financially. Britain was virtually prostrate. There is no reason to doubt that, but for the American Marshall Plan for Aid, the Union of Soviet Socialist Republics (USSR) would have spread its tentacles and taken a stranglehold on western Europe as it did in the eastern half of the continent. Between the end of 1948 and the beginning of 1951, Britain alone received a total of $9.6 billion in American assistance. Even so, in 1949 our proud nation had to devalue its once all-powerful currency against the dollar. Sterling was devalued nearly one third, from $4.03 to $2.80. The British monopoly on world influence had effectively shifted across the Atlantic. In my little world I, too, shifted. In October I found another job, but did not move far geographically. A publishing house located just off Fleet Street needed an assistant to the Sales Manager of the Burke Publishing Company.

When I did my rounds at the newspaper office, bidding farewell to the staff, I was subjected to a blatant example of English snobbery dispensed by the London editor who dressed more like a banker than the popular image of a newspaperman. I tapped on his closed office door and waited his summons to enter. He raised his head from his reading material and appraised me sternly over the top of his horn-rimmed glasses as I walked across the carpet to his desk. His majestic bearing always intimidated me, and I no doubt took more words than needed to explain my presence. He didn't respond; just stared at me as though I was a life form beyond his comprehension. By now I was opposite him across his desk, already rattled by his lack of response, and unsure what to do next. Impulsively, I leaned across the desk and extended my hand. He now directed his fierce gaze at my extremity, but didn't move and remained silent. With my arm extended, like a frozen old-time railway signal, I felt dumb and humiliated. After what seemed an eternity, he bent forward minimally to lightly shake my hand, mumbling "goodbye." I turned and walked out, deflated and embarrassed.

That editor no doubt felt copy boys didn't rate acknowledgment, even one who'd worked more than three years at his newspaper. I felt hurt, even knowing I became far too sensitive over such perceived slights. The incident just added another layer to my resentment of the English class-system. My intense dislike for this feature of English life increased considerably in my middle teens as I expanded my reading horizons and gained a deeper understanding of the composition of British society. I probably allowed my strong feelings to develop into a low-grade obsession. (Years later I would discover a tendency to obsessive-compulsive disorder runs in my family.) My opinions were many and adamant back then. Without realizing it, my tendency to be judgmental of people became excessive. The emotions of youth don't really allow for rational examination, and I became an angry young man.

Eddie, although a less complex person than myself, also displayed a certain dissatisfaction. I now suspect this disaffection formed, in part, a component of our long association. While most other acquaintances appeared to be content with, or resigned to, their life station and their foreseeable prospects, Eddie and I were ill-defined malcontents.

In attempting to understand it now, I believe Eddie had been psychologically sensitized by his polio-induced physical deformity. I was similarly afflicted by my lack of height. Additionally, I believe that of the two of us, because of my greater lack of confidence, I more keenly felt my inadequate education. Neither of us, I think, recognized this subconscious turmoil exerting its powerful influence in our lives.

The publishing company to which I moved produced a number of specialized and business directories. Its preeminent offering was "Burke's Genealogical and Heraldic History of the Peerage, Baronetage, and Knightage, Privy Council and Order of Precedence of the United Kingdom," known more familiarly as "Burke's Peerage." This annual tome, with its heavy cloth-bound cover and title inscripted in gold lettering against a wine red background, contained the names and basic family details of all the peers and baronets in the U.K. First published in 1826 by John Burke, it is considered the primary, authentic source on the ancestry of Britain's aristocratic families. These households together owned so much of the island's expensive real property they exercised enormous authority. World Wars I and II had diluted their wealth, and socialist taxation now squeezed them more, but they still represented a powerful British clique.

This plush, six-inch thick directory of the land's plutocracy could give one a hernia just to lift it from a bookshelf. The rich and influential were highly motivated to reproduce. They wanted to keep the money in the family. Each one of their new little-darling progeny had to be duly recorded in the book. If your name appeared in this directory, you didn't need to go to night school. I could imagine these families sitting around in their castles pouring over the latest edition to see who had been elevated by the Monarch, who was ahead in the procreation race, and whose fortunes were rising or ebbing. This publication was an efficient, albeit expensive, way of keeping track of those worth keeping track of. While I don't know what a copy cost, a subscription price undoubtedly precluded it from the best-seller list.

In 1949, the year I joined the publisher, they were cranking out the 99th edition. The volume came with a set of formal portraits of the extended Royal family. Surprisingly, it also carried advertisements, albeit imposingly stiff. On the page opposite the picture of her Royal Highness Princess Elizabeth (now Queen Elizabeth II) they placed, rather incongruously, an advertisement for Wright's Coal Tar Soap, an old-fashioned disinfectant soap recommended, I vaguely recall, for particularly soiled people. *Burke's Peerage* was continuously updated by a small staff of donnish-looking men and women who kept to themselves in a couple of offices on the top floor of the building. What was I, a left leaning, iconoclast-in-training, doing in this world of musty conservatism besotted with hide-bound privilege? Without realizing it, I'd wandered into the vast service industry that caters to it.

The year 1949 also proved to be a watershed in domestic and international affairs. The government pushed on vigorously with nationalization of major segments of British infrastructure and industry. Since 1945, the Bank of England, coal mines, electricity supply, railways and road transportation, had been transformed into government entities. It also completed the take-over of the gas and steel industries, and expanded its tax-based health and welfare programs. Soon the national government virtually guaranteed your transition from cradle to grave, regardless of the worth of your contribution to society.

It is said people tend to become more conservative as they age. That certainly happened to me, although hopefully more through life observation than mere aging. Initially I felt public ownership of services used by an overwhelming percentage of the population to be right and fair. In reality, government ownership gave birth to the mind-set that "my government must take care of me." It tolerated employee sloth, not good for either the individual or the nation in the long term. Years later in America, capitalism's fountainhead, I witnessed some public employees exploit the certainty of their job status. They developed an art for doing as little as they could just shy of dereliction of duty. They were secure in their protected idleness. I've observed both genders dawdle away workday hours relating mindless trivia about their uninspiring lives. This atmosphere tends to undermine work ethics of responsible fellow employees. Today I accept, in the final analysis, private enterprise, despite faults, produces most efficiently what society needs, where it needs it. A lot of human nature requires a solid push to bring out its best potential.

Even the USSR's enormous social experiment to create a new man, so rational in concept, fell victim to human perversity. Deep-seated corruption and rampant manipulation undermined communist dreams as government ownership embraced most aspects of life. After 60 years, the experiment collapsed from its own dead weight. But before that, the Soviets proved difficult to deal with after the 1945 Allied Control Commission division of Germany into the four zones of occupation. The Soviets' most brazen saber rattling came in 1949 with the blockade of Berlin, a four-power enclave, sitting 80 miles inside the Russian Zone. When they turned back trains and trucks from the west, the Allies, led by America, chose to call their bluff. An around-the-clock airlift kept Berlin supplied. The North Atlantic Treaty Organization (NATO), formed that year, served as the political and military deterrent to Soviet expansion. The costly 40-year cold war struggle began in earnest.

The tensions in Europe lessened late in 1949 following the end of the Berlin blockade. However, they cranked-up ominously in the Far East. A new communist regime in China seized the American Consulate General in Beijing in January 1950. The nations of the west had barely completed their military draw down from World War II. But with communism already holding sway in a good chunk of our planet's terra firma, and with their seeming appetite to consume more, the non-communist world had to reverse. With a collective heavy heart, some nations of the West began once more to re-arm. Then the Chinese moved into Tibet under the pretext of "liberating" that remote country. When Tibet appealed to the United Nations for help, the world organization did not respond. Late in June the North Koreans poured across the 38th Parallel on the Korean peninsula, almost a year to the day when U.S. troops withdrew from that country. This time the UN rallied and, again led by America, sent a unified force to assist the South Koreans who had been pushed far down its peninsula.

On 28 June 1950, the British Prime Minister, Clement Atlee, a man of peace, announced to the House of Commons that we would fulfill our obligations under the charter of the United Nations. The prospects for western civilization appeared decidedly bleak in the early months of 1950. As the old saw goes, however, there's always a silver lining in the blackest cloud. As if ordained by a mighty unseen force, I achieved the age of 18 in March and became eligible for military national service (selective service in the USA). At the time, I couldn't have pointed to the Korean Peninsula on a world map. But my life became entwined in these cataclysmic events.

As the time approached for call-up, I became highly agitated at the thought I might not pass the physical entrance examination. My concern was not based on any specific known health defect. In fact, I believed myself to be in quite good shape. Fortunately, I'd adhered to my 1947 decision to stop smoking. While I had a sedentary job, I was an active person because of weekend sports and I walked as much as possible to save on transportation costs.

My dread about possible rejection for military service started when a neighborhood teenager told me he'd been declared physically unfit. I became full of fear it might be my fate, and obscurely felt that would be a life-long disgrace. Had the subliminal message of the red-splashed maps in my school corridors been far more effective than I chose to believe? I liked to think I was just a little more subtle and fully capable of forming my own opinions free from the influence of state-directed brainwash. In retrospect, it's more likely to have been simple teenage macho self-image. Children want to be exactly like all other children. I wanted to play only with the boys who'd been identified as belonging to the healthy set.

CHAPTER 14

When the military physical examination day arrived in May, I went there with my heart in my throat. Along with everyone else, I winced a little when the doctor cupped his hand around my scrotum and told me to cough. I was even more mortified when he told me to bend over and spread my cheeks. Despite these and other assaults on one's dignity, they failed to cool my weird desire to be shown as physically capable as the next guy. This need must have come from the core of my being. Certainly I had no desire to carry the Union Jack to far-away places.

As it turned out, I passed the physical without any blows to my oversized ego. Examiners detected a degree of color-blindness in me, and a doctor looked extra long at my right calf that is somewhat emaciated. Mom always said it "had gone thin" when I was 18 months, and neither she nor I ever pursued it. Aside from these defects, the military might of the West could soon count on me.

An Air Ministry letter shortly directed me to join the Royal Air Force No. 10 Flight, C Squadron, 2nd Recruit Training Wing. It handled both volunteers and national service conscripts, the second category far outnumbering the first. This organization was charged with turning boys into men by two month's smart marching forwards, backwards, and reversing (but never sideways), all in a strictly prescribed style and format. At the end of this process we supposedly emerged as clean, keen and compliant members of His Majesty's third service. This improbable activity was to take place at RAF Padgate, a major boot camp near Warrington, Lancashire, about 20 miles east of the once mighty port of Liverpool, but known more nowadays as the birthplace of the Beatles.

My nervousness on the day I entered the service made me wonder if, after all my emotional upheaval about failing, I'd have been better off not passing the entrance examination? I'd been increasingly discontented at home, but when the time came to fly from the nest, it proved more difficult than anticipated. My sentiments pulled in opposing directions.

Now my emotional pendulum swung back again and, on the morning I walked to Manor Park station with my small tote bag containing only toiletries, I enjoyed the sensation of being a little pumped. Here was the proof I was as healthy as the next boy. But while the feeling of going on an adventure brought pleasure, I wrestled with the contradictory thought I derived satisfaction from my civilian life routines and didn't really want them disturbed. I didn't know it then, but these mental crosscurrents were an early manifestation of my tendency to be forever looking over my shoulder. The accursed "what if" syndrome.

During the approximate 200-mile train journey from London I tried to read *THE GUARDIAN*, the quality liberal daily ranking high on my list of favored newspapers. My concentration, however, ran amuck because of jittery anticipation, so I watched without registering the passing view of England's busy, orderly farmlands as the steam train carried me to military life. The neat colored rectangles of various crops, now advanced in their growing cycle, looked like large quilts laid over the land on both sides of the tracks.

Signs at Warrington's central station directed arriving recruits to a parking lot at the rear of the soot-blackened, Victorian terminal. Outside, under heavy, low-hanging gray clouds, two small, drab-painted buses stood on the far side. Both sported the Royal Air Force emblem: a red dot surrounded by a white circle surrounded by a blue circle. Lounging against the grill of one vehicle, two flat-capped civilian drivers smoked cigarettes looking as relaxed as a Chinese coolie sucking on a hookah pipe. They appeared singularly indifferent that morning to the Chinese antics on the Korean peninsula.

Another sign directed us to wait on the pavement for pick-up by one of these buses. The assortment of 18 year-olds who had arrived gathered obediently by the sign. Even though we'd soon be living in stark-naked togetherness, none made an effort at communication beyond a self-conscious nod of acknowledgment we'd soon be a band of brothers for better or worse.

Thinking back, even conceding the deep-rooted tradition of British reticence, our timidity must have been the first sign we'd fallen under the spell of military life. We were uncertain whether talking was permitted, and none seemed brave enough to risk it. I was only 200 miles from the home of my old freethinking self, and I seemed already a frightened military member. .

We stood looking across the parking lot at the two government-paid drivers who clearly operated at their own relaxed pace. When they finished their cigarettes, and no doubt offered their last drop of opinion on the local football team, one driver went on board, cranked the engine, and swung his vehicle in a broad arc to where we future men-of-the-blue stood, still silent. The bus maneuvered out of Warrington's narrow streets lined with the array of diminutive shop fronts repeated in their thousands in hundreds of small towns nation-wide. The camp lay just over two miles out on the road to Manchester. The RAF gate guard waved the bus through, and its motley cargo of nervous, new recruits became government property as simply as that.

The bus stopped in front of a square, cinder-block building identified as "Induction Point." Several groups of boys, arriving on earlier buses, stood around and silently watched this latest batch of civilian specimens stepping apprehensively from the RAF vehicle. We now formed our own quiet, uncertain group. I wondered who, beside myself, might be thinking, for the first time that day, about home.

A uniformed representative barged through the building's front swing doors. The grimace on his acne-marked face suggested his life was exceptionally onerous. He stood, feet apart, sneeringly eyeing the collection of raw recruits. All our heads turned in his direction; our gaze focused, and some slack jawed. His right hand tapped a short swagger stick against his left palm with the precision of a beating metronome.

"You shower, form a line quickly," the apparition barked. Apparently the standard civilized greeting between humans when they meet for the first time played no part in our new family. His military attire demanded the attention of all of us as we, luggage in hand, banged into each other in our frantic effort to comply with his impolite order.

He wore his beret at a rakish angle. The brass badge on this headgear, displaying the service's initials surrounded by a laurel wreath topped with a crown, shone like Inca gold. The brass buckle on his blancoed web belt glistened like the jewelry of a Pharaonic Queen. Other uniform garments were pressed so sharply the creases stood out like leading edges on racing yachts, including even razor blade ridges running down his blouse sleeves. The creases of his trousers looked so perfect I imagined him lowered into them like knights were once introduced into their armor. His trouser bottoms fit neatly into web ankle gaiters whose small double buckles also shimmered like the precious metal. Finally, black boots with toecaps, burnished to a brilliant gloss, outshone the Lancashire sun. The sun part I had to imagine because we stood under an overcast sky. This military mannequin must have primped with the devotion of a narcissistic debutante.

This specter of spit-and-polish then advised us he would be our drill instructor for the next six weeks. Our slovenly, disorderly, and unregimented minds and bodies were to be thoroughly made over so we would be a credit to the nation. Just at this very moment, he bluntly told us, he didn't know whether to laugh or cry. I couldn't summon much sympathy for his plight.

"I'll start your next six weeks by telling you I'm Corporal Gilbert. You will address me as 'Corporal' and nothing else. You will follow my orders promptly and completely. If you don't, while it's going to be a miserable time for me working with you slobs, I can make those six weeks spirit crushing for you! Do you understand?"

"Yessir," several of us stressfully bleeped.

"You fucking idiots! I've not been fucking knighted. Call me Corporal. Corporal. Corporal. Is that fucking clear?"

"Yes, sir," blurted a boy a few bodies down from me. Almost all of us turned our heads to catch a glimpse of this slim, bespectacled novice who seemed particularly nervous. The devastated new recruit, just at this moment, was trying to retract his head into his chest cavity like a tortoise.

The model-perfect Corporal spun around, lips pulled back like a snarling guard dog, and walked stiffly to the lost soul.

"You must be the village fucking idiot!" the Corporal shrieked, his face just inches from that of the now terrified recruit. "If you don't smarten up boy, you'll soon be wanting to climb back into the womb you claim you were excreted from!"

Corporal God wheeled around and returned to the front of the now quaking line of boys. His dramatic display of savagery effectively installed the right measure of fear in us, its very purpose. Each new group almost certainly went through the same routine. I knew boot camp was all about taking a thinking person and transforming him into an unquestioning fool. But I had been on earth for 18 years, and only half an hour in the Royal Air Force, yet already my sense of self had wilted around the edges.. The pace of change was happening far too fast for my tastes. All this gave me yet further cause to wonder if I'd been incredibly misguided in my eagerness to pass the entrance physical. But I consoled myself with the thought that several boys I knew had joined the Army and that service had the reputation of being even more ludicrous. I fixed this shining two striper with a disbelieving stare. He didn't look much older than 18 himself, and what's more, I noted smugly, he wasn't much taller than I.

With the tenderness of a late night TV wrestler, he then informed us we'd already enjoyed our last stroll. Our days of relaxed locomotion were finished. From now on we'd march everywhere. We were ordered to realign ourselves into two rows, with taller boys on both ends and short asses in the center to create two walls of bodies with the tallest at both ends. There was some disagreement among the shortest as to whose unhappy lot it was to be the center person. Miraculously, it wasn't me. A boy from Wales qualified. But it was a matter of centimeters.

A command came to "right face and by the left quick march," and off we went, a couple on the wrong foot, towards what would undoubtedly be brilliant military careers. Our gleaming guardian demonstrated the authorized hop step for the benefit of those dumb ones who had started their careers by thrusting out the incorrect extremity. For a moment, I became more conscious of putting forward one foot before the other than at any time since I first learned to walk. We tramped along cement pathways, luggage in left hand, towards the recruit sleeping area. Off to the right, we could see the camp's main parade ground where several groups, each with about 100 bodies, were marching, wheeling left and right, and about facing with what looked like smooth accomplishment. The Corporal let us know we'd be out there day after next.

In the recruit sleeping area numerous rectangular wooden huts stood mounted on short cinder-block columns about 18" above the ground. We halted at huts in the middle of the cluster displaying our flight, squadron and wing designation. Corporal God walked along the row randomly assigning boys to our different huts. He said we could select our own cots in the hut, and that we were to be outside after breakfast at 0730 hours next day. Then he pointed in the direction of the mess hall and said we could get dinner anytime between 1630 and 1830 hours. Fortunately, someone understood this new method of recording time or some of us would have had no dinner that evening. Our fearless leader spun around on his boot heels, crashed the right to the ground with a force that must have rattled teacups in Australia, crunched the swagger stick under his left armpit and, with his right arm swinging to the prescribed shoulder height, marched away with mechanical toy precision.

At the end of the next day we were far more like members of the big Royal Air Force family. We were strutting around in its coarse, woolen uniform, a silly beret on our heads, and black boots at the other end. Perhaps worst of all, we had been shorn of abundant hair like sheep in springtime. They were doing a good job of breaking our spirits. And after this first full day of my military life, I came closer to sustaining an injury than at any other time in the service. But it wasn't the kind that wins you medals. It would have been self-inflicted and right outside the mess hall.

RAF practice of the day included issuing each airman a set of cutlery to be carried to the mess hall for every meal. This arrangement was really, I strongly suspected, just an excuse to give us more items to clean and neatly display at inspections. After a feeding, we'd wash these irons in a large, multi-fauceted sink using scalding water. Many of the boys-in-blue would put them still wet into their pockets. But as a clear sign of my greater refinement, I preferred to keep them in my hand for air-drying. As I went around the building in the direction of my sleeping hut, an officer was striding toward me on the same side of the road. We would pass each other within perhaps fifteen steps. We hadn't yet received saluting instruction, but I'd noticed quite a bit of it going on all over the place. I knew it was my station in life to recognize this superior creature. I swung my right hand up toward my forehead. The knife tip and fork prongs stopped millimeters from my right eye. The moist eating utensils remained firmly clasped in my right hand.

Then, in panic, I realized my saluting style did not conform to Britain's hoary military code. I relaxed my hand to present the proper open palm salute with the index finger just touching the forehead between the beret band and the eyebrow. Inevitably, Newton's law intervened, and utensils clattered noisily on the sidewalk. I stood frozen in embarrassment and uncertainty. Surely this gaff warranted a court martial? The officer's face revealed he'd been suddenly overwhelmed by an assault of incredulity. He abruptly turned his head as though something across the street demanded his instant attention, and passed me by without a word or a salute. I don't believe in astrology, otherwise I could have read from this incident all kinds of dire signs for my future in the military. Despite this unpromising start, however, I settled into recruit training on a par with the rest.

The six weeks spent at boot camp are now a blur of almost non-stop physical activity. We drilled marching with rifles mornings and afternoons for six days, and on the seventh the Corporal God rested, and we did too. As he'd promised, we marched from billet to the parade ground, rifle storage shack, mess hall, lecture room, gymnasium, and virtually everywhere else at regular paced marching. Then we practiced slow funeral marching in case we ever had to accompany the coffin of a fallen RAF comrade. After 42 busy days, we 90 boys of No. 10 Flight, C Squadron, 2nd Recruit Training Wing, were highly polished at starting, turning, wheeling, reversing and stopping in unison. While we couldn't compete with the guards at Buckingham Palace, we were not the stumblebum stampede of six weeks before. In spite of myself, I recall feelings of pleasure derived from the sheer physicality of this transformation and the proficiency we achieved in clomping about noisily as one.

My employment history and knowledge of shorthand and typing made it a foregone conclusion to be assigned to the clerical trades. At boot camp I'd spent six weeks on my feet. Now I was assigned to an administrative course where I'd be made to sit down for about the same period.

RAF Hereford, located outside the county seat of the same name in rural, picturesque Herefordshire, pressed hard against the Welsh border. This farming community sits among rolling hills at the head of the lush valley through which the River Wye winds its way to join the Severn River flowing into the Bristol Channel. Hereford was one of England's many medieval marketing towns chartered by the realm. Its 1950 population counted 36,500. Our compact camp, in this restful corner of England, was so different from the fevered, sprawling boot camp in flat, industrial Lancashire. My training assignment was to the No. 2 School of Admin Trades, No.1 Wing, on a course for Copy Typists, Shorthand Typists, and General Clerks. There were four airwomen and eight airmen in my class. The camp had the capacity to conduct simultaneously some

30 such classes. Our instructor, a veteran sergeant, had served in Kenya and South Africa, both components of the red-colored territories on our school maps.

Because I was already a reasonably competent typist and shorthand writer, I didn't have to work much in this course. In fact, when it was over, I earned a proficiency rating sufficient to obtain the designation of "Leading Aircraftsman," shown by a cloth patch displaying a single aircraft propeller worn on the arm. This is not a rank, but shows a person qualified in his trade. My one and only award. The Air Force trade school daily typing practices and shorthand dictation and transcription was not much different from what I had been doing for three and a half years in night classes. In the civilian setting, the material was largely about company year-end reports; now I dealt with a lot of letters and reports to the Air Ministry in London.

Camp Hereford provided a relatively quiet and peaceful time for its students. There were no spit-and-polish corporals screaming at us future Air Force pen pushers. Our sergeant instructor's cap badge and jacket belt buckle were as dull as weathered brass inserts on headstones in neglected churchyards. His uniform suggested it hadn't seen the face of an iron in many moons. While he didn't strike me as at all scholarly, he was efficient and a gentleman. He would tell an occasional corny joke, but they always were decorous, presumably in deference to the airwomen in the room. I understand things are quite different today.

It is just remotely possible that when Air Ministry bureaucrats decided on the location for the administrative trades school, they matched its decidedly unwarlike mission to the tranquility of its geographic setting. About 60% of the county's workforce was employed in agriculture. These rural activities meant its people saw early mornings. Charming Hereford turned off the light promptly each evening when the animals bedded down. Nightlife was not available. To provide a little recreation for the trainees, the base held a weekly dance in the gymnasium. Although airmen outnumbered airwomen, the gentle sex had a good showing. In those days, women in the British military, all volunteers, were far more likely to be administrative staff. I had soon noticed one extremely attractive airwoman in my Wing class. What I really noticed was how she filled out the uniform shirt in a most unmilitary way. What's more, she was short enough that I considered myself qualified to make an approach.

On the first Friday night I went to the gym dance, my heart missed several beats when I saw her standing with a group of airwomen across the floor. I kept her under observation and soon noted her popularity. Men rushed to be the first to ask her to dance as soon as the local trio struck the opening note. Knowing I'd have to be that bit faster to win a chance to hold her in my arms, I maneuvered close enough to reach her before other contenders. As I stood poised, I was as nervous as a runner in track starting blocks waiting for the gun. As soon as the beginning bar of the next dance tune spread across the gym, I snapped into action. Moving smartly around her group of friends, I stopped squarely in front of this petite beauty. She just had to give her attention to me.

"May I have the pleasure of this dance?" I heard myself saying, trying hard to give off vibes of extreme male confidence. Her azure eyes were just about level with mine. They met and my bone marrow quivered. A pocket-sized goddess just right for me. Her gorgeous, made-for-kissing lips moved:

"Thank you — but no!"

She had tempered the blow somewhat, but it still stung deeply. Then, as I slunk away, she turned to her support group and I overhead the words, "I'm tired of short men pestering me."

All of the many refusals I'd experienced at Saturday night dances at home hadn't toughened me. Her comment crushed me and pain burned along my nerve tree. If I'd had some insight and courage, I'd have gone on immediately to another girl and invited her to dance like pilots say it is necessary to fly immediately after a crash. I retreated to the other side of the gym. I was too hurt to even feign uncaring and didn't approach another girl that evening.

I believe one reason for my hypersensitivity was false pride: I feared public embarrassment. Also at play was the ever-present oversized male ego. Like so many other men and boys, I wanted to dance with, and be seen with, the prettiest girl possible. This was desired not only for the thrill of her company, but equally to satisfy a need to be admired, even envied, by other males. Many years passed before I gained a tentative understanding of such youthful motivation.

Life at RAF Hereford during my six weeks there proved to be slow and gentle, very much on a par with that of the nearby villages. While we did parade twice weekly, one to collect pay, and the other probably just to remind us we were in the military. Our evenings were far less occupied than at basic training camp. I resumed some reading, in spite of our crowded sleeping hut. Reading for me had become both a deep pleasure and almost a must. Just prior to the end of the course, early in November 1950, we received notice of our postings to permanent duty stations. The twelve pen pushers in my class were scattered around the country, with one to Germany, as if blown by a mighty wind. I drew an assignment close to home at RAF Henlow, in Bedfordshire, only about 30 miles west of London.

RAF admin trade school (1950). Official graduation-day photo. Me at extreme left, seated.

CHAPTER 15

Although I didn't know until years hence, Henlow camp held a distinguished place in the history of the Royal Air Force. It opened in May 1918, the year the RAF itself was formed, following WW1's demonstration of the decisive role aerial combat would play in any future geographically distant war (1). From its beginning, Henlow had been a camp devoted to all aspects of the RAF's communication equipment. RAF Henlow was not an active flying base, although it did have a runway, a remnant of WWII. As I write these words, of the three RAF camps at which I served Henlow is the only one still operating.

My ignorance applied equally to the Henlow unit headquarters I joined in early November 1950. It started life as the WWII Signals Development Unit in September 1940. As ground and air communications grew more complex, the nature of its work changed. With an industrial mission now emphasizing producing, installing and maintaining radio equipment, its name changed to Radio Engineering Unit on 1 January 1950, a mere ten months before my appearance.

Following a late arrival, next morning I processed in at the headquarters, which would be my work site. Stuffed full of military marching, diamond-hard discipline, and administrative trade smarts, the RAF now wanted its pound of flesh from my hide. Right after inquiring my name and serial number, a different kind of corporal filling in the paper work asked if I played soccer. It turned out that the camp had a keenly competitive inter-section soccer league on Wednesdays, the official fitness and sports afternoon. As the numerically smallest contingent, the headquarters needed anyone who could hold up for 90 minutes to complete a match. As a result, I turned out for the headquarters' team almost every Wednesday afternoon of my 18 months at Henlow.

Sleeping quarters were again the standard 24-man wooden hut mounted on short cinder-block piers. When the corporal led me into it, most of the cots were already in use. Britain's November weather is cold, and the hut felt icy. Heating was by means of two potbelly, coal-burning stoves located in the center towards each end. Fires were not allowed during the workday; a clever rule that insured you went eagerly to your duty station.

The corporal gave me a brief tour of the Headquarters. The general clerks were herded in a large bullpen at the building's center. They worked at old, kitchen-type, wooden tables. Banks of government-green metal filing cabinets lined several walls. Commissioned officers had their offices against the outer walls, thus affording them a status window. A young pilot officer, the lowest RAF commissioned rank, headed the finance section. About half the clerks fell into his domain. They worked on the camp's budget and on-going finances, and the Gilbertian palaver surrounding the preparing and dispensing of the camp payroll. A seasoned Warrant Officer performed as the equivalent of an office manager. The remaining clerks reported to this WO. Their tasks involved the overall administration of the camp. In time I saw that he smoothly handled the interface between the brass and the rest of us lesserlings.

The NCO in charge of the mail room was a weather-beaten sergeant, with a deeply lined face whose coloration bespoke of years spent in a climate far more torrid than Britain's. He was reputed to be one of the oldest in the RAF, having been in the service almost since its 1918 inception. We called him Sgt. Methuselah behind his back. This old timer had spent a lot of his younger years in India, and married a native girl. This union between the Raj and the sub-continent produced 11 kids, the right number to form their own soccer team.

I made out somewhat better for my personal working location. As the only shorthand typist assigned to the headquarters, I was put in an anteroom adjoining the large office of the unit welfare officer, with the rank of Squadron Leader (equivalent of a Major in the U.S. military), for whom I primarily worked. After a while, it became apparent to me that whenever a task presented itself that didn't appeal to the Warrant Officer, he assigned it to this Mail Room NCO. The delegation ensured the smooth functioning of an understood, if unwritten, pecking order.

The corporal left me in the hands of this gnarled NCO, who provided a more detailed run-down of headquarters' work policies and guidelines of where I fitted in as we walked the building's corridors. No doubt this was one of the tasks the Warrant Officer didn't relish. In contrast, the India-veteran obviously enjoyed the opportunity of making nervous newcomers even more nervous with little stories about what befell the airman who screwed up. The old-timer had been around long enough to have as many work-place wrinkles in his head as on his face.

After Sgt. Methuselah's joke-a-minute escorted tour, he took me to my work site. Squadron Leader Ryman wasn't in his office, a frequent state of affairs as I soon discovered. The sergeant told me to familiarize myself with the Smith-Corona manual typewriter and the contents of the locked file cabinets. Those in my alcove contained documentation on airmen involved in compassionate appeals. Some reports were from outside agencies, including the Red Cross, on private matters relating to individual airmen. One of my responsibilities was to lock the cabinets when absent from the office and at the end of duty. The sergeant handed me the keys and took off rapidly along the corridor in the direction of the mailroom hoping, I assumed, to catch some of his own personnel goofing off.

Its government furnishings overwhelmed my small anteroom. The battleship gray metal desk faced an unadorned, painted cinder-block wall, no doubt so placed to keep the typist's mind on the job. One side of the desk housed a typewriter on a spring-loaded tray that hoisted the machine to work height. Standing at one of the file cabinets, I unlocked a drawer and took out a few files to thumb through. The contents were mainly routine letters on the RAF standard memo to Henlow unit commanders concerning their personnel. Sometimes they involved requests for removal from an oversea posting, getting an assignment closer to home or the need for financial assistance from the quasi-official RAF Benefit Society. As I skimmed these documents, I noticed Sgt. Methuselah walk pass my door-less alcove several times and look in. I figured the old geezer hoped to catch me asleep. But it never happened because I don't sleep too well standing up and several of the files were interesting. I made a note to get back to them to read later.

After thirty minutes I had an idea of the correspondence format which mostly complied with the work samples used in the admin. training course. I decided to give the typewriter a try. The spring on the desk tray squeaked a little as I raised it. Then I spun around to the drawer side to find typing paper. I pulled open the top one...and nearly fell off the swivel chair. Sitting in the middle was a medium-sized pile of human excrement.

As I pushed back from the desk in mild shock and strong disgust, I heard guttural chuckles. I turned to see Sgt. Methuselah in the doorway, grinning from ear to ear. He had just pulled off his favorite prank on another newcomer. It turned out that the distressing object in my desk was a gimmick brought back from India. It was a wood carving of a healthy human bowel movement, incredibly realistic in shape and color. The repulsion I registered at first sight stopped me from remembering that had it been real it would have stunk up much of the building. He'd been patrolling the corridor to catch me in my first moment of reaction. The elderly prankster retrieved his toy, put it in his pocket, and sallied back along the corridor, still chuckling. This charming memento, purchased for a couple of rupees in a street market in the swarming subcontinent, had brought him numerous mirthful episodes. So much for joining the service that had won the Battle of Britain!

Meanwhile, on the other side of the earth, fierce seesaw battles on the Korean peninsula during the second half of 1950 resulted in the United Nation's forces, again primarily composed of Americans, pushing the North Koreans back to the Chinese border. Then, in late November, Mao Se Tung ordered nearly one million of his soldiers across the Yalu River to stampede these UN troops out of North Korea. I couldn't believe Mao's rashness. Didn't the man know I sat poised with fingers hovering over the keys of my Smith-Corona manual typewriter at RAF Henlow a mere 10,500 direct air miles from the battle zone? But the British government must have decided I would be vital in the defense of the realm had the Oriental armies ever reached the Home Counties. No matter the fortunes of the war in Korea, I spent the next eighteen months in that anteroom trying unsuccessfully to get back at Sergeant Methuselah for his tasteless practical joke. Only later, after I arrived in the United States, did my war contribution receive a modicum of official recognition.

In my time at Henlow I settled into a pronounced dual existence, shuttling between the RAF and Mom. I stayed on base only six weekends when I was tagged for the high adventures of mess-hall detail, guard duty, or the pandemonium that engulfed the headquarters preparing the base annual budget which went on for some 14 fun-filled days straight.

The weekend pass ritual became ingrained for those of us who happened to live in the London area, of which there were four in my billet alone. Those draftees from the north and west of the country underwent a much closer bonding with the RAF because they went home far less often. On Fridays we finished work at 3:30 p.m., an hour earlier than usual. Then came a charge to the billet to change into civilian clothes, followed by a dash out the main gate to catch the first bus to Luton. We were always in a state of high expectancy, like boarding-school children going home for summer vacation. At Luton we connected with an express bus to London. I'd arrived home around 6:30 p.m., just a little later than when I worked in Fleet Street. Weekends for me were then no different from my days as a civilian.

I soon discovered that after four nights in the rambunctious, noisy hut, I wanted solitude on Friday evenings. After a good meal cooked by Mom, I craved settling down with an equally good novel. At the time I derived great pleasure from British authors such as Charles Dickens, George Orwell, Somerset Maugham, and E.M. Forster. In an effort to be a worldly person, in my mind I crossed the English Channel to sample in translation a few French authors such as Victor Hugo, Andre Malraux, and the earthy short-story writer, Guy de Maupassant. Our living room on the ground floor, however, was still the only area heated. This room held the wireless (radio) that provided evening entertainment for my parents. They had favorite weekly comedies and serialized plays that were one source of their pleasure. The stage was set for a showdown. My ego won.

I badgered my parents to shut off the radio so I could read undisturbed. They soon became listless without their outlet and started visiting nearby relatives on Friday evenings. When I look back now I see my behavior as incredibly egotistical. Possibly Mom didn't object that much to vacating the house. She had been in it for a good part of the day, and quite likely welcomed an outing. But Dad almost certainly would have preferred his evening at home. He always rose about 5 a.m. and departed for work thirty minutes later. He liked to catch the early taxi business at the Covent Garden flower market, and steal a march on a few other commercial pickings. No doubt by evening all he wanted was to stretch out in a fireside armchair, scan his newspaper, and listen to the radio. Dad could apparently do both at once, although I wondered how efficiently. But they went along with my selfish demands. Perhaps this was their way of saying, "we love you." I didn't know enough to recognize this.

I had far less enthusiasm for the journey back to camp late each Sunday evening. I'd leave the house with just enough time to catch the last train around midnight from King's Cross station. This popular service hauled several hundred military personnel returning reluctantly from London weekends to a number of Air Force or Army camps in the area. Invariably, many fell into deep sleeps from which it was irksome to rouse ourselves when the train reached Arlesley. Brain-dead and bleary-eyed, we stumbled out the carriages knowing we still had the painful one mile-plus walk to camp. We reached our hut around 2:30 a.m. If anyone made too much noise coming in, or turned on lights, they'd be subjected to a barrage of juicy curses from those already in the sack. These airmen were full of resentment because their home locations necessitated them remaining on a base with minimal recreation facilities. Included in this category in our billet were three fearsomely strong Scotsmen who went home less often than anyone. They would not brook any nonsense from the London clowns.

Now I've seen the extensive recreational outlets available on most U.S. military installations, I judge those at RAF Henlow in 1950/2 as pathetic. This permanent camp housed about 2,500 service men and maybe 250 airwomen. Of course, some of these people found recreation with each other, but the majority of us weren't so lucky. My own pet peeve was the lack of a library. If I remember correctly, there was a pitiable excuse for a reading room run by the Navy, Army, Air Force Institute, or NAAFI (equivalent to the American Exchange Service, or PX/BX system). It occupied not more than 300 square feet, containing four or five well-worn, overstuffed armchairs. In one corner was a built-in bookcase holding 30 to 40 dog-eared paperbacks, mostly westerns. That was the entire stock, and not to my taste. There were no newspapers or magazines. In a nation with a proud literary tradition, airmen with the reading habit were out of luck. To resolve this problem, on the weekend I'd get one or two books from my local library to read on base.

Anyone with a desire to further his or her education would have been thwarted as well. There were none of the on base extension education programs I later encountered with the U.S. military. As a result, evening boredom, as much as hunger, drove a few of us to leave the hut once a week in favor of an incredibly unsanitary, greasy, hole-in-the-wall for a meal, even though we'd already eaten supper by 5 p.m. Located not too far from the main gate, this fry pit operated in a tumble-down temporary building whose walls seemed to stand up only because of their many coats of coagulated cooking fat. Its short, bald and over-weight owner-operator always sported about a week's stubble. With a cigarette dangling continuously from his lips, I thought it probable this robotic chain-smoker kept one going during sleep. He certainly appeared covered in more grease than the mechanic at the garage did a few doors down.

His menu offered two entrees: the world's fattest hamburgers or steak that must have been the most utilitarian of the utility grade of beef. You didn't get any choice in the preparation method: everything fried including hamburger, steak, potatoes, tomatoes, even sliced white bread. All menu items received equal treatment: thrown into the hell-hot fat in one of two large, long-handled skillets wheezing and gasping on his gas stove from morning to night. Your meal choices were incinerated before your eyes. Like a Chinese fireworks display, fiery red, yellow, and orange flame licks leapt from his pans resembling a chemical plant conflagration. From time to time he'd disappear in choking black smoke billowing up and out as from an erupting volcano.

Eventually the spluttering chef, whose lungs must have been blacker than a coal miner's, emerged from the dense smog with our plates of seared, oil-drenched, high-cholesterol food remnants. There were no warnings back then about the dangers of fried, or more properly piromanticised, food. This haute cuisine guaranteed a 2 a.m. acid attack..

My primary function at the Headquarters was working for Squadron Leader Victor Ryman, the base morale and welfare officer. In a typically British way, I never learned much about the man for whom I mostly worked for 18 months. S/L Ryman was a sergeant at the 1939 WWII outbreak, obtaining a commission because of the exigencies of war. Even though he hadn't been aircrew, he no doubt worked long hours and incredibly hard during those hellish years. I guessed his age as over 60. Compared with Americans, British career officers serve far more years before qualifying for pension. As an example, General Montgomery, of Alamein fame, retired at age 70.

But in this job S/L Ryman was not overly busy. He handled a modest caseload of applicants for compassionate postings and a few men who'd run off the tracks. For most of these cases, S/L Ryman requested the British Red Cross to investigate the airman's home situation and render their findings. We also asked unit commanders to provide input on an airman's conduct and work performance. Our office gathered these documents and S/L Ryman presented the facts to the Henlow Station Commander, whose decision was put in a summary report, prepared by our office, and sent for disposition of the next higher Support Command. Only rarely did cases have to be referred to the Air Ministry, the final arbiter. To the credit of the 250 airwomen on the station, to my knowledge not one of them ever caused me to start an official file on their behalf.

Most of the cases were not worthy of headlines. Every now and again, however, a juicier one came along, and two of them have stayed with me. A married airman applied for a compassionate posting to the north of England on the grounds, as I recall, to help support a floundering family business. Normally, the Red Cross report reflected the folks at home strongly siding with an airman's request. In this case, however, his wife unequivocally let everyone know she opposed her husband's transfer nearer home. She claimed she was managing the business perfectly well by herself with some help from her parents. The report explained that when her husband was on hand she couldn't work because of his "constant and insatiable physical demands." That horny airman stayed at Henlow.

Another singular case involved a handsome airman who had an affair with a married local woman he met in the nearby village pub. The cuckolded, but still loving, husband found out and, in his utter distress, wrote a letter of protest to our Station Commander. In the resolution, if I remember correctly, the airman wanted nothing long-term from this little triangle. The surprised, chastened wife stayed with crushed, forgiving husband, and handsome airman went to another camp where, probably, the local women were delighted. I felt a bit like an advice columnist when I typed this report.

Another variety of case involved airmen who weren't meeting financial commitments and reneging on loans. Often this resulted from excessive betting on horse and dog racing. S/L Ryman had to sit them down and point out a few basic facts of life and I first became aware of the British passion for gambling. Today, "novelty betting" in Britain is where you can bet on virtually anything. For example, an English bookmaker is offering 500-to-one odds Britney Spears will capture the White House at a presidential election by year 2030.

When S/L Ryman discovered I could put together a sufficiently comprehensible report for onward forwarding, he began to leave the report preparation more and more to me. I relished the chance to do some writing, even though it was strictly "officialese." Then his absences from the office, noticeable from my first day, became even more pronounced. He now approached the career finishing line, and wanted his ease.

As time went by, it became known around the headquarters I could take and transcribe dictation with reasonable competency. Calls began to come from the Station Commander, a Group Captain, equivalent to an American Colonel, that I should report to him with my notebook. I could save him laborious handwriting. His material was routine and I could handle it without difficulty. Then I was called on to take dictation from the Air Commodore, equivalent of an American Brigadier General, Commander of the Radio Engineering Unit. His heavily technical material, involving analysis of radio airwave transmission and electronics systems, had me sweating. He authored reports through Support Command to the Air Ministry on these complex subjects that were pure black magic to me.

This extra work paid off, but not in money or promotion. When the boys in the billet learned I had face-to-face, one-on-one dealings with the station's two top-ranked officers, I sensed a small increase in their respect. But nothing to turn my head.

The one time the workload became onerous was when the annual budget submission to Support Command fell due. Each wing, squadron, flight, or other-named element on the station submitted next fiscal year's financing request. All headquarters' sections worked on it to produce a station total package under the orchestration of the warrant officer and station commander. The HQ financial section, led by the young Pilot Officer, had the job of combining all the arithmetic. Whoever could type got to put these numbers in the appropriate little boxes on the Air Ministry prescribed forms to be forwarded in six copies.

No big deal, until you remember there were no copying machines in those days. Inserting five sheets of carbon paper and rolling a wad as thick as a pancake into the typewriter made the second to sixth copies. When you made a typo, it was misery going back through all those copies to erase and start over. All right, not quite on a par with the servicemen hunkered down in freezing Korean foxholes. But still miserable.

CHAPTER 16

The limited on-base recreational activities threw us back on our own devices. Inevitably, this focused us on the 6x5 feet of personal space in our 24-man sleeping quarters, scene of frequent rolling waves of boyish boisterousness. Soon after we got back from the evening meal, the keen card-players would organize one, sometimes two, games for stakes on somebody's cot. Others would gather round to watch the proceedings and join in the racy banter. In the casino corner of the billet, the air would soon be thick from cigarette smoke. Whereas my guess is about two-thirds of all the boys smoked then, it seemed 100% of card players heightened their thrill of the bidding with cigarettes dangling from their lips. I didn't join in the card games because I lacked enthusiasm for seeing my measly salary disappear so rapidly. A few others shared my views to a lesser or greater degree. As a result, by mid-week we fiscal conservatives were likely to still have some money in our pockets. Requests for loans from the high rollers were frequent. After being stung twice, I hardened my stance and refused the habitual beggars.

The great British masculine characteristic of a sponge-like ability to soak-up large quantities of beer found its emulators in our billet. Half a dozen would go out most evenings for a few hours to a local pub. Fortunately, these regular imbibers rarely returned drunk. I seldom went, partly because I preferred spending my time and money in other pursuits, and partly because I didn't really enjoy the taste of beer. Quite remarkable among Brits and, I suspect, an early sign of my tendency to be a loner.

Our hut boasted two members who were seriously productive with their off-duty time. One was a keen amateur boxer who most evenings went to Henlow's deprived gym to work out. He fought in several service-level tournaments. The other, an aspiring drummer, sat for hours on his cot tapping on a small, round rubber practice pad. This would-be drummer went on to achieve notable professional success and eventually performed regularly with one of Britain's leading jazz bands. Among the rest, those who seemed to share habits and interests tended to instinctively draw together.

North Londoner, Albert Vaca, became a friend as 1951 progressed. He occupied a cot near mine and, in time, I saw that he didn't participate in the questionable or disconcerting ways of some of our roommates. Albert also returned home most weekends, and we sometimes met at King's Cross station and completed the Sunday night journey back to the camp together. To escape the frequent silly antics going on in the hut, we started to jog during some fine evenings. We ran outside the base along the country lanes around nearby Clifton village toward the tiny River Ivel. On our very first jog, he asked me if his Jewish religion bothered me. Somewhat perplexed, I replied it didn't. But he didn't realize my ignorance of religion was so great I had only a murky understanding of humanity's different faiths. In fact, outside of a few shopkeepers, he might well have been the first Jew with whom I had a conversation.

As we ran on subsequent evenings, we'd tell each other bits and pieces about our lives and our hopes and fears for the future. Actually, he didn't seem to harbor many fears. Albert had passed the 11-plus exam and went to grammar school until 16, and could have gone on. He willingly quit to join his father who owned a retail men's apparel shop. My newfound colleague had already worked for two years in his father's store when called up. The day would come when he'd take over its operation and eventually inherit the business. He was apparently perfectly content with his future that, to me, seemed too assured. On the other hand, my own future seemed obscure and indefinite. Although his sounded confining, in truth at my core I envied him his life certainty. These opposing emotions were surely a sign of my confused thinking. Although obvious, I didn't fully appreciate that anyone with a hankering to write should not be casting an eye toward a secure future.

On yet another jog he told me his ancestors were among the Spanish Jews who refused to convert to Catholicism and were driven into exile by King Ferdinand and Queen Isabella some years before 1492. His forebears had arrived in England to live for generations in the East London slums. With hard work and the passage of time, the family improved its economic status until they were now comfortably off and well placed socially. It embarrassed me because my ignorance of history was so pervasive I didn't know Jews had been driven out of Spain in numbers and some wound up in Britain. His chronicle did cause me to think my own ancestry hadn't achieved so much. Another instance of my tendency to envy?

When the base budget time rolled around each year, its preparation rated such a priority, we worked Saturdays and Sundays. It provided an opportunity to find out what life was like for those boys whose homes were too distant to reach on weekends. I suspected it was boring and, worse, lonely. Then a sad incident transpired which proved my suspicion. It involved the short Welsh boy with the dubious distinction of being the shortest man on the camp, and who proved to be a complex and confused personality. During a bleak weekend, with station life barely registering a heartbeat, he apparently let his loneliness and boredom take control. On the Saturday evening he broke into station living quarters to steal cash, a watch and jewelry from a junior officer who, with his family, had gone out for a few hours. By Sunday lunchtime the Welshman had been apprehended. The jewelry, the watch, and most of the cash were found hidden at the bottom of his footlocker. By Sunday evening he'd become a resident of the closest civilian prison. Sometime after midnight, while many of us were returning to station following home-side weekends, he hung himself with a belt in his cell. The military police quickly came on Monday morning to clear out his metal wardrobe and locker. They exchanged his mattress in preparation for the next occupant. It seemed to me his existence on earth had been eradicated within hours.

If my memory is correct, the station didn't conduct a church service on his behalf. At the time I didn't give it any thought, but since have come to believe this sad incident demonstrated how little the authorities valued us conscripts. One small, solitary, confused Welsh boy who didn't know how to handle loneliness reduced the esteemed, popular Royal Air Force. To break into a house on an RAF station, where people are always looking for aberrant behavior, wasn't too bright. Whatever his tangled motivations, it's possible even a few on-base recreational opportunities might have prevented this tragedy. Despite his crime, his life deserved recognition.

On an infrequent basis, I joined a small group of my billet mates on an evening visit to Bedford, the nearest sizeable town to our station, with late bus service available. Our time there would be spent wandering around the town center, making teenage-type, mindless observations about society, and stepping into a pub for an occasional beer. Even though

I didn't care for its taste, I'd soak up one or two in a rare effort to fit in. Mostly we consumed the suds modestly and returned to the station just as sober as we'd left.

RAF Station Chicksands is located about a third of the way to Bedford from Henlow. It was (and still is) occupied by the U.S. Air Force, which built an antenna, 400 meters in diameter, to listen to high frequency radio signals in the northern hemisphere. US airmen from Chicksands rode the same buses to visit Bedford for an evening's high jinks. Their jinks were, of course, always higher than ours because of the differing pay scales.

One evening when we returned to the Bedford bus garage to catch the 11.30 p.m. to our base, a group of American airmen were already waiting for that same bus back to theirs. They'd obviously enjoyed considerable elbow bending, were garrulous and animated, but by no means falling down drunk. In the presence of the self-assured, worldly Americans, we became subdued, a trifle intimidated, even overawed, by the men from across the Atlantic. When the lumbering double decker arrived, the airmen from both nations clambered noisily upstairs to the deck where men tended to congregate and where, in those days, smoking was permitted. The RAF contingent went as a group to the front. The USAF members sprawled in the rear. About the time the bus cleared the town and headed southeast on the country road, the conductor came up to collect fares. He moved to the front and took our money first. Probably, he too, was just a little intimated by the Americans. Then we listened to an exchange between the conductor and an older American wearing the inverted five chevrons of a Technical Sergeant.

"Hey, Man, I apologize but I've had a few too many of your great English beers. I need for you to stop the bus and let me take a leak."

"Oh! Er, sorry. Very sorry, sir. Yes, sorry. Operating rules don't allow random halts along the road. Only at designated stops." There were few official stops along these country lanes.

"Mac, I know you've got your rules. But you're looking at one guy who's seriously hurting. If I don't relieve myself real soon, we'll all get wet when my bladder bursts. Come on, man, break the rules just this once or I can't be responsible for the consequences."

"Oh! Er, yes, er, right! I'll just have to ask the driver. He's really the gaffer. Kind of like the captain on a boat."

"That's a great analogy, man! 'Cos if you don't soon stop this boat and let me pee, there's going to be goddam water enough to drown us all."

"Oh! Er, right! I'll just pop down and ask the gaffer. If you'll excuse me just a tick..."

The now thoroughly distressed conductor stepped back, turned, and fled downstairs. No doubt he'd never before had to deal with an adult bladder emergency on an English country road. But this conductor had been less than honest. There was no way for him to communicate with the driver with the bus in motion. The driver sits in an enclosed compartment practically on top of an 11-plus liter diesel engine roaring like a wounded elephant. I also suspected that particular conductor would be too embarrassed if there were lady passengers on the ground level to shout to the driver the urgent need for an unscheduled stop. This delicate conundrum, fraught with international ramifications, pitted the hoary tradition of intense British reserve against American informality and engorged bladders. The Tech Sergeant let a few minutes pass. Then he hauled himself heavily out of the seat and went to the top of the stairs towards the rear of the bus.

"Mr. Conductor, my need to pee ain't gone away. One more damn bounce on the road and I'm gonna lose it. I tell ya, man, give me a break!"

No response mounted the steps. I imagined the conductor was himself distressed enough to begin needing a pee. The sergeant waited another minute, returned to his seat, and gingerly lowered himself on to it. Obviously the Techie was to the point where any sudden movement could turn on his spigot involuntarily. The sufferer was now thoroughly angry at the bus staff's inflexibility toward his very human need. We heard him say to one of his cohorts that the matter was now out of his hands, as he undid the flap on his tunic pocket and drew out a billfold. He'd just have to pee into a condom and throw it out the window.

Up front we couldn't hear the sound of his gushing relief. The silence at the rear seemed to last a long time. But then we distinctly heard a muffled pop.

"Goddam it. She's exploded on me and I ain't finished yet. Hell! I can't stop...it's going everywhere."

He continued to pee profusely, to the accompaniment of an occasional grunt. His buddies were falling off their seats in merriment. The man had the bladder capacity of an adult male giraffe.

Nature and latex limitations had thwarted the man's best intentions. His bladder contained far more liquid than the expandability of a BX condom could handle. Even a fancy American one with excitation bumps along its side.

"I warned that Limey conductor. Hey, I'm sorry, you RAF guys up front. Get your feet up or you're gonna get wet socks."

We promptly complied. It was a nice gesture to his fellow men on the part of this now relieved American sergeant. We all kneeled backwards on our seats to watch his bladder output rush toward the front along the dusty floor. It flowed swiftly like fresh storm water of a new rainy season fills dry gulches in the desert. It hit the front of the bus, spread sideways, and started back down the bus under our seats. Every incline in the road sent the urine backward and forward; every turn sent this now discolored waste product lurching against one or other side wall. Although some of the recycled beer went running down the stairs, the conductor chose to stay uninvolved and never appeared again on top deck. In due course the bus got to Chicksands and the Americans alighted, including one relieved Tech Sergeant.

Despite this unprovoked American watery assault on British sensibilities, in Korea, following a year of fierce, fluctuating battles that swept up-and down its peninsula, July 1951 found the opposing forces sitting near the original 38th parallel border set at the 1945 division of Korea into north and south. The cease-fire signed that month introduced both sides to the wearying game of watching and waiting that persists to this day. Almost half the world away, I, too, had been performing a lot of to-and fro-ing in a military uniform during that time. Five days a week in the RAF, with weekends at home, became my unvarying routine. Although I saw myself basically as a creature of habit, I'd adapted to this Dr. Jekyll and Mr. Hyde existence. Even the requirement to live so intimately with 23 other males, who ranged from boys to men in mental maturity, had become tolerable.

In reality, the 24 males in my billet were an amazingly homogeneous sampling, with many traits in common, and all from tradesmen or unskilled working-class families. Drawn so randomly from across Britain, one might have expected a broader range of the nation's young men. But

I saw those who liked frequent pub-crawling excursions, even though their pay didn't support this conduct, became great drinking buddies. The avid, seemingly addicted, card-players soon found each other. The sports fanatics quickly embraced. Those of us who wouldn't, or couldn't, fit into these mainstream categories found a soul mate with whom we communed. There was even one who seemed to prefer keeping his own counsel. I felt it fair to think that we didn't have specimens from the extreme ends of the intelligence spectrum. We had no college graduates; they would have almost certainly come into the RAF as officers. Nor did we have anyone who could be characterized as bonehead dumb.

Then, as if to rudely disprove my anthropological theories, a serviceman arrived in our billet who could be truly characterized as completely different, and well off the range of our spectrum at the intelligence end. In his mid-twenties, his serious demeanor made him seem older. He had attended Oxford University, reading philosophy, but we didn't know if he had a degree. This tall, thin person, who wore thick horn-rimmed glasses, spoke with a moderate German accent. Possibly a German background kept him from being an officer, to which rank his education clearly entitled him. He was one who very much kept his own counsel. He would sit on his bed in the evenings, his long legs drawn up to support a massive tome on aesthetics, ethics or logic. He seemed to have the singular ability to block out the hut's ambient racket to concentrate on these arcane subjects. He didn't gravitate to anyone, and no one seemed to gravitate to him.

Almost inevitably, this unique individual aroused the hostility of one of our hut's more mediocre occupants. That enmity exploded in a combative northerner, one of the frequent pub-crawlers, and a few years older than most of us. This swarthy, boozing airman claimed to have served a tour of duty in Germany during a three-year stint in the Army. He said scars on his left arm were inflicted by a gang of German youths, leaving the limb permanently weakened. From time to time, the northerner harassed our philosopher by making within-earshot hostile racial comments. His victim ignored him, which no doubt served to heighten the tormentor's real or imagined grievance.

One night, after the billet lights were out and all of us in bed, the northerner returned drunk. He threw open the door, which banged against the inner wall, and fumblingly flipped switches until all lights blazed. He staggered along the aisle to the philosopher's cot, stood there swaying while struggling to focus on his intended victim who appeared to be asleep.

"Get up, you fucking Kraut, so I can knock you down again," he growled in a thick-tongued threat. A self-satisfied grin swept his jowly face as if he found his own words amusing. In his right hand he held a piece of tree branch measuring about three feet in length and three inches in diameter.

The philosopher woke, raised his head briefly to assess the situation, returned it to the pillow, and even shut his eyes. Everyone else by now sat upright, all heads turned to the impending battle between the Gods of Intellect and Ignorance. The aggressor suddenly switched the cudgel to his left hand, grabbed the foot cross rail with his right, and hoisted the cot off the floor a few times.

"Come on, you Boche bastard, I want to pound the sheisse out of you," he snarled, perhaps to impress the philosopher with his possibly one word of German (slang) learned in his three years in that country.

"Please leave me alone and go to your bed," the philosopher appealed calmly, without lifting his head while blinking a little owl-like. "I've done nothing to you. Why do you hold me responsible for the harm done to you by other Germans? I'm not my brother's keeper." Now we all knew his status. The English Neanderthal paused momentarily as if trying to fathom the words' meaning. I suspect he had no success.

"Piss off, German pig. I'll bash yer gob shut and shove your big books up yer arse."

Perhaps because he could add nothing further to the debate, the aggressor suddenly jerked the branch above his head as if preparing to hurl it at the philosopher. His advanced state of inebriation, however, impaired his coordination. The branch detached from his weakened hand and flew wildly in my direction, about 180° from its intended target.

It turned out to be one of the few times I was glad to be short because it passed uncomfortably close to the top of my head, striking the wall above me, and hitting my shoulder as it fell to the ground. It had wounded only my clean blancoed harness hung there as a constant reminder of our military status.

Now the intellectual sat up and retrieved his glasses from a jacket hanging above the cot. He must have decided he couldn't reason with the swaying oaf at the foot of his cot.

"If you think it's necessary we fight, I'll agree to it. Just let me put on my trousers and boots," he requested in a courtly tone that made me think of a gentleman accepting a challenge to a duel.

"Fuck you," the drunk screamed, "them German bastards that did my arm never gave me no time to prepare."

Our inebriated plaintiff seemed to suddenly realize he was no longer armed. He turned clumsily around and spent some moments trying again to focus his vision as he looked for his weapon. He didn't spot it lying next to my cot. After a few moments he turned unsteadily back and stood unsurely, no doubt trying to decide his next move. But his bleary gaze had to adjust to a greatly changed situation. The philosopher had seized those moments to improve his tactical situation. He now had boots on and was in the act of pulling the suspenders of his trousers over his shoulders. He read the confusion on his attacker's face, and moved swiftly to turn the tables.

Our gangling intellectual threw himself at the drunk in a rugby style tackle. The northerner's expression of surprise, as he collapsed to the floor with the brain on top of him, suggested he knew this was not quite how this war should be progressing. By now several of the braver boys were on their feet, and they closed in to separate the two. It did appear just at that moment the drunk was about to receive a second German thrashing. He would've certainly deserved this one, as he no doubt deserved the first.

This fracas symbolized, for me, a conflict started by an abysmally dumb working class man who wandered his world with nothing in his head and nothing worthwhile to do in his spare time. Fortunately, his reluctant opponent's intelligence won this day. The English dumb ass was dragged along to his cot, forcibly stretched out, and sat on until soon loudly sobbing of his frustration at life. But the sobbing quickly changed to snoring in a deep, alcohol-induced sleep. We had been treated to a show of brains over brawn. The philosopher thanked the boys who had intervened, and silence engulfed our billet.

CHAPTER 17

According to historian Arthur Marwick, Britain in 1951 still displayed many of the conditions that characterized Edwardian (1901-1910) working-class life. A post-war survey showed that one-third of houses in England and Wales had no bath; over one million lacked a water closet (toilet). Food rationing was still in place, although slightly eased, but it did not end completely until 1954. By way of ironic contrast, food rationing in Germany, the leader of the defeated Axis powers, ended in 1948, a notable six years in advance of threadbare Britain (1).

Against this bleak background, the Labor government found £8 million sterling (some $21.5 million at the extant exchange rate) to organize the Festival of Britain during the summer. This event was intended primarily as the "people giving themselves a pat on the back," in the words of Herbert Morrison, Deputy Prime Minister. It also commemorated the 1851 Great Exhibition held at a time when Britain loomed large as the world's industrial leader. Now, however, with its Treasury drained, its empire collapsing, Britain knew well it no longer led the world. On 27 acres of London urban blight, along the south bank of the River Thames, a number of permanent and temporary facilities were built to showcase Britain's modern achievements in science and arts (2). But the event was not confined to the capital; almost every town and village throughout the country funded its own local celebration.

For those more interested in having a good time than honoring Britain's accomplishments, the Festival Pleasure Garden provided a carnival offering the usual fair rides and sideshows. It also featured a huge tent housing a stage and dance floor. Records show that about 8.5 million people visited the festival, many as an antidote to their rationed, dilapidated daily lives. Among them were Eddie and I on a Saturday night on the town. After wandering the area, we settled on the dance tent as our non-cerebral way of rejoicing for Britain, and we quickly knew we had chosen the correct celebratory method. We spotted two girls alone;

their movie-star looks made them sparkling standouts. They both had long, black hair, carefully coiffured, and faces worthy of an artist's brush. From the way they filled out summer blouses, their bodies also should be captured on canvas while the painter was at it. With one taller and one shorter, the equation looked just perfect.

Eddie and I asked them to dance. I was overjoyed when they accepted our invitations. Not another turndown for the short-ass! I tingled head to toe as I raised my left hand to gently grasp her right hand, and my right forearm gingerly encircled that trim waist. We moved off smoothly in time with the band and melted into the flow of dancing couples. While my dancing was passable, my conversational ability with girls almost qualified as lalophobic.

"I think it's a little chilly this evening, don't you?" I smiled. Before I could stop these words slipping out, I realized my question sounded like that of a middle-class English twit, the world's worst kind. Dull-witted people in Britain spend a lot of their lives discussing the weather. My line would never win this exquisite creature. I executed a couple of glide sequences while I tried desperately to think of a brilliant follow-on. But, as if I labored under a curse, I went back to weather forecasting.

"Of course, coolness is relative. Guess it also depends on how you're dressed." Idiot! Now it sounded as if I was trying to get her to tell me if she had on warm underwear. She narrowed her eyes and shot a horrified glance at me, but said nothing. I felt the blood rushing to my face as my confidence evaporated like the value of money in a South American country. My mouth dried and I fell into silence. But a silence that made a lot of noise in my skull. I spun us around a few times attempting to demonstrate my suave composure. My mental torment mounted as I struggled to think of something bright and charming to say that would turn her to putty in my hands.

I looked at Eddie and his companion across the dance floor. They were engaged in an animated exchange. Eddie was so comfortable with girls. He had that enviable ability to be at ease and entertaining at the same time. Girls seemed to enjoy his idle chatter no matter how fatuous. His competence only magnified my swollen-tongue despair. But the more I racked my brains, the more autistic I became. How could someone who read so much be so tongue-tied? Now I perceived I'd committed the sin of allowing my attention to wander. Every atom in my body should be directed at making this enchantress feel she was the center of my universe. Just at that moment I hoped one of those London pea-soup fogs would fill the tent and I could disappear into it. I knew I had to launch into another spell of scintillating conversation.

"Is this your first time at the festival?" Bloody idiot, another gaffe pathetique. It was everyone's first time. It had only just opened! She was kind enough to murmur, "yes," even if in a decidedly bored tone.

"It's mine, too," I smiled, not knowing how to extricate myself from this inane line of questioning. "Always busy on Saturdays," I said, followed by another phony smile.

How bloody lame, I instantly thought. This sophisticated cutie would know instinctively that somebody like me had more unoccupied Saturday evenings than residents of an old age home. Still, I had forced her to utter one word. Great journeys begin with small steps! I performed a reverse double spin to avoid a traffic jam in one corner of the floor. Once in open territory, I launched again.

"Do you go dancing often?"

Wait, stupid. Often to one person is different to another.

"Well, like more than twice a week?"

"No, you meet too many dumb men in dance halls." She shot me a scathing sideways look.

When the last notes of this romantic fox trot drifted through the tent I knew I was dead in the water. My threadbare personality was as much on display that evening as Britain's threadbare economy. Eddie's powers of persuasion, however, had been great enough to convince his target to join him for an orange soda and a biscuit. Now her friend, my suffering dance partner, was, by association, caught in the net. Common politeness prevented her from skipping her friend's acceptance. I could imagine the earful she'd give her friend at the first possible moment.

In the refreshment area we sat on plastic chairs at a plastic table with four watery sodas and four apologies for biscuits on tiny tissues. I knew my initial encounter with this self-assured beauty had been a disaster. But, like the rest of humanity, hope still swelled in my breast. If I could only win over this doll, I'd be prouder than those Brits back at the 1851 exhibition.

Eddie kept up a stream of palaver to which I offered only a rare, careful contribution. I was terrified of making another pathetic utterance.

Yet, I believed the situation was getting better. My victim offered an occasional comment. I reassured myself that this indicated a warming trend. Then castigated myself for one more weather analogy.

As I sat across the table from this outstanding specimen of pultrichude, at this British festival, I wasn't thinking of the country. My mind was racing ahead with my plan of attack when I escorted her home. Hopefully she'd invite me in for tea or coffee. Then she'd discover that this tongue-tied little twerp had more feelers than an octopus. I could hardly wait.

In time, the girls asked to be excused. Eddie and I jumped up in the politest manner to hold their chairs. We fixed their retreating shapes with our undivided attention as they sashayed across the floor in the direction of relief. We sat back down and congratulated ourselves on this stupendous pick up we had made with these two stunners. Although I accepted my partner was the reluctant party in the foursome, my inflated male ego led me to believe a viable chance for a conquest remained. Perhaps her ardor would yet ignite on this Saturday evening in spite of me but as a response to British scientific achievement since 1851.

In truth, I inwardly gloated at the prospect of regaling the guys back at camp about my successful amorous London weekend. I'd inflame their jealousy when I fed them the succulent details of my session with a film-star look-alike. I'd be the hut hero of the week. We waited patiently, blown up like balloons with self-congratulatory wind. Five minutes passed, then 10, then 15. We assumed they were carefully prettying themselves for us. Still our Mediterranean beauties hadn't returned. They hadn't even finished their cookies or sodas.

Slowly unease began to overtake us. Surely no one required so long in the toilet. Perhaps the cubicle doors had locked themselves and they were trapped inside. Even our boyish fantasies found fault with that theory. I secretly and deeply hoped the delay was because Eddie's partner was telling mine to be more accommodating. She just needed to see I was obviously a real warm-hearted charmer, just that I came in a plain package.

After another 15 minutes we had to acknowledge our two knockouts had walked through the toilet's front door and fled out the back. They weren't returning. They had outwitted us and escaped our fumbling clutches. My hubris dissipated faster than a politician's promises after election. I returned to Henlow the next night downhearted and without a glowing tale of conquest to lay on the boys in the billet. Just another wasted weekend.

Whether it stemmed from the RAF's marching boots which we paper-pushers even wore to the office, or defective genetic code, I started having problems with an ingrown nail on my left foot's big toe. Please don't misunderstand; toenails have never loomed large in my life. Their mention here is justified simply because a medical mix-up represents the only time I might have laid down my life while in the service of my nation. Early in 1952, in the last six months of my National Service, this condition caused my absence from the weekly parades, which concerned the RAF, and Wednesday soccer matches for the headquarters' eleven, which concerned me. A young RAF doctor at the station clinic eventually decided the troublesome nail needed to be removed. The Henlow primary clinic was equipped to conduct limited surgeries. I checked in late one afternoon for the operation scheduled the next morning. Patient meals were delivered from the regular mess hall. Another clever arrangement presumably intended to dissuade personnel from reporting sick too often.

Alone in a ward, it was like being at a hotel—not that I had much hotel experience then. No one bothered me after the 5 p.m. evening meal. A heavenly quiet enveloped the ward as compared to my hut and I was able to read in peace until lights out. A rare pleasure. It made up for my toenail discomfort. At 6.30 a.m. an orderly arrived with a food trolley. The baked-beans-on-toast breakfast wasn't my favorite, but I didn't decline. Never have been one to miss an opportunity to eat. A mug or two of tea helped wash it down.

About two hours later I was wheeled into the operating theater, with little more apparent interest from the medical orderly than the one who delivered the baked beans. Not too long after that the anesthesiologist rendered me harmless. While drifting in the ether-induced void, I distinctly felt the doctor yanking vigorously on my left big toe nail. Whether it was this or the involuntary eruption from my upper digestive system I don't know, but I came to, still on the operating table.

As my consciousness falteringly returned, I felt sharp pain in the area of my left big toe. I lay on my back squinting up at the theater's high-intensity neon lights. But they had succumbed to an attack of

German measles. They resembled acne-vulgaris-spotted teenage faces. I blankly pondered this strange vision for a few seconds without reaching any conclusions.

The diseased bright lights began to bother my dulled brain. I swiveled my eyes sideways without moving my head. The young doctor and a theater sister, both gowned and gloved for their life-risking work, swam into the area encompassing my amorphous field of vision. They, too, were afflicted by the same measles strain that had struck the overhead lamps. Most unmilitary and puzzling.

In my nebulous state of being, I couldn't understand what I saw. Then it registered that, perhaps, German measles had struck the whole world while I lay unconscious. Probably seeing these two sullied medical professionals, both of whom appeared in a state of disgusted shock, caused me to turn my head away. The nearby instrument tray was the next floating object that slowly came into focus. This, too, appeared blotched all over. But now this image was closer and clearer.

The measles pimples looked more and more like the remnants of my mess hall breakfast. I suspected my stomach had erupted like a long-dormant volcano and splattered its contents over medical staff, RAF equipment and a wide area of fixed real estate assets. No doubt it was all too much for my enfeebled mind. I returned to unconsciousness and missed the highly informative exchange that must have occurred between the doctor and the operating theater sister.

Ever since, I have suspected my eructation stopped the half-completed surgery in its tracks. The doctor was so pissed he just downed tools and walked off the job like a prissy, union plumber. He didn't bother to remove the nail matrix. As a result, I've lived with a nail bed that looks like a coastal outcropping of ragged rocks. I don't clip that remnantal nail with scissors, but use a file to laboriously wear it down.

I know I'm on solid medical ground when I put my accusation of a doctor's malfeasance in black and white. Subsequently, Roy had both his large toenails extracted properly and aesthetically at a civilian hospital. Mine looks as if the military doctor belonged in the motor pool rather than the medical corps. I've since been told that drowning is a real possibility when one vomits under anesthesia. I could have expired, rather messily, right there in His Majesty's clinic, growing cold along side the breakfast baked beans.

My military discharge took effect on 1 July 1952. The service didn't honor me with a parade, bugles blazing and flags fluttering, but S/L Ryman gave me a brief, positive letter of reference. I had worked for him outside his office since arriving at Henlow that wet November 1950 night. We never did bridge the gap between officer and enlisted man: a relationship more like that of master and servant persisted to the end. This despite what I believe was the officer's own modest background and limited education.

Notwithstanding, the S/L's laudatory words included the statement "... his loyalty to his superiors and his keen desire to accord them with faithful service...has been marked." What S/L Ryman didn't know was that I had started to hold the view there were fewer and fewer people in the world in which I moved whom I looked upon as my superiors.

CHAPTER 18

Because I'd been at home so much during the last 18 months of my national service, my transition back to civilian life was a non-event. There may have been some neighbors who never even knew I'd just spent two years guarding them from the big, bad Communists. Certainly there was bliss in not having to make the hated return journey to RAF Henlow each Sunday night with the rude awakening from a deep sleep on the train that turned me into a zombie. The pain of the mile trek, conducted in a dyspeptic silence, from the rail station to the camp gate, each week caused me to vouch I'd stay on base the next weekend. Of course, it never happened.

I spent a few heavenly days luxuriating in my mother's warm attention. In the morning she'd bring me tea and digestive biscuits, a traditional wheat-flour and semi-sweet cookie, in bed where I stayed late dozing or reading voraciously. No noisy, naked roommates to disturb my sweet peacefulness. But I soon felt aimless and returned to work. Under British national conscription law, the company for which a conscript worked at the time of induction was required to accept him back when he completed military service and received an honorable discharge. I went back to the publishing house near Fleet Street.

In the interim, my previous employer, Burke Publishing Co., had been sold. The parent company offered me a position with another of its small components, Business Publications Ltd., as admin. assistant to the circulation manager. I accepted it, harboring vague hopes of one day getting on to the editorial side of the house. My weekly salary was £4 sterling, or $11.20 at the existing exchange rate.

Business Publications produced a handful of trade and craft magazines, all with small circulation. Ironically, the most popular of the periodicals it offered was "The Royal Air Force Review." This title suggests an official government publication, but it had no direct connection.. To publish this magazine there would have been, I assume, coordination between its editors and the Air Ministry, but none of it involved my section, which hid in a back street warehouse not far from the River Thames. It soon became apparent that little effort was expended in attempting to increase the circulation of any of the titles, a couple of which were available only through subscription. The company seemed quite content to let sales find their own level, which tended to ensure a static situation. In a typically British manner, the business ethos was reactive rather than proactive. Trying for a bigger piece of the pie bordered on the impolite.

My job consisted of an assortment of administrative and secretarial functions, none particularly exciting or challenging. Because the circulation manager was frequently out of the office, I fielded a lot of phone calls. I spent a large percentage of my time pounding a manual typewriter producing individual invoices each month on a printed form for about 350 magazine subscribers. Most of its circulation, thankfully, was from newsstand impulse sales. Not too many months passed before I concluded this dull routine had little appeal. It appeared to me I had landed in one more treadmill, dead-end job. I have learned since that any job, with the right attitude, can be interesting.

In August I resumed night classes. I went back to the free county evening program rather than the expensive private Pitman College. I selected an English composition class, the only one offered, intended for people in engineering. There were no women in the class, and I was the only student not working in engineering or construction. Perhaps in an unrecognized effort to emulate the education of grammar school graduates, I chose French for a second course. I really needed elementary mathematics, but couldn't dredge up the necessary enthusiasm. My poor grasp of arithmetic partly made me reluctant to expose my ignorance of this subject. What backwards logic! On the evening I enrolled, I thought of my first enrollment at night school six years earlier when I had trouble spelling my own middle name. Yet, my objective then in going to evening classes was lucid. I hoped for a newspaper career. Now I could manage my name, but my reason for resuming adult education was no longer that clear. Was I merely returning to a comfortable routine?

Further indication that I had undergone some kind of metamorphoses manifested itself in my changing attitude toward soccer, the love of my life since childhood. I'd been an avid supporter of West Ham United, the nearest professional team, from the time I returned from my third evacuation in 1944, at age 12. Mom gave me the six pence to be faithful in my attendance at their home games. Those Saturday afternoon matches were always a sell-out. If I remember correctly, the stadium at Upton Park held about 40,000 fans. All vocal. We were packed into the standing-only terraces tighter than rush-hour riders on the Tokyo subway. Friends and I always went several hours early to get into the front row so we didn't have to look around tall men in front. Women were almost non-existent on the cheaper terraces in those days.

Even before call-up, however, my presence had steadily decreased during my mid-teens because of the demands of studying for night school. After leaving the service, I went to a few games, but somehow the old enthusiasm didn't come back. Although I had continued to play the sport with great enjoyment during RAF days, I began to feel alienation at the West Ham engagements to the mass of spectators, predominantly blue-collar men, with their Cockney accents, crude ways, and empty bluster. I started to feel a disdain for the uncontrolled emotionalism on display by a majority of that yesteryear crowd. Their loud cries of support for the home team, alternated with childish barracking of the visiting opponents, or the hard-working referee, began to seem a form of mass hysteria. I found it sheep-like behavior. I thought this conduct both dumb and distasteful and felt a need to distance myself from it. On the other hand, I never witnessed any violence, no matter how worked-up they became. Today's pathetic hooligans are of a different breed, likely with causes in the excessive generosity of Britain's state welfare.

One day at the office we received publicity on the Society of British Aerospace Companies (SBAC) annual civilian and military air display each September. It is held at the Royal Aircraft Establishment, a government research facility and airfield, near Farnborough, Hampshire. It showcases British-built aircraft to potential buyers around the world. The initial two days are reserved for civilian and military aircraft buyers, government and industry officials, etc., with the last three days open to the public. It has always drawn large crowds of people interested in aircraft and flying. It occurred to me this event would be a great opportunity to increase public awareness of our "The Royal Air Force Review." I proposed to my boss that Business Publications seek permission to sell it at the air show, which he promptly did.

The printer shipped two thousand copies to the Farnborough train station to be available on the first public admission day. The circulation manager arranged for a local newsagent to collect Eddie and me and the magazines early from the station and drive us to the site in his small delivery van. The show organizers provided an eight-foot folding table, and two metal chairs as our rudimentary sales point. These we collected near the airfield's entrance and jammed into the van. As it turned out, we didn't have far to drive. We were positioned in a vendor area about halfway between the entrance and the runway. Here, merchants sold refreshments, military memorabilia, model and toy airplanes, children's kites, sunglasses, plastic raincoats, and umbrellas to cover the spectrum of the fickle English weather.

The air show consisted of a static display mainly of then propeller-driven aircraft with flying demonstrations at 2 p.m. It didn't take us very long to set up the table, unpack and spread out some magazines, and tape a few posters to the table. We were finished by around 10 a.m., still an hour before the gates opened. We spent that time taking turns viewing the exhibition and having an early lunch.

I remember the de Havilland Aircraft Company displayed its Comet jet airliner, the first in the world, flown initially in 1949. Since May 1952 it had been in regular passenger service between London and South Africa. The company placed the plane's development and testing on fast track in a desperate effort to beat the giant American airplane manufacturers in rolling out the first jet airliner. In January 1952, after three years of testing and refinement, the British government awarded it an airworthiness certificate. Huge foreign currency earnings were foreseen from exports of this revolutionary plane to airlines preparing for the anticipated expansion of world tourism.

The first Comet put into service carried 44 passengers, had a range of 2,400 miles, and cruised at a speed of about 490 m.p.h. It had four 7,000-lb. thrust jet engines, close to the fuselage, configured as an integral part of slightly swept-back wings. Its only problem then appeared to be that it carried just about half the passenger load of propeller-driven planes of that time. Behind the scenes, de Havilland had started work feverishly to launch a model with significantly increased carrying capacity (1).

De Havilland also displayed the D.H. 110, a prototype jet fighter. It had twin booms, with the pilot and observer cockpit located in a pod at the center of a straight wing which supported two jet engines, closely resembling the U.S.-built P-38 Lightning of WWII fame. Its manufacturer hoped the D.H. 110 would become the fighter of choice around the world. Many air forces were then switching to jets. It would perform later in the flying display.

When the gates opened at 11 a.m., a surge of humanity headed in our direction as it stormed toward the runway. We hoped they would all stop first at our table to purchase our magazine, a Time-sized publication, with color and monochrome illustrations, and articles aimed at aviation aficionados. But almost all of them streamed passed, intent on securing a favorable runway spot. Around noon, however, the tide began to turn. People who had wandered through the static display still had time before the flying began. More and more drifted back to the merchandise area and we received our share of attention. While it was still not gold rush business, the magazine moved modestly. Our best customers were teens keen on flying. Americans were one rich vein we struck. The US Air Force personnel stationed in Britain, then numbering around 35,000, were well represented. They tended to purchase our magazine even after they found out it was not the show's program. Its price represented the equivalent of about 20 American cents to them.

Not unexpectedly, once the flying started, we saw no more customers. This let us watch the action from our chairs. The active display finished around 4 p.m. and the crowd began to flow by again, headed for the exit. A few sales materialized from the Walter Mitty-types among the boys and younger men who had imagined themselves behind the controls of the planes that had performed daredevil maneuvers above the crowd.

The same scenario transpired the next day, Saturday. Attendance was higher, and our sales reflected that. By 2 p.m. on Sunday, when the flying began, we knew sales would be few during the rest of the day. We talked about shutting down early and beat the masses by calling the newsagent to advance our planned departure. We'd already watched the flying for two days. It couldn't provide any new excitement by seeing it a third time. In the end, it wasn't the flying that kept us there, but the mercenary hope of achieving just a few more sales, to add to the total of about 1,200. After all, we were on a small commission.

Promptly on time, the flying display commenced. A number of civilian and military aircraft went through their paces. As old hands, Eddie and I watched perfunctorily. We paid more attention to the last act of the day, de Havilland's D.H. 110. The program said it was flown by test pilot John Derry, one of the company's most experienced pilots, together with observer, Anthony Richards. Following take off, their routine began with a climb away from the airfield to where the plane was no longer visible. Then it turned and dropped back toward the show venue accelerating through the speed of sound to cause a sonic boom. Although the plane was still not in sight, the boom was audible to the 100,000 spectators, and everyone turned to catch the first glimpse of the aircraft. Then a small object appeared high in the sky that was quickly followed by all heads rotating in unison, like viewers at a tennis match, as it streaked at altitude over the airfield. With the plane soon beyond our vision again, the pilot decelerated, turned, and then descended to make a low-level pass at perhaps 2,000 feet, directly over the runway, still at a high, but subsonic, speed. Although we had seen the performance twice, for us this was the highlight of the air show, and we watched with a mixture of fascination and admiration. Most people were hearing, for the first time at close quarters, an alien noise harshly heralding the beginning of a new era in human transportation. It seemed to me there was an air of respectful doubt among the spectators possibly akin to people exposed for the first time to the loud, hissing steam locomotives nearly 150 years before.

Suddenly, above the thunder of the jet engines, a detonation boomed across the sky. I had looked away just at that moment, but looked up to see multi-sized shards of aluminum-alloy swirling in all directions in specter-like slow motion. Pieces of the fuselage bounced and twirled through the air like trash newspaper blown by blustery winds. As it roiled about, its silver color reflected the bright afternoon sun providing a brief aerobatic light show. The D.H. 110 had disintegrated.

For a few seconds, an eerie quiet engulfed the airfield. One moment our hearing was assaulted by a tornadic thunder; the next by a deathly but palpable silence. Then a scream of horror rose from the crowd, which was followed by what sounded like a mass gasp—a gasp of disbelief that a pleasant day's outing had turned into bloody carnage. People in panic ran toward the exit. By the time they passed the vendor area most had slowed to a fast walk. Many looked intensely distressed; they wanted to put distance between the runway and themselves.

Amateur cameramen captured the disaster on film. We learned

days later that the leading edges of the outer wings buckled. In seconds, the entire wings ripped from the fuselage and the tail broke off. The two engines sheared from their mountings and then, impelled by their own momentum, surged through the air like torpedoes through the ocean. One tore into spectators, killing 28, and injuring 60 others, many seriously. The other engine fortunately carried farther before burying itself in an adjacent farm field. The pilot and observer died.

Eddie and I could not see the slaughter at the runway, and didn't know the extent of the accident. We decided our appropriate response was to close. Then, as we wrapped unsold magazines, the SBAC had another D.H. 110 take off. It taxied to the runway, quickly throttled up its engines, sped down the airstrip, and became airborne. Later, newspaper articles reported the organizers wanted to let the public know the neoteric jet airplane was a safe machine. But this action further disturbed many people who formed a second wave of frightened spectators surging toward the exit.

None of us knew on that terrifying afternoon that a similar fate awaited the much-vaunted Comet passenger airliner attracting significant attention at the static display. Within 20 months, Comets were in four accidents, all involving fatalities. Two were attributed to pilot error, but two involved the break up of the planes in mid-air, and metal fatigue became suspect. In April 1954 the government withdrew the plane's airworthiness certificate. De Havilland had not done enough research on airframe design and materials' strength. The thrust of the new jet engine placed such stress on the metal, especially along rivet lines, that it ripped after relatively few flying hours.

Britain lost its chance to preempt America by making available a jet passenger plane to the world's airlines. De Havilland barely survived its mistakes. If the company had not erred so badly on materials' stress, it might have beaten the world by several years in pioneering the first commercial jet passenger aircraft. In 1958 Boeing rolled out a prototype four jet-engine passenger plane that went into commercial service as the 707 jetliner. America became the manufacturing hub for large commercial planes. Britain never again competed in this field until it formed a consortium with France, Germany and Italy to build the Airbus series.

In an ironic and remarkable incident of art preceding life, Neville

Shute's prescient novel "No Highway" had appeared in 1948. Its plot involves an aeronautical engineer who predicts that a new airliner will fall apart catastrophically after a specific number of flying hours. His prediction focused on inadequate testing of airframe materials used with the new, more powerful jet engines. The novel virtually foretold the fate awaiting the Comet airliner just a couple of years into the future. It was made into a 1951 movie titled "No Highway in the Sky" starring James Stewart and Marlene Dietrich. Perhaps the moral of this has to be that if de Havilland's directors and engineers read novels or attended movies, they just might have avoided their costly mistake.

My 21st birthday, in March 1953, provided another indication I did not conform to the ways of the average young man with an East London heritage. Mom wanted me to have a party to mark the occasion. I resisted. She pushed harder. Since my early teens, I'd harbored feelings of superiority towards people who seemed content to comply with traditional ways of the working-class culture. In my assessment of life at that time, I had reached the austere conclusion that many accepted celebrations—such as birthday parties and large white weddings—served the primary purpose of feeding human vanity. I'd not achieved anything yet in life that would justify a celebration. The required ascent to the mountaintop to commune with the guru about the meaning of it all was still in the future. Mom could not understand my twaddle. She was disappointed, and let me know it. This might have been the occasion when she told me she was glad she wasn't a young girl who might meet me and make the mistake of marrying such a self-absorbed person. But Mom had transmitted her own hard-headedness to me. There was no 21st birthday party. Instead, my parents gave me a quality wristwatch.

During this time, Eddie began to raise the idea of emigrating to Canada. He knew of someone who'd gone to Toronto two years before and now sent back glowing reports. He asked me to consider going with him. I said I would think about it, half seriously, half in jest. Since the end of WWII Britons had emigrated to some of the bigger British Commonwealth countries such as South Africa, Australia, New Zealand, and Canada. At the time, it appeared Britain's post-WWII economic prospects would be bleak for years. Ironically, about this time, a new social phenomenon began to manifest itself. Immigration into Britain of peoples from poorer Commonwealth countries such as India, Pakistan,

Trinidad and Jamaica started. This reverse flow would, in a few years, become a torrent, and change the island's demographics in a huge way.

At first I believed Eddie was far too attached to his own home life to go through with the idea. One less appealing aspect of his personality was prattling on about his extended family. A lot of this babbling about family I found childishly fulsome. But Eddie persisted over the next few months in raising the subject of Canada to the point where I became convinced he was serious. I knew Eddie to have a lot of initiative and courage. His proposal to leave the country must have reflected his own deep-seated restlessness. In me, of course, he found a receptive but uncertain co-conspirator. My own discontent was never far from my thoughts. Emigrants, by definition, are dissatisfied people. In this respect, at least, we were the perfect candidates.

Even though I'd grown discontented at home, and had few friends, I harbored a great reluctance to tear up roots to go live in some place where I didn't know a soul. I wrestled mightily with this fearful prospect. One is inevitably most comfortable in the setting into which born. Yet my reading, which more and more included foreign authors, was firing a yearning in me to see other parts of the world. While there were aspects of English life which contented me, there were other aspects I disliked, a few passionately, from the anachronistic Monarchy to the various layers of titled aristocracy which continues perpetually whether the newer generations are worthy or not.

While it is true the British Monarchy is not directly a part of the drive train that moves the country, I have long suspected it exerts an enormous influence among the 400 core families that hold the potency and wealth of Britain as depicted in Anthony Sampson's book "The Anatomy of Britain" (2). These families make up the core of the British Establishment, the nation's true power brokers. My biggest personal animosity was the limited educational opportunities for people born into the working class. Until WWII, only four or five out of every thousand students from British state schools reached a university. In truth, however, during the time I so loudly decried these circumstances, great changes were afoot in the British educational system. A number of new universities opened during the 1950s and 1960s, making available higher education to a much broader range of the population. I harbored ill-considered resentment that these new opportunities were a generation too late for me. Whether I would have made proper use of educational chances, had they been available, in truth remains a huge question in my mind.

Eventually emigration became virtually the only subject Eddie and I talked about during our outings. We even went so far as to write each other letters in an effort to clarify our thoughts in a retainable format as to the pros-and-cons. Eddie was always positive. He didn't seem to have the problems in making up his mind that I had to make up mine. After endless conversations between us, I finally decided I would go. Eddie pushed for leaving England as soon as we could. I took a day off from work to visit Canada House on Cockspur Street near Trafalgar Square to pick up the visa application. At home, in the privacy of my bedroom, attempting to complete the form, my doubts overwhelmed me. I did another flip-flop after deciding that emigration was a bridge too far.

Eddie was none too happy when I told him, but carried on determinedly with his own arrangements. We were to have one last small adventure together before he sailed to Canada and a new life, and I continued with the old one in the Old World, or so I thought.

Selling "RAF Review" at the 1952 annual British Air Show at Farnborough, England, at which a deadly accident foretold immediate fate of the British attempt to launch an early jet airliner.

CHAPTER 19

The death of the British Monarch, King George VI, in late 1952 brought the 26-year-old Princess Elizabeth to the throne as Queen Elizabeth II. Historical meteorological records indicate June to be England's least wet and most sunny month. She was not, therefore, immediately crowned, but did about eight months of on-the-job training after the powers behind the throne decreed June 1953 would be the month for the inaugural. This interim period gave the printed press much time to speculate about whether this fresh, young queen would inspire a new age of glorious exploits by Britain comparable to her predecessor's. During the 45-year reign of Elizabeth I, Drake completed his three-year voyage of discovery around the world in 1580. With an assist from prevailing weather patterns, England defeated the mighty Spanish armada in 1588. But, alas, Britain's light has tended to grow dimmer during Elizabeth II's tour of duty. Meanwhile, she has already exceeded her namesake's throne-time by seven years as I write these lines. If she's anything like her mother, she'll be still around for a goodly chunk of the first half of the 21st century. Time yet for plenty of catch-up, glorious exploits.

A newspaper reported that Lyons & Company, Britain's Starbucks of that day (now Forte, the large catering and hotel operator), had been awarded the contract to provide food and beverages to the coronation's noble invitees. It also mentioned that London college students would be hired for the day to work in the basement refreshment area in Westminster Abbey. I had the idea to write to Lyons presenting Eddie and I as students seeking catering work at the Abbey. Amazingly, we were recruited on the strength of my letter alone. No one verified our status. Security was a tad more relaxed in pre-terrorist times! The creme-de-la-creme invitees included remaining European Royals, heads of state from many foreign countries, all ambassadors to the Court of St James, and assorted aristocrats. If you received an invite, you had it made!

On the big day, Tuesday, 2 June 1953, Eddie and I were up well before dawn to beat the crowd that would head to Central London to line the coronation parade route. With the aid of the ornate passes we'd received in the mail, we were ushered through the various police barriers to get into Westminster Abbey, to play a somewhat less-than-historic role in England's 38th coronation since William the Conqueror's on Christmas Day 1066.

We were assigned to the cathedral's basement washing-up detail. All utensils used that day were washed twice—before usage and after. Eddie and I, working stiffs who left school at 14, joined students from London University with high-profile futures. For now, however, we were all equal and all up to our elbows in soapy water washing the already spick-and-span cups, saucers, plates, glasses, knives, forks and spoons arriving from a Lyon's warehouse packed in straw in wicker crates, each duplicated about 1,500 times. Lyons' staff randomly checked our dedication. After the washing and drying, we ferried the chinaware and cutlery to the basement's large open area outside the kitchen. They were placed on long tables draped with impeccable, floor-length white linen cloths. Cups had to be inverted and arranged in pyramids; plates and saucers stacked to an exact prescribed height. The cutlery required sorting before placement in wicker baskets lined with white muslin napkins edged with lace.

Lyons' personnel and a few students were preparing food in a second kitchen. In time, they brought out trays of small, stemmed crystal glass bowls containing lobster, crab and shrimp cocktail. Then came trays of finger-food sandwiches of pate foie gras, smoked salmon and smoked turkey, garnished decoratively. Dessert included strawberries with Devonshire cream, chilled melon slices, and petit fours in individual doilies arranged in colorful displays on silver trays. A third group of staff and students prepared the tea and coffee, and then carried the large silver tea pots and coffee urns to the tables. A selection of juices came in individual-sized bottles. The food was self-service; while white-gloved Lyons' personnel in company livery poured the drinks. Patrolling Lyons' staff made sure we grunts didn't sample the delicate refreshments soon to be enjoyed by the illustrious ceremony's exalted guests.

When assembled, the buffet had the appeal and elegance of one prepared at Claridges Hotel in Mayfair. A sumptuous spread to nourish the nation's most powerful and richest men and women. We washers-up were given a break and provided with a cheese roll and jelly tart, fare ordinary mortals ate in Lyons' work-a-day snack bars. Then three of our kitchen's wash-up contingent, Eddie among them, were chosen to move among the honored guests when the time came to remove dirty utensils no longer needed. I wasn't selected. In fact, those not chosen were warned not go out of the kitchen while guests were present. Eddie's height, wavy hair, and straight teeth won over me! I felt left in the scullery like Cinderella.

Not too long after this, the charade going on one floor up concluded. Shortly after I heard an increasing mass conversation like a concert hall audience before the conductor taps his baton. I inched open a swing door to gain a view of the outer chamber. The world's blue-blood gentry, clothed in the robes of high office, streamed from several stairways across the basement stone floor towards the sumptuously laden tables decorated with silver candelabra. This wall of humanity's favored was arrayed in a profusion of colorful ceremonial uniforms and formal gowns, gold and silver plastered all over. The spectacle excelled any opera or fancy-dress ball and transported the onlooker to an earlier age of British imperial pomp and circumstance at its grandest.

It appeared that the shoulders of all the men's uniforms were adorned with epaulets. The side seams of their trousers were braided from waist to cuff. Some draped shoulder sashes with medallions identifying their status. Others had banners around their necks which carried insignia indicating their exact position in the complex heraldic hierarchy of Europe. Medals enough dangled on their jackets to stock a dozen new military museums. The women were all in full-length gowns and gloves, many wearing tiaras. Their necklaces were emblazoned with enough diamonds to match the annual production of South Africa's De Beers mines. Yet while the women were elegant, they were noticeably less ornate than the men, in deference to the British heritage of male domination. Boys could play dress-up to their hearts' content; girls had to employ restraint to avoid out-shining them.

Among this large gathering of European royalty and aristocracy, were no doubt representatives of all 400 families that control the lion's share of Britain's wealth. It's certain that any British subject who received an invitation was in attendance; death the only acceptable excuse to stay away. These members of the Brahmin class, with a certified grade-A genealogy, were doing their darndest to retain their gentility and dignity, while pushing and shoving to get to the tables a step or two ahead of the advancing line. I stayed in my peeping position just long enough to see them reach the tables and register the vision of many arms outstretched for the sandwiches, especially the smoked salmon. The hands of men protruded from sleeves circled with gold braid. The hands of ladies were all encased in elegant, elbow-length silk gloves. But all hands were just as grabbing as those of the homeless at mealtime in a church charitable mission. As these Brahmins demolished the eye-appealing spread, in a most plebeian display of hunger abatement, I thought about what an enlightening figure the net worth of all these frenzied feeders would be. Then my pleasant peasant musings were interrupted by a member of the Lyons' staff who tapped me on the shoulder and reminded me sternly I wasn't being paid to spend my time checking out the noblesse oblige. I needed to be changing the water in the large sinks ready for the utensils after their usage by my superiors.

Our new Monarch never paid a visit to the buffet tables or kitchen, so didn't witness my hard work on her behalf that day. I've never received another gilt-edged bearer pass for access to her presence. But perhaps once in a lifetime is all one should expect.

Eddie departed for Canada early in summer. I continued with my now well-rehearsed lifestyle of twice-weekly night classes, studying on the other workday nights, and pursuing my concept of pleasurable activities on Saturdays and Sundays. But I missed him, especially on the weekends, more than I cared to admit. No one else in my limited circle of acquaintances went to the theater or to art movies. As a result, I became more of a loner than I really wanted. Yet I fought my loneliness by telling myself I enjoyed my own company. It wasn't healthy psychologically, and certainly less than the truth.

I went for more Sunday bus rides out of London into Essex County to walk alone in Epping Forest. While I found it troubling to accept the biblical theory of the beginnings of life, it felt right for me to perceive the manifestation of a God in the natural world. And during these all-day excursions, I believe I started to sense a primal being in nature. The magnificence of a large, mature tree; the life renewal imparted to meadow grasses by early morning dew; the sublime beauty and fragility of wild flowers in fields or hedgerows. Although my increasing mental turmoil was never vanquished by these outings, I did experience an exquisite feeling of oneness with these relatively modest vistas of the natural world.

Ever one to look back, within a few months of Eddie's leaving, I began to regret not going with him. He'd taken the best paying job he could find; lathe operator at a Canadian aircraft manufacturer. He'd never worked a manual job before, but it demonstrated his flexibility. Very soon after arriving, he purchased a small British-built Ford, and spent much of his leisure time visiting areas of interest in Ontario. It sounded adventurous and exciting while I felt stuck in the proverbial rut. Such thoughts, of course, added to my seemingly eternal turmoil of the need for a job that would give me some kind of social standing. I don't now believe it was simply a matter of ambition; my longing probably had a neurotic component. I arrogantly assumed no one at home understood.

Now, in my old age, I believe that these thoughts represented the beginning of feelings of a totally unjustified intellectual superiority. I had read a few too many novels, and even if literary ones, they were still just fiction. My outlook was out of balance, weighed down by tons of make-believe with no counter-weight solid reality. Many years later my brother, Roy, told me how difficult I made it for my parents during this period. They were no doubt happy when I finally decided on a major change of work, which also involved leaving home.

Ironically, the one bit of good that came out of my generally difficult domestic behavior involved Roy. Then 15 years of age, he was due to leave school because he'd also failed the all-important 11-plus examination for entrance to a grammar school. One evening I berated my parents that they needed to get Roy more time at school so he didn't become just another school leaver without skills to bring to the labor market. I must have been persuasive because Mom and Roy paid a visit to the local education board where it determined he could go to an intermediate technical school for two more years. When asked what interested him, Roy told the board official that he liked drawing. The official thought he meant mechanical drawing: Roy had in mind animals and people. Based on this misunderstanding, Roy wound up enrolled in a program that leads in the direction of drafting architectural and engineering schematics. Although Roy didn't get to sketch horses or dogs, he stayed with the technical program. From that intermediate school he moved on to a technical college where, after much hard grafting to acquire the advanced mathematics involved, he eventually earned a degree in civil engineering.

Mom and Dad were, of course, more than willing to support him while he stayed at school. Our parents, I believe, just never focused their sights to a life outside their working-class traditions. Fortunately, their economics had recently improved. Driving a taxi in London had become a more lucrative calling. A much broader spectrum of the population now used taxis as a result of the modestly greater spending power of ordinary citizens and the more subtle social equalizing effects of WWII. Roy was the first member of a wide swath of the Davies family to obtain a college education. I enjoy the thought I can take a measure of credit for playing a small part in this happy occurrence.

In my own life, however, I floundered on. Then somewhere in this time frame, I think I had a "vision." Not a religious one. I'd settle for a garden-variety epiphany. One cold, gray, Saturday morning, I rode a red double-decker bus along several of Central London's busiest shopping streets. It moved slowly because of the traffic volume. I sat upstairs looking down at thousands of my fellow Londoners scurrying on the sidewalks. Mostly garbed in dark, heavy topcoats, scarves, and hats, their shoulders hunched against April's blustery wind, they made me think of programmed robots. Some of them disappeared into the stores along the route while others emerged carrying bags of merchandise. In my reverie, the revolving doors became treadmills with the robots trapped to perform tasks not according to their own will but by tyrannous tradition. The activity before me seemed so mechanical and pointless. My mind formed a picture of an ant colony whose members' behavior is set unalterably by their genetic chemistry. What was the purpose of all this tedious hustle and bustle?

From the perspective of my new intellectual mountaintop eyre, I decided most people, especially the blue-collar masses, conduct their lives slavishly. They follow safe, well-trodden paths complying with patterns that unquestioningly conform to a life dictated by societal traditions. It struck me as so predetermined and tawdry. The ordinariness of it seemed stifling. I didn't want to become one of those ants. I wanted to live a more meaningful life, and hopefully leave, if not a mark on history, at least a small footprint in Longfellow's sands of time. Perhaps this musing amounted to nothing more than youthful braggadocio. But at the time it felt real and could be the under-girding of my seemingly endless life dissatisfaction. I felt a strong need to break the common mold and devote my life to a higher calling. No more pointless clerical work routines for me. I couldn't be a doctor, but nurses were in great shortage, and hospitals were constantly advertising for people in their late teens or early twenties to take up nursing. I would abandon my approximate six years of clerical work in favor of something with social purpose. Given my tendency to equivocate, and to complete my night classes, it took me two months more before I acted on my vague concept. Then I applied for and was accepted as a trainee nurse. .

The general hospital in Bishop's Stortford, Hertfordshire, a small town about halfway from London to my beloved Cambridge, would be the site of my nurse training. I traveled there on a green, single-decker country bus one sunny day in early July. At that time jobs were still plentiful and nursing, which paid poorly, experienced a large turnover. The government-run National Health Service had just had its fifth birthday, but already groaned under a large expense burden.

I picked that particular hospital because it meant I had to live on the premises. This provided me with a valid reason to leave home, a step I wanted to take for some time. There was something of a tradition among British working-class families that children don't leave the parental home until marriage. It might well have an historical basis in low wages and accommodation scarcity. Mothers, in particular, seemed to perceive it as personal criticism when their children move out earlier. My mother was no different. I just felt a need to leave home as a step toward personal growth, although snobbery might have been at play. In switching to nursing, I also hoped I'd find status and work fulfillment doing something of help to society. In truth, my reasoning was as nebulous as summer's cirrus clouds drifting over the orderly English landscape that I watched from the bus trundling along country lanes on my way to the hospital.

A kindly, gray-haired chief matron talked to me at the screening interview. Her blue cotton uniform, with starched white collar, cap and pinafore, well befitted the hospital, a gigantic, grim, gray-stone building dating from the turn of the century. Its sheer massiveness reflected the overbearing confidence the Victorians felt about Britain's place in the world. Acceptance or rejection for the job was based on this single interview. There was no examination to pass, which was just as well, because I didn't know a metacarpal from a metatarsal. The matron focused her questions on my interests and particularly on why I wanted to join Florence Nightingale's brigade.

It seemed prudent not to reveal the true reason I sat before her: my confusion over life and my place in it. My responses emphasized altruistic motives. She said she spoke with many applicants each year, and felt by now she could accurately judge those made of the right stuff. I worried that this experienced lady might detect my continuing uncertainties. My responses, however, must have been satisfactory. She concluded our meeting by telling me I appeared to be someone with the character and motivation to make a good nurse. Since I faced more than a 50% drop in weekly wages as a trainee nurse, my life confusion cost me some hard cash. But room and board came with this job, and without a commute, it was not all loss. By mid-July I was back on the green bus headed for Bishop's Stortford, and this time accompanied by two suitcases containing most of my worldly possessions.

My hospital accommodation consisted of a small room containing a narrow single bed, a clothes closet with built-in chest of drawers, a table/desk, and a wooden upright chair. A diminutive well-worn throw rug next to the bed provided the only covering on the gray, vinyl-tiled floor. On the desk, positioned to serve as a nightstand, stood a minuscule reading lamp. A rectangular window high on the outside wall admitted a modest amount of daylight. Communal washing and toilet facilities were down the hall. Meals were served at prescribed times to the nursing staff in a dining room near the huge central kitchen. This set-up was rather spartan compared to what I'd left at home. But since I was there to help sick humanity, I could forego creature comforts for the good cause.

Next morning, attired in a fresh white linen jacket supplied by the hospital, I reported at 8 a.m. to the nurse station at a large, general ward for men. The age range of the patients was wide, but geriatrics predominated. The head duty nurse told me that for my first six months I'd be classified as a nurse-attendant under the wing of the registered nurses in this ward. Later I learned a nurse-attendant is the bottom rung of nursing's pecking order, on a par with a cleaner with seniority. Over me were aides, practicals, and top-flight RNs.

The ward staff comprised both females and males. I was genuinely pleased not to be the only staff member who had to shave each day. Two of the men were already Registered Nurses. . The third, a small, middle-aged, almost-bald Scot had joined the staff after many years in the Army. He carried the nurse-aide title. One of the male RNs, aged about 45 years, struck me from the start as somehow remote and defensive. I couldn't put my finger on it. I learned to take my questions to the younger one who seemed more open and approachable.

My preconceived idea that I'd spend my days in lectures on anatomy, physiology, nutrition and pharmacology was quickly shattered. My days involved delivering and retrieving urine bottles and bedpans for the elderly bed-ridden. I took the used containers to a sanitary room where the contents were tipped into high-sided circular sinks with pressurized water faucets that flushed with a roar, like those on commercial airplanes. On my third morning I had to help a doddery octogenarian to a hallway toilet. This no-nonsense man insisted on using a regular toilet because he didn't like bedpans. Neither did I by this stage. I was happy to support him on his journey at glacial speed to a joyful bowel movement in solitude. When we were finally in the cubicle, I loosened his pajama tie, and slowly lowered him onto the commode. He indicated I should leave and return in fifteen minutes. When I went back I found him still sitting there, a look of satisfaction smoothing his wrinkled face. He rasped he'd finished. I heaved him upright, not knowing a long, thin sausage dangled from his anus. The motion of lifting him upright caused this object to swing forward, break away, to land neatly on my left shoe upper where it stuck fast looking like the hood ornament on an automobile. I didn't know whether to escort him back to bed while this thing still clung to my shoe, or sit him back down and clean it off. I chose the latter course. This little incident seriously jangled my exaggerated sensitivities. Body wastes had suddenly assumed an enormously significant role in my life.

At mealtimes I worked at the other end of the patients, spoon-feeding some of the oldest men. Unfortunately, I soon found this important activity also didn't provide me with a feeling of accomplishment. Staring into toothless mouths required something like saintly fervor, and I was coming up short. I began to think being a clerk/shorthand typist wasn't so bad in the final analysis.

All these gritty, menial functions were very necessary. Regrettably, they provided me with no satisfaction. My own immature impatience could not accept the thought of years performing a type of work that I found unpleasant. By my third week, I started to feel I'd made a huge mistake, both costly and embarrassing.

Then another incident helped unnerve me in a more fundamental way. One afternoon I passed a partially open bathroom door and glanced in just as a male patient, probably in his mid- thirties, stepped out of the high-sided, old-fashioned, cast-iron bathtub. The senior male RN, seated on a stool, had his right hand cupped under the man's testicles. The man was, in fact, the victim of an arm injury sustained while operating farm machinery. There appeared to be no medical necessity for the type of testicular support being rendered. It looked distinctly like gratuitous fondling. Given my uncertain impression of this nurse, I immediately categorized him as a sexual deviant. Another of my black and white snap judgments about human beings. Years later I learned nursing is a calling that attracts homosexuals. I used this incident to help convince myself I'd made the right decision to leave. It hadn't taken any time at all to reveal I didn't have a genuine desire to help others. After only a month I gave two week's notice to the matron who had so recently said I seemed to have the right ingredients to make a go of it. I felt sorry to ruin her track record, and was back home in London before the end of August 1953. My impulsive change of employment now strikes me as bordering on the irrational.

CHAPTER 20

Returning to my parents' home so quickly from such an inglorious attempt to start a new kind of life, I castigated myself as the prodigal son. No one in the family censured me, but I wallowed in a tubful of self-criticism, my mood bleak. In order to reestablish a sense of personal order, I resumed night classes when they began in September following the summer recess. Going to night school helped anchor me.

After a few days of regretful idleness, the vigorous economy let me quickly secure a job with an up market leather goods manufacturer and retailer. Swaine, Adeney, Brigg and Sons Company Limited, established in 1750, sold quality leather belts, gloves, handbags, billfolds, briefcases, riding whips, and sporting sticks, et al, with some items entirely hand made. They had some small manufacturers under contract to produce goods exclusively for them. Leather goods from this outfit set the standard, and their prices reflected it. Their clientele was the aristocracy and wealthy professionals. Adjacent to Mayfair, the shop's location on the south side of Piccadilly about half way between Regent Street and Green Park, situated it in London's most prestigious commercial real estate. Their property taxes must have been daunting.

My position involved taking dictation from Mr. Adeney, one of the owners, and transcribing his letters. Most of this correspondence answered customer inquiries and the very rare complaint. Mr. Adeney's replies were couched in the most deferential terms with profuse assurances of satisfaction, value, reliability and unending appreciation of the customer's esteemed patronage. I learned that the well off is most careful in spending its coins. With my lukewarm feelings towards the upper classes, again it was not the ideal employment for me. Mr. Adeney's obsequious tone and flowery wording soon grated on my liberal leanings. However, the workload was modest and the company atmosphere pleasant. Then, a few weeks after I'd started, a new female sales assistant arrived on the shop floor, making the atmosphere more pleasant.

I learned she was from Wellington, capital of New Zealand, and came to London for a six-month lay-over while working her way around the world. She'd already spent six-months in Johannesburg, South Africa. From London she hoped to move to Vancouver, Canada, before returning to New Zealand. What a fascinating life!

Given my enamored state for all things foreign, I enjoyed drawing her into conversation. This attractive girl with bobbed, brunette hair and large brown eyes told me that many young people from Australia and New Zealand have a strong pull to see Britain where so many of their ancestors originated. This motivation stems from a sense of being born far from the world's major cities. Many like to make a two- or three-year world odyssey before settling down.

I told her about how I'd contemplated going to Canada with Eddie, but chickened out. Pamela Ashton told me I'd missed a great opportunity, while still young, to experience something of the world outside my own backyard. Talking with this sophisticated girl made me feel good. She was a cut above the average type of female I met at public dances. She knew something of life—the very kind of life I hankered for. After a week or two of these pleasant little conversations, I asked her if she'd go dancing with me.

We met on a Saturday evening at Aldwych subway station, the closest stop to the popular Lyceum dance hall, just off the Strand, which is the south side of the entertainment district of Central London. In my eagerness, I'd arrived nearly 30 minutes early. Normally I would have stuck my nose in a newspaper, but now a pleasant anticipation dominated my mood. I selected a spot where I could survey the subway exit, and watched with fascination the hundreds of jostling people, mostly young, leaving the station. This time my reaction to the sight was different than the bird's eye view of the shoppers when, as I looked down from a bus, I likened them to ants. Perhaps a measure of humility had entered my consciousness after my false attempt to do good for mankind.

The scene at Aldwych Station represented one vivid facet of the pulsating life of a metropolis of eight million plus people stirring itself in search of Saturday evening entertainment. Those spilling out onto the sidewalk were intent on cutting a slice of happiness. Some elected the numerous live theaters staging plays and musicals in the adjacent entertainment district. Others headed for the pleasures offered at cinemas, dance halls, pubs, and private clubs. A few selected the more aesthetic pleasures of opera or ballet at the nearby Royal Opera House. No doubt some of the lonely men, if the price was right, paid for the quick thrill of a lady of the night parading on adjacent streets.

Among the dance hall subgroup, youths from blue-collar backgrounds predominated. Britain's plenitude of jobs helped boost wages for the country's hordes of these unskilled workers. Most labored in the grungiest jobs Monday through Friday. This infusion of money allowed them to indulge their weekend desire to be seen in the hottest fashions. Now they arrived in Central London from outer boroughs like preening fighting cocks.

Males overwhelmingly favored the wool-gabardine zoot suit. Their single-breasted jackets hung way below the seat, with narrow waists, and shoulder padding sufficient to make each look like a Mr. Universe contender. Trousers were tapered from the hips to a peg-top cuff. Crepe-soled shoes the required footwear. The mandatory long hairstyle resembled the rear end of a duck and was known, most appropriately, as a "duck's arse."

When it came to the females, once again I saw evidence of the unwritten law of male-dominated Britain. I seem to recall that the men were more decorative than the females. My memory is of imitation leather skirts being the number one choice of the girls. The length was still modest. The incredibly short skirt craze was yet some years away. I'm vague about the lower garment, however, because my eyes rarely got down that far. The girls chose to emphasize their upper figures with wonderfully skin-tight sweaters encasing bras that uplifted and molded their breasts to look like Roman spearheads.

At last Pamela appeared at the top of the stairs. Radiating a country freshness and naturalness, she spotted me almost immediately and smiled recognition as we moved towards each other. Her cherry-red, flared skirt, navy-blue jacket with ornamental silver buttons, and white silk blouse, weren't fashions favored by the London dance hall majority of that time. It reflected her staunchly middle-class Auckland family, now 12,000 miles distant. Best of all, I noticed her shoes were flat-heeled. I much appreciated her thoughtfulness because she was several inches taller. I read all kinds of amorously hopeful meanings into her gesture.

The regular denizens of the Lyceum were the zoot-suited and tight-sweatered crowd. Pamela and I, in our conservative attire, didn't quite meld in. This was also the time when big band music started slowly losing out to rock-and-roll. Further, London dance halls were usually so crowded there was no room for proper ballroom dancing. More and more couples shuffled lazily around the floor in time with the music as a spot-lit, rotating ceiling globe reflected an almost hypnotic pattern of silver squares. As it turned out, dancing was not one of Pamela's passions. She hadn't done much and I soon discovered she really didn't know how to ballroom dance. But while I preferred that type of dancing, I could suffer the hardship of the slow shuffle with a pretty girl.

Between dances, over a glass of a standard watery orange soda, she told me that when she finished district high school she entered a teachers' college. But a strong case of wanderlust caused her to drop out when about half way through. Her descriptions of the places she'd seen kindled in me the sense I'd made the wrong decision not leaving for Canada with Eddie. I now pined to see something of the world; if this girl could, why not me?

The dance hall became even more packed as the evening progressed. I took sly advantage of the conditions to hold her tightly. If she objected, she didn't protest. While the lusty side of my brain bubbled happily with the sensation of her body against mine, the other half began to race with thoughts of forgetting Canada and instead striking out for New Zealand. There I'd spend the rest of a contented life with Pamela Ashton. Perhaps her well-placed father would endow us sufficiently that my concerns about obtaining a good job would be a thing of the past. I'd just read, travel, and write for the rest of life. These daydreams were over as soon as the bars of the last dance, a sentimental waltz we danced cheek-to-cheek, faded away. The air of magic seemed to vanish when the rotating globe stopped and the reflected silver squares faded. We retrieved her jacket from the cloakroom, and retraced our earlier steps to the subway station. We stopped in the entrance hallway, almost at the same spot we'd shook hands about five hours before. She laughed softly as she fumbled in her small black handbag to find her return ticket to Hammersmith, in West London, where she rented a hotplate room. Her warm smile, playing gently on her lips, momentarily let me hope for an invite to her pad for a nightcap that might lead to a cupful of passion. But no invite came. I didn't want the evening to end. "Pamela, I'd like to take you out again. A movie next weekend? We could see something in Central London or one in your area." She turned so that we looked at each other directly. Now there was no smile in her eyes or on her lips.

"Alan, it's only fair to let you know I've got a fella back in Wellington. We're unofficially engaged. I'm really making this world jaunt so he can complete his engineering studies without me distracting him. It wouldn't be right not to tell you."

It didn't surprise me. There'd be lots of interest in such an attractive female. I didn't know what to say. In spite of all my reading, I could be rendered speechless easily.

"That's OK," I added shortly, knowing it really wasn't. An awkward silence ensued. Finally, she rallied her quick wits, and a soft smile changed to an expression of apology that tightened her mouth.

"See you at the leather merchants bright and early Monday morning."

Then she leaned forward in this decidedly unromantic location and planted a brief, tender kiss on my cheek. We never went out again.

I continued with English composition and French two nights a week at the East Ham County school. The only vivid memory of this time occurred one night after class when I walked home along East Ham High Street, a distance of about three miles. Attired in a raincoat, walking with a brisk military step, carrying a cheap briefcase, I must have looked like the teacher's pet school snitch now blossomed into a constipated office clerk. And alone.

En route I passed a group of five teenage boys, probably 15 to 17 years old. They slouched along, prattling animatedly and laughing loudly. Each ate fried chips out of hand-held, newspaper wraps. From their voices and appearance they were typical of a kind of east London working-class youth, uneducated and intent on staying so, but full of themselves when surrounded by their mindless mates. As we came abreast, I anticipated some cutting comments from them, but they kept silent. Then, after I had gone a few more steps, I felt something hit me softly on the shoulder. I assumed instantly one of them threw a chip. Because it occurred along an unlit section of the road, I couldn't see where the missile fell. However, my anger, impulsiveness, and hot head, demanded a reaction. I spun around and shouted they should stop. Which they did. Oh, shit! I realized ruefully that I'd started something. They arranged themselves in a semi-circle across the width of the pavement (sidewalk.) Now I could be subject to a frontal assault and on both flanks. Regardless, I wanted an accounting and strode back to them. An unplanned high noon showdown in the making on one of England's ubiquitous high streets!

"Did any of you throw a chip?"

"No, mate," came their chorus, almost in unison. I hadn't anticipated that: more like "Yer, wot you gonna do about it?"

"Well, something hit my shoulder just now."

Silence. I decided to put the question to each one.

"How about you?" I asked, turning to the first one on the left flank.

"Not me, mate."

So on, down the line. Each answered almost identically. An impasse! But I felt I'd seized the moral high ground and made my point. Had any of them admitted to it, what could I have done? The good guy hopelessly out-gunned! Yet I felt proud about single-handedly challenging all five of these yobos, even if it could be characterized as imprudent. I really didn't want to be found in the morning smeared all over East Ham High Street. Time to terminate this confrontation.

"Must have been a pigeon shitting on me from high," I said, hoping to defuse the tension with humor. Again, silence. They didn't get my joke. I turned on my heels and marched off. As the distance between us grew I heard catcalls and laughter. But I ignored it and told myself I'd faced down a black hat bunch. At home I checked the back of the raincoat: a visible dark spot, imprinted by a thrown greasy chip, just as certain as the leaves will come down each fall.

The first month of 1954 found me changing jobs yet again. An advertisement in an evening newspaper led me to the Ford Motor Company. Money was the principal draw to this latest position as a stenographer. It paid £9 sterling weekly, £3 more than the Piccadilly leather goods merchant. Ford's huge principal production site in Dagenham, Essex, east of London, on the north bank of the Thames, had its own ocean terminal. At the time I joined, it produced, I believe, three passenger car models and a number of commercial vans and heavier trucks. As my first exposure to the working environment of an American company, I'd stepped into a whirlwind. While it paid employees relatively well compared with prevailing average rates, it worked at a pace faster than I'd ever experienced.

Years later I read a comment that seemed to capture the reality of work experiences in Britain and America. In Britain, school children study hard, but then take it easy during the rest of their working lives: in America, children play in school, but as working adults must hustle like squirrels gathering nuts. The big-brother aspect of this manufacturing giant also bothered me at first. I'd always worked in small, rather quaint, family-type firms. Business was conducted behind closed doors, at a restful pace, and almost in whispers. In Ford's headquarters, other than for top executives, each office consisted of a glass enclosure on a corridor, and my desk was up against it. Anyone passing could look in. I felt as on display as tropical fish in an aquarium.

My job involved stenographic and office routine handling a range of endeavors from fairly major matters to trifles, sometimes dealing with space layout and allocation in a new, much-needed main office under construction. I also handled employee claims against a petty cash fund for damage to their personal clothing because of cramped office space. A few women had discovered a way for Ford to keep them permanently in new nylons and constantly claimed they'd snagged their hose on furniture in crowded offices.

Initially, with my new job and comparably good salary, I believed my future had resolved itself. In fact, I wrote to Eddie telling him I no longer contemplated emigration. He responded without rancor; his letter even made him sound a bit home sick. But although I had put my decision in black ink on white paper, my true feelings were still equivocal. I continued reading massively. While I should have been absorbing books on business and economics, I mostly had my nose in novels involving the human condition, travel books, and true adventure stories. Not the best diet for an emotional ditherer. My yearning for the writer's life, no matter how illogical, was always just below the surface.

Then a new source of yearning started to agitate me again over the idea of emigration. On finer days at work, I'd stroll along Ford's dockside during lunch. At that time the River Thames was still a busy shipway for cargo vessels headed to and from London Docks another 15 or so miles upstream. As the ships steamed past, not more distant than 200 feet, I noted their names and registry. Far-off places such as Buenos Aires, Hong Kong, New Orleans, Panama, Singapore, or Valparaiso stirred me. When ships were heading downstream toward the North Sea and unknown points beyond, the crews were often assembled on the bow watching England slip by. They appeared to me from that distance to be adventurous and worldly, like the men in the travel books I gobbled so voraciously. Such dreaming and longing worked mightily to unsettle my workday serenity and satisfaction. I was now with one of the world's leading industrial organizations, but it was tough to get enthused about returning to the glass box and the pile of routine work. I liked the pay and security of an 8-5.30 job in a big company, but secretly craved excitement. After about 18 months of irresolution, I forced myself to make a decision. I would go to Canada.

On 10 March 1954 I feigned sickness at work to spend most of the day at Canada House applying for an entry permit. There I underwent a lengthy interview with an Immigration Service officer, completed paperwork, and took a screening x-ray for tuberculosis. The whole procedure consumed about six hours. Based on the day's process, the officials must have felt I would not become a ward of the state. My vocation as a shorthand typist, and my savings of £75 sterling, made me a reasonably safe bet. By the time I left the Canadian authorities in the late afternoon, I knew I would emigrate to that vast country!

I walked the short distance from Canada House to Trafalgar Square, site of the statue of Admiral Horatio Nelson standing on its 180-foot-high column. Probably London's most prominent statue, the cocked-hatted, one-armed Nelson, commemorates his 1805 victory over a numerically superior French and Spanish fleet. His triumph is credited with thwarting Napoleon's plan to invade England. Four massive cast-iron lions rest on four stone rectangles projecting diagonally from the corners of the monument's plinth. I leaned against one of the lions' bases hoping I had finally achieved my own victory; this one over myself. As 5 p.m. approached and dusk enveloped the swarming metropolis, I stood there observing the evening rush hour. Droves of warmly-dressed office workers left nearby places of employment and headed single-mindedly for their home-bound transportation. Big double-decker, red buses, and compact, boxy, black cabs snarled their way around the square. The ubiquitous pigeons reclaimed roosts on well-stained window ledges of adjacent tall buildings.

It was a scene repeated each workday, year in, year out. I knew this city and its rituals well. Since age 14 I'd worked almost continuously in Central London, and its daily routines had been imprinted on my adolescent brain. Now I was contemplating the almost unthinkable act of tearing myself away from it and going to live in an unknown place. It didn't help that I knew millions had preceded me nor that I was joining Eddie who had already done it alone and survived. The experience promised to be as jolting as when the umbilical cord was cut and a midwife slapped my butt. On that occasion, however, I'd been wrapped in a towel and placed in my mother's arms in that new world. In this New World there would be no soft towel and enfolding arms awaiting me. I was plain gut wrenching scared.

CHAPTER 21

On the morning of my departure, 20 May 1954, I was up early to take leave of Dad who left the house for work by 5:30 a.m. I managed to restrain my tears when we said our partings, but I could feel my inner calmness rapidly slipping away. Reg, Vera's husband, followed about 30 minutes later. I knew it was going to be an ordeal when it came time to leave Mom and Vera. The little things that had irritated me about life at home suddenly seemed so unimportant. In fact, my upset was such I couldn't eat a bowl of corn flakes. Only tea with milk would go down, the beverage that helped so many Britons through WWII.

When I said goodbye to Mom, Vera and her three-year-old son, Christopher, I could no longer suppress my emotions. They burst out under pressure like water from a ruptured main pipe. The break seemed to come from deep down. Tears flowed freely. Not only was I embarrassed; my outburst confused me. An inauspicious beginning for someone who saw himself at least one step above the armchair adventurer. Here was the extra bold family member off to the New World blubbering like a baby. Had I understood psychology, I'd have known I was acting beyond my personal comfort zone.

Once the steam train lurched forward to clank out of Euston Station for Liverpool, probably as many earlier emigrants, my thoughts diverted and the constriction in my chest abated. When a dining-car waiter came through taking lunch reservations, I felt restored enough to order. Eating on a train: a first for me. Liverpool, with seven miles of docks, is situated on England's north west coast at the mouth of the River Mersey, and boasts a long commercial history. It became Britain's most important trading port after the settlement of America, rising in importance because of the slave trade and the subsequent cotton industry (1). At one time most British transatlantic passenger lines also made the city their principal terminal.

My train shuddered to a halt at the foot of the pier at which the

Cunard Line ship "Ascania" was tied. Built in 1923 specifically for taking emigrants from Britain to Canada, it was one of Cunard's older, slower liners (2). Its tall single funnel gave a dated, utilitarian appearance. Later I learned the Ascania had performed important service during WWII. Converted by the government to an infantry landing ship, it carried invasion forces to Sicily, Salerno and Anzio, places my father went through. None of us boarding the ship that afternoon knew that two years hence, again under Admiralty control, its future involved troop voyages from England to Malta during the 1956 Suez Crisis.

I declined porter assistance and struggled with my suitcases from the train to the ship, perhaps trying to display a bit of manliness after my earlier pitiful bawling. My trunk, I assumed, was already on board. Roy and I had sent it ahead a week before. A place card in a small, third class, four-person cabin, announced me as the rightful occupant of one of the lower berths. I returned to the top deck to join most other voyagers lining the ship's rails to look out on the Liverpool skyline under gray, lowering clouds that threatened rain. The stiff breeze blowing inland from the Irish Sea kept many in the small crowd assembled on the quay, and some of those on board, in raincoats and hats.

As the 3 p.m. sailing time approached, the Ascania thundered its fog alarm several times. The blasts rumbled away among the wharves on adjacent piers. A team of flat-capped workers rolled back from the bulwarks the mobile stairway, which, mounted, on small iron wheels, resembled a mediaeval siege catapult. One connection with the old country had been removed. The same workmen slipped the knots and unwound the thick Manila hemp hawsers from pier pilings holding fast the ship's bow and stern. With a combined effort of several men, they threw off the heavy lines, which splashed heavily into the river. When winched aboard through the hawser holes, the ropes writhed and sprayed water like eels caught on a fishing line. Now the second, and final, physical link to the old country had been severed.

A scruffy tug, belching black smoke, pulled the Ascania into the central channel of the muddy waterway by a towline to the liner's prow. The two vessels exchanged meaningful blasts. Passengers waved hands and scarves to the dockside well-wishers. I waved along with the others. Since I didn't know anyone, perhaps I was waving a symbolic farewell to my fellow countrymen. At times I'd been haughtily critical of them, but now felt pain at leaving them. .

Passengers stayed at the rails watching, me somewhat in disblief, as the people on the dockside shrank and the cityscape receded. Once in the wide estuary, the vessels indulged in a maritime duet again. Two crew seamen detached the towline, which the tug speedily retracted. Then it turned in a tight circle, blowing several lusty bon voyage toots, and headed back. The tug left wake forming more than half a giant zero, which rapidly dispersed. Now under its own power, the ship headed into the Irish Sea.

As soon as the Ascania reached the Irish Sea, the ship started to roll, and not too long after, I started feeling queasy. We were only a few miles from land and the sailing profile of this 14,000-ton tub didn't augur well for the Atlantic Ocean. We still faced nine more days at sea during spring's temperamental weather. Perhaps consolation could be derived from the emigrant crossings of the early 1800s, which took forty days from Liverpool to New York.

Someone told me it's best to stay in the open at the first indications of mal de mer. So I sat alone reading on the upper deck on a bench behind an aft superstructure wall affording some shelter from the brisk, cool wind. Eventually we rounded the Anglesey headlands of north Wales. Since the sun was obscured, our direction was sensed, rather than observed, from a rough knowledge of the geography. Low gray clouds melded with the gray sea to form a close horizon. Even the hilly coast was not visible at that short distance.

Try as I might I had trouble concentrating on my Russian novel, *The Idiot*, by Fyodor Dostoevsky, a challenging book requiring my full attention. I kept glancing up from the page to study my unusual surroundings. The black liner plumed black smoke from its tall stack. The only color relief within my view was the red blur of two flags snapping from the stern. Mounted on the poop deck's mast was a "red ensign," the official British merchant marine pennant with its Union Jack in the upper left corner against a red field. Just below flew the Cunard Line's flag with its rampant, crowned lion holding a globe in its forepaws, also against a red background. These emblems of British nautical prowess struck me as ill used on this elderly, plain jane already buffeting before wind and waves.

Once in St George's Channel, squeezing the sea between the rocky coasts of Wales and Ireland, the swells increased. Our modestly sized liner, built before the advent of stabilizers, promptly responded. And I responded myself about an hour later by losing my railway lunch. While I stood retching into a Victorian-era tall commode in the men's bathroom, the public address system squawked an announcement that dinner was being served. I retched a few more times. Much as I disliked forgoing something for which I'd already paid, my sick body ordered me to forget it.

After I made my uncertain way back to the cabin, it appeared only one other passenger would occupy it. The printed name card on the other upper bed identified my roommate as Peter Mason, now presumably at dinner. This was the first of a majority of the meals I had to forsake because of my pathetic performance as an ocean-crossing adventurer. Once in bed I lay still feeling the steady throbbing of the laboring engines and the more erratic lurching of the ship. What was really happening seemed somehow beyond my comprehension. With a churning stomach and a churning head, however, I managed to fall asleep.

When I awoke next morning I felt more or less recovered. My roommate was sleeping on his right side with his back toward me, his left arm outside the covers. As I swung myself out of the bunk, I was conscious of the ship being motionless. Were we in the doldrums or had I found my sea legs and could now stay upright even in a typhoon? I went to the porthole to find the answer: none of the above. We were tied up in the port of Cobh, or Queenstown, as renamed by the imperious British, on Ireland's south coast.

There was no bath/shower, or toilet, in the cabin. These were in communal facilities along the passageway. I washed my face and brushed teeth in the cabin's small metal sink. In spite of my efforts to perform these chores quietly, my roommate awoke, rolled on his back, swept long hair from his face, and introduced himself. Peter, from Winchmore Hill in London's northern outskirts, was bound for Vancouver, British Columbia, where he had relatives. We talked animatedly for the next 30 minutes as though we hadn't been face-to-face with another human being for years. Presumably we shared a subconscious nervousness about the circumstances in which we found ourselves early that Friday morning. Yet he seemed to have made the tough emigration decision with a lot less anxiety than me. Our conversation ranged over our family backgrounds and the sports we enjoyed. When I told him I'd been earning £9 sterling a week with Ford, he unnerved me further by saying he wouldn't have left England if he'd earned that much. Another doubt added to my quavering resolution. He had a significant other who would join him later if things panned out on the Canadian west coast. Instantly my envying ways had me wondering if I should have made the effort to have a significant other? Peter broke my reverie by suggesting we go to the restaurant. Despite having chatted so long, we were still the first at our assigned table.

The next to show was Charles Bigley, an older, sophisticated Englishman, now resident in Hamburg, Germany, who traveled the world for an oil company with its headquarters in Canada. Finally came Tom and Jenny Ripton, a couple originally from Bristol, in Somerset County. The Riptons had emigrated to Canada in 1947. After a few years, he elected to join the Canadian Air Force. They were on their way to an air base near Ottawa following a tour of duty in Germany.

Absorbing all this geography was exciting for me because I had long liked pouring over maps and atlases. Now it wasn't theory; I was really out loose in this big, wide world. I did more listening than talking at that breakfast because I was interested but also intent on packing away a huge breakfast. I was hungry and probably ate more than healthy to recoup some of the value from the previous evening's missed dinner. Everyone at our table seemed to settle into a relaxed mood, swapping background details and expanding into other subjects, as we sat leisurely for a while after stewards cleared our table. It made me think of rich people in their ornate dining rooms who never have to gobble their food and rush to catch a bus to reach work at a prescribed time. A most agreeable experience.

We weren't allowed off the ship during the stop at Cobh, and a small number of new passengers came aboard. When Peter and I reached the top deck after our table group finally dispersed, the Ascania again went through its departure routine with a small, peppy tugboat. Peter and I, fully satiated, stood by the rail observing the procedure. When Ascania reached the mouth of Cork Harbor, its engines again rumbled to life and the ship shortly arced westward. The partly sunny day encouraged us to take a few turns around the upper desk. Mixing with these people at breakfast, and now strolling with Peter, helped considerably to ease my fears. We sat on the starboard side to watch the south coast of Ireland slip by, although it was already too distant to make out features. By the time the lunch clarion call sounded from the public address system, I felt almost as buoyant as the seagulls looked wheeling above the stern. This world voyager was ready for another hearty meal.

When we passed the southwest tip of Ireland, location of the aptly named Roaringwater Bay, we entered the broad expanse of the Atlantic Ocean. The wave height promptly increased, as did the Ascania's pitching. My vertigo responded with alacrity to the vessel's every precipitous plunge, roll, and quiver. In short time I'd lost the earlier conversationally-interesting breakfast and my recent hearty lunch, to spend the rest of the afternoon and evening writhing on my bunk. Apparently totally unaffected, Peter came and went, offering kind words of encouragement which accomplished absolutely nothing.

Days three through five are a vivid memory of infrequent appearances at the dining table. When I did make it, my general queasiness prevented any enjoyment of the company or food. I ate only the lightest offerings, and immediately after went to the top deck to try the fresh air trick, which mostly didn't work. There were a few times when I retched to such a degree nothing was left to bring up save my shoelaces. Such spasms were painful and most unpleasant. I'd creep gingerly back to the cabin and stretch out on the bunk. There was no question of reading. In fact, I'd keep my eyes shut to block out the Dervish-like spinning world. I just wanted the ship to sink to the ocean floor where its motion would be stilled. Unfortunately, I'm a poor patient. Peter initially irritated me as I lay dying on my bunk. Probably in a gesture of friendliness, he'd bound into the cabin and launch into a description of each meal. With irritation, I told him I'd rather not know and he kindly stopped.

But the tormenting sea didn't relent. In fact, the fifth day was so turbulent the Ascania was forced to decrease speed. It slid into wave troughs at such a steep angle that the twin screws were rising out of the water on each forward pitch. This removed the pressure against the propeller blades and the drive shaft raced. Given the vessel's age, the engineer officer had concern such stress could cause a power-train failure. I didn't leave my bunk for 24 hours. Late that night Peter brought me some crackers and a soda water, which was all I consumed during that entire period.

Then on the sixth day, Poseidon took pity on my miserable state. He calmed the sea and parted the clouds. Nearly all the passengers flocked to the upper deck to soak up sun and pretend we were on a cruise rather than an emigrant passage. That day proved to be the most pleasant of the voyage. As could be expected, we quickly paid a price for our calm, sunny interlude. That very evening we ran into a dense fog that reduced visibility ominously. We were still several hundred miles from Newfoundland where we were due to stop at St. John's. There was talk among the passengers of icebergs in the area, and May is the most active month for icebergs heading south from Greenland glaciers. The captain slowed speed again, this time for about eight hours. We heard the engines turning over at the minimum speed required, I believe, to keep on a straight course. Seamen also posted watch in the forward mast crow's nest.

After a restless night, I went on deck the next morning around 5 a.m. The fog had lifted, save for wispy vapors drifting just above the ocean surface, like smoke from a contemplative man's pipe. Off to the starboard side, at a distance I guessed to be two to three miles, was the ragged outline of a sizeable iceberg. Against the darkish sea it glistened brilliantly white in the early sun. Although I desperately wanted this trip to be over, I didn't mind arriving late to avoid sharing the fate of Cunard Line's Titanic, which went down in that very region 42 years earlier. Around noon we sighted Newfoundland and some hours later docked in the deep water of the well-sheltered port of St. John's. We'd made it across the world's second largest ocean. I had even attended all meals in the last 24 hours. But the sea wasn't finished with me quite yet.

Ascania left St John's in darkness and followed a southern course around Cape Race and then westerly through Cabot Strait, between Breton Island and Newfoundland's southern Cape Ray to emerge in the Gulf of St Lawrence. Here the Atlantic collides with the outflows of the St Lawrence River, said by experts to pour a volume of fresh water into the sea second only to the Amazon. By that afternoon the ship roiled almost as severely as in the open ocean. I soon discovered I hadn't gained sea legs and promptly performed the same sad act I'd done so often. Half of my seventh day at sea, and the first full day within Canadian territorial waters, was spent flat on my back, eyes shut tight, head spinning.

Next morning found us moving through the Honguedo Strait between the northern coast of New Brunswick Province and Anticosti Island. Along the Gaspe Peninsula I could just distinguish a few hamlets.

The harsh landscape of the island appeared uninhabited. As we entered the great estuary of the St Lawrence River, nearly 100 miles wide, the waves abated. We still had about a thousand miles to Montreal, the final port of call. But there would be no more grim, gut-busting retching that converted non-believers.

The St. Lawrence remained too wide to clearly see its banks as we steamed quietly along. When it narrowed, the land on each bank appeared rugged and wild, with few signs of the hand of man. As the afternoon progressed we started to see a few cultivated stretches. At a place called Father Point, we picked up a river pilot and a bevy of immigration officials. For our last dinner, the oilman treated for two bottles of champagne. We all toasted each other's health and good prospects, and promised faithfully to stay in touch. That evening an immigration official checked my travel documents. Had he rejected me, he might just have faced a loud protest. The bubbly had made me uncharacteristically confident.

We reached Quebec City around dawn on our last day and disembarked some passengers. Those of us going to Montreal were not allowed off the ship even though we remained at the dock until 11 a.m. Once the ship pulled away we had only an approximate 200 miles to Montreal, in those day's Canada's largest city. The river had narrowed to an average width of somewhat over a mile, close enough to distinguish features. We passed a verdant landscape spotted with colorful small towns. The orderly, brightly painted houses were capped with red-tiled roofs. They appeared new and different from anything I'd known in Europe. We saw the occasional car traveling along roads that in places ran alongside the river. Their size made me think of houses on wheels. I am sure all passengers still on board lined the rails to take in the views and try to absorb the atmosphere of this huge, new country. As I surveyed the scene, I had moments of doubt whether this was what I really wanted. A clear indication my mind still struggled with indecision.

Almost exactly at 4 p.m. on Saturday, 29 May 1954, the Ascania tied up in the Montreal Harbor on the west bank of the river. The city occupies a huge portion of the Island of Montreal. We docked under the Jacques Cartier steel-girder bridge massively spanning the river. Many houses on wheels streamed across. A small crowd of people waited on the quayside. Scanning anxiously, I eventually spotted Eddie toward the back. It was too far to shout, even with my loud voice, but my frantic waving eventually caught his attention. Seeing a familiar face in this unfamiliar place helped lessen the grip of my personal fear demons.

Today's airplane travelers would not be happy with the length of time it took to retrieve our hold baggage from the bowels of the ship. Mine wasn't brought out until about 6:30 p.m. Another half hour passed before I cleared customs, with my trunk and two suitcases on a trolley. Fortunately, Eddie still waited outside the exit. Our arguments forgotten, we exchanged warm greetings. In 1941 I'd helped Eddie carry a phonograph along our street when his family moved there after German bombs destroyed their dockland home. Thirteen years later, in a different land across an ocean, he helped me load my entire worldly goods into his car. That day I landed in the New World. Would the New World ever be in me?

We started south to Toronto on an early version of Highway 401, today's principal motorway between Canada's two largest cities. Back then it was a narrow, two-lane road, with many junction crossings, making for a slow ride. Eddie's small English Ford Prefect, his first car, looked rather intimidated by the passing heftier, faster vehicles. It had been built for export at the Dagenham plant I'd just quit. The highway followed the course of the St. Lawrence River through a fertile countryside of low hills and shallow valleys. To my European eyes, passing through miles of empty landscape gave an impression of Earth still waiting the arrival of humankind. At the same time, huge fields were planted with vegetables and grain crops. Capacious pastures were populated by enormous herds of what I assumed to be dairy cows. Later I realized one would be in a real fight to extract milk from what were actually steers bred for meat. That was the first of several instances of me in the role of innocent immigrant loose in North America.

Daylight began to fade after we'd driven about 90 minutes. Eddie had been up early to make the long, slow journey once that day. We both thought in terms of British distances. A drive of 350 miles from London would put one some 25 miles north of Edinburgh, Scotland. To us, a long way. We decided to spend the night in roadside accommodation and finish the trip next day. A motel with an adjacent restaurant was our choice near the small town of Cornwall, the same name as the western-most English county. Already I was responding to a vague but urgent need to identify with anything remotely British. What I was clear about, a little later in the restaurant, was the size of the plate and the pork chop, which covered so much of it. The accompanying mixed vegetables and mashed potatoes were heaped into small mountains, about double the quantity one would receive in most British restaurants at that time.

After we were in our motel beds, we talked long into the night. I wanted to know Eddie's impressions of Toronto and Canada, and exactly what a machinist at the aircraft plant did. His personal flexibility impressed me. He wanted to know how things were back in our local London area and the sceptered isle in general. I told him nothing had changed. East London was still a grungy, limiting place to live, although just at that moment it tugged mightily at my heart.

Every time we thought all interesting subjects had been talked out, one of us would venture down a new memory lane that consumed another 30 minutes. It was after 3 a.m. when sheer fatigue finally silenced us.

On one of my Atlantic crossings. Me, trying to look self-assured and worldly.

CHAPTER 22

I spent my first week in Canada performing various logistical chores to get set up, including that of finding a job. Somewhere I learned that both the Canadian National and Canadian Pacific railroads employed male stenographers. By Thursday I'd been accepted for such a position in the General Superintendent's office in Pacific's Express Company that handled freight haulage. Located in the heart of downtown at King and Simcoe Streets, in 1954 that area was strictly a commercial segment, functional but unexciting, although convenient for a streetcar commute.

The job came with a weekly salary of C$66, which then translated into sterling at nearly £24. My new wage level seemed handsome indeed, but typing railroad freight memos and letters was far removed from my vague hope of work involving creative writing.

A newspaper advertisement for a self-contained, two-bedroom apartment on the 2nd floor of a private home on the western side of York aroused our interest. Eddie called and arranged for us to visit and view the premises. When she opened the front door to our knock, the widowed owner let it be known at once that this assembly was far more a matter of allowing her to assess our suitability than vice versa. We knew immediately we were in the company of one of Toronto's old, solid British-descended families, which were socially dominant for many years, but nowadays, fraying somewhat at the economic edges. With gray hair pulled back in a bun, a starched white blouse with frilly cuffs, and a long floral patterned skirt, Mrs. Somers looked and sounded life a leftover from the Victoria era.

"Should have told you when we spoke on the telephone, I much prefer renting to young business ladies. They're more reliable, at least mostly. And certainly tidier. But come in anyway. Don't forget to wipe your shoes!"

She watched us carefully to make sure our shoe sole wiping was adequately brisk. The second-floor apartment was unsullied and bright. It geographic location, however, required about a 15-minute walk to the nearest streetcar before a lengthy ride to reach downtown. We surmised young business ladies found this a problem. But this place was a light-years improvement over Eddie's dark basement apartment where I'd bunked for the first week. We voiced our mutual liking of her property. We knew she was warming to us by her next utterance.

"Males living here must keep the apartment in its present condition, and conduct themselves like respectable gentlemen. Absolutely no women guests allowed on the premises."

Mrs. Somers closed her eyes and grimaced briefly as if contemplating the choice between her negative cash flow and us. Money soon conquered up bringing when she concluded, with a haughty expression, that we at least looked clean and sober.

We moved into her house within a few days. This apartment appealed initially to my innate snobbishness because of its up market street name, Humbercrest Boulevard. That would, I thought, impress my family members back in England. I didn't know of any boulevards in the old country. This name derived from the nearby Humber River flowing into the city from the northwest to meander through it before emptying into Lake Ontario. A number of parks have been built along its banks giving a particular legacy of natural charm and repose in that city section.

In a month or so I felt at ease on the job. Primarily it involved taking dictation from the superintendent or several assistants about tariffs on rail bulk shipment of mined ore and harvested agricultural products. I produced memos destined for freight agents at strategic initiating and switching points along the company's seemingly endless tracks. But railroading wasn't newspapering. All too soon it represented, as I had feared, dull, dull work.

Canada, for me at least initially, felt like a "small" country in spite of being one of the geographically largest nations on earth. Perhaps the "provincial" quality of the Toronto of that day gave me this impression. The city eagerly embraced quiescence by 10 p.m. like an octogenarian. Although I partook minimally of the cultural life London had offered, and nothing of its night scene, it was then noticeably non-existent in Toronto. Indeed, my new city had the reputation of being "Toronto the good." A lifestyle of early to bed, early to rise, and adequate laxatives.

On my work-bound streetcar one morning I read the obituaries in *The Toronto Globe & Mail*, which called itself "Canada's national newspaper." The biographical sketch of one stalwart citizen mentioned, among the good man's other lifetime achievements, his "long-standing subscription to TIME magazine." Insights like that into the life of a city with an approximate population of 625,000 did nothing to diminish my natural skepticism. During that summer, however, we made a number of sightseeing trips offering more insight into our new country.

For our first excursion, on the very next Sunday after we moved to our new apartment, we visited Niagara Falls. For me it boggled the mind to see natural splendors crafted in such monumental dimensions. Britain has its share of scenic marvels, but they tend to be on a Lilliputian scale. North America has even more marvels, and they come in gargantuan sizes. To see a river spilling 500,000 tons of water a minute into a steep walled gorge on both sides of the international boundary is a humbling spectacle. This awesome scenic wonder drew huge numbers of tourists and we just merged into the gawking crowd.

From Niagara Falls we followed the Queen Elizabeth Highway south and crossed the border on the Peace Bridge at Buffalo, New York, to make our first sally into America. We wound up in the city's downtown, parts of which shocked me. We were amidst rundown streets and buildings that looked more blighted than any parts of Toronto I'd seen. Of course, I didn't know about America's seemingly intractable problems of inner city decay. White flight was a social condition still years away for Britain. I believe it never came to Canada to the degree of its southern neighbor. I made one more instant judgment when I promised myself I'd never live in the U.S.A.

Another of our early trips was to Ottawa, Canada's capital. We started after dinner one Friday and drove the 300 miles through the night to arrive at 5:30 next morning. It would be more accurate to say we crawled there. The previous winter's heavy frosts had undermined the road base in many places, and now its surface crumbled. We learned later that Ontario was locked in legal battles with contractors, with maintenance halted while the lawsuits ran their course.

Ottawa, situated on the south bank of the Ottawa River, proved to be a show-place city; pleasant, green, and dignified. Its 48 square miles contains 1,600 acres of parks. We visited most of the city's principal sights including the Parliament Building where we joined a highly informative tour. Then we climbed the adjacent 292 foot-high Peace Tower, Canada's tasteful memorial to the nation's war dead. I left the parliament complex believing I discerned a smaller gulf between public officials and the people than I think pertained in Britain. The Canadian bureaucracy seemed to have a more human face than its British counterpart.

Another highlight was Rideau Hall, residence of the Governor General, the British Monarch's representative in Canada, sited near the mouth of the Rideau River where it plunges over cliffs to join the Ottawa River. Until 1952 the Governor General always came from Britain. That year saw the first Canadian, Vincent Massey, appointed to the position. Henceforth the appointee followed the directions and advice of Canada's Cabinet. Another brick fallen from the British Commonwealth edifice.

Next day, after spending the night in the cheapest motel we could find, we decided to explore in Quebec, the province of the French-descended Canadians, across the Ottawa River. Once outside the riverbank city of Hull, we didn't have to drive far before we were in a vast rural area that appeared sparsely populated. I don't recall that we had any particular destination in mind, merely idly turning this way and that, and were soon lost in an immense hinterland with atrocious roads and few directional signs.

Somewhere in this vast void we passed a dilapidated, large car flying Quebec license plates, windows down, and stuffed to the upper deck with local unkempt young bloods. As we overtook it, their driver saw Eddie's Ontario plates and indulged in a horn-blowing frenzy. At first Eddie thought they were signaling for assistance and, like a Christian, slowed down.

As their old boat drew closer, numerous arms suddenly appeared ending in single fingers or fists. This didn't appear to be in the friendly spirit of nautical tradition where vessels exchange identifying signals as they pass at sea. We quickly realized we'd encountered a boatload of youthful hotheads who had probably enjoyed more than their ration of grog. Presumably they wanted to discuss passionately held opinions on the French-English rift that so troubles Canada to this day.

We realized that our Ontario plates marked us as Canadians of English descent. Furthermore, if we stopped to debate their historic beef, they'd discover we were, in fact, two rather soft specimens of the genuine thing — two Englishmen adorned in cheese cutter cotton hats who had even showered that morning. We knew it would be a one-sided, messy discussion. Eddie stomped on the gas and his modest Prefect lurched into unmanly flight bouncing drunkenly in what must have been the world's longest pothole.

Although their vehicle was considerably larger, it was ancient, and probably had never seen the inside of a garage. In addition to its motley crew, it no doubt had a cargo of six packs sufficient to lubricate all of Canada's lumberjacks coast-to-coast. Thankfully it soon fell behind. We hightailed it back to and across the Ottawa River, pledging that from now on our explorations would be confined to the Province of Ontario.

These early trips gave rise to a wanderlust that would grip us and guide our lives for the next few years. Since neither of us had professional skills to offer the job market, we should really have spent our early 20's building a career with a corporation. Instead, we tasted the heady, broadening pleasure of travel and our appetite developed for more of the same.

Eddie's position at the aircraft plant offered overtime on Saturdays. He chose to work about half of them. He also moonlighted at a men's clothing store as a salesman. This let him work Friday evenings, and also some Saturdays all day. On my second Friday evening in Toronto I tried my hand as a salesman. But the management told me politely I didn't fit the mold and not to return. Probably I lacked the extrovert enthusiasm they wanted. I was a little miffed, but also pleased to reserve more time to read. Daily chores now consumed so much of that treasured commodity.

But with Eddie's extra job and his plant overtime, I frequently spent Saturdays on my own. I began to explore Toronto on foot, often undertaking lengthy walks to and through one of the city's approximate 100 parks or open spaces known as ravines. Wise Toronto city planners had left many trees in place. Comparing it with east London, Toronto streets offered a lot of eye-appealing shade trees that made even ordinary roads look inviting and somehow free of urban tension. Maples (the leaf of which is Canada's national symbol) and oaks predominated.

These rambles became little voyages of discovery as I wound my way along unknown streets. Even though I never found anything out of the ordinary, they provided me with a diluted sense of adventure. As I played no sports at this time those walks provided some exercise. In hindsight,

I wish I'd become involved again with soccer, and opportunities for it were available. Toronto had sizeable populations of Britons and Italians. In fact, in a few of the parks where I walked, amateur league games sometimes were in progress. But I stuck to my solitary ways.

This choice was wrong because I needed more camaraderie, to say nothing of the healthy exercise the sport provides. My way of life turned me ever more inward.

During my early months in Canada, I began a habit that became a way of life well into the future. Since age 15 I'd been a borrower of library books. Now I began to spend hours in some of these places of wonder. Although I was there alone, it was not as alone as reading in one's own room. I liked best the main public library located near the University of Toronto downtown campus. This spacious branch made available some English political magazines, such as *New Statesman* and *The Nation*, which I'd read in London. Nowadays I had a palpable ache for news from England.

Then I found out the general public could use the university's John B. Robarts library, with its extensive humanities collection. I especially relished the time I spent there. The perhaps 200 students bent over their books at numerous long rows of tables, with individual green-shaded lamps, generated an atmosphere that resonated deeply in me. Because a university education was still to my British mind a attainment beyond reach, I always felt humbled yet exhilarated to be allowed in.

Time spent there reminded me of my bittersweet trips to Cambridge where I mingled with, but was unnoticed by, the intense students on the streets or the banks of the River Cam. Now I was inside a college facility where the fascinating process of knowledge transfer was in progress. I doubted the general public would be allowed into the libraries of Oxford or Cambridge universities. One up for Canada!

During that July we became involved with a group of young men who had formed the Canada Queen Sailing Club. Exactly how we learned about it I no longer remember, but almost certainly through someone Eddie met. This club had been established with the purpose of building a residential house, and with the profits from its sale, purchasing a 65-foot ocean-going yacht to sail around the world with a crew of some ten aboard. It would be christened the "Canada Queen."

With club members performing most of the weekend construction work without pay, the anticipated hefty profit from the C$20,000 house would be sufficient to buy the ship and provision it. The club required an initiation fee of C$100, refundable upon profitable sale of the house. By joining, Eddie and I thought we were on the threshold of a world of real adventure!

Barely two months had passed since I proved to be the wimpiest passenger on the Ascania sailing across the Atlantic. No one else seemed to miss as many meals as I did on the 14,000-ton ship. Now I was willingly contemplating a world cruise in a 65-foot yacht weighing perhaps all of 30 tons.

The club's two founders were Toronto freelance travel filmmakers who'd successfully produced several documentaries on South American countries and one on England. The planned voyage would be the subject of a film for them and its proceeds would remain with them. They'd come up with the original idea and the money to buy the building plot in the East York section of Toronto, then still possessing acres of undeveloped land.

Among the members was an older Canadian who'd lived a checkered life. The only person who knew construction, he became our de facto work foreman. The rest of the Canadian contingent consisted of three or four university students who yearned for a year's wind-blown freedom sailing before the mast. The others were all immigrants: two from Holland; one each from Australia, Hungary, Netherlands, and South Africa, with three from England, including Eddie and I. Some seriously hoped to join the pantheon of world circumnavigators.

Once Eddie and I signed up we began to spend our weekends on the site. Because of his job commitments, Eddie didn't make it on some Saturdays and I would catch rides with other members. The project was still at its earliest stages when we signed on. A few trees had already been felled. We helped take out the roots manually. We next cleared the thick undergrowth covering the house plot, and then leveled the house plot with pickaxe and shovel. We dug four-feet deep perimeter trenches for the footings required by Canadian winters. Just clearing and preparing the ground, and digging the trenches, took about two months. There was no shortage of exercise in my life once this involvement began.

Nowadays I think becoming associated with this venture demonstrated just how much I lived in the clouds. But it also told me that, having made the hugely painful break from home, I could now easier consider another grandiose, far-flung undertaking. At least in theory. But much as I desired a few years of true adventure, something inside forever nagged I should settle down.

With the approach of fall I returned to night school, and elected English Composition and French offered at the Harboard Collegiate. As far as I can remember, this school was something between High School and University, perhaps on a par with an American Junior College. A vigorous, crew cut Canadian, an M.A. graduate of the nearby University of Toronto, hustled and harried us through the English course. A quiet, self-effacing young German exchange teacher, in the mildest-accented English, gently led us among the labyrinth of the French language. The differences in their new and old world approaches registered strongly.

After one Sunday of hard grafting on the site, when we returned to the apartment, persnickety Mrs. Somers awaited us as we came through the front door. She got straight to the point.

"When I rented my accommodation to you it was, I thought, for the benefit of two young business gentlemen. Lately you've started to come into my accommodations in old clothes, mud on your feet, and looking quite disheveled. You never disclosed this undesirable aspect of your persons when we first met."

It was true we mostly returned home on weekends looking more like coal miners than young business gentleman. We attempted to explain to her the clever, exciting plans of the Canada Queen Sailing Club. We hadn't quite reached the part about the glory it would bring to Canada when we sailed triumphantly up the St Lawrence River to Toronto after circumnavigating the globe in the best tradition, we fully expected, of some of the great ones.

"Building a house! Sailing round the world! What rampant nonsense!" she soon squealed, and stepped back as though she suddenly found herself conversing with two disreputable men. The neighbors might notice!

"I want you to vacate my accommodations as soon as possible, but certainly no longer than one month."

She turned and walked away stiffly, nose tilted heavenward, toward her ground floor living room. We'd only been in her apartment for about four months and already we needed to find new digs. Our response was to quickly put an advertisement in the evening *Toronto Telegram* for rooms with full board Monday through Friday. Eddie didn't seem to mind doing all the chores involved in apartment living, but I disliked it. I wanted more free time to study for my night classes and keep up my self-imposed reading load. I also made a mental note that when we reached Tahiti on our yacht, I wouldn't send Mrs. Somers so much as a postcard! During the weekends as we worked at the building site, Eddie and I would listen eagerly to the past exploits and hopes of some of the Canada Queen Club members. They were all people who had traded in the conventional life, perhaps temporarily, for one involving risk. Heady stuff for us. We were now so susceptible to the lure of far away places. A 9-5 job, building a corporate career, just couldn't compete. My adventure/travel reading increasingly convinced me I more treasured the intellectual life over worldly goods. Ironically, at the stolid Canadian Pacific, I encountered two men who intrigued me.

The first, whose name I don't recall, was a Canadian who, immediately out of high school, worked for three years at a remote nickel mine near Flin Flan, in the snowy wastes of northwest Manitoba. He received a site salary well above Toronto averages. Utilitarian accommodation came as part of the pay. The company canteen food was adequate. Best of all, there was nowhere to spend wages. When he quit the mine he left with about C$25,000. A healthy sum in the early 1950s. Back in Toronto, he married his high school sweetheart, and built a house. By the time I met him, he had two children. Now he seemed content with his life including his relatively safe and steady railroad employment. He was just 25, and seemingly set. The other man, Robert Banting, became even more fascinating to me. This tall, thin, laconic New Zealander had an intensity that radiated. His enthusiasms wafted around him like morning mists around Japan's Mount Fuji. He worked in the Accounts Department, for me about as dull as the Freight Department. After we became acquainted, I'd pester him to tell about his travel experiences. He came from Auckland, New Zealand's largest city, and had been roaming alone for several years. He lived first in Sydney, Australia, and then moved to London, England. Now he scoped out Canada. His next keen goal was to emigrate to America and live in San Francisco, a city he described as Shangri-La and of which I knew nothing. I was soon in the library reading up on his dream destination.

Eddie and I were extremely receptive to the strong influence of these birds of passage we encountered. Just the exposure to this emphasis on wanderlust soon had us thinking about what we could do to take in more of this earth if the circumnavigation project sailed over the edge of the world. We came up with a different idea almost every day. We wrote to the provincial governments of Alberta, British Columbia, and Manitoba for work possibilities at remote mining or construction sites the following summer. Our vague idea was to make a modest bundle that would finance a few years of living in one or two idyllic spots — Tahiti, Bali, or the Andaman islands came to mind — dotted around the globe. None of our probably amateurish efforts met success. But our very readiness to make these serious inquiries demonstrated the prospect of moving on again didn't faze us. We'd evolved into reckless dreamers.

Meanwhile, our immediate domestic situation needed attention. Few replies came from the newspaper ad we'd placed, so we accepted the responder who came closest to meeting these requirements. Mrs. Hogan, with a large but unkempt house on Havelock Street in an older area closer downtown, offered us full board for the five workdays plus laundry of shirts and underwear, but without ironing. We would have individual rooms, furnished with items that should have been carried to the landfill long before.

Its location meant a greater drive to work for Eddie, but it cut my streetcar commute almost in half. I could also walk to the night classes I'd recently started. But after initially believing we'd been lucky, it soon became apparent we'd left a middle-class, sanitary environment for a decidedly grungy, blue-collar one. From our first morning there we discovered "full board" meant we prepared our own breakfasts of toast or cereal, as Mrs. Hogan didn't rise early enough. She prepared the evening meal for daughter Joan, who went to work, Eddie and me, and herself. The food proved to be mediocre and skimpy. But I was prepared to tolerate almost anything if I didn't have to cook and do laundry.

After a few evening meals I gained the impression that the two women enjoyed new people with whom to talk. Each had a tendency to start separate conversations with the two of us, as if trying to outdo the other. They didn't talk between themselves that much. In fact, their relationship appeared to be rather tense. This belief was confirmed within a couple of weeks when we heard them from our rooms shouting at each other.

We also found out that Joan, who I guessed to be in her mid-thirties, had lost her husband exactly ten years before in 1944. He'd been in the Canadian Air Force assigned to a bomber squadron in England. His plane had been on a raid over Germany when hit by anti-aircraft fire. It didn't crash immediately, the pilot managing to keep it aloft until over the English Channel. Then the remaining engines failed and it crashed into the sea killing all aboard.

Joan seemed to be a troubled person. She often appeared forlorn and despairing. She seemed to have little zest. She was quite attractive and shapely, but we never saw a boy friend. During several nights I awoke to hear her crying. She slept on the third floor in a room immediately above mine. Thinking back now, the loss of her husband, whom she said she deeply loved, could have plunged her into a depression. In those days I knew nothing of this insidious condition—the common cold of mental illness.

Another mild shock came after we'd moved in to find there were two other renters in rooms somehow hidden away in this rambling, creaky structure. They came and went at odd hours. This development concerned me when we discovered there were no keys available to secure our rooms. The landlady hadn't mentioned these two extra tenants when we made our initial arrangements with her.

After a few sightings of these two mystery lodgers, during which we never communicated, we asked Mrs. Hogan about them at dinner one evening. Emitting an embarrassed laugh, she said she'd completely forgotten them when we first met her. They weren't getting any board or laundry service, and kept pretty much to themselves. She asserted they'd give us no problems. One was a night warehouse worker and the other a gravedigger. Both as honest as the day is long.

Her association with honesty was put into question when, over the course of several weeks at the meal table, we found out she also had a grown son living overseas. We assumed he'd emigrated. It slowly emerged that, in fact, he was running from the police. Although she selected her words cautiously, the son became involved several years before in a racket offering hot, quick profits in a business we never learned. The scheme was rumbled and her son made an overnight flight. Now he lived in Mexico separated from his wife and children.

Perhaps in the third month in our new digs, I was propped up reading in bed one night about 11 p.m. I suddenly heard my door handle turn, the door opened, and the gravedigger stepped into my room. He scared the holy bejeesus out of me! This huge man had scraggly black hair and beard, deep-set eyes, a prominent hooked nose, and shaggy, black eyebrows. Now, without first knocking, he stood in my bedroom.

What unspeakably bad manners! This violation of my privacy outraged my English sensibilities! One side of my brain tried unsuccessfully to think up words strong enough to express my indignation. Meanwhile, the other side was telling me this was the time to let our English sensibilities be trodden into the mud without protest. I was in bed, in pajamas, in reading glasses, and with telltale wimp soft carpet slippers placed neatly on the floor next to it. I hardly presented the picture of an opponent likely to launch a meaningful resistance to his imminent physical assault. In fact, I'd already decided it was my time to die. Murdered brutally in my own bed. Perhaps this monster was an enterprising gravedigger who kept up his productivity by supplying his own steady flow of corpses needing cemetery plots. Killed and buried at the same hands. That had the ring of New World efficiency. Almost like one-stop shopping then sweeping America. But the brute didn't advance. He just stood there, looking at me with his penetrating eyes. Finally, I broke the pregnant silence with a squeaky voice.

"Oh, hello, nice to meet you at last. Seen you around, but don't know your name. I'm Alan Davies. Eddie, my best friend, is just down the hall. We're very close. Within easy shouting distance. We watch out for each other. One always knows what's going on with the other..."

My impression was the barbarian hadn't listened to any of my carefully chosen words. Eddie was probably sound asleep by now as his day started earlier than mine. This situation was taking on an alarming aura of foreboding. This was the first gravedigger I'd met face-to-face. Right then and there I elected in favor of cremation. Dying was tough enough, but then having to endure such a malevolent trench maker was more than a body should have to bear.

At last this creature gabbled something in what sounded like French/English patois spoken by a Quebec native of limited erudition. It flashed in my mind that we might have escaped the carload of Frenchie rednecks in Quebec, but I was about to meet my end at the hands of one of their lesser charming expatriates! I hadn't understood anything of his brief dissertation but the words "need" and "argent." I recognized the French word for "money," and knew this meant trouble.

Now much as I feared dying, making injudicious loans was right up there in second place of my most distasteful activities. I remembered my ill-advised loans in the sleeping hut of my RAF days.

"Oh, I'm very sorry, I've got no argent myself," I lied without guilt. "Have to send all my spare argent to my work-house poor family in England."

He scowled at me, didn't look convinced, but turned on his heel, and shambled out of my room. He uttered no mercies or pleasant good nights. And he didn't even close the door!

I slept fitfully that night, fully expecting him to come back to help himself to the contents of my billfold which I'd tried to protect by subsequently rolling it into a clean pair of socks in a middle drawer. We quickly knew we weren't too happy with our second choice of digs, but moving was already becoming a bore.

Canada Queen Sailing Club building site in summer 1954 began as a program to raise money to buy yacht and circumnavigate globe. First wall cinder block put in place. Project fairly soon sank.

CHAPTER 23

When we learned that the Labor Day holiday provided an extra long weekend in both Canada and the USA, we visited New York City, which metropolis for us most enshrined America's image for the world. These two countries, the bastions of capitalism, were the first industrial nations to officially recognize the grunt work of millions of their men and women. Casual observation so far convinced me blue-collar workers in both countries enjoyed a higher social status than their counterparts in Britain.

Having been warned that a car in the Big Apple is a liability, we traveled by overnight train, leaving Toronto's Union Station at 7:30 p.m. and arrived about the same time next morning in the heart of Manhattan. We entered the U.S. at Niagara Falls where relaxed, friendly U.S. Customs officers boarded to non-officiously inspect our documents. We could see why this border enjoyed a reputation for peaceful, amicable crossings. Before day turned into night we had passed long stretches of attractive evergreen forests. The small towns we encountered indicated rural life in western New York State enjoyed a good level of prosperity. At that time I couldn't reconcile this impression with the abjection we'd seen in downtown Buffalo. It didn't seem rational these widely divergent scenes were aspects of the same state. We still had much to learn about our new continent.

New York City, with its dramatic skyline, is many things to many people. It is the cultural offerings of a great city; the dazzle of Broadway; the non-conformist life of Greenwich Village; the horse race of Wall Street; or finally, and perhaps mostly the synthesized, roiling energy of eight million souls jostling for a living within the confines of just a few postal zip codes. After securing accommodation at the YMCA, we launched ourselves in fast-track tourist mode. We went immediately to the observation floor of the Empire State Building, for many years the world's tallest building. At the Rockefeller Center, we took an elevator in the RCA tower that ascended 70 stories in 37 seconds. I still remember how nervous it made me looking down from such heights for the first time. People were turned into ants and cars into Tonka toys. While I doubted the fear felt in my stomach qualified as acrophobia, it felt real enough.

Next we walked through bohemian Greenwich Village, where aspiring artists, writers, musicians, and actors live and work. On holidays they emerge from their tiny apartments to congregate for fellowship, especially in Washington Square, which attracts thousands of tourists who want to observe something of a lifestyle freer than their own.

As Eddie and I ate lunch at an outdoor table of a sidewalk café, we watched a tall, scraggly middle-aged male walk past our eating-place. He spotted three dollar bills left on a table as a generous tip by a group that had just departed. When he reached that table he grabbed the money, glowered at us as if daring us to raise an alarm, and strode on nonchalantly. Life in the big city! Later, on our way to the financial district, we detoured into the Bowery, the city's infamous skid row. Here we had our first sightings of real human derelicts. These were men, aged well beyond their calendar years, mostly done in by alcohol. Their outward appearances aroused in me a contradictory mixture of compassion and disgust, tinged with fear. At the same time they strangely fascinated me. Why and how did human beings allow themselves to sink so low? In this wealthy society, theirs was a poverty and degradation eclipsing anything I'd ever seen in East London. I like to think the would-be writer in me struggled to understand this grim feature of the human condition.

In the evening we lined up to gain entrance to a television studio taping a talk show. Its producers wanted live audience participation. The name of the show I don't recall. No loss! It was so idiotic and phony I was glad I didn't even own a TV. During the taping, a prop man held up cards telling us to applaud and laugh. The dumb public being blatantly manipulated!

On our last day, the return overnight train didn't depart until 5 p.m. After breakfast we spent a couple of hours in Central Park, and then had our first disagreement as to how to pass the day. Eddie had developed a liking for baseball and wanted to ride the subway to see the Yankee Stadium in the Bronx. That had no appeal for me, so we went our separate ways. Since the famous city public library wasn't open, I preferred to randomly explore more Manhattan streets alone. Everything went fine until the simple matter of lunch.

A drug store window sign advertising a 25-cent liverwurst sandwich and a 10-cent soda won my business. At that time I was not familiar with the various beverages that satisfied America's enormous thirst for soft drinks. The sign said "7-Up" and I misread the "7" as a "Z."

"What'll yer have?" The table waitress was the personification of the stressed, over-worked, middle-aged waitress dealing each workday with more than her fair share of male jerks.

"A liverwurst sandwich and a glass of zup, please." (I can no longer be sure exactly how I pronounced this mythical drink, and in my timidity I probably mumbled, making the exchange even more aggravating for the long-suffering lady).

"Say again, Mac."

"I'd like to eat a liverwurst sandwich and drink a glass of zup, please." I mimed these actions to clarify the words as a traveler might do ordering a meal in remotest Mongolia.

"Hey, buddy, I know yer solids. It's the liquids you ain't communicatin'."

"Zup!...ZUP!...ZUUUP!" I persisted, raising my decibel level with each utterance in the hope sheer volume would bring comprehension. People nearby turned to take in this increasingly noisy exchange. In yet another wave of acute embarrassment I sank lower on the bench seat.

It was obvious that Anglo-American relations were quickly deteriorating to those prevailing in 1776. Through my mortification I sensed I was up against the native-born New Yorker's infamous nanosecond patience level. At any minute she might lean over and slap me.

"A liverwurst sandwich and a glass of milk, please."

Just lately a newspaper article related the ever-declining share of the soda market nowadays won by 7-Up, leaving the impression the drink could become as extinct as the dodo bird. Its maker can't blame me; I once risked life and limb for it!

After lunch I resumed trudging through towering canyons. Perhaps the waitress had rattled my nerves or the liverwurst and milk combination didn't fit, but I soon needed a rest room. Careful reconnaissance failed to locate any city-operated public toilets as available in civilized places like London or Paris. My prayer seemed answered when I stumbled on the New York Port Authority Bus Terminal. The by-now desperately necessary facility hid in the basement. Then joy turned to despair. The builders had forgotten the stall doors! Again my mind couldn't reconcile the world's richest nation didn't have doors on its sanctum sanctorums! Now if there's one thing a shy Englishmen likes, it's his privacy at such sessions. And this bus restroom seemed as busy as a 4th of July parade. But, as it must, the call of Nature prevailed. In mental agony I used the commode without even a newspaper to hide behind. Yet half the male population of the eastern seaboard seemed to saunter by, not at all shy to look in on my humbled state. While I hadn't been subjected to one of New York's infamous muggings, I certainly felt rather roughed up.

Even though I'd been gone from home eight months, I still experienced distressing bouts of homesickness. These feelings were overlaid with a degree of guilt as I acknowledged to myself that I'd been cold-blooded in the way I'd broken bonds with my parents and home. My feigned iciness had really been a mask because I found it so difficult to tear myself away. My family would be more than justified in simply forgetting I existed. But they didn't. When I tried to explain my confused actions to Mom and Dad in a rather mawkish letter, they responded separately with replies full of understanding and love. Mom and Vera showed their affection by sending hand-knitted woolen sweaters, and a pair of leather gloves. Dad faithfully each week wrapped and mailed a copy of *The Observer,* London's literate, liberal Sunday newspaper that had won my undying loyalty. This publication, which covered the arts world extensively, had been my favorite since about age 17. When it arrived I'd indulge myself in a reading orgy, devouring its contents, especially book and movie reviews, and travel features. Knowing my parents bore no resentment comforted me in my bouts of homesickness.

To keep my mind occupied with more positive thoughts, I applied myself to the English and French language courses at night school. Class attendance occupied two evenings. The other three work nights I stayed home and studied in my room or one of several libraries I frequented. The amount of studying necessary in these matriculation level courses proved heavy, and I struggled to keep up. In the English course we covered Shakespeare's "Macbeth" and "Romeo and Juliet" and a selection of classic poems. When the weather abated, I decided I'd not resume spending the whole weekend at the Canada Queen Club building site. One day at least had to be reserved for studying.

As it turned out, when the climate mollified around the middle of March, we never went back to the site. The outer walls were in place to the height of 10 or 12 cinder blocks. It was then necessary to come up with the cash for the lumber and plumbing supplies, but the Canada Queen Club was out of funds. Two of the Canadian university students, no doubt under pressure from their parents, withdrew from the club to resume their studies. One of the Dutch immigrants returned to Europe. The rest of us began to feel the scheme might not pan out and became skittish. No one, me included, wanted to put up more money. Eventually, the plot and improvements in situ were sold and the photographers retrieved their investment. Much as I was annoyed to forego my C$100 contribution, mine would be one of the smaller losses. I believe Eddie had invested C$250, and others C$500, to roam the oceans blue. Red ink was all we would-be sailors saw.

The collapse of the CQC, admittedly an improbable scheme from the start, served the purpose of solidifying the constantly changing ideas of Eddie and me about moving on. We hadn't found employment at any remote Canadian mining or construction site. From time to time I still saw Robert Banting, the peripatetic New Zealander, pouring over books about San Francisco in the downtown library during the lunch break. He continued effusive as to the wonders of that California city.

In February our second landlady gave us the abrupt notice of two weeks to find alternate accommodation because she and her daughter decided to move. We scurried without success to locate full-board rooms together. There were apartments available, but I didn't want to again have all the associated domestic chores. The best we could do in that short time was to find rooms with Monday-to-Friday board in separate houses not too far apart in a much swankier area of Toronto. My new small room came well appointed with red maple furniture in an attractive home. Its location was as far from downtown as the original quarters from which we'd been evicted. This second ouster doubled my living costs and my commute. Toronto's subway system opened late in 1954, but it didn't serve my area. Back to riding the slow, clanging Dundas Street tramcar.

It is almost inevitable that immigrants to Canada, while registering the kaleidoscope of fresh impressions of their new country, are soon drawn to the dynamism of the restless giant beyond their long, southern border. Just the sheer gravitational force of America's 1954 approximate 162 million enterprising people, when compared with Canada's approximate 15 million, exerted a powerful attraction (1). We decided to respond to that draw. Eddie and I took off from work to visit the American consulate in Toronto to apply for resident alien entry visas with the right to work. We planned to move in June 1955 after I'd taken my matriculation examination. Eddie had decided to make a May visit to England to see his ailing mother.

At that time, I believe U.S. law allowed an annual quota of 60,000 British immigrants; however, it was usually only 50% subscribed. Indications were we'd be accepted because we had sufficient cash to tide us over until we obtained work. We were advised, however, that male aliens of a certain age would be subject to the military draft after six months in the country. The sobering requirement to join the military concerned me. I'd been in one military and really didn't want a second round. We quickly decided we'd stay in San Francisco for six months only before moving to Australia, from where we'd return to England, thus going around the world despite the sinking of the yachting project. In fact, to prove our point, on 2 March 1955 we paid deposits on two berths on the British Pacific and Orient Line "RMS Orsovo" to sail from San Francisco to Sydney on 17 February 1956, nearly a year in the future. I assumed that once I showed the kindly American authorities my berth receipt to leave California, they'd just strike me off their list of military-bound immigrants and turn to more pressing matters. Things were to prove that's not what happens.

After a few weeks, a surprising notice regarding our applications for working visas came from the American Consulate: mine had been approved; Eddie's, for unstated reasons, had not. Although he made several phone calls, and at least one more personal appearance at the Consulate, he was unable to obtain a definite answer. Nor could he find out why his application had snagged. This unexpected turn-of-events could scuttle our globe-circling travel plans. Meanwhile, Eddie had already booked passage from New York to England sailing in late April, to be gone about a month. We planned to leave for the west coast as soon as possible after his return to Toronto. In preparation, he'd already sold his Ford Prefect.

This worrying development brought into sharp focus our personalities. Eddie was calm, indicating he'd follow-up at the American Embassy in

London, and seemed confident he'd be approved. I panicked. If he wasn't successful, would I have the fortitude to go west alone? That question began to take on obsessive-compulsive aspects. Like Scarlett O'Hara, I'd try to stop this constantly revolving problem by telling myself I wouldn't think about it today, but put it off until tomorrow. During daylight hours I felt I could do it; at 3 a.m. blasts of doubt and fear transformed my iron resolve to earthworm limpness.

Eddie's departure for England made extra time available for studying. Night school final examinations were scheduled for the end of May, and I needed to do a lot more sweating. Alone in my room during the next few weekends I studied harder and read more. Just as I thought things were under control, Mrs. Finch, her eyes red from crying, waited for me as I arrived at the house from work. She told me she needed my room quickly as her single daughter, Maude, was unexpectedly returning in the middle of the state school term. Mrs. Finch offered no further explanation. I knew the daughter held a teaching position at Masan, a village at the end of a rail line near James Bay in northern Ontario.

Mrs. Finch knew of an attic room with board available just a few houses along the road. I immediately said I'd take it sight unseen. The need to search for new quarters so close to exam time, and our still unannounced but hoped-for departure in June, would just add to the hassle.

So on the next Saturday I moved into the house of a Mrs. Roper on the opposite side of Runnymeade Road. This was my fourth move since arriving in Toronto one year prior. Although I did moan about the need to move, true to my nature, it really didn't present a problem. My possessions consisted only of personal clothing, footwear, and a few books. I filled my two suitcases loosely and trundled them the 200 feet to the new quarters. I had to return a couple more times and the transfer was complete, trunk and all.

A letter arrived from Eddie saying he hadn't made headway at the U.S. Embassy in London with his visa. He still didn't know their objection. On the surface, he appeared a better candidate for entry than I. He had more cash than I did. Also, his work potential was broader than mine. So I wallowed anew in my fears and self doubts about going it alone.

Later I learned from Mrs. Roper that Mrs. Finch's daughter had been put on medical leave by provincial authorities because of a clinical depression. I did see a tall, youngish-looking woman once coming out of the house. She looked tense, withdrawn, and kept her eyes downcast. Although I didn't understand her illness, she had my sympathy as recently I'd had a few black spells more severe than just fleeting moods.

On Monday, 13 June 1955, in the afternoon, I sat the senior matriculation in literature at the Collegiate. I had read "The Tragedy of Macbeth" twice, only one-fifth the number of times the teacher urged. The paper seemed more difficult than I'd anticipated, and I answered just over half the questions. When the results arrived through the mail, my exam scores were even worse than I dreaded. Out of a possible 100% in each subject, I'd managed 62% in French. The English course examination was taken on two separate days. I slipped to 57% in English composition, and fell to the bottom of the mountain with 27% in English literature. Anything below 50% represented failure. I'd found the literature questions difficult and long, and I'd worked at a snail's pace. I cringed as I read the result believing it true I'd worked hard. This piteous score crushed me. Even though I'd scraped together the highest of my scores in French, this subject, too, was a disappointment. In the mid-term I'd achieved an 80% pass, which put me on top of the class. Quite a precipitous plunge between that and the final. While I'd made progress in literature appreciation since age 15, my understanding level remained abysmal. I rationalized I didn't know how to study, nor how to take examinations at this higher level than anything I'd tackled in Britain. A sad and sobering experience.

Eddie came back to Toronto that same evening. He returned about two weeks later than originally planned. I didn't know whether because of his mother or his visa complications. I rushed from the school to the Union Station to meet his train, but arrived too late. We eventually encountered each other at the intersection of Runnymeade Road and Annette Street. As I crossed over, I saw him reach into his jacket inside pocket, and flourish an envelope. He smiled broadly. He'd obtained his American visa in London. We would, after all, move to the land of round doorknobs together. Eddie had left the aircraft company before going to England. After returning he worked part time at the men's clothier. I quit the Canadian Pacific Railroad on 10 June. The chief freight clerk gave me a kind letter of reference. It had been a dull but easy-paced workplace. I had no complaints, but earnestly hoped I wouldn't have to earn my living in railroading again. With all arrangements completed, we departed on Sunday, 19 June 1955.

I had to acknowledge Toronto had been a pleasant enough experience. That said, I did subscribe to the general opinion that Toronto was a little too stolid and staid. As life worked out, during the next decades, Toronto blossomed. Up market high-rise towers of steel and glass have come to dominate its squat brick and stone structures of my time there. It is now almost a Japanese-like mixture of old and new. In this process, the city metamorphosed from a repressed Victorian provincial capital to a vibrant, cosmopolitan city bursting with ethnic diversity and liveliness. It shed its British-style conservatism as waves of immigrants arrived. And arrive they did, from Asia, Africa, the Caribbean, and Europe. Today some 2.5 million people enjoy its many cultures and joie de vivre. Each group carved a niche in the city's pragmatic mosaic to offer and imprint its own language, cuisine, music, dance, religion, and daily rhythm of life. Toronto now has Canada's largest immigrant community. More than a hundred languages are spoken. The place hums. Normally people arrive somewhere too late; Eddie and I arrived there too early!

CHAPTER 24

At midnight on Sunday, 19 June 1955, we left Toronto aboard a Greyhound bus to Detroit. We were scheduled to arrive at seven next morning. Stowed in the luggage compartment were our two ocean-going trunks, three large suitcases, and two canvas holdalls. We chose to travel through the night to avoid the cost of one night's lodging. We hoped to purchase a car by noon on Monday and be moving west by afternoon, with San Francisco, the far-off destination. But first we'd meander across the continent to take in Vancouver, British Colombia. From there we wanted to follow the glorious Pacific coast highway south with its stunning panoramas through Washington, Oregon and northern California. Our excitement at being at last underway on our odyssey kept us from sleeping on the bus. We talked into the wee hours. Eddie filled me in on his England visit during which he'd called on my parents.

At long last, from a seat across the aisle, a burly male, no doubt a production worker at one of metropolitan Detroit's 7,000 industrial plants gruffly told us to pipe down. His manner struck me as impolite, but his brawny bulk suggested we heed his demand. With the ink on our American visas barely dry, I didn't want to create an international incident so soon.

At Detroit's Greyhound downtown terminal, we checked our trunks and suitcases at its storage room. We asked a cigar-chomping cabbie to take us where we'd find the motor city's best selection of used cars. There our disbelieving eyes surveyed acres of car lots stretching to a restricted horizon. Vehicles of seemingly countless shapes and hues, solid and dual-toned, lined up like packages of cookies on a supermarket shelf. Vividly colored flapping bunting and multi-sized balloons bobbing in the breeze, garnished these lots. This ocean of vehicles, and the array of dealer advertising gimmicks to catch a buyer, looked like a vast fairground. It wouldn't have surprised me if the salesmen wore clown costumes. I wondered if all this razzle-dazzle really influenced customers. The few used-car lots of East London in my black-and-white memory offered no more than half a dozen automobiles, and not a single balloon. Standing amidst motor city's cornucopia brought the realization that America is the most mobile society on earth, both literally and figuratively. At that time, some Europeans in their entire lives never journeyed more than ten miles from their birthplace. By virtue of car ownership, almost every American traveled at will, narrowing the gap between social classes.

My knowledge of cars then was absolute zero. What lurked under the hood, and what went on there, equated to black magic. My mechanical know-how didn't go beyond the workings of a two-wheel pushbike without a derailleur gear. Fortunately, Eddie's ownership of automobiles, in both England and Canada, gave him a basic understanding of these mechanical chariots. As we wandered these car lots, however, we became more confused. The choice was too broad. We knew we needed something bigger than an English Prefect to carry our luggage across the continent. And we'd capped our spending limit at $500.

After couple of hours we encountered a salesman at a Nash/Hudson lot who seemed especially helpful and friendly. A smile never left his face. He quickly ascertained our first names and used them constantly as if we were his long-time friends and he relished our company more than that of his own wife. He asked where we were from, and where we were going. When he heard California, he said he'd been stationed there during the war, and would have returned save for a Michigan wife who wouldn't leave. His bonhomie made me think that if all Americans were like this, it really would be a whole new world.

After we described the amount of luggage we were hauling, this amiable, friend-for-life salesman focused our attention on a 1951 Nash Rambler Super Station Wagon. In a lowered voice he said he had the boss's authorization to let this beauty go for only $594.25 if good people came along. Apparently, we qualified. Then to ice the cake, and without a sign of embarrassment, he pointed out the vehicle's hood ornament, a chrome angel with outsize wings outstretched to form a "V". This supposedly added a distinct touch of class. In truth, the car was a utilitarian box on wheels adorned with an out-of-proportion, kitsch statuette.

However, the car's practicality appeared to meet our needs. We settled on it, and Eddie and I each contributed $300 in cash. A frenzy of hand shaking followed, with ear-to-ear smiles, as he wished us bon voyage. Off we went in our second-hand green wagon to retrieve the stowed luggage. Eddie decided we should follow the salesman's recommendation and have our new baby's oil changed and chassis lubed at a specified nearby garage. Telepathically, the mechanic on duty seemed to expect us. While performing the work we wanted, he told us the car needed a couple of jobs done to make it really road worthy. Without these repairs, he gravely advised, he wouldn't risk his own life in it to drive downtown, let alone across the continent.

I don't now recall what the repairs were because I didn't understand then, but do remember how mad we felt. The car had cost us nearly $100 more than we wanted to pay, and now we faced another $125 expense. But wait, surely that friendly salesman would underwrite this work as he'd said the car would carry us in style to the Golden State? We knew he'd be unhappy if we left Detroit just a little in doubt about his good character. Before letting the mechanic proceed, we headed back to the used car lot.

Unlike when we'd first appeared, the salesman didn't emerge brightly from the garden-shed office at the rear as we weaved our way through the lot's huge inventory. In fact, we had to go inside to get his attention. It surprised us his face never broke into the smile that hadn't left it when we were there originally. In fact, he acted as though we were strangers. Nearly three hours later, Eddie still argued the point he'd said the car was in good shape. I wouldn't have had the moxie or fortitude to debate so long, but Eddie possessed some British bulldog tenacity and a lot of self-confidence. Even Eddie, however, could finally get the guy to pay only for the parts, the cost of which the mechanic had written down, and we paid for the labor. His $25 joined our $100, making the car $200 more than our original price cap.

We arrived back at the garage too late to get the job done until next morning. We then motored to the "Y", only to find it full. We had to take our first commercial accommodation in the New World, a rather non-descript Hotel Norton at $6 for a double room. Because the area looked decrepit, we moved all of our seven pieces of luggage into this hotel that appeared not above renting a room by the hour. Before going to bed, my journal tells me I wrote a letter to Mom. By the time I drifted off to sleep, I hadn't resolved if our first day in America as permanent residents had been triumph or trouncing. I suspected the latter.

Although I don't believe the repairs performed were major, the car wasn't ready until after lunch. We finally departed Detroit's sprawling automobile reservations, with their hustling salesmen skilled in the art of snake oil, around 3 p.m. Even though super-efficient interstate highways remained for the future, the roads were good enough to drive steadily, stopping infrequently, and giving us the illusion we made up lost time. About midnight we pulled off the road to sleep in the front seats for three hours. Our plan for the trip included unpacking the car's rear cargo area to stretch out at night. But in this early part of the journey, transiting well-populated, north-central USA, passing cars were too numerous to feel safe leaving our luggage just piled high and unsecured outside.

We roused ourselves at 3 a.m. to continue. The road carrying us west curved around Lake Michigan's southern end. It then flung us northwesterly like a planet's gravitational field swings a space probe on a course correction. The dawn slowly climbed the sky in our rearview mirror as we passed row upon row of assorted industrial plants on Chicago's west side. I enjoyed a brief sighting of the star of the east before increasing light obliterated it from view. An unseen hand painted giant brush strokes of orange and red across the sky's fluffy cloud backdrop. It seemed particularly incongruous to witness this glorious spectacle of nature's daily cycle amidst this grim hardness of man's manufacturing world.

During that day we continued our northwesterly tack across Wisconsin. Known as America's "Dairyland," its farmlands showed to be well maintained amidst a verdant lushness. This state's highways were a considerable improvement over those in Britain. We cruised many miles on roads as straight as railroad tracks. Around midnight we stopped just short of the Mississippi River, which flows north-to-south for virtually the entire USA. Here, at Wisconsin's western border, we were in a true rural landscape. Our headlights picked up a large, pitch-dark building set back from the highway. Too big to be a residence, we assumed it to be a commercial establishment, now closed for the night. It wasn't the structure that attracted us, however, but its rear, paved parking lot. We drove around to park, unload, and sleep prone. Our selected spot must have been about 200 feet from the unlit building. From the luggage area, we unloaded Eddie's trunk and our three suitcases to stack them in a pile on the pavement next to the car. My larger trunk was roped onto the roof rack, not to be opened during the journey. We put the holdalls on the front seat, giving us space to stretch out. We crawled in the back fully clothed, rolled up the windows, and locked the doors. It felt so good to be supine, even on this hard surface, I fell asleep instantly, no doubt from the lack of it during the previous night. Sometime around 2 a.m., however, we started awake at a heavy metallic rapping on the window. When I opened my eyes I was partially blinded by a light shining in on Eddie's side. He lowered the window an inch.

"What the hell are you doing here?" demanded a tobacco-husky, female voice. We smelled her breath and felt her anger, both wafting in the slightly opened window. She continued to focus a nightstick flashlight beam on us. I saw nothing but concentric light circles through the dirty side window.

"Come on, what are you two up to?" Her second question sounded just a little less ferocious. She might have expected to surprise a couple who didn't want to pay for a motel, but she could see we were two tired, disheveled males.

"Just sleeping," we volunteered, almost in unison, as we struggled to rouse ourselves from deep slumber.

"What's in them cases stacked here?"

"Just clothes," Eddie responded.

"You must have lots of duds."

I think about now she realized she was dealing with foreigners, not locals, Chicago hoods, or extraterrestrials.

"You men are trespassing on private property. This is my parking lot for my restaurant and club. You can be cited for violating a county ordinance." She gave the name and paragraph number of the county code we'd broken.

"You sure it's just duds in them go-away bags, eh? Nothing illegal drugs or moonshine?"

As the flashlight moved slightly in her left hand, I noticed something glitter at her other side. I gulped. Her right hand held a silver, long-barreled revolver. Just then Eddie, whose eyesight always worked better than mine, whispered he could see a man standing fifteen yards away with a rifle, raised to the firing position, and pointed at us.

Now we both felt we'd arrived in the Wild West, somewhat ahead of its true geographic boundaries. We could be cut-down by a hail of hot lead as happened in the Saturday morning serial movies of my boyhood.

Once again, the smooth-talking Eddie, in his best English accent, rose to the occasion.

"We're awfully sorry, Ma'am, for our mistake. We're not familiar with, or understand, trespass laws. All we've got in our suitcases are personal possessions. We're new British immigrants driving to California. We'll move on if you want, but would prefer to wait till daylight."

I thought this was not the ideal time to remind Eddie that the principle of trespass has been a part of English civil law since the Magna Carta of 1215 and perhaps even since compilation of the Doomsday Book in 1086.

"Well, OK. You guys better learn up on them trespass laws in America. People need to respect 'em. Make damn sure you're out of here by daylight."

"Oh, thanks. Thank you very much. Good night."

She didn't respond. Eddie rolled up the window. We silently watched the flashlight beam bouncing on the ground as the good lady made her way back to her building. Our eyes now adjusted, we saw the shotgun man fall in beside her.

We were up promptly and quickly reloaded the car. We wanted to get away before the chance of another visit by Annie Oakley and her sidekick. Eddie jumped in and cranked the engine. The SOB failed to start. Eddie tried again and again. We were concerned lest the noise bring the owner out in another rage. Our luck might not hold twice.

Fortunately, the lot was level and the car could be moved by shoulder power, but it seemed a long 200 feet back to the road. A vision of our night visitor using my protruding rear end for target practice as I doubled over to achieve more traction made for sincere effort. Once back to the road, Eddie turned the dead vehicle in a westerly direction and I pushed on until we'd put a little distance between the restaurant and us and parked on the soft shoulder. I raised the rear door, and we sat on the cargo bed facing the oncoming traffic. We awaited our fate with a measure of calm after we'd survived our first encounter with gun-happy America.

Lady Luck came to our aid on that long-ago morning in western Wisconsin. Two men on their way to work in a pickup truck saw us, slowed to a stop, and asked our problem. The driver kindly offered to push us with his vehicle to a garage in the next town, only a few miles up the road. So little traffic moved that our bumper-to-bumper caravan presented no hazards. In those days bumpers were made of materials that would withstand a little pressure. No more!

The mechanic who checked our car could find nothing wrong. It seemed the manual choke, pulled out too far, flooded the carburetor. He charged $1. I'm sure he went to heaven!

We crossed the historic Mississippi River and stayed true to our northwesterly direction through Minnesota. Again we put in a long day crossing the state on excellent roads, with few curves to slow us down. Unfortunately, and for reasons now unclear, we were slaves to the feeling we had to keep to a schedule. As a result, we chose not to spend time in St Paul, the capital, or its bigger twin, Minneapolis.

In central Minnesota numerous dairy farms and cattle ranches, with hundreds of plump livestock, passed in review as we wheeled across the state. Gently rolling hills, carved by glaciers in a former Ice Age, were now covered with countless acres of corn, flaxseed, and hay. Enormous barns and silos attested to the scope of its farming activity, dwarfing British counterparts. Slowly it sunk in that one needed to think on an entirely different scale in the USA. In the area of Fargo, we crossed into North Dakota, turned north and followed a road that in places paralleled the Red River. The terrain became flatter than a lake on a calm day. Here we saw fewer cows and far more beef cattle and sheep on sprawling ranches whose acres were delineated by wire fencing stretching for miles to the horizon and beyond.

Darkness had spread over this thinly populated, quiet area by the time we reached Noyes, on the border with Canada. At the crossing checkpoint, an older, fatherly INS border guard checked our passports and immigrant visas.

"You guys only entered the USA three days ago. What's the matter, you fed up with it already?"

He raised his eyes from the paperwork and scrutinized our faces. We were suddenly nervous he had it in his power to veto our plan. We earnestly assured him that we merely wanted to drive across Canada on the Trans-Canada Highway to Vancouver and then return to America on the Pacific coast.

"I've heard Trans-Canada's in bad shape further west. Hope you young fellas know what you're about."

He smiled sagaciously, and waved us through. As we drove away,

Eddie quipped he'd had enough trouble getting into the country. Now it wouldn't let him out!

We reached Winnipeg, Manitoba, at 10:30 p.m. and again sought the cheapest hotel we could find in another decrepit part of another downtown. From then on our crossing of the continent would be noteworthy for the dingy, forsaken hotels selected, almost as if we were compiling the Zagat North American hotel guide for deadbeats. Our plan was to spend a few hours in the morning seeing something of Winnipeg, then Canada's third largest city. Next day we slept until about 10 a.m., stuffed our gear into our holdalls and ran to the car. We were relieved to see no one had broken in. But once again it refused to start. There was no choice but to return to the hotel and call for mobile service.

Winnipeg has a sizeable Indian and Metis population, and our choice of flophouse seemed to be their first choice also. As they went in and out of the lobby, its faded wallpaper peeling, they cast suspicious glances at us as we waited for the service truck. I wanted to read a book but felt it might appear too wimpy or snobbish. I didn't have the courage to do my own thing. So we looked over and over the same three torn, ancient auto magazines cluttering the cigarette-burned lobby table. It was nearly midday when the truck arrived. The mechanic tinkered for a while, adjusted the automatic choke, and fairly soon got the thing running for a $5 fee. He cautioned a proper cleaning of the carburetor was necessary. By then we were disgusted with the hotel, its lobby, our car, and the world in general, and chose to push on westward regardless, now for the first time on the Trans-Canada Highway. We traversed Manitoba, Saskatchewan, and Alberta, a total of about 900 miles in 48 hours, on Canada's #1 route, memorable for long stretches where winter-inflicted potholes created an obstacle course. On one stretch of about 70 miles there was no macadam surface at all. We drove over a clay subgrade that, in one section, had been turned into a quagmire by a recent downpour. Had our temperamental vehicle failed along this section we might well have been seriously marooned because of light traffic and widely spaced towns. We took night catnaps on the roadside, avoiding hotels or unloading the car to stretch out.

We reached Banff National Park on the eastern slopes of the Alberta Rocky Mountains in the early evening. Established in 1885 as Canada's first park, it offers monumental landscapes, with glaciers, high moraine lakes, and rushing rivers. We found accommodation in a small log cabin complex that posted a notice telling us we were at 4,500 feet above sea level. Next day I wanted to spend the morning hiking a mountain trail. Because of his unsure gait, Eddie didn't care for walking on uneven ground. So he explored the valley while I set off about 6:30 a.m. to hike nearby Sulpher Mountain, which, at 7,495 feet, made it one of the lower mountains in this area. It was June 28th and all of the valley peaks were still mantled in snow. My journal reflects it required about two and one half hours to reach the top and about one hour less to return.

I encountered only one other human being, an older man, on the trail. We met close to the summit; he was descending while I ascended. We talked for a while and he told me his age was 70 which I've passed as I write this. I was so impressed that a man of his years had walked up there. He modestly pointed out he'd been born locally and had been an active hiker since boyhood. Nowadays 70-year-olds are reaching the top of Everest.

Eddie and I left the park around 7 p.m. to drive through the night again, with one sleeping while the other drove, or to restore ourselves with an occasional roadside catnap, during which we left the engine running. In retrospect, a dumb decision. That night's driving required both of us to watch the road. The still uncompleted Trans-Canada Highway zigzagged up and down mountains to reach passes through the extensive area encompassing the Rocky, Purcell and Selkirk mountain ranges. Some of the surrounding peaks reached above 12,000 feet. Along much of this stretch of hairpin turns, the narrow road fell off on one side precipitously mostly without guard barriers. Again we encountered lengthy reaches where the road surface had been undermined by winter frosts. Grandmotherly restraint characterized our driving.

By early morning we reached Revelstoke, elevation 1,495 feet. We were at last descending to the rich farmlands of the interior plateau. At a restaurant, however, we learned that the highway ahead had been severed in no less than five places because of flooded rivers and overflowing lakes. To reach the west coast meant a long detour through the United States. Since our ultimate destination was San Francisco, we decided to head back into the United States and keep bearing southwest to reach our goal. Vancouver would have to wait until later. In fact, I didn't get there for another 45 years!

Late afternoon found us at Lind in wheat-bountiful east Washington. As we drove into town and a sign announced its population as 494, I thought vaguely that they would all fit into five London double-decker buses. With minds begging for sleep's blissful unconsciousness, we holed up there for the night in an old-fashioned wood hotel, with a 2nd floor, covered veranda along the entire front. Straight out of my cowboy movie serials of the 1940s..

Following a restful night, we set off in high spirits. At the time I wrongly felt people living in these vast stretches of western American must be almost as remote as Aborigines in the Australian outback. I didn't credit the connectivity of train, telephone, automobile and, increasingly, television and airplane. Our morning started as a relaxed drive across a moderately rolling landscape of the Columbia Basin, which we'd read, makes up part of the largest lava flow plateau in the world. But, alas, our buoyant feelings were transitory. We'd driven about 80 miles, admittedly at speeds higher than our recent stints, when the car developed what, in my utter mechanical ignorance, I noted as a "wobble at the front." I suspected it had something to do with a few too many of those Canadian potholes. The glib words of that especially friendly used-car salesman who vowed this vehicle would deliver us trouble-free to the Pacific Coast went through my mind. We seemed to be making the acquaintance of every mechanic between Detroit and San Francisco. We limped into Pasco, the next town on the road, which sits where the Snake joins the Columbia River. We later learned the Lewis and Clark Expedition had passed through this exact area 151 years before on their historic journey to the Pacific coast. Of course, their progress was much better than ours. They used canoes and horses; nothing manufactured in Detroit. Whatever the cause of the wobble, it took three hours to correct. I didn't record the diagnosis, or what it cost to fix, probably because I couldn't spell the mechanical malfunction, and the expense put me in shock. Soon after we crossed the Columbia River and headed south through eastern Oregon. The undulating road at times climbed to reach low passes. The modest mountains hereabouts had elevations from four to eight thousand feet. Late that evening we arrived on flatter terrain and rolled into Burns, on the Silvies River, bursting at the seams with 2,000 citizens. Our latest auto repair costs only strengthened a mutual feeling we needed to reach San Francisco quickly as though we could outrun the car's defective genetic code. Since accommodation expense was the only category over which we had control, we resolved to scrimp even more on our already low-budget motel/hotel choices. Here we out-did ourselves at Hotel Real Dump that, in truth, should have paid us to stay there. Yet it had the effrontery to charge us $3.00 for a double room. Fittingly, its pauperized clientele looked extra down-and-out. The ramshackle building threatened to become a rubble pile if someone slammed the hotel's front door too robustly. Once in the room we observed the fixtures must have been the best pickings from the local landfill. When we turned back the single bed covers, the sheets were gray with age, having probably been in use continuously since the hotel's erection for early Oregon territory settlers. It's best not to talk about the bathroom.

After we left the next morning in bright sunlight we crossed a leveling terrain. A dry, sand and stone landscape encircled us. Trees were scant but stumpy bushes and shrubs proliferated. A road sign told us we had 55 miles more to reach the California border. Between that objective and us, however, we could see another ridge of higher ground we would have to top before we attained it. Eddie was at the wheel when a curve clearly required a slower speed. But as he negotiated it our tires squealed.

"Best take it easy, Eddie," I suggested unnecessarily.

"I'm trying, but the bloody brakes didn't respond just now."

"Don't make jokes like that."

"Trouble is, I'm not joking. The brakes *have* quit," he repeated, as I now watched his foot uselessly pumping the brake pedal.

Eddie spoke the truth. Now the brakes on this piece of junk had failed. He engaged a lower gear and the car slowed. He used the hand brake to bring it to a stop at the side of the road. Once again, there were so few cars we presented no problem in this sparsely populated area. Since leaving Burns we had passed only a couple of clusters of roadside bars and basic eateries. We doubted they possessed a garage that could fix our latest mechanical trouble. We didn't, of course, relish the prospect of climbing to traverse the now close mountain range, but Lakeview, the only town worthy of the name, still lay about 25 miles ahead. So regardless of sans brakes, we elected to head up and over. By maintaining a slow speed, engaging the lower gears going up and especially coming down, and with me working the hand brake, Eddie piloted us into Lakeview. Once again, a garage was the first place we looked for.

We were underway once more about 2:30 p.m., crossing into California late in the afternoon. Ours was the only car at the border control point where a lone state inspector checked for forbidden fruit and plants. We confessed to a few apples and, apparently to his amusement but true to our miserly dispositions, we chose to eat them right then and there rather than tossing them. As we stood munching two apples each, the sun shone brilliantly from a cloudless California sky to reflect blaring from sheared rock faces still raw from the dynamite of road-builders who blasted their way through nature's obstructions. Standing in this warm, still, quiet spot induced a feeling of being far from everything known and comforting.

Soon we again traversed winding, narrow roads at elevations around 6,000 feet, through spectacular, wild landscapes. Dense forests of spruce, oaks, juniper, sycamore, redbud, and varieties of pine and fir, climbed the mountains. We crossed overpasses under which cascaded clear, raging streams down torturous, rock-strewn beds. Off to the east were individual peaks rising over 9,000 feet. We decided to spend our last night on the road in the car. At these high elevations, however, it felt too cold to park. So we continued to twist and turn until mid evening. By then we had dropped several thousand feet into the northern end of the Sacramento River Valley stretching through much of the state's center. The pleasantly warm night air soothed our tired bodies. I don't know where we parked, unloaded the luggage, and climbed in the back for that final night, but it could have been near Red Bluff. Mercifully, no middle-of-the-night, gun-toting woman disturbed us. In fact, we slept so well it was 9 a.m. before we woke with the sun streaming through the dirty windows. A mere 200 miles remained.

As we got closer to San Francisco we observed an extremely heavy flow of automobiles away from the Bay Area. We hoped this mass exodus had nothing to do with our impending arrival. The dizzying stream of vehicles passing on the other side of the road was mostly full of life-reaffirming young families: teenage-looking parents in the front; bountiful children in the rear. The backs of station wagons, and roof racks on sedans, carried enough camping gear to make a weekend in the woods as comfortable as home. We felt better once we remembered the day was Saturday, 2nd July 1955, and Bay Area residents were heading to spend their holiday weekend in the mountains.

We reached our final destination via the Oakland-San Francisco Bay Bridge, an 8-mile long suspension/cantilever monster resting in the middle on small Yerba Buena Island at which point you enter San Francisco county/city limits. Because we'd heard hotels in the city were expensive, we headed to the YMCA, on Turk Street, in a lesser desirable section of downtown. We stayed true to our record of cheap accommodation in the grungy Tenderloin neighborhood.

Our troublesome Nash Rambler (1955). Caked in Alberta mud of unfinished Trans-Canada Hwy #1. My old ocean trunk on top.

CHAPTER 25

On our first San Francisco Sunday we prepared ourselves to attend church. I don't recall what inspired us. There is a remote chance we wanted to say "thank you" for our safe arrival in California. There is also the possibility that we knew in two days we had to start the distasteful chore of seeking employment. A little help from above would be welcome. We had also become aware that Sunday church visiting constituted a major activity in America. We just may have been curious enough to check out what we'd been missing.

As it turned out, the Tenderloin had a marked dearth of churches. In San Francisco's version of New York City's once infamous namesake, there was, of course, no shortage of seedy bars and liquor stores with the contents of their shop windows protected by security grilles. Our Sunday good intentions defeated, we went for a walk that led us to busy Chinatown, then centered around Grant Avenue, where neighborhood morning life already pulsed. Since neither of us had been in Asia, the scene struck us as genuinely exotic. The opened crates, boxes and barrels of pungent fruits, vegetables, spice, nuts and herbs on display at many Mom-and-Pop stores, into and out of which we wandered, roiled olfactory senses. Intense and subtle colors of some of these items pleased the eye. Tasting them, I thought, might be a different story.

Later we climbed one of the steep streets running east to west to reach the Nob Hill district. We paid to go up to the observation tower in the Top of the Mark Hotel. From there we had a 360° view of the city. My first impression was of its closely built homes and apartment buildings stair-stepping up the many hills to which they cling. Their whiteness and density conveyed the flavor of the Mediterranean, although I'd never been there either. As a dramatic backdrop, the waters of the bay, sprinkled with sailboats, wrapped around two sides of the peninsula. On the third side, we knew the Pacific Ocean, beyond our view from here, spread westward to Asian shores. This introduction whetted our appetites to discover more.

During that long weekend I prepared a list of names and addresses of newspapers, press services, and magazine and book publishers in San Francisco. Armed with this, I launched myself to find employment bright and early on the first workday by visiting each, starting with the *San Francisco Examiner.* I yearned for some kind of media work. Eddie proceeded to the California Labor Exchange located quite close to our quarters.

Downtown San Francisco is reasonably compact. I walked in crystalline sunshine to each of my addresses, at first in high hopes. As the day wore on, my spirits began to dissipate as my efforts bore no fruit; at each personnel office, a gentle, courteous declination, but declination no less. My lack of a college degree or local newspaper reporting experience proved my Achilles' heel. By mid-afternoon I'd run through all the names on the list. Scared of being jobless for too long, I also made my way to the Labor Department. It knew of one opening for a railroad stenographer, exactly what I'd been in Toronto. After lying about being interested, an interview with the company was arranged. Next morning, upon walking through the front door of the Southern Pacific Railroad's large main office at the lower end of Market Street, I immediately sensed the conservative atmosphere of a desiccated, stodgy organization ensnared in petty protocols. After completing the employment application, I took a typing test. My prideful disdain shattered when an unsmiling official announced I'd failed it. Return in two days to try again.

Somewhere I learned that the Labor Department was not the only way to locate work. Because of the steady influx of new residents from other states, indeed other countries, on any given day, there were thousands of newcomers seeking work. In this free for all, a number of private employment agencies had opened to perform the service of finding vacancies. If an applicant obtained work through them, he/she paid a fee to the agency. The fact that the employee, and not the employer, had to pay, struck me as outrageous. Having to pay to find a job was one of the great eye-openers for me in coming to the United States. When I left England, there were so many jobs available a person could quit one office, walk into another down the hall,, and be back at work that same day. In quick time I came to feel that ordinary Americans generally held their jobs in greater respect than ordinary Brits. Presumably a legacy of the Great Depression. Much as it galled me, I spent the next few days visiting employment agencies, filling in their applications that always ended with the statement that if employment was secured through the agency, one third of the first month's salary was theirs. I seemed to have forgotten I'd moved to the capitalist nation el supremo.

Off I trotted to a number of interviews, however, through the auspices of these agencies. They were organizations as disparate as an oil company, a ship chandler, and a flag manufacturer. Nothing came of the first two, but I could have had an administrative job with the flag maker. A far cry from media work. The flag company owner, however, offered only $250 a month. Although less than I'd made in Canada, I was on the verge of accepting. As I sat facing him feeling he held all the aces, his phone rang. He had a lengthy conversation and it gave me time to summon my courage and decline his stingy offer. When I later relayed this story to Eddie, who had an enviable inner fortitude in such situations, he said I could be proud of myself by keeping the Union Jack flying high. That sounded good. He'd found work as a stockman in a warehouse. I was still without.

Each time I checked, the Labor Department had nothing new. I returned to the Southern Pacific Railroad to re-take their typing test. On the fourth attempt I passed. By then, however, their position had been filled. I'd be considered again if another vacancy arose. I just had to cool my heels. As a result, after a second week in the YMCA, we elected to move on the Saturday to a nearby hotel whose weekly rates were lower. With prices less than the "Y", this accommodation looked remarkably like some of the flophouses we'd used crossing the country. This one even lacked an elevator.

We carried our ocean trucks one at a time to our room on the third floor. On our last trip from the car, we banged through the front door laden with two large suitcases and the holdalls. We dropped them in the lobby at the foot of the stairs and sank down on a couple of nearby tattered easy chairs to rest briefly. Just then an American enlisted sailor in uniform and a dyed blonde with a few miles on her odometer emerged blinking from the hotel's darkened bar into the lighted lobby. She led him by the hand towards the stairs bound for a floor above. Our baggage blocked their way. Jumping up to move it, we apologized.

"Well, bless my li'l ol' soul, where you boys from?" asked the blowsy, but not unattractive woman, in a slurred, singsong voice. She wore a tight fitting, low-cut dress that outlined a still sexy body. A small hat, sporting an ornamental feather, had slipped to one side of her head to complete her overall disheveled appearance.

"We're from England, just arrived via Canada," a smiling Eddie answered.

Her rouged mouth dropped open. A bemused look passed over her heavily made-up face as she struggled with the geography.

"Well, now, that's mighty interestin'! That's where my friend here's from, isn't it...what's your name again, darlin'?" she bleated toward the sailor. "You tell me your name agin, honeybunch, and these nice gen'lmen jus' where you're from."

We could see the sailor was uptight, his jaw closed like a vise. In fact, the young sailor was antsy, almost hopping from one foot to another in excited anticipation. He obviously had other things on his mind than this idiotic exchange in the public lobby.

"My name's Pierre, and I'm from Montreal," he half snarled, without looking at us.

"Come on, sugar, let's go, the clock's running."

"Oh, Perry honey, jus' don't you rush me. It'll be real thrillin' for both of us. Jus' know you won't be disappointed."

The eager, but highly irritated sailor, stood glum and silent. His lady friend turned her slightly unfocused focus back to us.

"It's jus' so wunnerfull you boys come all that way to see us here in ol' Frisco. Now, Perry, you be real nice to our visitors and help 'em with those there bags."

I glanced at Pierre. He was ready to commit murder. He had no desire to use his energy carrying our luggage. He drooled in anticipation of a different activity.

After throwing us a death-threat look, this representative of the U.S. Navy shoved a holdall under each arm, grabbed both of the suitcases, and charged up two flights, two steps at a time, to the third floor, where we had a room. The third floor must have been for the transients because it's where their commercial exchange, just down the hall, would take place. He'd already deposited our bags at the end of the hall when we reached it. Pierre proceeded to his room, unlocked the door and went in. The desultory companion of the antsy Pierre was still raining praise on our heads for the miracle of our arrival in her city as she unsteadily mounted the stairs. We walked to ours further along. After arriving on the floor, she stood waving at us from their doorway. Then a hand shot out and seized her arm. She almost came out of her high heels as she flew over the threshold. The French-Canadian would wait no longer.

Each day on my way seeking work I stepped out of our Tenderloin flophouse into bright sunshine to walk through the scruffy streets to the financial district where most of the private employment agencies congregated. The earlier bounce in my step had gone. It had become increasingly apparent that my only saleable skill was my shorthand/typing. The fund of general knowledge with which I prided myself, acquired from persistent, if random, reading since age 15, seemed to mean nothing. Eddie was settling into his job located in an industrial area near the International Airport on the southeast side of the city. He drove the car each day because he again had the advantage of a reverse commute. Inbound commuters already endured hectic traffic, and this would grow steadily worse as the Bay Area's population grew exponentially.

By the Wednesday of our third week in San Francisco I still didn't have a job. As I wended my way back to our dingy room that afternoon, following another fruitless day, I stopped at the YMCA to see if it held mail for us. It did, and also had a message, by now two day's old, for me from one of the first agencies whose agreement I'd signed. I called as soon as I reached the hotel lobby, as telephones were not part of our room's furnishings. The agency knew of an opening with the Chicago-based Atchison, Topeka and Santa Fe Railroad. The job required a stenographer in the freight rates department of their west-coast branch office in San Francisco's financial district,

The agency arranged for an interview the next morning at which I passed their shorthand/typing test first time. Perhaps the prospect of long-term unemployment focused my attention. I was taken to the regional general manager for the interview who, several times over, emphasized the railroad's need to hire only people who would join the company for life. His pronouncement made me squirm because I knew my true interests lay elsewhere. But I wanted an immediate income. As I reassured the elderly gentleman of my foreverness, I thought of the P&O Steamship Line reservations we already held to Australia. My mea culpa now for my behavior then is I knew nothing of economics. I didn't understand that jobs exist only after a company or individual risk capital, direct and indirect, in a venture. The job would not be available without this investment capital. The adventurous life is only for the wealthy. If you need to earn a living, it's logical you step on the treadmill and stay on for the full ride. Yet I must have put on a good enough act to convince the man. He hired me to start the next day, a Friday, at the handsome salary of $375 a month, $125 more than the flag manufacturer. Sadly, that latter amount from the first month's wages had to be surrendered to the employment agency.

My worksite in the large freight office was at one of the desks set out in orderly rows of four abreast, all facing in one direction, like tanks on a battlefield. There must have been 25 rates clerks and half a dozen stenographers. At one end of the room the chief clerk and his assistant occupied desks on a raised dais. They looked out over the small army of clerks and stenos beavering at the complexities of the Interstate Commerce Commission's railroad rate structures. The scene, for me, evoked an office from the Victorian Era. But my reception in this workplace couldn't have been more cordial. The steno corps comprised three young men, one from Canada, and three older women. Although I didn't realize it then, American railroads in the mid-1950s were still a male dominated industry. I learned later that male stenos could advance to rate clerks, but not women. A barrier based on the whimsy of industry tradition. The women had been there many years typing basically the same short memos to freight agents located at different key stations along the railroad's thousands of miles of track.

Today's office custom of having a desk emblazoned with framed photos of family didn't exist in that department. Only work-related materials were allowed. At the railroad I thought I saw the work ethic that helped build America into an industrial colossus. Very little of the idle chitchat I encountered years later in government warrens occurred in that freight office.

Now employed, Eddie and I selected permanent individual rooms at a guest residence operated by two men, buddies from the Second World War, in a formerly large, four-story private home, now sad from years of neglect. The owners didn't seem inclined to have maintenance, let alone improvements, performed on the place. But the price was right. The rent included breakfast and dinner Monday through Saturday, and breakfast on Sunday.

The residence's occupants made up the proverbial motley crew; men and women of a wide range of ages holding varying jobs, and hailing from many different states. There were several students, including one from Korea. But apparently we all had one thing in common: we wanted to stay alive with the least cash outlay. Another economical feature was its adjacency to a stop to catch a bus to work, exactly 21 blocks from door to door. Occasionally I walked it in the morning; and always after work, except for rain days. San Francisco's cool, maritime climate let one do this without arriving like a wet, limp rag.

Within a short time I remembered my resolve to give church a try. Thus on at least two Sunday mornings I donned suit and tie and walked to the Gothic Episcopalian Grace Cathedral atop Nob Hill. James A. Pike who, three years later became the bishop of the Episcopal Diocese of California conducted one of the services I attended. Then, in the mid-1960s, he publicly expressed discontent with several of his faith's doctrines, resigned his seat and later left the church. In 1969 he went to Israel to investigate the origins of Christianity and, in mysterious circumstances, died in the Judean desert.

All these dramatic events were in the future when I stood in the imposing nave, listening to this sincere man, and struggling to understand his sermon. Perhaps feeling out of place, I cast glances at the congregation and saw people decked out in their Sunday best as if attending a business conference. Most had driven to the cathedral, parked, and walked only a short distance to their pews. After the service, many would return to their cars to drive to a restaurant for a hearty brunch. It struck me as too comfortable. I believed I needed something more demanding. I didn't know exactly what or whether I was really receptive, but the superficiality of these proceedings didn't do anything for me. Perhaps because I'd turned up in a city with Asian ties, at this time I read several books on Buddhism. That religion seemed more real and substantive. In Buddhism, as I understood it, its adherents must suffer to reach Nirvana. Full of doubt and confusion, I made one of my black/white judgments and did not pursue church attendance in San Francisco further. Later, while living in the Sun Belt, where churches stand on every corner, several phony evangelists were exposed. Their acts shut the door to religion for me forever.

When Eddie and I arrived, San Francisco's population stood at approximately three-quarters of a million. With its 47 square mile land area, it boasted a density of 16,500 p.s.m, more than double that of London. Working downtown, one could commute faster and far less expensively by public transportation than private car. As a result, both to save pennies and to exercise, I mostly walked. Even so, I felt I didn't get anything like the exercise I once obtained from playing soccer. Long before jogging became the de rigueur national pastime, I decided to take up evening jogs as during my military service days. Two city parks, Alta Plaza and Lafayette, both only two blocks square, were located about a five-minute walk from our guesthouse residence. After the evening meal, I'd wait a couple of hours reading in my room until about 9 p.m., before stepping out into the darkened streets to run around the perimeter of one of these public areas.

Both parks were near the top of one of the city's many hills. They were often enveloped in nighttime sea mist, especially in the summer months, drifting inland from the Pacific Ocean. Clouds also sometimes masked the moon, but when they broke, it shone through the wispy fog like a ghostly face. The quiet streets and swirling vapors made it for me an eerie atmosphere.

What I might have stumbled across in my attempt to get exercise in these two small natural islands, however, were meeting grounds for the city's male homosexual population. In 1955 this lifestyle was still in the closet and I had no idea San Francisco was a significant venue for it. Through the misty dimness, I'd sometimes see shadowy lone male figures standing quietly off the pathways. Once I think I saw two men kissing in an embrace behind some bushes. As I circled the park, it seemed to me a few of these night apparitions moved a little closer to check out this small jogger. Thankfully, no one ever spoke to, or propositioned, me but I was concerned enough to maintain a faster than normal pace. Apparently, a few city bars then existed at which homosexuals congregated, but as far as I know there were none of the highly publicized bathhouses that opened later and which the city eventually closed for health reasons. Certainly neither Castro nor Polk Streets were such established gay community strongholds as today.

The San Francisco peninsula, about 50 miles long and averaging 35 miles wide, in 1955 still boasted numerous highly fecund fruit orchards. I doubt a single one remains today. With California's population growth, the price for land for housing brought far more than fruit growing. We learned a little cash could be earned for a day's fruit picking at such orchards. For this reason, and for a different experience, one Saturday morning we rose early enough to arrive by 5 a.m. at the Agriculture Department at the state office complex near City Hall. At that pre-dawn hour, only this office splashed light on to the sidewalk through its front windows. When we entered we were nonplussed to see our day's workmates. About 40 odiferous derelicts lay or sat on the floor or lolled on the few available chairs. Their hair flowed down generously from beneath battered baseball caps or wool ski hats to reach hunched shoulders. It looked as matted and mangy as a Dartmoor wild pony's mane. The wardrobe of this canaille was wondrously unorthodox and decidedly unfashionable. Torn, filthy, ill-fitting jackets or parkas, long discarded by original owners, seemed in vogue for this outing. Mismatched trousers, afflicted by even grosser stages of decrepitude, stayed up only by a piece of string. Their footwear complemented their day's ensemble.

In the current politically correct atmosphere, I guess they'd be characterized as "homeless." I suspected many of them waited at the front door, not really for work, but to get inside as soon as the office opened as San Francisco streets can be cold at night. We signed a form to comply with state agriculture regulations and were shunted aboard a commandeered school bus when it arrived outside about 5:30 a.m. The rag-tag army of sorrowful humans clambered listlessly up the two steps to shuffle down the vehicle's aisle like prisoners in ankle chains. When selecting a seat, they glanced suspiciously at each other with red, rheumy eyes. Around 6 a.m. the driver climbed up front and our trip started, still under the cover of darkness.

The rules to which we'd agreed by signing the form forbade drinking alcohol on the bus or worksite. It permitted smoking and most did. The bus hadn't rolled more than a few miles when I saw half-pint bottles of whisky unsheathed from inside pockets and stuffed into mouths camouflaged by unkempt facial hair. Cowboy gulps, rather than society sips, were the rule. Soon cured ham could have been smoked in the bus' acrid atmosphere.

The drive to the orchard, located I believe near San Jose, capital of today's Silicon Valley, took the better part of two hours. This included a stop at a roadside gas station shoppette to eat breakfast and buy lunch items. Virtually everyone got coffee. Only a few ate a pastry or bought something for lunch. The majority ignored food as if on diets, but most spent money on half-pints of booze or small bottles of cheap wine. Cigarettes and chewing tobacco were also popular items.

By 8 a.m. we arrived at an apricot orchard. We debarked to follow on foot a foreman's truck to a nearby grove. Here he distributed wooden boxes with canvas shoulder straps from the back of the truck. Each worker received a pair of slim, lightweight, eight-foot ladders from a trailer already on site. We were warned not to damage the smaller branches when picking the apricots. Finally, the foreman reminded us the more we picked, the more we earned. However, with a filled box rate of 15 cents, and the boxes quite large, the odds favored the house.

By 10 a.m. the work and temperature took its toll on one of the hoboes. He began laboring painfully for breath, made even more difficult by frequent coughing convulsions. His hands trembled to the point where he almost couldn't hold an apricot once he'd detached it from a bough. The foreman, stationed at the truck to pay the workers for each box filled, gave this pitiable creature the lighter task of distributing empty boxes as needed presumably for some fixed paltry sum payable at day's end. Each time I returned to the truck with a full box, I found the wretch engaged in sycophantic efforts to retain the foreman's good will. No doubt the man feared being told his labor wasn't needed and he'd return to San Francisco without money for Saturday night booze.

At the lunch break we sat in small groups under trees to escape the hot sun. Eddie and I chose to sit by two men who didn't appear quite so wild or fearsome. Our talk was sporadic and perfunctory. Shortly, however, we learned that the taller one had been a medical doctor, license now revoked. The other, originally from Switzerland and still carrying the distinct accent of French speakers, had a banking background. Both fell victim of their bibulous excesses. I wondered the obvious question of why educated men could so lose their way. I didn't understand then the hellishly addictive power of demon rum. Nor how some poor souls, because of genetic chemical precursors, are goners with their very first drink.

The workday ended at 4 p.m. We walked back with our boxes and ladders to deposit them on the trucks. Most of the men hadn't bothered to start another box when quitting time approached. But others combined their less than full box loads to split the 15 cents between them. It seemed their suspicion had been overcome and a bond formed during the long, hot, dusty day. Once the bus rolled out of the orchard, a palpable, if unspoken, sense of relief swept through it. Whoever still had a drink soon swigged, shared with others, and finished it off.

As we trundled along the Bayshore Freeway towards the city, a younger-looking Hispanic occupying a seat a few rows behind us passed out, slid to the floor, and wound up in the aisle on his back. He appeared to be unconscious, but his body trembled violently, he emitted low moans, and his face shone with sweat. Several men called for the ex-doctor who left his front seat to attend the victim. As he went by, I thought I saw a look of confident compassion on his face as he possibly enjoyed the sensation of again being needed professionally. The good Samaritan said he believed the prone patient was a victim of delirium tremens. He asked for coats and when volunteered he folded one and placed under the man's head, put several over him, and said the victim would come around after a sleep. My first exposure to someone suffering the affects of prolonged, excessive alcohol consumption.

But by now I had a problem of my own. During the first couple of hours on the job, for every half dozen apricots going into the box, one went into me. In those days I knew nothing of the miracles of fiber. One would think the toddler who greedily ate a box of Ex-Lax, believing, or hoping, it was chocolate, would know better. I was about to discover apricots work just as effectively. Perhaps more so. My need grew more insistent with each passing mile. The DT's victim awoke enough to be helped back to his seat, his immediate choice of medicine: a few slugs of cheap wine. But my condition only worsened. When we reached the state office complex, I still clung to my dignity. I assumed the agriculture office would be open. It wasn't. There were several cafes near by that catered to state government employees. But this was Saturday, approaching 7 p.m. Government doesn't work Saturdays. None of their eateries were open. There were no gas stations in the immediate vicinity. And, of course, as in New York City, sophisticated San Francisco didn't have public toilets. I sprinted down a nearby alley. Along the way I found a herd of trashcans. I pulled them into a circle, like pioneers positioned their Conestoga wagons at night, and squatted in the middle, not a second too soon. And I offer sincerest apologies to the city's municipal street cleaners.

We arrived back at our rooms about 8 p.m. I had picked a total of 19 boxes of apricots as my contribution towards the annual multi-billion dollar agriculture production of California. My share of these impressive billions came to $2.85.

CHAPTER 26

John Barry, one of several elderly residents at our frayed guesthouse, unknowingly served to alarm me about our grandiose around-the-world plans. I'd learned Mr. Barry came from England as a young man and spent years in Canada's Yukon and Northwest Territories. I wanted to know more of his fascinating life. However, he never came to the dining room when most of the residents collected there. If ever he did appear, he chose a table in a corner to sit alone, apparently happy in his own company. He had an offset arrangement whereby he kept tidy the small gardens, front and back, in part payment for a portion of his rent. When I left in the morning for work, he'd sometimes already be pottering among the plants. We exchanged pleasantries, but nothing more. Even after all these years in North America, a baseball cap and T-shirt were not for Englishman Barry. He gardened in an old but neat suit, shirt and tie, and a battered, stained fedora.

One Saturday morning I came down for breakfast almost at the cut-off time. The only diner remaining, Mr. Barry sat alone finishing a cup of coffee. Although I knew better, I asked permission to join him. He looked up with an air of mild affront but slowly nodded his affirmation. As soon as I occupied the chair, I launched into a selfish interrogation.

"Mr. Barry, I've heard you were in the Yukon and the Northwest Territories as a young man. How long were you up there, and what did you do? Were you looking for gold?"

He had kept his head down and remained silent for an uncomfortable length of time. Then he slowly raised it to fix me with his tired, sad, rheumy eyes.

"Please excuse me, but I don't like talking about those long-ago days."

This withdrawn, formal man looked down again, and I felt embarrassed, a little hurt, and a lot confused. How could he not want to talk about his days of high adventure? Only years later did I learn something about human depression and a frequent accompanying symptom, regret. Possibly he suffered from that condition. Ruminating about his young life, which he may well have viewed as misspent, might have caused great anguish. Had I been more astute, I would have realized he could hardly regard himself as successful when, at an advanced age, he lived in a low-end, paint-peeling guesthouse, and paid some of his keep by casual labor. While I saw his adventurous life as something heroic, he might have felt himself a failure. I thought a lot about Mr. Barry and came to be vaguely concerned I'd end up in a similar state. Eddie and I had committed ourselves on a handshake for the next three years or so to live and work in Australia, South Africa, and, at least for me, Paris.

My motivation derived from the desire to follow an adventurer's life that would lead, I unclearly and uncertainly believed, to the writer's life. Yet here in California, I was again a member of a large, conservative organization, doing work that had no appeal. But all my office acquaintances were building careers for the long haul. I was a transient interested only saving money enough to fund our next global relocation. Being in this conflicted position was tolerable during daylight hours; if I woke at night, such thoughts didn't let me return to sleep. While I tried to resist this drumbeat of worry about the future, in truth I began to ponder this dichotomy more and more. On a few days black clouds settled to envelope me for hours. My colon seemed to be warning me I couldn't take the life of a rootless roamer. I felt under pressure to do something concrete to convince myself that my ill-defined aspirations to be a writer were not beyond the pale. I decided to write an article for our hometown newspaper about our travel experiences so far and future around-the-world plans. When word came from Roy that *The Stratford Express*, in East London, had sent a reporter to our house to verify my claims, it was highly elating. I spent a few weeks in tense anticipation waiting to see if they would use my piece.

The weekly published my article, without changes, together with a picture of Eddie and me taken with the eye-appealing Golden Gate Bridge as backdrop. Just to make the event sweeter, it gave me a by-line in a neat little printer's standout box with brief biographical details. Heady stuff indeed for this confused 23-year-old. Conceit helped me believe this "break into publishing" held hope that a writing life was, indeed, possible. Had I been even a little smarter, I'd have realized the newspaper got by far the best of the deal. It received an article of interest from a far-off, famous city to brighten its pages of mundane coverage of the gray, grimy life of an East End neighborhood. It didn't pay me a penny. .

Now emboldened by my break into the holy circle of published writers, I ached to expand my life and report my experiences on the printed page. But about what? I had become fascinated by the down-and-outers who roam America's back byways to congregate in such infamous enclaves as New York's Bowery and Chicago's Madison Street. Both of these I'd glimpsed on our visits to these cities. During our apricot-picking escapade, the most interesting aspect of the day for me was the exposure to this culture of alcoholic derelicts. My curiosity represented an effort to grasp the "why" of people falling so far in society. To be again at close quarters with this sub group, I spent a Saturday evening alone in San Francisco's Skid Row, a leftover remnant of the city's hectic, free-spending days as a major west coast shipping point for WWII in the Pacific. In the mid-fifties, the city's Skid Row mainly encompassed the streets south of Mission to Townsend, and west from Embarcadero to 5th. Here, run-down bars and cheap rooming houses rotted as inexorably as their besotted clientele.

Donning my fruit-picker clothes and shoes, and leaving untouched a two-day growth of beard, I set out with trepidation to pass inconspicuously in this tough world of deadly serious drinkers. It was already dark as I started on my surveillance walking east from 5th along Townsend Street. Soon I passed solitary, shuffling figures of former men, with their threadbare, disheveled clothing and haggard, blotchy faces, their lives unconditionally surrendered to alcohol. They were moving between their shabby accommodations and cheap bars, or the reverse, as fixed to this circuit as birds migrating between summer and winter-feeding grounds. Mostly they passed seemingly unaware of my presence, their faces displaying benumbed, twilight expressions. Every now and again, when through the stupor one of them sensed my observation, he glowered back a bitter reproachfulness as if to tell me I had no permission to try to see into his withered soul. But I missed the best chance of seeing into their world because I didn't have the courage to engage any in conversation.

When I reached the Embarcadero, hugging the San Francisco Bay shoreline, I turned north and walked along its inland side the six blocks to Mission Street. Along here the bars were both more numerous and more grungy. In one doorway of a closed pawnshop a man lay, breathing sonorously through open mouth. I edged closer to inspect. A pale yellow streetlight let me see the head of this sorry creature swam in a pool of fresh vomit. His jaw, neck and matted hair were speckled. The stench, overwhelming. Three empty Gallo wine bottles stood like conquerors silently mocking his downfall. The scene shocked and revolted me. I wondered if this man had a wife somewhere, or perhaps his mother still lived, passing lonely days, wondering about this long-departed man. They could be thinking he made his fame and fortune and was too busy to communicate. Would it be better if they never learned the truth? Through the midst of the swirling fog hugging the bay's shore came the muffled moan of a fog siren. It jolted me. I moved on.

That evening I made a rectangle and wound up back on Fifth Street at its intersection with Townsend. There I hesitated before a bar watching the smoky interior through open doors. I debated with myself how far it was necessary to go to write authentically about the stark realism of this world of abandoned hope. Although reluctant, even scared, to drink alone in this hangout for the lost, I felt the would-be writer must subject himself fully to such rawness. As I dithered, a taxicab slid to a halt and discharged its human cargo, a foursome out on a night's spree. The women in gaudy, inexpensive-looking dress, with heavily made-up faces, resembled children at Halloween. They stood talking together in raucous tones, while their men joked with the driver after paying the fare. The women were soon exhausted of their store of conversational tidbits, and one then turned impatiently to their escorts:

"For chrissakes, let's get in this place and have some drinks. We didn't come to no corner bible meeting."

They swayed inside. But I couldn't. I didn't have the nerve. Skid Row was too stark for my exaggerated sensitivity. I thought of a recent encounter when I wandered into this grim area during a lunch break. On one of its forlorn side streets I passed a less decrepit wino leaning against a wall. I noticed that he watched me closely as if assessing my potential as his mugging victim, and then glanced in both directions to check if the coast was clear. Fortunately, a man had just turned into the street, and I suspected this happenstance might have stopped me becoming a victim for that day. Literary career or no literary career, I balked. Not a good omen for a would-be writer trying to absorb something of life.

If Toronto had been suburbanly quiet, San Francisco jumped. After a couple of excursions to the North Beach bohemian district with its tourist strip clubs and bars, we settled into routines more normal for us. The city's nightlife had no lasting appeal. Eddie soon started a part-time job at a Union Square men's clothing store on Saturdays to supplement his income. The salary I received as a railroad stenographer was healthy. I preferred to spend my free time studying or reading and now fed my fiction passion with American top-flighters. I started reading the works of Caldwell, Crane, Dreiser, Wolfe, Hemingway, London, Steinbeck, and Twain. As with British literature, there were so many writers who deserved one's attention, again I put myself under some pressure trying to absorb as many as possible. Intermixed with all of what I believed worthwhile works, I also indulged my long-standing liking for good adventure/travel books.

I enrolled in a literature appreciation class and a writer's workshop at the Galileo Senior High School night classes. An Englishman, supposedly a graduate of Oxford University, who now worked for a publishing house, taught the workshop. He'd arrived on America's west coast after time spent in Sri Lanka and Australia. His widely-traveled background fired my by now travel-mad imagination. It never dawned on me that if any good as a writer, he wouldn't be a part-time high school teacher.

For exercise I supplemented my occasional jogs with a good measure of walking. San Francisco's temperate climate made it enjoyable, and trudging up some of its 40 hills is rewarded with great views. One walk I did regularly was to the main public library, some 23 blocks from the guesthouse. With Eddie now working, I began to spend Saturdays there. When I started to haunt the place, I discovered a small contingent of the habitual vagrants who fascinated me also passed a goodly part of their day in the facility. These men usually picked a magazine or book for a prop. They sat down at one of the long wooden tables, braced their heads on an arm, unkempt hair falling across their faces, and went to sleep. Some soon snored. I could tolerate their noise, but found other behavior more disturbing. When their mouths fell open, saliva dribbled over their chins, puddling on the table as little mounds of spittle. Then I opted to move.

I spent my days there working on exercises assigned at the writer's workshop, studying material set in the literature appreciation class, and reading short stories. I became acquainted with such American short story masters as O. Henry, Harte, Cather, Tarkington, and Aiken. I feasted on their creative telling of pulsating life in the United States. In fact, reading now occupied a great amount of my free time. And, without family or any friends, except Eddie, I really had a good many hours to indulge myself in what had probably passed from passion to obsession. If a day or two passed without spending time with a book, I sensed almost a physical hunger for it. The role of books for me at the time is, I believe, accurately captured in the lines of poet Emily Dickinson:

There is no frigate like a book
To take us lands away,
Nor any coursers like a page
Of prancing poetry (1).

A few years into the future, I'd come to believe that so much of what I read was simply escapism. Without a balanced education in other subjects, in my innocence I'd stumbled into the phantasmagoric world of novels and opium described by Matthew Arnold, the English Victorian poet and literary critic, in his work "Literature and Dogma." My choice of reading provided profound pleasure, but didn't help to keep an impressionable person's feet firmly on the ground.

About this time it dawned on me I'd become more interested in life's misfits than those with whom I swam in my segment of American society. This inconsistency bothered me, but the exterior similarities of the male freight rate clerks at the Santa Fe Railroad office struck me jarringly. Although they were from various parts of the geographically diverse United States, speaking with a variety of dialects, a majority of them presented a noticeably standardized appearance. There must have been unwritten but firm rules to follow in attaining the apparent mandatory corporate image. It prescribed pricey, conservatively colored, single-breasted suits. Creased pant cuffs needed to meet with a slight break at sturdy, well-buffed brogues. White shirts, their full-length sleeves joined by large ornamental cuff links, were adorned with narrow ties clamped in place by a decorative clip. For sorties into the outside world, banded fedoras and belt-less raincoats completed their armor. This standardized appearance of these hard-working rate clerks generated the thought they were highly efficient end products from the J. Edgar Hoover's people plant that cloned G-men. Their dress code homogeneity, and more particularly a certain mental sameness, did not appeal to my rather individualistic outlook of that time. I tended to consider most of the rate-clerks uninteresting and narrow. My hasty judgment failed to do them justice

Almost in a perverse way, I chose to become friendly with the office night janitor. Not the best end of the hierarchy with which to consort in the button-down corporate milieu. However, Sidney Joiner, a pipe-smoking, bull-chested, ruddy-faced, 55-year-old, with a full head of healthy black hair only just surrendering to streaks of gray, had lead a unique, colorful life. I was drawn to this man as to no other in the office. He'd be starting his 5-12 p.m. shift just when I finished for the day. We encountered each other sometimes in the hallways. His outgoing personality soon had us stopping to exchange greetings. Then, when he disclosed his birthplace as Winchester, England, and later that he had a interest in writing, our chats became more intense. I took him to dinner one weekend and encouraged him to tell me his intriguing life story.

Leaving school at age 13, he signed on as a drummer boy with the British Army Royal Fusiliers (the regimental name deriving from when muskets first became part of a foot-soldier's weaponry.) This boy saw action in the Great War in France. Following the Armistice, his unit moved to Ireland where civil unrest spread. Ordered to be a member of a firing squad, he refused. A military tribunal had him cashiered. After six years in the army he returned to London where he found work as a low-grade civil servant at Somerset House, former site of the National Registry of Births and Deaths, now at Kew. The army, however, had roiled his spirit and given him a taste for life overseas. Unable to resist his restlessness, he emigrated to Australia in the early 1920s. He roamed that country's vast hinterland, doing different jobs at remote sheep farms. The second half of the 1920s, however, found him back in London after working his passage on a freighter. With unemployment high, he spent months without wages. For a period he worked nights in a Hammersmith bakery at six shillings a shift, and lived in Rowton House, charity quarters for the indigent. There he became acquainted with the then-struggling writer George Orwell. The writer's meager living at that time of his life formed part of the basis for his gripping tale *Down and Out in London and Paris.*

Eventually, Sidney Joiner worked his passage to Canada and

shortly entered the United States. He arrived in the depths of the Great Depression, and again couldn't find work. He joined native hoboes riding the rails from coast to coast. His harrowing stories of these days were, for me, spellbinding. At the outbreak of WWII, Sid shipped out as a supply man on American freighters. He made several grueling winter voyages from east coast ports to Murmansk, Russia's Arctic Ocean year-round port on the far-northern Kola Peninsula, during which conditions were brutal. Although the pay for U.S. merchant sailors on this voyage topped any other, he eventually moved to the west coast and shipped out of San Francisco into the Pacific Ocean.

Sid told the story that on one voyage to Papua, New Guinea, he encountered the captain of a British freighter. Over a few drinks in a bar, their British reserve melted. At some stage of the congenial evening, they started comparing what they earned. Sid made more money as a supply man than the British captain of a medium-sized freighter. Although he'd salted away a nest egg by war's end, during a long period of poor health immediately after, he watched it soon dwindle. He'd been working as a night janitor for about five years when we met. He liked the low pressure, easy pace of his current calling, which paid him enough to live modestly in a small downtown apartment. Sid existed without an automobile. It seemed his only indulgence was the occasional services of a lady of pleasure, whose rates he reported to be more modest during daylight hours.

Although he'd made a few perfunctory attempts to publish segments of his extraordinary life, he hadn't met with any success. He felt he lacked the polish to turn his adventures into sellable articles. It scared me to think that living a life beyond the fringe did not necessarily a writer make. My plans for the next few years could result in me joining Sid in the ranks of night janitors. In reality, for all my desire to be a writer, all I had to show were two puny items published, neither of which had brought in a penny. That made me nervous.

CHAPTER 27

Our reasonably priced, conveniently located, guesthouse stood atop the hill where Buchanan and Pacific Avenues intersected. The four-story building, plus a basement, had once been the private residence of a wealthy San Franciscan family. It had a red-brick facade with two tall arched, capstone windows, and a similarly shaped entrance reached by a dozen steps leading from street level. The other three levels all boasted three rectangular windows, almost floor-to-ceiling in height, beneath decorative stone lintels. But its solid appearance was deceptive.

The slim house, squeezed between more substantial properties, measured about two-and-a-half times long as wide. Clapboard siding nailed to a wooden frame covered the other three sides. I don't know the date of its construction, but probably after the 1906 earthquake and fire, and before the city adopted robust building codes for anti-earth-movement protection.

An advantage to living on top of one of San Francisco's hills, at least in my westward-facing room, were the occasional dramatic sunsets served up. As the sun went down, its spreading rays turned the sky into boiling, orange-crimson cloudscapes. With structures to the west now starkly silhouetted, the scene took on a surreal, brooding aura, announcing the imminent arrival of the nightly low-hanging sea mist.

The next free excitement in my room occurred one evening when I sat reading in an old wicker chair. Shortly after eight the window suddenly rattled violently. The house shuddered and swayed about a foot out of true on both sides. This extreme movement, accentuated on the top floor, lasted about 30 seconds. The overhead hanging light, with its cheap, soiled shade, continued swinging for a minute or two after the house came to rest. Even the worn out bedspring joined in the melee with a creak. A solid reminder of this city's vulnerability for huge damage from earth movements. With our guesthouse already on the city's vulnerable buildings list, this vigorous shaking resulted in a visit by public works inspectors who declared the premises in need of a thorough engineering survey. All residents were alerted to the possibility of a move in our futures. For Eddie and I it would mean relocating just months before our planned departure for Australia. As events transpired, human nature rather than Mother Nature finally determined the fate of our cheap lodgings.

The owners' income from the reasonable weekly rates they charged would never make them wealthy like the building's original owner. At the same time, their business ethics were somewhat flexible. They weren't above purchasing discounted food beyond its shelf life. I recall several bouts of mild food poisoning at their establishment. To cut their operating expenses, they hired a town drunk to wash the dishes from the two scheduled daily meals and perform other menial tasks. Although paid a pittance, the derelict also gained use of a basement room next to the trash storage. The turnover in this position was brisk, but San Francisco offered a seemingly endless supply of these lost souls.

Early in 1956 the lamentable creature holding this job angered the operators. They fired him summarily. A few nights later, in a state of intoxication and revenge, he returned and gained entrance through an unlocked basement door. Probably muttering curses at his former employers for his perception of their injustice, this failed dishwasher piled newspapers against the exposed wooden frame of the house, and struck a match. The fire took rapid hold of the desiccated framing timbers. Fortunately for all residents, the elderly, taciturn English adventurer, John Barry, occupied a rear room on the first floor, where he sat next to an open window, his radio quietly playing. He fairly soon smelled smoke when it started billowing through the trash room open door and called the fire department. A single tender and its efficient crew soon arrived and brought the blaze under control. I believe a man who possibly saw his life as a failure might well have saved about a dozen other still-unfolding lives that evening. Yet the quickly-apprehended, dipsomaniac dishwasher, who spent only a few nights in the city jail, succeeded in having us all thrown on the street and ended the livelihood of the laid-back owners. Following the engineering inspection, the city condemned the building. Its variegated residents scattered to the winds. Some years later when I returned to San Francisco, the guesthouse had been demolished and a nearby hospital's parking lot occupied its space. Eddie and I found a facility on Bush Street, closer to downtown, offering about the same deal. It was a newer building, but far less atmospheric. We remained there until we departed the city by the Golden Gate.

When I received my selective service notice through the mail, I wrote advising the authorities I'd be unable to be part of America's military muscle. My time in their country was limited as we'd soon be moving on to Australia. Thanks, anyway, for their kind offer. I forgot to wish them well in their historic tussle with the Russian Bear.

By return post I received an imperious reply testily stating I was already several months overdue in registering with the Board: do it forthwith or face a fine of not more than $10,000 and/or five years imprisonment. Their heartless attitude seemed utterly disinterested in my development as a world citizen and, even worse, failed to comment on my planned launch of a writing career. Just in case they weren't kidding, however, I took myself promptly to the downtown address where this inconsiderate Board did its thing.

Right off, I had to write a statement explaining in detail my failure to comply with the law of the land. Whatever I wrote must have calmed them. This was just as well: I didn't have ten grand on me. Still they must have thought it best to test me right away in case I slipped north or south of national borders.

Stripped to our underpants, a few nervous young men, me among them, went through the physical examination. It blew my mind when one guy calmly declared he wasn't wearing underpants. These tough authorities let him go through the process in his street pants. In the richest country in the world, in its most avant-garde city, guys run around without underwear! What must go on in Podunk, Iowa?

Despite my lack of enthusiasm, I passed their test. They found out I'd been in the British Royal Air Force and seemed to conclude, a priori, I'd just love being in theirs. In nothing flat I was seated before two Air Force recruiting officers who collectively opined my shorthand skills were just what the USAF needed. They assured me I'd hear from them promptly.

Dejection dogged my next few days, with meals eaten in gloom. Donning the military uniform of yet another nation seemed but a step away. It looked like our life plans were torpedoed. It also occurred to me being a raw recruit at age 18 is, in itself, disconcerting; being one at the advanced age of 24, in the barrack's life of a different military, would be intolerable. Then, somehow and somewhere, both of which I no longer recall, I learned immigrants from countries sending forces to Korea for the United Nations' "police action" of 1950-53, were exempt from U.S. military service unless Congress declared war. I fell into that category!

A copy of my military discharge certificate, obtained from the Air Ministry through the British Consulate in San Francisco, facilitated my escape. Once delivered to the eager Board, I received a little card saying I was now in category "F-4" and didn't have to serve in Uncle Sam's war machine. So my picayune RAF service of 1950-52, during which I never left England, saved my quaking butt, and Uncle Sam's welcoming draft notice never arrived.

Despite a few elated days after this brush with the law, I became more aware of depressive spells. Mornings arrived and I'd awake devoid of customary life force. Confusion and tension built as I wrestled with the thought of moving across the world's biggest ocean to live in Australia. I began to seriously suspect my nervous strength was not adequate for the wanderer's life. The attraction of the summer 1956 Olympic games in Melbourne began to wane. After all, at the first games following WWII held in London in 1948, I didn't attend even one event.

It seemed my self-confidence was ebbing, and I struggled with my emotions. I believe I kept my turmoil to myself for a few weeks, but finally told Eddie I'd lost interest in living down-under. My new, urgent goal was to return for a brief visit with family in London before moving to Paris. The time had arrived to make a line-in-the-sand attempt to become a writer. The French capital had been conducive to launching a few commendable literary careers. Why not my own? I'd admired Englishman George Orwell, a brilliant, socially poignant writer, who did a stint as a starving, fledgling writer in the French capital. I knew Orwell had survived the city of light by washing dishes at a fancy restaurant during the hours of darkness. My railroad job, however, had let me save nearly $2,000 and I hoped this would tie me over until adoring fans lifted me on their shoulders when my first masterpiece appeared. A much tried, patently autobiographical, tale of a rags-to-riches East London youth germinated in my imagination. Perhaps I could pull it off without the dish washing!

Then my fanciful writer's dream received a boost from recent news from England of a young man with a working-class background who had written, not a mere novel, but a scholarly work on philosophy. The critics generally lauded the book, although many of them expressed blustering dismay someone with such a background could produce a philosophical tome. This squawking all worked to make his book an overnight success. The saga of Colin Wilson, the neophyte at the center of London's literary teacup tempest in early 1956, really gripped me.

Born in 1931 to a factory worker in the industrial city of Leicester, he didn't read until age eight. But by ten he'd become an avid reader, guided by a book-loving mom. At 11, Wilson won a scholarship to a grammar school where he stayed until 16, showing an interest in chemistry. Following his formal education, Wilson held positions as a laboratory assistant and a clerk with the government department collecting income taxes. Conscription into the Royal Air Force came in 1949. Not finding service life congenial, he falsely declared himself to be homosexual; in those days a basis for discharge. The Air Ministry, not quite as courageous, officially attributed the dismissal to "health reasons."

Migrating to London's streets of jostling anonymity, the 19-year-old spent his days as a construction laborer, and later a hospital porter, while vastly broadening his intellect through reading the philosophers. The boredom of his menial jobs probably clashed violently with the activity of his searching mind. Something of Wilson's thinking can be gauged from this verse he penned:

I wander through each dirty street
Near where the dirty Thames does flow
And on each human face I meet
Marks of weakness, marks of woe.

He left England to live about two years in Paris and Strasbourg. When he returned to London, he undertook his boldest life decision: he would sleep rough on Hampstead Heath to save money while spending his days at the seven-million volume British Museum library writing a novel and a philosophical tome. *The Outsider*, Wilson's interpretation of man's alienation in the universe, was published in 1956, four years ahead of the novel.

I can still clearly remember the Saturday morning at the San Francisco public library when I read in *TIME* its review of *The Outsider*, with the fascinating details about Wilson's background. An English working-class boy had pulled it off! To climb out of the festering bog that then was the British working-class child's inheritance is a singular achievement, especially for a lone seeker. I walked back to the guesthouse that afternoon with a sprightlier step. In this dream state I resolved that the time was definitely now for me to etch my own literary mark.

CHAPTER 28

When I told Eddie I'd lost interest in moving to Australia, he at first opposed scrapping our plan. I, too, regretted giving up a visit to the nearly three-million square mile continent. As was our way, we debated, sometimes argued, back and forth. Finally, we came up with a new scheme that would still let us have one last great travel adventure before we ended this phase of our lives. We'd first make a month's trip to Brazil, especially Rio de Janeiro. Our interest in that country had been fired by a Stanford University professor's slide show and lecture we'd attended. When I priced such an excursion, however, it would wipe out my modest nest egg intended to let me abandon ordinary life for a left bank existence on the River Seine. Our dream had to be modified. We'd merely travel through Mexico and Central America to the Panama Canal from where we'd try to work our passage on a cargo ship back to Britain. Research soon determined this battle plan, too, presented numerous obstacles with visas, inoculations, and transportation. The airplane age hadn't yet dawned for us: we were wedded to buses, trains, and ships. Even these curtailed wanderings appeared likely to consume much of my savings. Once more I backed out.

We finally agreed to, and shook hands on, a plan to hitchhike across the USA to New York City where we'd embark for Britain. Our route would be south through California, down the west coast of Mexico to its capital city, returning along the Mexican east coast to reenter the US in Texas. As we moved in a big "V" across North America, we'd hit several highlight cities and sites along the way. To set this idea in concrete, we soon shipped our trunks and suitcases to New York City to be held for our later arrival.

Terminations were given at our jobs. Santa Fe's "old dry balls," whose decision it had been to hire me, said he'd never felt I would be permanent. One of the freight clerks, with whom I'd developed a modest friendship, presciently warned me that "we all like to dance, but eventually the piper has to be paid." No doubt I cockily dismissed his words as I had my father's when he gave me the "rolling stone gathers no moss" dirge. For me, the future was tomorrow. I didn't want to do an ordinary job for the next 45 years or join the contented cowherd.

On Saturday, 28 July 1956, a helpful friend from the Santa Fe files office picked us up at 6 a.m. and took us across the San Francisco-Oakland Bay bridge to the outskirts of Hayward whose 60,000 habitants at the time were not yet stirring. We were starting on Highway 99, then the main north-south corridor through California's San Joaquin Valley, years before Interstate #5. My friend dropped our backpacks and us on the southbound side of the road. During the drive we had cracked jokes about him coming to collect us in the evening at the same spot because we'd failed to get a single ride.

When he spun his Ford Fairlane around to head back to San Francisco, we watched his retreating vehicle until it disappeared into an undulation of the road. A thick quiet enveloped us in the thin, early morning light. We stood silently but critically surveying a road littered with human refuse. Volumes of discarded aluminum drink cans glinted like lights reflected in water. Years passed before adoption of a national anti-litter campaign. As we waited in the quiet, my thoughts returned to our immediate situation and feelings of alarm surged. We'd launched irrevocably on our approximate 6,000-mile expedition. Despite what others said, I refused to call it a vacation.

Long waits became the discouraging pattern that day. Several hours passed before a hardscrabble farmer and his wife, chugging slowly toward us in an early, dilapidated pick-up truck, halted to offer a ride for about 25 miles. An 18-month-old toddler sat between them in the cab, while the woman held a baby in her arms. The truck's open bed already swarmed with six bare-foot children, the oldest probably ten years. We scrambled over the tailgate and squatted down on the bed to join the kids. I thought it wasn't only the land that was fecund in California.

One of the girls, aged about six, wore a pass-me-down, torn, yellow cotton dress with a petticoat now closer to battleship gray than white. While her brothers and sisters kept up a raucous banter back and forth, this child intently sang the opening words to the Sunday school hymn "Yes, Jesus loves me, the bible tells me so." She sang this line over and over, indifferent to the scenery, 18-wheeler diesel trucks thundering by, and the two funny-talking strangers now on board. Her small face registered the earnestness of a cathedral choir lead caroler. .

We arrived in Fresno about 8:30 p.m., after 14 hours on the road in a hot July sun, a bare 175 miles between our starting point and us. An hourly rate of only 12.5 miles, it had taken half a dozen vehicles with kind drivers. It promised to be a long time to the east coast. Each night, when we bedded down at the cheapest motel available, before turning out the light, I kept a log of the day's events. I retained those notes during the intervening years and can thus accurately recount our escapades, none of which, in the final analysis, would make headlines.

Our second day on the road, a Sunday, brought extra traffic which provided a few more rides. We reached Bakersfield in about three hours and were dropped at the intersection with Highway 466, which headed east. After an hour's wait in near 100° F heat, a lone driver in an early 1950s two-door Plymouth slowed and pulled over. Luggage in the rear reached to the roof. This Air Force captain was transferring from McClellan base, outside Sacramento, to Dyess, a base near Abilene, in north-central Texas. Forcing a holdall occupying the passenger front bucket seat onto the hillock of his chattels, he most kindly let us squeeze on to the free seat with our packs on our knees. I assumed he must be lonely to make this much effort.

The captain told us almost immediately he offered the ride only because we were carrying backpacks and didn't look like "professional drifters." This quickly broke the ice and we conversed animatedly for much of the next 200 miles. He drove across the Mojave Desert along heat-shimmering tarmac looking like a wide paintbrush stroke of black on a giant tan canvass. Passing through this mineral-rich wasteland we discussed with this sharp American his country's emergence as leader of the free world. While the divorced officer exuded a great confidence, it emerged he wasn't convinced of the wisdom of America undertaking this role. For himself, he said laconically, all he now wanted from life was "a library, an armchair, and a bottle of scotch." When we broached the subject of travel, Eddie's and my most passionate pastime, he again offered a jolting, fresh perspective: "Singapore looks just like Kansas City."

My mind instantly rejected his second contention. But I bit my tongue because I didn't want to be invited to walk. If he was correct, Eddie and I were jackasses. We had just uprooted ourselves again to really see and experience some new parts of the globe by the not-so-easy travel method of hitchhiking. For me travel equated to education. Years later the Air Force pilot came into my thoughts when I read the words of Isaac Beshevis Singer, the Polish-born Yiddish writer, who opined "... one place is pretty much like another; if they are on the face of the Earth, they are all the same." A further crack developed in my granite conviction on the merits of travel when I learned the Internal Revenue Service does not allow travel as a form of education. Did the flyer, the writer, and the IRS, know something I didn't? When it came time to part ways at Barstow, we treated the captain to a sandwich and a beer believing this was the first hitch that approximated what we'd hoped for. And I trust that somewhere the captain's still reading in an armchair and enjoying a scotch or two!

We walked the short distance through Barstow to reach the highway to Las Vegas. I didn't record its number, but believe it must have followed today's Interstate #15. Once in place, we took up our now well-practiced stance of arm extended and thumb vertical. Nothing happened in the next 90 minutes. That late afternoon tested us with a temperature of 107°F. We decided that the trickle of traffic now winding across the eastern segment of America's largest desert was unlikely to provide our onward transportation, and walked back to the town center to the Greyhound Bus Terminal. We hated to surrender, but the heat became almost debilitating. Fortunately, in those days, the bus system offered frequent departures and greater area coverage. Despite the cost, we luxuriated in the comfortable seats and air-conditioned clime of the fast, silvery aluminum bus with its uniformed driver.

We glided smoothly the approximate 160 miles to Las Vegas across the sagebrush-dotted desert with interspersed sprinklings of the gnarled Joshua trees, one of the few kinds that survive such limited annual rainfall. Aside from the roadway itself, for many miles the only signs of human intrusion were abandoned mineral excavations on nearby hillsides. Suddenly, instead of driving through what I saw as a brittle landscape, we bowled down the wide main boulevard of boomtown Las Vegas. It had its beginnings only in the 1930s with the 3,500 lonely men working on the nearby Hoover Dam to collect the waters of the Colorado River. Now Lake Mead, with its 10-trillion-gallon capacity, is one of the largest man-made lakes on earth.

In 1956 Las Vegas already prided itself as America's leading gambling town. But it was a small town carnival compared with the stupendous conglomeration of casinos/hotels/show venues of today. We spent only one night there. The outrageous $10 cost for a motel room might have influenced my feelings toward the entertainment capital of the USA. The next morning we elected, with the disdain and certainty of English superiority, to depart the glitz in favor of what we considered the highlight of our trip through the southwest — Arizona's Grand Canyon.

After sleeping later than usual, we walked through Las Vegas to reach the road to Boulder City, site of the Hoover Dam, planning to devote half a day seeing the immense facility. That plan was forgotten when, after waiting again for well over an hour, we were offered the chance of a ride that put us back on our original schedule. A peppy salesman in a new 1956 Ford, apparently imbued with his own and my share of life confidence, stopped. He valued an audience and needed to reach St. Louis, Missouri, about the middle of the country, in two days. Both of these desires accorded with ours. His way through Arizona would be along the famous route #66 passing close to the south entrance of the Grand Canyon.

As it transpired, the road he followed in a southeasterly direction passed across the top of the quarter-moon-shaped Hoover dam at a height of 725 feet above the water release level. Thus we enjoyed a brief external view of this engineering masterpiece set in the earth-red, craggy rock faces of Black Canyon. Years passed before I saw the dam's gigantic interior. Our salesman-in-a-hurry, while regaling us of his joy at having been born an American, pushed his shiny, two-toned automobile hard. On straight stretches on the flats of western Arizona, at times he hit 110 mph, in a vehicle without seat belts. Had he experienced a tire blowout, I thought, all three of us would be hitching rides to the next life. Fortunately, Detroit's policy of planned obsolescence built into its products was still about 15 years in the future. The tires didn't blow and the car didn't flip or fall apart. Later the ponderosa pine-covered mountains of the central part of the state slowed his progress and I had no problem with that.

In the early evening, when he dropped us at the small town of Williams, we had only about 60 miles to reach our destination on an almost straight road that ran north to the Grand Canyon National Park. By now, however, darkness had arrived, and hitching, difficult in daylight, was a lost cause at night. Williams, and its motels, reflected their adjacency to one of America's most popular national parks. We inquired at several lodgings, but soon decided our splurging in Las Vegas couldn't continue. One irritated motel owner, when we declared his $8 charge exorbitant, told us disdainfully that down-and-outers could find accommodation at the town's one-cell police station/jail if unoccupied. We high-tailed it to the quarry-stone facility to beat out competitors for the freebie. A uniformed officer, sprawled at his duty desk, didn't seem at all surprised when we asked to spend the night in his company. The cell occupied one end of the square building with a security wall of floor-to-ceiling 2" diameter steel bars. Anyone apprehended who needed detaining overnight, he warned, would have priority; we'd have to clear off, no matter the hour. He swung open the cell gate, ushered us through, and locked it behind us

The cell's gray, grungy decor discouraged any thought of personal hygiene. We quickly used the steel commode in a corner, stowed our packs on a bare shelf, and stretched out fully clothed on the wooden bunks. Because the night temperature cooled at the town's 6,770-foot elevation, I had little choice about pulling the mangy blanket over me, trying to keep it away from the face. Eventually my concerns about bed lice receded, and blessed sleep came. Fortunately Williams' 1,500 citizens all behaved lawfully, and we stayed in their jail until 6:30 next morning.

After washing and shaving at a nearby service station, over breakfast we decided on a new strategy for the remaining 60 miles to Grand Canyon. We'd noticed drivers sometimes looked as if they'd stop for a lone hitchhiker, but didn't have space for two. So when we reached the road to the national park, I withdrew behind bushes and Eddie thumbed it alone. Sure enough, Eddie soon disappeared up the road with a young couple driving a late 1940s car with California plates. I entered from the wings and, although my ride took much longer to materialize, we met as planned at the park's south rim entrance just before noon. We rented a park cabin for two nights and spent much of the afternoon sleeping and repairing the damage of the road by washing clothes and ourselves. That evening we walked to a rim observation point to see the sunset when light dramatically colors the canyon's jagged buttes formed over eons by erosion. The effects of the Colorado River, wind, rain, sun, snow and frost have created this spectacle of nature that focuses the mind on the transitoriness of human life and leaves a powerful sense of humility.

Next day we dumbly decided the rim-to-river trip by mule cost too much. Tackling the mile-deep switchback trail journey on foot, said to take around four hours, with the return climb consuming another six, seemed too much. Just as dumb. We trekked to the east under a cloudless sky and warm sun to an observation point free of people for the first 30 minutes. The silence enthralled. We marveled at the canyon view from this promontory. Its width varies from 600 feet to 18 miles. Many buttes are composed of reddish Supai sandstone that the sun inflames while casting deep shadows. That morning half a dozen buzzards circled effortlessly on the upward air stream rising from the canyon's floor. Eventually a group of tourists arrived and shattered my reverie. I listened to their homely comments like "gees, honey, it's a long ways down there." In my superior mind set, with my excessive judgmentalism at full bore, I sneered at their shallow appreciation and fully believed they weren't drawing anything like my degree of celestial inspiration from our surroundings. Oh, the snobbery of some English!

It now seems inexplicable that we didn't give ourselves at least one more night to provide a second long day to perform the hike to and from the bottom. After all, the Grand Canyon, one of the world's natural wonders, was our primary stop in the southwest. It had taken much effort to reach and we failed to do it, and ourselves, justice. I don't believe the missed opportunity stemmed from a concern we weren't up to its physical demands, but from a silly sense we weren't covering distances in the time we hoped..

Our experience as hitchhikers thus far proved enlightening. We gained the impression that, for the average American, the idea of such an undertaking is beyond comprehension. When they saw our knapsacks some thought we were in the army; a few in the southwest assumed us to be prospectors. As with the Air Force Captain, several more said if we'd been carrying a suitcase they'd never have stopped. In terms of efficient use of time, I sometimes felt we'd make almost as good progress if we flat out walked. Rides often took more than an hour, and a few over two, before materializing. When these extra long waits occurred, my spirit would sag and I questioned the sense of it all and a fear surged through me. If we'd thought it hot standing at roadside in southern California, we were now crossing the desert landscape of Arizona where temperatures of 105°F regularly prevailed. My office-bound, sedentary body was severely challenged.

When we resumed the trip from the Grand Canyon, we took a local bus to Flagstaff, former lumbering town set in the pine-covered San Francisco mountains, about 75 miles to the southeast. Once again, well over an hour passed before we, in desperation, accepted a short ride with a loquacious Carnation Milk traveling salesman whose destination was Camp Verde, in a southerly direction toward Phoenix. But en route he had half a dozen off-the-track client calls. My watch showed 3:30 p.m. when the salesman dropped us, only about fifty miles beyond where we'd been at eight o'clock in the morning. But then the dice rolled favorably and we secured a hitch in the back of a farmer's pick-up truck that was headed in a hurry straight to the northern suburbs of a rapidly expanding Phoenix. Wind-blown and grubby, we reached the outskirts of Arizona's capital, which sits on the Salt River in a valley ringed by low mountains. Again, deciding our linear progress more important than sightseeing, we took a local bus through the city to the southern suburb of Mesa so we could hit the road next day early for the Mexican border some 175 miles away. There we'd have completed 1,400 miles of our estimated 6,000-mile trip.

In the morning we secured two quick, early rides, each of short duration. A sheriff on routine patrol stopped and took us a few miles to his turn-around point at the Maricopa County limits. We decided he did it just to get us out of his jurisdictional territory. If a passing vehicle had hit us, he'd have to do paperwork on two unknown wanderers. This theory was proven when several more police officers offered rides.

Of all the rides so far, the next was the most interesting, if the most zany. We'd learned we were beggars, and thumbed almost everything going in our direction. Without realizing who sat behind the wheel, we thumbed an ancient jalopy puttering wearily along. A little old lady dressed in the fashions of a former era, pulled her 1938 Buick off the road to offer us a lift. This woman was the first and only female to give us a ride. That should have alerted us we were in for an eccentric hour, at speeds never surpassing 25 mph.

Probably her cotton, floral-print dress had, in distant times, been a pretty summer creation. Elbow-length gloves, once white, were now more yellow. Her legs were encased in light gray stockings and her feet in white, buckled shoes. I thought of the Charleston dance craze when I looked at her. To set off her quaint wardrobe, she had chosen a wide-brimmed white hat that once might have graced the Royal Box at Ascot, but now looked part of the ensemble of a bag-lady with airs. In the short distance she drove us, she managed to tell her life history in considerable detail. According to her tale, she'd been born to a comfortably off, solidly middle-class family in Pembroke, Ontario. An upbringing of genteel finesse led through debutancy to a society wedding. But her important, pillar-of-the-community husband departed this world at an early age. Many years ago she moved to Arizona on account of an anemic son who was now, in her own words, "married to some conniving whore." Undaunted, our dressy chauffeur had married again, but this husband, too, had gone to his maker.

She then revealed more of her fantasy world with a sub-plot of Royal duplicity and intended state-to-state repercussions. As she gripped the wooden steering wheel of her 18-year-old auto, she shot us repeated glances to see how we reacted. In tones of absolute conviction she claimed that Queen Elizabeth II — at whose coronation Eddie and I worked in Westminster Abbey just three years before — had "robbed" her of a Canadian castle, a property of the lady's uncle, to which she was the rightful heir. As a result, she thought seriously of returning to her native land to lead a movement to bring about the secession of Canada from the British Commonwealth. One of us must have been gauche enough to question the likelihood of this change to world order. With renewed vigor to her grip on the wheel, and nostrils flared, she declared herself to be "an educated woman who could talk to anyone." The last time I checked, Canada remained in the Commonwealth.

Hitch-hiking across USA (1956). On back roads in Arizona under a fierce sun.

CHAPTER 29

Having little interest in the grimy border town Nogales, early next morning we boarded a 2nd class bus to Guaymas on Cape Haro on the west coast, 250 miles south. We didn't count on hitchhiking in Mexico because of sparse private automobile ownership. There is, however, an elaborate public bus system that links the cities and everywhere else down to the smallest rural communities.

During this expedition we hoped to study differences between Mexico and her northern neighbor. Some were quick to reveal themselves. In Arizona we'd seen huge farm tractors, enclosed for operator air-conditioned comfort, pulling 20-foot wide plows with 10 or more furrowing blades and trailing colters to break up residual clumps of earth. Nimble crop-dusting planes skittered across vast tracts of freshly planted sorghum to aerially spray powerful pesticides in a matter of minutes. Now we were passing sombreroe'd farmers ploddingly following a single walking plow pulled by a mule or donkey team. At times the bus had to move over as we drove farther south to pass burros groaning under a load of farm products or kindling wood.

Many of the rural Mexicans lived in small square adobe huts or tin shacks, standing on a tiny cultivated plot enclosed by a low mud-brick or woven-branch wall. Inside, a few chickens scratched, a pig rooted, and a lone burro futilely flicked its tail along its back to scatter flies in the relentless heat. Their cattle, mostly thin, weary-looking beasts, roaming in the surrounding cactus-covered scrubland, bore the marks of owners' branding irons.

Although a relatively short drive of only 250 miles, we didn't arrive until 5:30 p.m., or eight and a half hours on the road. It seemed the bus stopped about every 50 miles for pauses lasting up to 90 minutes. This slow mode of travel, however, put us in close quarters with Mexicans of Indian descent. We were quickly aware we were observing a simple-living, deeply religious peasant people. These Mexicans were poor, it appeared some desperately so, but they were ever ready with bright, flashing smiles. They displayed a warm, humble humanity.

A young, bare-foot, dark-skinned, woman in a white blouse and colorful long skirt, boarded the bus at one stop with a boy about four years. Her boundless love for her child fascinated me. Cuddling him close on her lap, whispering into his ear, she occasionally brushed back his black hair to plant a kiss on his forehead. Once he saw me watching, whenever his mother kissed him, he wriggled vigorously and gave a look of pained protest.

Almost from earliest days of Spanish rule, the strategic importance and commercial potential of Guaymas' large natural harbor was recognized. Today it is Mexico's seventh largest port. At the time of our visit the town had an infant big game fishing activity and embryonic commercial shrimp and oyster markets, all now well established. In our peregrinations there we didn't encounter a single paved road. Great poverty and modest wealth seemed mingled to a peculiar extent. Not more than 25 yards from a collection of Spanish-style, ornamental homes, with noticeably high security/privacy fences, were the tin shacks and wooden huts of peasants.

As we made our way from the bus station to the street skirting the bay in search of a cheap hotel, we passed a couple of young Americans walking bent forward from the large packs on their backs. Their longhaired pony tails, flowing beards, mountain boots, and sun-tanned faces showed they weren't garden-variety tourists. We exchanged greetings to learn they were law students from the University of California at Berkeley on their way back after 45 days in Mexico. They'd hiked the exact route of Hernan Cortez, the Spanish Conquistador, who conquered Mexico in 1519. Their footslog had taken them 26 days, covering about 300 miles, or about eleven and a half miles daily. Hernan Cortez had set out from Vera Cruz with about 450 men and reached Tenochtitlan (meaning "the Place of the Cactus Fruit" in Aztec), today's Mexico City, 86 days later. These student adventurers had both been plagued by dysentery as they hiked through forests, over mountain passes, and across long stretches of rural Mexico. It would be tough settling back into study routines, they laughed. Eddie and I were impressed by their expedition that made our plans tame in comparison.

After selecting a hotel with rooms for $2.00 a night, we headed to the bay front about 7 p.m. to find a reasonable, if not up market, restaurant for dinner. We chose one where Saturday evening diners thronged the typical eatery with its exuberant activity. About halfway through my chicken fried steak meal, I happened to glance at the wall behind the counter. A nine-inch diameter metal exhaust pipe spanned the length of the wall a few feet below the ceiling. A large rat minced along the pipe, pausing every few steps, its head raised and sensitive nose twitching. I stopped eating when I noticed the color similarity of the rodent's brown coat to that of my fowl's batter covering.

From there we strolled to the bay front and found a large beer garden with many trees where a sizeable cross-section of local people were gathered. Christmas-type lights wound around branches gave the place a festive atmosphere. It was a warm, humid evening, but breezes off the Gulf of California gently rustled the leaves and kept us almost comfortable.

Several amateur mariachi bands took turns on a central stage to entertain the crowd, which was not backward in showing its displeasure at one of the groups by hoots and catcalls. But for me the most enjoyment came from the antics of two American male tourists, both probably in their early twenties, who arrived to occupy the table next to us. They came complete with jeans and huge belt buckles, tasseled cowboy shirts, calf-high boots, and wide-brim Stetsons. My instant impression was they were weekend trippers come south of the border for the cheap booze and Latino comfort women.

A waiter arrived to take their order. They asked in English for bourbons and soda. The waiter looked blank and advised he "no comprendido Ingles." Regardless, the Americans persisted in ordering the same item and always in their native tongue, only with each rendition they cranked up the decibel level. I'd tried the same tactic in New York City to obtain "Zup." But this approach had no more success in Mexico. Higher volume didn't produce understanding. The waiter remained just as non-comprendido. One American suddenly gave up on the hard stuff and said grandly "OK, OK, bring us a bottle of red wine." But this switch still didn't produce a meeting of the minds. Both customers were by now agitated and vociferous as they pleaded for red wine in a tone suggesting the waiter was intent on denying them their civic rights.

The negotiation seemed to be at an impasse. Then presumably tension in the brightest cowboy triggered a brain surge. He suddenly exploded, his volume carrying widely despite the considerable ambient noise and the heavy, warm evening air, spelling out the letters "R…E… D W…I…N…E" to form the two English words just then closest to his heart. The waiter's face didn't change. Eddie chose this anti-climactic moment to motion the patient, befuddled waiter over and say "vino rojo" to diffuse the dangerous build up of cross-border misunderstanding.

We moved the short distance from the beer garden to occupy an ocean front public bench on the quay. Here the entertainment came from watching the horde of shoeshine urchins line up on the quay to urinate into the bay in full view of the passing crowd. The boys directed their stream to achieve the highest arc before it plunged into the sea. Overhead streetlights illuminated their display almost like the stage in an open-air theater. The boys bandied back and forth making obviously derisory comments at their comrades and boasting of their own prowess. It reminded me of the competitions we conducted at my middle school playground bathroom in East London, now a wide continent and mighty ocean away.

Believing our luck had changed mightily for the better, next morning Eddie and I left Guaymass as passengers in the 1952 convertible of a pair of newly-weds in their early thirties whom we'd met while exploring the town. We learned the Los Angeles couple, Armand and Nancy Succar, were on honeymoon, the second marriage for both, and were driving south along the coast to Acapulco, and their next port of call would be Mazatlan, another emerging coastal resort. They planned an ambitious 450-mile drive to reach there by evening. They offered us a ride that would cover in one day what would take three in 2nd class, bone-rattling buses. Soon we were rolling along unimproved Highway #15 in true American comfort.

For about two and half hours Armand kept the car moving at speeds that made it seem likely we'd reach Mazatlan by late afternoon. Suddenly, about 1 p.m., we all noticed steam coming from under the hood and the temperature dial gauge spun to hot. At this time we were on a desolate stretch of the road south of Navajoa and north of Los Mochis. Fortunately, we were approaching a curbside ramshackle structure on the right. Armand turned off the engine and guided the bouncing car in neutral gear across the rutted, hard-baked mud to halt outside.

Closer inspection revealed it to be a primitive carport with six bays covered by a corrugated tin roof. Two end bays were enclosed by canvass that we assumed to be living quarters for the proprietors. The other four bays, open front and back, contained metal chairs, tables, and a few wooden benches. Nailed to the support posts of this snack stand/bus stop were several Coca-Cola signs, so ubiquitous in Mexico. About a dozen men in their white cotton shirts, baggy trousers, and straw sombreros, occupied some of the chairs and benches. They observed us disinterestedly as we climbed from the car and Armand raised the hood to survey the engine's burst upper water hose. The rest of us crowded around to peer somberly into the compartment with almost as much grief as if viewing a relative in a coffin.

We later learned that about half of the men were from the nearby village of Estacion Don enjoying a Sunday cerveza on their only day off. The remainder were waiting for a bus to Navajoa, said to be already about three hours late. Eddie used his embryonic Spanish to explain our situation to the two men behind the makeshift counter. Miraculously, one of them owned a pre-war Cadillac and offered for a few dollars to take Armand back to Navajoa where a replacement hose might be found. Nancy, Eddie and I would remain guarding car and contents. The Cadillac owner said they'd be back in not more than two hours. Four men waiting for the bus promptly crammed themselves into the back of the car, no doubt happy to pay the same fare in lieu of a bus that might never arrive.

An hour passed. Then two. Then three. The ferociously hot day dragged on. A breathless oppressiveness cloaked the area. The high humidity proved we were only ten miles from the Pacific Ocean. Our dessert surroundings seemed scorched to a stupor. From time to time, during the long afternoon, men on horseback arrived from local sugarcane fields, tied their mounts to a post, and flopped on to chairs for a restorative beer or two. Browned arms rippled with muscles. Hanging from waist bands were machetes as enormous as pirate cutlasses.

Nancy grew increasingly antsy. For a while she'd sat in the car flipping through fashion magazines. But when these ran out she couldn't seem to relax and started pacing outside, presumably increasingly concerned about the safety of her new husband. But I grew more worried about her safety and, inevitably, Eddie's and mine. She was an attractive, statuesque, California blonde. Her attire, or lack of it, a tight tube top, pink short shorts, and sandals. Finger and toenails painted red. After all, she was on honeymoon and dressed for a recent, but now overdue, husband. Few would pay her attention on the Santa Monica beach. But we were in Catholic Mexico, where women dress modestly.

I could see in the local hombres' fixated eyes the intense libidinal interest she aroused in them as they swigged their beers, tongue-swabbed wet lips, and dried them with the backs of strong hands. My concern, of course, was that in all this heat their close scrutiny of this tantalizing creature might boil over. I envisioned the biggest, meanest one seizing Nancy, throwing her over his horse, and galloping off in a cloud of dust. What he might do to this shapely gringo female was both scary and exciting to my mind. Eddie and I, if we offered any resistance, would be cleaved by those outsized machetes like abattoir carcasses.

But Armand did arrive back, about 7 p.m., some six hours after he left. He couldn't get a universal hose, but had a length of flexible hose that could be fitted to serve the purpose. It had taken so long because a bald tire on the old Cadillac punctured, and there wasn't a spare. The car owner had to then locate a tire. Amazingly unruffled, Armand soon fitted the pipe, filled his radiator with water from the snack stand, and at about 8 p.m. we rolled south again. Nancy, angry but unviolated, and me profoundly grateful I'd not had to reveal my essential cowardice in an inept effort to protect her honor.

By now it started to grow dusk. Armand found he had to drive slowly because of cattle and donkeys that roam the open countryside and sometimes stray on to highways. After it became dark our headlights illuminated a cow in the northbound lane that looked as if struck by a passing vehicle. An animal that large could inflict huge damage.

About an hour into our resumed journey, we entered the outer edges of the first tropical storm Eddie and I had ever witnessed. As we penetrated deeper, the more spectacular it became. Lightning forked through the sky to briefly but brilliantly light vast stretches of the flat desert rendering it a shadowy landscape. Thunder rumbled among the clouds like artillery duels of the Great War. Raindrops hit so fiercely on the convertible's top each thud sounded capable of ripping the canvass.

As we passed through darkened shanty settlements we saw men, rolled in their colorful blankets, sleeping on sidewalks pressed against exterior walls to gain some protection from the rain under roof overhangs. Perhaps after 45 minutes the storm abruptly stopped. Armand drove on for another couple of hours, but by midnight said he'd had enough. Meanwhile, we were still 125 miles shy of our planned destination. The day had started so promisingly but turned into a long, arduous, but interesting ordeal.

By noon of the next day, however, we completed the drive to Mazatlan, then a fledgling resort. It boasted Mexico's longest uninterrupted beach (16 miles) and planned to develop itself into a serious challenge to Acapulco, 900 miles further south. Its promoters were betting Mazatlan's shorter distance from the U.S. border would make its location a strong draw. And it has. It is now one of the country's major tourist attractions. Our kind chauffeur and his wife were pre-booked into the Playa Mazatlan, located about eight miles out of town, then one of a few luxury motels catering to Americans. The white, two-story building offered a balcony with each room, shaded by abundant, well-watered palm trees. Sited on the ocean, the motel apparently owned the wide sand beach that sloped gently to the sea. But Eddie and I chose to stay in town at a medium-level hotel at about a third of their nightly rate.

Next morning Armand collected us and we spent half a day playing tourists on their golden beach laying in hammocks under open round shacks roofed with palm leaves, and wallowing in the gentle surf. But we hadn't come to Mexico to vacation: we'd come to observe and discover. Hardy explorers should not indulge the flesh. We had already determined to move on by taking a second-class bus to Guadalajara leaving at 9 p.m. that evening. So after a lunch on us, we bid goodbye to our newly wed friends of the last 48 hours, and walked back to town along a hilly path above the beach but below the road overlooking the scenic bay.

When we boarded our bus to Guadalajara we found it almost full. Some passengers had been waiting at the depot for hours to get on early. Our only seat choice, if we wanted to take that last bus of the day, was two places on a backbench with most of its padding missing. Already ensconced was a woman with a baby in her arms and three dark-haired, big-eyed boys lined up next to her ranging in age from 3 to 6 years. We wanted to get close to ordinary Mexican people and again this transportation mode certainly honored our wish.

The three young boys had scrunched themselves to make room for Eddie and me. Despite their kind act, I'd been leery of sharing the backbench with them during the scheduled 12-hour overnight bus ride.

I expected sleeplessness and constant uproar. But as it transpired, and as if to demonstrate the meanness of my suspicion, they proved to be the best behaved children I'd ever encountered. They didn't utter a whimper during the entire trip. Even the baby, whom the mother modestly suckled under a cloth from time to time, remained peaceful. The real challenge proved to be hard jolts of the old bus, rolling over poor roads, delivered undiluted to our backsides.

The night brought little abatement of the sticky heat as the bus followed the coastline for about half of the journey. I could doze only briefly before a bump started me awake. There were, of course, no passenger lights to read by. Around midnight the bus blew a tire. This involved everyone alighting with their inside luggage and some from its bay so the driver could get to the jack to raise the vehicle. Then additional luggage from the roof needed unloading to retrieve the spare and lighten the vehicle's weight. While I was ready to spit bullets, the Mexicans endured it all with a dignified stoicism. The disruption was accepted with resignation, and in good humor. I suspect I was the only passenger who became irritable by the discomfort of that infamous bus ride. The only defense I can offer is that my stomach had become queasy which I attributed to the back seat shaking.

When the morning at long last slowly revealed itself around us, we were climbing moderately on a narrow mountain road with a steep incline on the west side. The countryside in the valleys here was both more attractive and more arable. Grazing cattle looked plumper. To the southwest a high range of mountains, their peaks shrouded in white clouds, stood out starkly against an azure sky. This spectacular landscape helped assuage the miseries of the night.

We chose Guadalajara, Mexico's second largest city, set on a mile-high plain of the Sierra Madre Mountains, as a primary destination because of its importance during Spanish colonial rule. We'd read of, and were interested in, the city's many historic buildings, tree-shaded plazas, and pleasant parks. Founded in 1531, it now has a population of about 1.25 million. Because of our speedy realization that scrimping on hotels in this country resulted in vermin-disturbed sleep, we selected one with a medium price. The wisdom of this choice revealed itself all too soon. The stomach discomfort I'd felt on the bus during the night exploded into a dysentery deluge. Many times during the afternoon I sprinted between the bed and the bathroom, and steadily felt more debilitated. By early evening my distress necessitated having the desk staff call in a doctor. The elegant Mexican medico, obviously a descendent of Spanish ancestors, prescribed some foul tasting but efficacious powder. Even so, my weakened condition required another 24 hours in bed.

This unpleasant indisposition denied me nearly two days of playing tourist. When I returned to this role we spent only half a day touring two colonial era buildings in Guadalajara, both of which house dramatic murals by Jose Clemente Orozco, among Mexico's finest painters. One, "The Man of Fire," considered his best work, is claimed by some to be second only to those in Rome's Sistine chapel.

We made our way by city bus just five miles north-east of Guadalajara to the small community of Experiencia, just outside of which is Barranca de Oblatos, touted by locals as "Jalisco's Grand Canyon." Even with its waterfall, it proved disappointing in comparison with Arizona's. But the excursion provided more exposure to ordinary Mexicans as we walked through Experiencia going and returning. Here we saw some of the more extreme poverty so far.

Most of the small adobe-brick homes had tin or thatch roofs, with a few tiled. Since at many the front doors stood open, we could see inside their dirt floors. Chickens and pigs apparently enjoyed tenant rights. We saw only a few with tiled floors and this made for a huge improvement in the appearance of cleanliness. The community's unpaved roads were deeply rutted by the daily peregrinations of the residents and the steady plodding of their diminutive burros. These busy thoroughfares must be burdensome quagmires in the rainy season. Younger children, black haired, brown eyed, and barefooted, played in the streets. As we walked slowly along, taking an occasional photo while trying to absorb the sights and sounds of their town, they began to fall in behind us. Soon there were perhaps 25 of them as though we were modern Pied Pipers of Hamlein. Eddie's elementary Spanish enabled him to communicate at a level most appropriate for their ages. Any shyness they harbored soon dissipated. They seemed to find immense pleasure in the back and forth banter. When asked to pose for a group picture they tussled each other to be at the center. Our encounters with such good-natured youngsters were among the more enjoyable aspects of our trip.

Set in the midst of the material poverty of their small town was an ornate Catholic church, with characteristic twin bell and clock towers. The interior was not as elaborate as some we'd seen, but still looked profusely decorated. I wondered how the limited size and relative destitution of the congregation of Experiencia could support this rich-looking institution. For me there was conflict in this, so widely seen in Mexico. The predominant role of the church in Mexican life left a distinct impression on me. Was Marx right when he called religion the opium of the masses? Or is it justified if people find solace in it for their daily hardships?

For our last Guadalajara evening we attended my one and only cockfight, a gruesome, cruel spectacle. I blame my naive lust for new experiences. Unadorned testosterone predominated in the tattered marquee. Violence and greed exuded from the pores of intense, eager punters. The feathered combatants wear razor-sharp steel spurs on their legs to slash each other open. In a particularly hideous duel, one rooster blinded the other. The sightless entrant floundered around presumably lunging when it heard or sensed its opponent, but sustained many horrific slashes in these vicious encounters. Its fat, sweaty owner, in blood-splattered white cotton pants and shirt, loudly goaded his bird. Pierced so many times, it collapsed in the ring and bled to death.

Our earlier resolve to travel only in transport that kept us close to ordinary Mexicans had been, for me at least, seriously called into question by my bout with Montezuma's revenge. On the following morning we elected to take a first-class Fletcher Roja bus to Mexico City, some 500 kilometers distant. What a difference the upgrade made! Nowadays, it would compare with flying first-class versus the discomfort of economy coach class. Not only were we assured of a seat, but also for a great deal of the trip we shared the bus with only half a dozen other passengers. From Guadalajara's altitude of 5,200 feet we climbed another 3,000 feet before dropping to the central plateau on which today's megalopolis is located at about 7,500 feet. Much of the agricultural land along the way appeared fertile and gave an impression of relative prosperity. Stone shrines dotted the roadside, normally housing a cross or carved wooden figure of the Virgin Mary. Sometimes flowers had been put in place.

We saw much poverty among the people who worked the land. In one of the small towns the bus stopped for passengers to eat, we saw a beggar who looked not more than 35 years old. His clothes were filthy rags and bare feet mud-caked. His lean, weary face was covered with the stubble of months. One becomes used to this and somewhat hardened. But this beggar had at his side a boy of about two years. A heart-ripping concern for that innocent child, knowing the life it faced, would penetrate even the most insentient. Another noticeable feature along the way in 1956 was the ubiquitous, steel-helmeted military. Armed soldiers were posted in virtually every community we passed through. Indeed, the troops seemed to enjoy their authority and literally strutted in their cotton uniforms, rifles at the ready.

We arrived in the capital city at 11:20 p.m., just 20 minutes late, and the closest adherence to the official schedule for any of the numerous bus lines we used. We dove into the first hotel we came to outside the bus terminal. During the five days we spent in Mexico City we visited some of its major attractions. The fine national museums display art pieces depicting Mexico's three great periods: pre-Columbian, the colonial, and the modern. At the new, vast University of Mexico we saw ultra-modern buildings raised on pillars, with many glass sides. One structure had an exterior of stone murals depicting the country's complete history.

We spent a Sunday afternoon drifting in a flat-bottomed, canvas roofed boat, poled by an attendant, among the man-made islands in swamp-like Xochimilco Floating Gardens. Around these popular points of interest vendors operated stalls or carts offering tourist trinkets and nick-knacks. If we paused to look at their merchandise, we soon found out they were offering more than that on display. Several asked if we wanted a woman, a young girl, even a young boy. We never accepted. This had nothing to do with morality, but amounted to the fear of walking into a trap. Cash-laden male tourists could be lured to a house on a deserted back alley. There they'd be stomped and enthusiastically relieved of money and valuables. Although sexually transmitted diseases were not daily newspaper fare at the time, they were always in the back of my mind. But my favorite excuse for being chicken had to do with, for want of a better phrase, innocent idealism. At age 24 I believe I still harbored a genuine hope that my first complete liaison with a female would be a more aesthetic experience in a more romantic setting. Proving my genuine democratic tendencies, I wanted the partner to be as eager as me.

Next day we were up early to visit Teotihuacan (House of the Gods), about 15 miles northeast of Mexico City. On our way through the city the bus stopped first at the Basilica of our Lady of Guadalupe where, according to tradition, the Virgin of Guadalupe appeared to the Indian Juan Diego in 1531. This shrine has become a Mecca for many pilgrims. As we milled about at its entrance, people approached the holy place on their knees. This sight stirred my non-believing soul. In July 2002 Pope John Paul II canonized the 16th century Aztec Indian at this Basilica.

Teotihuacann is a well-preserved area of ruins of the Aztec Indian Empire capital, Tenochtitlan. Here we climbed the 244 vertigo-inducing, narrow steps to the top of the Pyramid of the Sun, covering more than 10 acres, and rising more than 200 feet. On the summit, historians believe, Aztec ceremonies of human sacrifice occurred. If it was difficult climbing, the descent was more so because of the six-inch step width. Only years later did I learn this small step width served a real practical purpose: it's believed once the beating heart of human sacrificial offerings had been cut out, the body was flung down the steps to the crowd waiting below. The steep, narrow steps prevented the body from lodging as it rolled down. It is further speculated that cannibalism may have been an accepted part of the ritual. But the large number of chattering tourists, attired in gaudy outfits, clambering up the challenging stairway, tended to disrupt one's contemplation of the site's macabre history.

Vera Cruz, on the east coast, would be our final Mexican destination. We had chosen it because it's where Hernan Cortez landed in the New World to start Spain's 350-year colonization. Also, we had returned to the idea of trying to work our passage on a freighter sailing from this busy port to one on the U.S. Gulf Coast. That would be a glorious culmination to what we perceived as our bold exploration of the colorful, exotic land of Mexico.

Shortly after leaving Mexico City on the 200-mile bus ride to the Gulf of Mexico coast, we passed the snow-capped volcanoes of Ixtaccihuatl, 17,343 feet, now dormant, and the occasionally active, Popocateptl, 17,887 feet. The former, some 33 miles southeast of Mexico City, is called the "sleeping woman" because its mass resembles a reclining lady. The latter, only another 11 miles due south, is shaped like the classic volcano. They loomed, magnificent and alluring, into the sun-brilliant, azure sky of the morning. They were the first volcanoes these two East Londoners had seen, and their majesty humbled.

This journey to the coast involved dropping from 7,525 to 10 feet above sea level. Before that, however, the road at one stage reached an elevation of nearly 10,000 feet. Here, as if flying, we drove into clouds clinging to mountain peaks. Then suddenly, as the road curved and dropped., on either side would be valleys flooded with a golden sunlight, with the land looking rich and fertile. For more than an hour the narrow road clung to mountainsides curving around, descending slowly. The driver pumped the brakes almost constantly and the old, 2nd class bus rocked like a small boat on a choppy lake. When traversing a few high valleys with straighter roads, he gunned the motor and the vehicle shuddered jarringly when it encountered the frequent potholes. This ride wasn't one for little old ladies.

As we reached lower altitudes, the vegetation became denser and tropical and the climate more humid. Open windows provided a draft in the bus, which helped. The cultivated land hereabouts was taken up with coffee plants, sugar cane, and papaya trees. At one small roadside community we saw a young girl walking a two-foot lizard tethered on a thin rope like a dog in a public park. Yet the highlight of the seven-hour bus ride was, once again, people we met.

When we first entered the bus, no seats were available. We stood in the aisle in the rear thinking it would make this a long, tiresome ordeal. A family of two adults and four children occupied the backbench seat. Before long they had made room for one of us. Then the two daughters, aged about 11 and 7, squeezed together more to make room for the other of us. This now meant there were four adults and the two girls sharing the backbench, with their parents holding two younger boys on their laps. All the children of this poor family were, as seemed usual to us by now, well behaved. A sense of responsibility seemed to be inherent with them, presumably developed by the hardness of their lives. The oldest girl had a pretty face with sparkling hazel eyes and lustrous black hair. She wore a pale blue silk dress rather the worse for wear. Even in a nation blessed with pretty women, she promised to become an outstanding beauty. She seemed pleased when Eddie attempted to converse with her parents about our English backgrounds and travels in Mexico. Later we took the two young boys on our laps and tried to play hickory-hickory-dock with them. That seemed to make the 11-year old so happy she gave us each an apple from a few her father bought for her. A wonderful human encounter with strangers that makes one feel good about the human race.

Immediately after arriving in Vera Cruz in the mid-afternoon, we booked into a modest hotel near the in-town bus terminal to dispose of our knapsacks. Under a scorching tropical sky we walked to the Malecon, the boulevard forming the waterfront. Initially we joined a small group of people watching several boys diving off the high quay into the water retrieving coins thrown by crewmembers from the stern of a rusty freighter out of Buenos Aires tied up alongside. A few mariners leaned over the poop deck railing next to the ensign staff. The Argentine flag, with its sun mask in the white center band, bordered on both sides by light blue bands, hung limply in the still afternoon. This scene, so Joseph Conrad authentic, rekindled our idea of taking a ship back to the U.S. as we'd hoped could be done from Panama.

This city, founded in 1519, was the first Spanish settlement in Mexico. Today it is an industrial center but is known best as the country's principal port handling the bulk of its exports and imports. The large natural harbor accommodates many ships and we counted 12 what to us appeared to be ocean-going vessels docked at quays, and another five anchored in deeper water. The pickings looked good! All we needed was one to take us to New Orleans, Houston or any port along the eastern U.S. coast as far north as New York City.

Next morning we went first to see the city's large open-air market. One sensed in the market's hubbub as much emphasis on social interactivity among those manning the stalls as the business of commercial trading or merchandise bartering. Fruits and vegetables, vibrant in color and pungent in aroma overflowed from stalls, and blankets lay on the cobblestone street. Boxes of fish, fresh from the Gulf of Campeche, attracted a few serious customers and a few of the town's stray dogs. Huge stalks of bananas bore fruit all of 18 inches long.

As in every country, we had detected in Mexico more common humanity among small town inhabitants as compared with those in Guadalajara and the capital. We breakfasted on fruits and juices, the freshest I'd ever eaten. Succulent fruits like mango, papaya, and guava were tasted for the first time. This abundant, sticky meal required a quick wash of the face and hands in the plaza fountain in front a few town elders seated on adjacent benches who seemed to enjoy the spectacle. Then we made our way to the waterfront to begin the quest of finding a freighter needing two deckhands and bound where we wanted to go.

We intended to visit only the most modern, streamlined ships and avoid the old tubs in case we were put to work on one that hadn't seen a paintbrush or deck mop in many voyages. The first ship that appeared to meet our demands was a Swedish-America Line vessel across whose boarding ramp we walked confidently to come face to face with its boatswain. He turned out to be a friendly Canadian who, after we explained our hopes, said he might be able to arrange something. The Captain was ashore today, he explained with a wink, and wasn't expected back until late at night by which time he might have trouble understanding or even speaking. Success on our first try! Now we could play tourists. We spent the day wandering through the narrow streets of old Vera Cruz with its selection of colonial buildings.

After dinner we returned to the Zocalo, on the Plaza de Armas, to study the Mexican evening ritual where single women, many of whom were most attractive, circle the fountain in one direction. Eligible bachelors form an outer ring to promenade in the opposite. No doubt there were well-established, subtle signals passing between the sexes we didn't see. It was all very proper as chaperons sat on benches nearby monitoring these charming rites. I couldn't help equating the process with the mating rituals of some of our feathered friends.

Next morning, full of the hope of a new day, we returned to the waterfront to again step aboard the Swedish-America ship. The Boatswain informed us that the Captain was now so drunk he could not be disturbed. Furthermore, and he'd forgotten this yesterday, there was a seaman's union rule about scab labor, so it'd be smart if we checked with other vessels in port.

For the rest of that day and most of the next we clambered aboard a German, British, Finnish and another Swedish vessel. But like unsuccessful door-to-door salesmen we were cut off in mid-sentence and our services firmly declined. While climbing on and off these vessels, we inevitably met a number of crew members of varying nationalities and they all seemed in agreement on one thing: the prostitutes of Vera Cruz were exciting and the price was right.

Finally, the "Dalesman," out of Liverpool, owned by the English Harrison Line, remained the one ship to be propositioned. Somewhere we'd heard that a little backing by the national Consular Corps might help. Ever hopeful, we paid a visit to the British Honorary Vice Consul.

He proved to be most charming, diplomatic and totally unhelpful. The only thing we gained from our effort was we found out the "Dalesman" would be loaded with Mexican Heneqen plant from which rope is made. While interesting, this closed the door on our efforts to sail off in glory.

Disappointed but accepting, we knew we would leave Mexico the same way we arrived — on a bus. But most likely on a first-class one, because we were beginning to feel a little worn from the exposure to the country's 3rd class bus system.

In a classic example of abandoning one bad idea in favor of an even worse one, we were determined still to perform a substitute feat of boldness that would leave our footprint on Mexico, perhaps not on a par with Cortez, but something more than the average American tourist. We resolved that a land-based, derring-do stunt would be almost as good as one on the ocean. Who first suggested the idea I don't recall, but climbing mountains was the rage because of the first ever-successful assault on Everest three years before. We nonchalantly decided to hike to the summit of snow-capped Ixtaccihuatl, 17,342 feet, via a trail leading to the top. We selected the "sleeping woman" because her brother, Popocatepetl, was another 545 feet taller and his reputation for being less dormant. We wanted to be heroes, but not dead ones. In the afternoon of the day our entreaties to the British Consul were rebuffed, we left Vera Cruz on a bus that would deposit us at about 9 p.m. in Huejotzingo. This village would serve as our base camp for our strike on the summit. We would step in the still warm footprints of Hillary and Tensing.

CHAPTER 30

Now veterans of Mexico's bus network, it came as no surprise to us we arrived in mist-shrouded Huejotzingo approaching 11 p.m., some two hours behind schedule. We alighted at the central plaza and all evidence indicated the village's population of a couple of thousand souls had already battened down for the night. The few streetlights provided minimal illumination as we walked along cobblestone alleyways diverging from the square in our search for a hotel. But we were unsuccessful and eventually wound up back at the plaza, where we sat on a public bench, weighing our seemingly non-existent options. The bench started to look like our only choice of overnight lodging. At an altitude of 7,480 feet, however, sleeping outdoors would make it uncomfortably cold.

Then Eddie noticed a wooden sign reading "Policia" on the front of a squat, stone building at one corner of the square. The sign was visible by virtue of one of the few streetlights. No interior light showed through the station's windows. It appeared the police station, too, had closed for the night. In our desperation, however, we decided to see if anyone was on duty in the hope they'd let us stay in a cell as we'd done in compassionate Arizona. We crossed to the police station and knuckled the heavy oak door, stepping back to wait. Three bare-footed Indian women in rebozos (shawls) and wide-brimmed straw fedoras skimmed in single file like dream phantoms through the plaza shadows. As they padded silently with short, quick steps, their billowing skirts swayed from side to side in chorus-line uniformity. They were the first people we'd seen since stepping off the bus. Perhaps a little spooked, we knocked again, this time more energetically.

Light suddenly sprang through chinks in the window shutters, from within came several alarmed voices, and after another pause the door opened slowly, on a chain, and a beam of laser-like illumination cut the darkness as far as the road.

"Buenos noches, Señores, my amigo y yo..." said Eddie, launching into a prepared speech, in his best Spanish, trying to explain we'd just arrived, couldn't find a hotel, needed a place to sleep, and hoped to climb Ixtaccihautl in the morning. He spoke rapidly to get his message across, like a telemarketer trying to sell something before the listener/victim hangs up. The door closed again, we heard the chain slipped from its slot, and then it swung open wide. A young, startled policeman, struggling to wake up, draped in a colorful, patterned serape over his knee-length white underpants, stepped out in unfastened sandals. Eddie repeated his explanation, clarifying points with inventive gesticulation.

It appeared Eddie's performance brought the policeman back to the land of the living with a bump. In between blinks, he presently smiled, nodded, and seemed full of kind understanding. We'd already noted the easy friendliness of the ordinary Mexican people we'd encountered. Now this yawning, young man of the law graciously offered his wood bunk to us and he'd move in with one of his compadres. We didn't need to sleep on a park bench, or in a cell, because we bedded down right alongside the constabulary. The Gods that night were on our side.

Next morning that same helpful policeman told us of an early-morning bakery just off the plaza where we ate some plain rolls and purchased four more for the climb. Eddie filled his flask with strong, black, bitter coffee. Our lawman amigo organized a ride on a logging truck to drop us higher on our volcano. With their kind permission, we left some of our gear at the station, taking only useful items like sunglasses, hats, a sheath knife, matches, binoculars, and our cameras. I carried an old raincoat, but doubted it would be needed.

We'd learned from the lawmen that simple food was available at a rough, overnight hut at the approximate 15,000-foot snow line, which now became our day's upper objective. We decided we'd settle for that and let Hillary and Tensing later climb the remaining 2,342 feet to the summit and the real glory.

Dawn had not fully lit the new day when, at a little after six, we departed the village's mist-dampened, narrow cobblestone streets. At first we were the only occupants in the open bed of the truck bouncing along rough dirt tracks climbing gently across the oblong mountain. Now and again it stopped at one-room adobe huts lost among plantations of tall, green sugar cane, to pick up forest workers. Swinging aboard their axes and day's food wrapped in white cotton cloth bundles, they scrambled up the tailboard chanting a gay "Buenos Dias, Señores." A lack of language, certain shyness, and a loud, growling engine precluded further conversation. They busied themselves with their breakfast of tortillas flavored with thin strips of a raw, red chili. The truck jarred on for more than an hour. We were set down at about nine-o'clock at what we calculated as something less than 10,000 feet. We tipped the driver and his fat, stubbly face broke into a grin as he pointed to the summit trail. The truck rumbled out of sight, and when the snarl of its straining engine died away, the silence was absolute.

The trail wound through open forest of pine, fir and alder, with unfamiliar evergreen shrubs, bushes and herbaceous species forming dense thickets on either side. Results of the woodsman's axe was in evidence here and there. We also saw a surprising number of trees that appeared to have been snapped off and blackened by lightning. We were making our personal, proud statement, however, in glorious weather, and a threat from electric storms never entered our minds. In our early enthusiasm we walked for some 90 minutes, although our pace slackened as time passed. Crossing open, sacaton-grass glades afforded brief views of the broad summit, its whiteness blending with wispy clouds contrasted against the turquoise sky. We walked at a most modest rate. Neither of us were jocks and had spent a week at sea level before coming to this high altitude. Our bodies hadn't had time to acclimate. Eventually in a wooded gully the trail crossed a swift stream forded by a few conveniently situated rocks. The water was clear and cold, the day's first wash invigorating. Lulled by solitude, we sat listening to the gurgling stream as we fashioned staves with my sheath knife to aid ourselves along. In time, we passed a herd of black bulls peacefully grazing on an unfenced grassy ledge forming a giant step in the mountain's side. These muscled animals were probably destined to meet their fate in the world's largest bullring in Mexico City. They displayed no interest in us, merely raising their heads to look us over, and then returning to their important job of keeping the grass short.

Now the trail steepened and became more difficult with rain-worn ruts. Already the altitude began to be a factor. We both found it increasingly difficult to breathe, and at best could maintain only a mañana pace. Shortly after noon we halted to eat. We expected to reach the overnight cabin by late afternoon. Even though we were both in our mid-twenties, we responded to the food like old men: an overwhelming drowsiness induced a 30-minute sleep.

After this we walked in 30-minute segments, and rested for ten. Each step required increasing effort. The thin air produced a peculiar feeling of suffocation. Topping a vantagepoint, we searched the wide area ahead through binoculars. No sign of the hut. About six hundred feet higher the trees were sparse, shrubbery almost disappeared, and purple lupines contested tufted grasses to dominate the boulder-studded slopes. The Alpine meadow terrain appeared to stretch endlessly upward. It would probably take two hours more to reach the snow line. We convinced ourselves we didn't have the stamina to accomplish that, yet didn't want to retreat so ignominiously from Ixtaccihuatl.

At 4 p.m. we decided to stop, make a fire, sleep under the stars, and at daybreak, refreshed from a night's rest, find the cabin. We decided it wiser to make camp among trees rather than on the more open terrain. The trees, we hoped, would offer us some protection from sun and wind. In the warm afternoon this didn't seem too unpleasant a prospect. We estimated we were bedding down at about 13,000 feet. Although early to halt, we naively hoped we'd be rewarded with quick success next day. We located a small campsite in a grassy hollow, not very wide, but with room to stretch out and for a fire pit. The site, close to the edge of a deep gorge, offered an immense panorama.

From our eyrie, rugged, wooded slopes tumbled down to a plateau 1,600 feet below where Lilliputian cattle grazed. We assumed them to be the bulls we'd passed earlier. In between, half a dozen turkey buzzards wheeled on updrafts. Beyond and below, the undulating mesa, spotted with clumps of trees, stretched away to merge with a hazy horizon. Yet much as this majestic vastness inspired us, we harbored foreboding. The unknown night waited.

Wind-felled branches from nearby trees offered an adequate supply of wood to make a fire. We spent an hour collecting and breaking sufficient branches to keep it going through the night. We had no food left and the remaining coffee had to be diluted to provide one last cup each. Eddie remembered seeing a snow melt trickle down a rock face higher up. He went there again to fill the aluminum casing of the thermos bottle. This required nearly an hour. I spent the time finding loose rocks to contain the fire that would foster a night's child-like sleep in our warm, cozy encampment. It was now about six-thirty and the sun had slipped below the mountain's western slope. The dusk transformed the forest into a dream-like shadowscape. We sat by a healthy fire sipping the hot coffee, talking over the things, good and bad, seen in Mexico.

Soon we prepared for a night under the stars. We donned our warmest clothes — light sweaters and jackets. I put on my old raincoat, for warmth, not moisture. Face towels became pillows. We stretched out on the rocky ledge close to the fire and lay waiting for the darkness to close around us. Inwardly, I acknowledged pangs of fear, intermixed with a sudden yearning for my more normal London office 9-5 existence. Eddie, I suspected, entertained none of these qualms. My mind taunted me with images of Mexico's fauna—bear, mountain lion, jaguar, tusked wild boar, and a variety of reptiles up to two meters long. In time, I convinced myself that we were at least too high for the reptiles. Then, as if Old Man Pluvius found us too much of a temptation, the rain started. The first spots softly tickled our upturned faces. The rainfall increased perceptibly until, in about 30 minutes, the fire sputtered and soon started to dim. Decision time!

In the darkness it seemed madness to go higher seeking the cabin. Staying put seemed perhaps the safest if most uncomfortable as the ever-heavier downpour continued and temperature dropped. We chose the third, perhaps equally dangerous, option. We elected to start walking down in the doubtful hope of discovering a natural shelter, like a cliff overhang. We threw the towels and thermos bottle parts into our knapsacks and set off. My watch showed almost 8:30 p.m.

It didn't take long to find what we believed to be the trail. However, our one flashlight helped little to illuminate the many clefts as we picked our steps carefully on the precipitous path. Torrential rain continued and now the occasional drone of distant thunder carried across the wide sky. The wind surged to move the trees warning Ixtaccihuatl that it barred the path of a significant summer storm. The thunderclouds marched in relentlessly. In about half an hour we walked through a deluge of obese, tropical raindrops that clung like a saturated woolen drape. Thunder roared immediately overhead and lightning flashed vertically, horizontally, diagonally. It momentarily lit the mountainside with a dawn grayness silhouetting the gaunt, roiling pines. All vegetation leapt and whirled like dervishes to the frenzied overture.

Nature's awesome anger left us cringing. The depth of our terror caused us instinctively to link arms. We could not admit our fear and said clinging together was necessary to hear each other above the storm's tumult. I admit to believing we were destined to die on this Mexican mountain. Fortunately, this paralyzing fear did not last too long. Calm resignation replaced it. I learned that we could face death with a little dignity. As the storm center passed overhead, dense cloud, more like fog, clung to the slopes and plunged us into a blackness the flashlight did not penetrate at all. We laboriously probed each step with the staves.

Thus the night's long hours dragged by with us prodding our slow way, checking constantly the trail's course. When overcome by tiredness, we would just sit down back-to-back on whatever part of the pathway wasn't running like a river. Sometimes we dozed for a few moments, to start awake, cold and shuddering, only to realize it was not a nightmare, but reality. Then, stiff with a chill wetness, we started trekking again to warm up. We castigated each other and ourselves for forgetting August is part of Mexico's precipitation season.

After three to four hours groping along and concentrating on each footstep, we did not perceive the path lost its steepness. Suddenly, right in front of us, there was a ferocious snort and something lurched furiously to one side. It sounded like it slithered down a bank and plunged with a mighty splash into a water-filled ditch. Seeing nothing, we froze, and after a petrified few seconds, turned and stumbled back to cower behind the first tree. Whatever made the noise did not pursue us. As our wits settled, Eddie suggested we'd missed the trail and wandered onto the bull-occupied ledge. Toro either saw or smelled us and just might have been terrified of the one-eyed apparition of our flashlight coming straight at it out of this wild night. At the time, the feat of scaring-off the powerful beast of the bullring, if that is what happened, seemed no more unlikely than any other aspect of this bizarre experience.

We sat huddled together like Hansel and Gretel at the base of that tree. We were wet through and our boots squished. We started to chill again. Although we had descended for hours we still needed to keep walking, while making a better effort to stay on trail. This was a tall order in such bad visibility. A mistake could yet have us plunging off a precipice to certain death.

About three a.m. we awoke from a longer nap to find the rain had ceased. A clear sky now blazed with a myriad of radiant stars, each one circled by a silvery aureole. The dazzling tropical night sky, shimmering brilliantly like the surface of a becalmed, sun-drenched ocean, lit the way almost as clearly as daylight. Our spirits soared. For the first time in many hours we were out of danger. In spite of our hubris, and exceptional stupidity, we had survived!

As we reached lower heights it grew less cold. The trail lost its declivity, changing from a narrow rock-strewn gravel one to a sand-colored clay track, pockmarked with many rain pools. The lush vegetation, tall and leafy, looked like what we remembered seeing from the truck. We ambled on in a daze for several more hours. Eventually the stars started to dim and a dull-grayness edged across the satin sky to the east. If our aspiration to ascend Ixtaccihuatl represented youthful braggadocio, our abject descent represented rapid converts to a belief in Nature's superiority.

Just before six o'clock we rounded a curve to enter a valley. In the distance we saw habitation, which proved to be a Forestry Commission hut. As we pushed open the gate to start the dogs barking, the sun's rays were coloring the eastern clouds a pale orange. We looked back at Ixtaccihuatl, its forested slopes now still and well behaved. The outline of its broad summit was silent, even inviting. But our ordeal was not yet over.

When we thumped on the door of the Mexican Forestry Commission hut, the ranger who responded was already in his uniform. The hut's half dozen male occupants, preparing for their workday, came to the entrance when they heard our voices. Our situation didn't need much explanation because we weren't the first lost hikers within the 63,500 acres of the Ixtaccihautl-Popocatepetl National Park. But we may have been the wettest. Again, these Mexicans were beyond kind and helpful. They quickly made a wood fire to let us dry our clothes on the backs of chairs placed close to the pot-bellied stove in their hut's main room. Meanwhile, we took sponge baths in their rudimentary washhouse.

To our amazement, but not surprise, it turned out that rather than following a descending trail down the mountain's eastern flanks to get back to Huejotzingo, we had stumbled in error along a trail that circled the volcano. We were now on its western flanks. To this day I don't know whether we wound around the volcano on its northern or southern side where a saddleback ridge joins the two volcanoes, known as the Paso de Cortez, with a road running between them at an elevation of just over 12,000 feet. Cortez and his Conquistadors crossed this pass on their trek from the coast to the Aztec capital in the central interior. They just had a better sense of direction!

With the aid of a well-worn park map taken down from a wall, a ranger indicated it could take us 9 hours to walk the trail back to Huejotzingo, making the unlikely assumption that we wouldn't lose our way. An alternative would be to head for the nearest community, San Antonio Tlaltecahuacan, at the base of the western slopes. There, a logging road terminated, and we could hitch a ride on a truck to our starting point to collect our stuff and then catch a bus to Mexico City. But even the hike to San Antonio could take four or five hours. I believe by now they knew they were dealing with two gringo babes in the woods. They asked if we could ride horses.

Probably Eddie answered positively and I dithered. I couldn't remember ever riding a horse, only a donkey along a stony beach at a forlorn English seaside resort. The Rangers decided for us. They'd escort us to San Antonio Tlaltecahuacan, with four rangers and Eddie and I mounted on Forestry Commission patrol horses. The prospect alarmed me, but the walking alternative was even worse.

One ranger held the reins of our assigned powerful-looking stallions, and one cupped his hands for a boost onto the saddle. With two rangers abreast in front, Eddie and I in the center, and two rangers in the rear, we rode slowly out of the compound like a cavalry detachment on a mission.

For a while the lead rangers allowed their horses to walk. My noble steed dutifully fell in behind. After perhaps 10 minutes my nervousness abated. Of course, I held the reins very loosely out of concern of doing something that would annoy the creature beneath me. Above all, I wanted it to like me. I began, in fact, to feel quite comfortable, even a little in command, as though riding a horse along trails on the lower slopes of volcanoes was something I did every other day. After all, this was the true adventure we wanted.

Our ranger friends must have had other duties to perform and could not let this escort mission, said to take about two hours, last all day. Suddenly the leading pair nudged their horses into a trot. I swear I didn't do anything, but my mount just accelerated behind the leaders as if the thing was in automatic cruise control. Now it was swaying and bouncing in a most scary manner below me. I grabbed the saddle horn, eyes closed. When the reckless lead Rangers boosted their mounts from the canter into a gallop, mine just tagged right along as if it had no mind of its own. Incredibly, no one fell off during that memorable morning's ride, even though Eddie and I were more dead than alive from our antics of the night. Possibly the flexibility of my semi-comatose state helped me stay in the saddle. Or was it fear-induced sweat trickling down my spine that stuck me to it? Since then I've suspected these dumb animals know when they're carrying an even dumber passenger.

At last we passed from a trail to a dirt road that led to the hamlet of San Antonio Tlaltecahuacan. As soon as we came to the first humble habitation, its resident children were sufficiently intrigued by the six-man mounted troop they fell in behind. Word must have spread through the village with the speed of juicy gossip forbidden by the local priest. Children flowed out of the side streets like cookies out of a carton. Soon an audience of bemused youngsters followed.

Our lead riders led us to the square, also unpaved, fronted by a couple of official-looking buildings plus the inevitable church, this one of modest proportions and appearance. Our mounted troop halted next to the church. Fortunately my horse did faithfully what its buddies did so no one could really tell I wasn't in control. The children, by now numbering as many as 150, with remarkable orderliness formed a semi-circle to gaze with their big brown eyes at this unusual band of unequal brothers that had arrived in their square.

The rangers leapt from their horses with adroit manliness. Eddie straightened his left leg in its stirrup and swung his right over his mount's back to let himself slide slowly down its side until he landed on his two feet. Not quite with the macho competence of the rangers, but still a commendable show for someone with little more equestrian experience than I. I tried to follow the rangers' example, rather than Eddie's, but then my dismount turned traumatic. My choice of footwear for our Mexican campaign had been my black military boots from RAF days. Their cleat-less, flat leather soles made them singularly dangerous on stony surfaces, especially with an incline. But rather than part with the price of proper hiking boots, I'd persisted with this makeshift substitute.

With the considerable rough terrain walking we'd done, the stitching at the rear of the half sole at the instep on the left boot had broken. It'd happened weeks before, but so far hadn't presented any real problem. Now, as I applied all my weight on my left stirrup, it slipped forward from the pressure of my boot instep and wedged fast beneath my flapping leather sole. My tall horse and my short legs came into dispute. As my right foot hit the ground, my left remained firmly ensconced in the left boot, which, in turn, was firmly ensconced by its sole in the stirrup. I performed a kind of half split, lost my balance, and fell backwards heavily onto the dusty square. There I lay, my buttocks lifted off the ground and only my shoulder blades touching, my left leg and its attendant foot, pointing heavenward. Because the horse was so tall, and my leg so short, I couldn't unhinge the RAF's black boot.

Terror seized me. In an instant the horse would buck and its rear hooves would crush my skull like a moldy melon. Or it might be time for a healthy bowel movement and cascading chunks might splatter across my face. Worse yet, the frightened beast would bolt, dragging me across the earthen square, along cobblestone alleys, through rock-strewn mountain passes, and out into the endless expanse of cacti-covered desert. This intelligent horse would seize the opportunity to repay two-legged Man for all the cruel indignities our species has inflicted on Equus since they evolved through the natural selection process. It seemed unlikely the horse would make allowances I was, just at the moment, only a one-legged specimen. I cringed at the thought of what would happen to my essentially office-clerk, sedentary body. I had horrifying visions of my bones being splintered on rocks as I bounced over them and great shards of flesh ripped off by the cacti and other needle-wielding flora.

Then I realized absolutely nothing had happened. Yes, I was still trapped by the stirrup and laying at about a 35° angle on my shoulders, but the horse hadn't moved a muscle. The four rangers stared, wide-eyed, in utter astonishment. Their identical expressions revealed very clearly they had but one thought: this idiot gringo can't even get off a tame horse, the most docile in their stable!

In a state of petrified embarrassment, I turned my head and, through the archway formed by the belly and legs of my long-suffering mount, I saw the faces of the village children. Their expressions showed they were, from first to last, of the same mind. After several more what seemed like self-confidence destroying minutes, one of the rangers came and released my entangled boot and I clambered to my feet silently vowing that the RAF boots had to go. I also accepted instantly, without reservation, I didn't belong in the ranks of the world's great adventurers.

Then these incredibly friendly and helpful rangers arranged a second truck ride for us back to Huejotzingo, on the eastern side of the volcano, where we could retrieve our stuff from the police station, and where this nightmare had started.

One of the trails up Ixtaccihuatl volcano (17,343 feet) only about 50 miles from Mexico City.

CHAPTER 31

One more bus ride from Huejotzingo took us the approximate 70 miles to Mexico City. From there we would head north for the USA. That night we charged again into the hotel nearest the bus terminal, regardless of price. By 9 p.m. we'd showered and collapsed into our beds. It felt so good we doubted even a five-star inn could have given any greater sense of comfort to our tired bodies and bruised egos.

We certainly hadn't left the kind of imprint in Mexico we had envisaged when we hit on the idea of hiking Ixtaccihuatl. More like a smudge. Many years later at a writers' group, I read the piece I'd written about our Ixtaccihuatl bummer. A woman said it sounded as though there were "two guys on a mountain without a brain between them." A rather apt comment, I thought.

But several good aspects came of our expedition: discovery of the Mexicans' great kindness to strangers; the Mexican rain season is May to September; and we did, in fact, survive. Six days later we crossed back into the USA after traveling the 700 miles between Mexico City and Laredo, Texas, along a main highway that opened in 1936. Since the second half of the 1940s, American influence moved south along this main road requiring just a few years for tourism and the transfer of manufacturing work under license to become a tidal wave.

Back in the land of potable water at the turn of a faucet handle, we resumed the rigors of authentic hitchhiking. During the next two days we made slow progress in covering the approximate 550 miles from San Antonio to New Orleans, the last major USA destination we wanted to visit. During the afternoon of the first day we crossed the flat, monotonous Texas coastal plain to reach Houston. Long waits between short rides under the lone star state's fierce sun started to grate as I still didn't feel 100%. We hitched rides with a disparate group of drivers. One industrial salesman boasted of earning $1,950 a month, a healthy salary at that time. We didn't offer to buy him even a cup of coffee.

An elderly African-American man, driving a worn out 1946 Ford that apparently couldn't run more than about 35 m.p.h., picked us up for a short ride. When we offered to buy him lunch, he told us he was not allowed in any of the roadside eateries. When we stopped, anyway, we paid for his lunch but had to take it to him outside while we, the real roadside beggars, ate inside.

Eventually we reached the far western side of Houston, already a fast-growing, well-spread-out metropolis of 556 square miles, and approaching one million residents. We knew it to be a useless exercise hitching across a big city and found the transit bus that would take us through to the outer eastern suburbs where we'd resume our thumbing. Feeling grimy and disheveled from the day's roadside exertions, when we boarded the public bus we purposely walked to the back in an effort to be unobtrusive. In the best spirit of goodwill ambassadors, we didn't want our redolent selves upsetting other passengers. As we sat down on the hindmost bench, the booming voice of the driver, who had watched us in his interior rearview mirror, immediately informed us gruffly "you guys can't sit back there. This bus won't move until you come up front." We dutifully complied, odorous dirt and all. Segregation still ruled in the South in 1956.

We counted our time in New Orleans, often touted as America's most interesting city by virtue of its periods under French, Spanish and U.S. governance, as a highlight of our tour. In the heart of its old city we visited the French Quarter, famous as the birthplace of jazz. Music erupting from numerous clubs and bars, some of which never seem to close, create a charged atmosphere. Brawny sidewalk barkers add to the cacophony with their raucous, insistent appeals to win the patronage of passers-by.

We walked down Canal Street to its termination at the Mississippi River, which, at one time, formed the southern end of this hustling municipality. The activity along the riverfront, still operating commercially at the time of our visit, provided a real international port atmosphere. An ethnically diverse work force of Creoles, African-Americans, and muscled whites toiled among the wharves bringing the "Ol' Man River" song to mind. We visited the Cabildo, the Old Spanish Courthouse, scene of several major events in the early days of this city, now a state museum, where we devoted several hours.

In the relative cool of the evening we again joined the throngs drifting through the French Quarter. We dove into two clubs at random to drink a beer and listen to excellent jazz groups. But I found that after hearing a few jazz numbers, even though they were toe tapping good, they all started to sound similar. It seemed to me that in each tune a single theme is repeated over and over. It became tedious once I'd detected this, and my enthusiasm waned.

We left New Orleans mid-morning on U.S. 90, a road skirting the eastern shore of Lake Pontchartrain, and which today runs close to the route of Interstate Highway 10. Our target was Atlanta, Georgia, a distance of nearly 500 miles, which we optimistically hoped to cover in two days. Eddie had been invited to call on an acquaintance from our hometown street in London who married an American during WWII. He was now stationed at Fort McPherson in south Atlanta. But it took us until 8:30 p.m. to reach Mobile, Alabama, a day's measly progress of 140 miles.

The next day we again experienced little success. We waited two hours before getting a hitch with a salesman who chose us as a captive audience to listen to him voice his case against the 1954 U.S. Supreme Court ruling for integration of public schools across the country. In the South, however, there was much foot dragging. Our driver, an intelligent man, pleaded his case against segregation on practical grounds. His arguments seemed reasonable, if immoral, but the details I've forgotten.

Our third road day since New Orleans also started poorly. Feeling rather desperate, we decided to split up again with the intention to meet at Fort McPherson in Atlanta, hopefully by late afternoon. I succeeded in obtaining three short rides the last of which put me down in La Grange, Georgia, only 20 miles inside the state border, with 70 miles still between me and our hoped-for destination.

Our route had followed a two-lane road traversing large tracts of farmland, with only a light sprinkling of small towns along the way. At one point I'd been let out on the road with nothing in sight but a roadside fruit stand. I tried my first Georgia peach, liked it, and ate three or four more. By the time I reached La Grange I felt lousy and soon knew a recurrence of Montezuma's revenge had struck. That night I bedded down in the town's most modest motel and fervently hoped my problem would be gone by morning. It wasn't. Greyhound Bus Lines came to my rescue and carried me in style to Atlanta. Later I learned Eddie made had it on schedule.

The American-Anglo military couple made us most welcome. It so happened that the woman's mother, a classic East London Cockney, was vacationing with the couple when we arrived. This peppery Londoner had formed a few opinions about life in America and wasn't backward in voicing them in her inimitable speech pattern. One custom in particular apparently perplexed her mightily. She wondered aloud, notably when her daughter and son-in-law were out of earshot, why she found so many "fings" (contraceptives) stashed in odd places around the quarters.

"I fink 'e must want it when 'e wants it," she giggled, nodding her head, "no matter where the mood takes 'im. Then they jus' does it right there as casual as when I makes a pot of tea."

I relished our 24 hours spent with them because it meant the certain availability of a bathroom at short notice. Fortunately, my problem eased by next morning and we set off in the early afternoon. We separated again with our next meeting place planned at the Greyhound Depot in Charlotte, North Carolina, nearly 250 miles on. Once again our hopes and reality were leagues apart. I never made it out of Georgia, but only to Toccoa, near the South Carolina state line, 80 miles short. Even then, I'd been extremely lucky. Our late start, and my slim pickings, found me after dark on a stretch of highway with no human habitation in sight. I didn't know the next town with a motel, or Eddie's whereabouts, and thought I'd be in for another long night under the stars. Almost no traffic moved by this hour. Getting a ride at night just didn't happen.

After a while a vehicle approached from the rear and, with a rush of hope surging through me, I turned to signal the slow-moving car as I stood blindly staring into its headlights, my right arm rigidly perpendicular. The car passed me and I dejectedly wrote it off as a lost opportunity. Then it slowed even more and pulled over, perhaps 100 yards ahead. I hadn't seen who drove it, and suddenly became apprehensive of why it traveled slowly, past me up, and then stopped. Had the occupant seen this short nutcase hitching on a deserted road in the dark? Was he now donning brass knuckles and drawing a switchblade for my personal close inspection? Although fearful, my desperation was such I ran to catch up.

My lucky moment had arrived. The lone male driver was a man of the cloth, a young Baptist Minister. After he told me he was going as far as Toccoa, which boasted a motel, my spirits soared and, in a great wave of relief, I clambered aboard, almost ready to finally take up religion. Ironically, I could tell he was as nervous of me as I had been of him. He shot frequent glances in my direction for the first few minutes, and seemed to be watching my hands. Was he wondering if I was about to reach for my switchblade? That kind man saved me from a lot of outdoors reality I didn't need that night.

A series of short rides brought me to Charlotte next day by about 3 p.m. where Eddie snoozed on a Greyhound bus terminal bench. We'd decided to make the station our meeting place because getting rides now seemed more difficult. Although rather early to quit, neither of us wanted to risk any more night-time hitching, so we stayed in Charlotte, named after King George III's wife, in the state that was the 1585 site of the first English colony in North America.

Our last port-of-call before our final destination of New York City was Washington D.C., still almost 400 miles distant. Next morning we separated again and, as I watched from the sidelines, Eddie obtained an early ride and disappeared up the road for points unknown. I now moved to the side of the road and signaled anything going to the northeast. After ninety minutes passed, my hopes sank ever lower. I began to believe I'd have to return to the bus terminal to make any forward progress. When I'd almost given up, a car with Texas plates pulled over. A ride at last! And what a ride! With Baltimore his destination, the driver would pass near Washington D.C. This savior from Heaven proved to be a Yugoslavian physician, resident of Houston, en route to Baltimore. During this best hitch for me of our entire journey, he told me something of his interesting personal history.

In repayment for serving six years in his country's small navy, the communist state funded his education to qualify as a physician. Then he won a United Nations' scholarship for specialized study in Paris and from which he eventually refused to return behind the Iron Curtain, claiming political refugee status. After three years in Paris, during which time he contemplated emigrating to various French colonies or a South American country, he obtained a visa to enter the USA. Now, after a three-year residency requirement, he was eligible to sit for a state medical license and Maryland was one of the few states to accept his application. He dropped me off in the outskirts of D.C. at 4 p.m. All I'd done for his fabulous hitch was buy him coffee. I considered offering him a few bucks for gas, but didn't. My rationale: he'd soon be a well-paid American doctor, while I was about to become a starving writer. I regret my tightness yet.

Eddie and I wanted to see the capital's historic highlights, and were also attracted to the city because Robert Banting now lived there. The New Zealander, whom I'd met in Toronto, had played such a big role in our decision to move to San Francisco. He'd yet to move west, and now worked at the New Zealand Embassy. Eddie and I had his apartment address and would meet up there. With my fortunate last hitch of nearly 400 miles, I reached the small apartment of Robert Banting in the northwest section of the District of Columbia about 5 p.m., for once ahead of Eddie, who arrived later that evening. Here we didn't have to concern ourselves with accommodation because Robert kindly let us bunk down on his living room couch and a sleeping bag on the floor.

For the next three days Eddie and I played tourists, joyfully free of our backpacks. We visited the Library of Congress where I was in awe of its 22-million book collection, the many rare editions, and other literary exhibits. Early on our second evening in town, we returned to Robert's apartment, and then the three of us headed for one of the less pricey eateries in the area. Robert brought us up to date on world events over dinner. It turned out there'd been a lot going on while Eddie and I wandered in Mexico. The tall, gangly New Zealander was a bit of a homespun philosopher, with a head full of arcane facts.

Egypt's new strongman, Colonel Gamel Abdel Nasser, following several years of social unrest generated by a rising tide of anti-colonialism, seized and nationalized the Suez Canal on 26 July 1956 — the very week Eddie and I left San Francisco. The British and French, joint owners of the canal, were outraged, and feared Nasser might stop laden oil tankers bound for western ports. The owners landed a combined military force to regain control of the canal. The Soviet Union warned it would rain rockets on Britain and France, plus send troops, accompanied by Chinese "volunteers", to defend Egypt. Meanwhile, Nasser was playing America against Russia as both nations sought to garner influence through partial funding of the Colonel's pet project, the Aswan High Dam, from which he anticipated great benefits for his country's backward economy. America successfully applied pressure on Britain and France to quickly withdraw. Israel, seizing the moment, attacked Egyptian military posts in the Gaza Strip and Sinai Desert in response, they claimed, to repeated border violations. Middle East tension skyrocketed.

Meanwhile, in Eastern Europe, disputes intensified between the peoples of Poland and Hungary and their communist puppet governments, backed menacingly by Russian garrison troops present since the end of WWII. In Poland the widespread anti-Soviet sentiment so alarmed the Kremlin's top leadership, it feared Poland's defection. Also, in the summer of 1956, social unrest in Hungary, active just below the surface more or less from the 1948 communist usurpation of power, broke out with limited fighting in the streets against the police and state security forces. These daily tussles erupted into major street battles on 23 October 1956. Moscow sent 200,000 soldiers and 2,500 tanks. About 50,000 Hungarians died in the ensuing urban combat, and approaching 200,000 fled the country. The tanks razed large areas of Budapest, much only recently rebuilt after WWII. The Russians crushed the popular uprising by savage brute force. Europe hadn't been so tense since the 1949 Berlin blockade.

Against this unstable world backdrop, Eddie and I were about to return to London for Christmas of 1956. But as I pondered the volatile scene, I became alarmed another war could be in the making. Although Eddie's future didn't include any military obligation in Britain, in a national emergency, if domiciled in the U.K., I was subject to recall to the RAF until age 40. Having learned how much better the pay and conditions were in the U.S. military, the RAF had lost its appeal for me. If war raised its head again, and my invaluable services were required, I wanted the best conditions!

We both decided to remain in the USA for six months more to see if the war clouds moved away. Now we needed to find temporary work, but Uncle Sam, the biggest local employer, accepted only U.S. citizens. We didn't qualify. Robert had lived in the District of Columbia for about a year after moving from Toronto, and knew something of the foreign embassy scene through his employment at his own country's legation. He said that the large British Embassy at 3100 Massachusetts Avenue had a frequent turnover in low-paying clerical and custodial positions. We called there and, following a brief interview with an assistant in the security section, both of us were accepted for positions as messenger-guard starting on 1st October 1956. We were given lengthy application forms to fill out and bring back, but probably our presentation of British passports sufficed for background checks. Ironically, I managed to lose the application and had to return for another blank. Not an auspicious start for someone being hired to deliver mail reliably to the many Embassy offices.

For permanent quarters, we moved into a massive, modestly-priced boarding house that accommodated several hundred residents, some working and some studying at nearby Georgetown and American Universities. We had individual basement rooms, the price of which included breakfast and dinner each day. Its location meant we could walk or ride a bus to work.

On my second workday, Montezuma's revenge returned. While not as bad as the attacks in Mexico, it made me feel grim, listless, and devoid of energy and interest, to say nothing of the embarrassment. I still had some of the Mexican powder and, reluctant to pay to see a physician, when I got back to the guesthouse I took it. For a day or two it seemed to help, but then the distressing condition returned. I saw a local general practitioner whose name was on file at the Embassy. The doctor suggested a hospital test to determine the exact nature of my illness. The anticipated expense of that made me feel even worse, and I asked him to prescribe medication based on my description of the problem. The good doctor complied with my dumb request. Almost predictably, this approach to the problem didn't effect a cure.

During the next couple of months my digestive tract malfunctioned intermittently. I dragged myself to work most days feeling poorly, but because the job merely involved internal distribution of the mail, I could perform that without too much expenditure of mental or even physical output. Soon the blahs, discomfort, and my own exasperation wore down even my tight-fisted ways. Stool culture examinations lead the doctor to prescribe a different medicine, which helped somewhat but by no means totally. Another four visits and different medications were required, including a barium enema x-ray, before my volcanic digestive tract finally fell dormant. During this process the doctor also diagnosed me with colitis and, just to complicate matters, told me he believed I'd also developed a condition he called "anxiety neurosis." He prescribed tranquilizers, and they improved my sleep, but he said I needed to change long-term my intensity and worrying. Now I really worried this illness would eat my $2,000 capital earmarked to launch my writing life.

Walking the Embassy's corridors delivering mail to offices soon lost its charm for me, except perhaps offices containing pretty women. A better paying job came open in the Diplomatic Mail Room with two requirements — British citizenship and 60 w.p.m. typing. For once I qualified. The need for a competent typist must have been urgent because I applied one morning and started that afternoon. The work involved listing all mail leaving the Embassy for oversea locations, with the majority destined for the London Foreign Office. The modest amount of extra money was welcome, but best of all I didn't have to wear the ill-fitting mandatory blue, coarse, woolen uniform of the Embassy guard detail. About six weeks after my new job, Eddie learned of an opening at the United Kingdom legation to the United Nations in New York City. It paid somewhat better because of the higher cost of living there, and Eddie thought the Big Apple would be livelier than D.C. He applied, got the job, and he and his luggage moved the 200 miles north in the Embassy panel truck that went regularly with official mail for transport to Britain on Cunard Line ships.

Although my digestive system had improved, I didn't feel 100% most of the time, and I noticeably lacked what I perceived as my normal zest for life. A listless disinterest took over. Now alone, except for an occasional Sunday outing with Robert, I became something of a recluse. To occupy my spare time, and hoping it would mark the start to my writing career, I began work on an article about our nocturnal experiences on Ixtaccihuatal. I thought the affair both bizarre and amusing enough to sell itself to an adventure or outdoors magazine. All I had to do was capture it on paper. Researching the flora on the mountain's slopes took me to the National Geographic Society's marvelous depository of information on our world. Reading good literature and writing it are not the same, I wondrously discovered. It also introduced me to the stark reality that getting published for free is a world away from getting paid for one's scribbles.

The confrontations in the tinderbox Middle East and Eastern Europe hadn't ignited WWIII by the end of 1956. Although both situations had been touch-and-go since mid-year, they now seemed to be defusing. To allow a few more months for the tension to fully dissipate, and to avoid the British winter, I decided to remain in the U.S. until early spring. I booked passage on one of Cunard Lines smaller and older passenger ships, sailing from New York City to Southampton on 28 March, hoping this crossing would be far gentler than my May outward passage.

During December I finished my article on Ixtaccihautl, added an accompanying letter, included the mandatory postage-paid return envelope, and let my fervently hopeful package of literary effort join the millions of Christmas Cards that month.

In preparation for my planned writer's life launch, I visited the nearby French Embassy to inquire as to the laws on taking up residency in Paris. A charming staff member advised that British subjects could visit France as a tourist without documentation for three months. If I stayed longer, a visa would be needed. So, excluding the outbreak of war, and as long as I didn't need to work to live, there appeared to be no reason why I couldn't move to Paris and launch my new, shining career. The fact I didn't have a head full of plots for award-winning novels didn't occur to me as a problem. I'd find my inspiration in a writer's garret overlooking the rooftops of Paris.

Passing the three months to departure, I spent most evenings reading in my room. With the doctor's direction to loosen-up fresh in mind, I tried to break my strong compulsion to read most of the world's good novelists. This was my first conscious effort to change an excessive diet of fiction. I tackled Will Durant's "The Story of Philosophy" and some Montaigne essays. Neither of these choic4es seemed relaxing. I also attempted to resume studying French by listening to language records at the local library where I borrowed books. But I became aware of a concentration problem. Nothing would seem to stay in my brain, no matter how often I read a phrase or heard it through earphones. Because of my ignorance and overweening pride, I didn't accept I had a condition as demeaning as "anxiety neurosis." I attributed my mental difficulties to my dysfunctional intestines!

If I thought I'd been lonely at times in Toronto and San Francisco, now I really wallowed in it. But I couldn't seem to muster the get-up-and-go to change things. To escape monotony of the plain walls of my room on weekends, I made solitary walks through bright, crisp sunlight in nearby Rock Creek Park which I could enter two blocks from the guesthouse. These improved my spirits as I walked but soon after returning to my room a heavy sense of aloneness, even hopelessness, moved in like morning mist in high valleys. Despite these emotional upheavals, I tried to stay focused on writing because everything else seemed to have slipped away. For the first couple of weeks after I mailed my article to the magazine, each day I eagerly went to the residence front desk in the hope of finding a letter from a grateful editor, accompanied by a check with at least two zeroes in the amount box. Nothing came. As more weeks passed, I checked less and less, until I more or less forgot about it. Then, just two days before I departed for New York, I found my self-addressed return envelope in my pigeonhole. There was no return letter and certainly no check. Someone had merely scribbled in the right-hand margin of the first page the words "not suitable."

With my heightened sensitivity, I responded to this rejection with more emotion than appropriate. This represented one more life blow, when I already struggled with an erratic physical illness and a weird mental state. I'd always enjoyed good health; now even that was in doubt. Although this article represented my best effort to get published, there were, no doubt, many valid reasons why it didn't find favor with that editor. Amid all my self-doubts, this rejection added an extra reason to question my plan to move to Paris. Regardless, by this time I was committed to return to Europe.

A few days ahead of my 28th March sailing date, I left the Embassy, moved out of the residence, and headed for New York City on another Greyhound bus. For my last few nights in the United States, I bedded down in Eddie's rented room in mid-town Manhattan. Eddie accompanied me to the pier for the afternoon sailing of Cunard Line's "Scythia," another steamship of the class that brought me to Canada nearly three years earlier. We'd done and seen much together in that time. I believed I'd learned a lot about the three components of North America (Canada, Mexico, and the U.S.) through reading and travel. If a writer's life wasn't in my future, perhaps this knowledge could lead to an interesting, well-paying job in another field.

CHAPTER 32

On the morning of our arrival at Southampton, a brisk, sparkling day, I went on deck after an early breakfast. The liner moved deliberately through the last few miles of the English Channel after an eight-day voyage. Once close enough to shore to let me make out land features, the clear conditions showed off the green, lush English countryside at its best. In my subconscious I compared the seemingly endless dry, barren land Eddie and I passed through as we hitched across the American southwest.

Soon the Scythia maneuvered cautiously through the Solent around the north side of the Isle of Wight. At the mouth of the Southampton Water, a tug came alongside. The pugnacious little vessel guided the ship up the waterway to finally nudge the liner into a berth alongside one of the projecting finger-like piers. When the ship was tied, I looked down on what struck me as a Lilliputian world. The automobiles, and especially the rail freight wagons, resembled toys in comparison with their American counterparts. This assessment of things British versus things American became almost an obsession with me.

My parents, now owners of a small car, their first, met me. Whatever disagreements we'd had before I left England were not remembered as we greeted each other. Once I'd answered a few, almost nonchalant, questions posed by an Immigration Service officer, and satisfied Customs, we started for London.

The drive took us along two-lane roads through numerous quaint villages that filled me with nostalgia. The British government was still some 10 years away from its construction of expressways spanning the country. I thought back to the rarity of seeing people in the open in rural America. Now, on these English country lanes, we didn't go too far before spotting a person walking or cycling and those working fields.

When we reached the outskirts of London, the traffic became much denser than I remembered. London's eight million people seemed to be sitting behind the steering wheel of a compact car, on their faces a look of bemusement at the new experience of a modern traffic jam. Early glimmerings of a recent, modest prosperity had spread across a wider segment of the British population. Average weekly earnings of male blue-collar workers increased 107% between 1946 and 1955 (1). Furthermore, the American notion of selling on credit —known as "hire purchase" in Britain —had been introduced during my absence. Total 1951 hire purchase debt of £208 million rose to £461 million by 1955 (1). Happiness equated to your own wheels!

The circumstances at our row house in Forest Gate were also different. Vera and Reg had moved to their own rented apartment. The living room now boasted a small black and white television, another first. A quieter house, with Roy and I having our own bedrooms.

I had the second floor back room with a window looking out at the merano cherry tree and, beyond, at the trees behind the cemetery wall. I'd spent happy, carefree times climbing all of them. Now I seemed to be weighed down by a life concern holding me in a debilitating grip.

I soon registered with a government-paid local General Practitioner. Once I told him I'd picked up dysentery in Mexico, he referred me to London Hospital for tests to see if a parasitic infestation remained. It proved negative. I asked the hospital doctor the reason for my persistent nervousness, erratic sleeping, bodily fatigue, and general lack of zest, which he attributed to my stressful, itinerant lifestyle. He recommended I "settle down" and my health would restore itself. His advice, of course, flew straight in the face of a move to Paris.

My doubts intensified. If my condition, whatever it was, became permanent, it looked insane to make the leap to a writer's life in the French capital. All of my former zest for, and interest in, life had dissipated. Not only in religion could I not make the great leap. I started to believe I simply didn't have the courage or energy to undertake this huge change of direction. In my notable naiveté, I hadn't given serious thought to my ability and talent. But the greatest restraint to my will power now came in the form of a terrorizing fear, not unlike the experience when I first contemplated emigration to Canada.

In truth, I had only one life passion that might contain the seeds of a worthwhile novel plot: a gut dislike of the British class system that, for me, fostered a life malaise for most blue-collar workers. The pathetic education provided to their children continued this social sickness that, in the final analysis, was the root of these social problems as I perceived them. But this theme had been already well covered in the works of Arthur Morris, Charles Dickens, and George Orwell, to name a few. At decision time, the writing life seemed another leap too far.

The best thing I felt I should do would be following the doctor's advice to settle down, at least to the extent of finding work while I decided where I'd spend the rest of my life. Despite the doctor's advice, I still felt driven to try for a job satisfying my compulsion for work providing the status my ego dictated. If not, America and I might waltz around together again. But at this early stage, I pushed that thought to the back of my mind.

For my first step, I sought out Mr. Trevor Bennington, the reporter at the Birmingham newspapers' London Office who had been so instrumental in motivating me to get an education. During my three-year absence, he'd returned from Australia. Now he was the London reporter/editor for another provincial city newspaper. We had a brief and, for me, unpleasant, meeting. In fact, I sensed he considered it impertinent I'd even contacted him. He seemed uninterested in what I'd done since our last encounter. It didn't produce an offer on his part to help me find a newspaper job, which was my deep hope. I left with tail between legs.

In the print media's trade publication, *Journalist*, I saw an advert for shorthand reporters at the Associated Press, a major news wire service, for their London Fleet Street office. I must have satisfied the man in charge of this small crew that included several with employment records as messy as my own. The job involved shift work taking dictation from domestic and foreign reporters phoning stories to the newsroom, and transcribing the pieces for sub-editor review. The AP phone bank was covered by shorthand typists around the clock every day of the year. Two started at six a.m., increasing to four in the afternoon. At five p.m. the number started to decrease, until only two stayed on duty to 11 p.m. One note taker staffed the night shift from 11 p.m. to 6 a.m.

In my early months at home I felt at a loss during my leisure time. During my absence I hadn't kept in touch with my few acquaintances. Nor did I resume any of my former activities such as soccer or attending public dances. Rightly or wrongly, I felt to do so would indicate a lack of personal growth. In fact, I happily turned to Roy to fill some of my inner void. At age 19, Roy had recently finished his three years at the East

Ham polytechnic college and now worked at his first full-time job as a technical draftsman for Essex County. He, too, had lost touch with most of his state elementary school friends when their paths diverged at age 15 — he into further education and they into the working world.

We began to make occasional trips to central London to visit museums or take in a quality movie. Although I was six years older than my brother, for the first time in my memory we seemed to have common interests. Yet compared with my own dissatisfied personality, Roy was quieter, calmer and reflective. I felt he had a life wisdom that I, the older person, should display. Hiking, another activity we mutually enjoyed, occupied several weekends, with an overnight stay in one of the many private B&Bs available in rural Britain. A weekend hike still in my memory took us across the unspoiled Sussex Downs to the English Channel at Littlehampton. We rode a steam train from London to Petersfield, Hampshire, which left us about a 25-mile hike over the two days, with a return home on Sunday evening. Petersfield is embedded in the Downs, so as soon as we stepped off the train we were following undulating footpaths in a southeasterly direction towards the coast. Views from hill high points afforded us gentle, peaceful vistas every few miles. Villages crouching in valleys appeared to be frozen in time since the 1800s. Finding a quaint country pub for a plowman's lunch was a highlight of the excursion. Yet in this so pleasant landscape I found aspects of English life that raised the hair on my neck.

During the morning of the second day we reached the village of Slindon, about five miles from the coast. As we walked through this quiet hamlet, we spotted an older man pruning in the flower-festooned front yard of his tiny, thatched-roof cottage. We crossed the lane to ask directions, and fell into a brief, illuminating conversation. Although puttering in his garden, he wore a shirt and tie, and a short cotton jacket that, when he bent, revealed his suspenders and belt supporting his trousers; double protection is said to be the sign of an insecure man. He told us he'd been born and raised in Slindon and, in fact, never lived anywhere else. Now in his late sixties and retired, since age 13 he'd worked always as a laborer on nearby farms. He'd never visited London, only about 60 miles distant, and vigorously shook his head when I asked if he'd any interest to see the nation's capital and seat of government. "What'd be the point?" he retorted? A concept apparently beyond his ken. Indeed, he seemed to have no interests outside the old wooden fence enclosing his garden. Although a civilized man, for me he represented the typically truncated human produced by the British education system for working class children until well into the 20th century. Our brief exchange over, he turned back to his flower tidying.

As we left Slindon and headed south into the open countryside, now sloping gently toward the coast, I could not resist continuing to contemplate this man's circumscribed life and accepting attitude compared with my own. He absolutely fit the "contented cow" category of humanity, the demeaning tag I applied in my teen years to such people. Now I'd had a chance to see and experience a little of the outside world, and knew in the months ahead I'd be struggling with the decision of where I'd live for the rest of life. This man's feet were anchored in his one-eighth acre of pastoral Sussex County and his interests equally narrow. But I have to admit that while I dismissed his limited horizons, deep down I felt he was the happier person. A cold sense of emptiness and uncertainty swirled through me.

Our route soon took us past Arundel Castle rising, on a Brobdingnagian scale, above the River Arun. From the far bank of the river we confronted an imposing symbol of the other side of class-ridden Britain. This restored Norman fortress is the family seat of the Duke of Norfolk. Ranked as the premier British peer, his is one of the few dukedoms outside the Royal family. As my vision registered this sight, my brain just as quickly challenged what it represented. The palace's restored castellated round towers, and the huge 16th century manorial house addition, personified the incredible distance between the Duke of Norfolk and the old man who lived almost literally in the shadow of his castle walls. Nowadays the Duke finds it necessary to open his castle for revenue-producing public tours. The unwashed take guided tours of portions of the palace between April and October. The social pendulum has centered itself just a little, but my antagonism to Britain's social structure reignited. This subject roiled me for the rest of the day, certainly distracting from the pleasure of the surroundings, and strongly suggesting my mind could not let go of what, for me, were disturbing subjects.

In the summer Eddie came back to England. At the time he said he didn't know whether it was to stay or just a family visit. He moved into his mother's apartment on Capel Road where she lived alone now that her other children were married. We were both back to our home roots. But for me there was an unsettling feeling that somehow my tie to home had been broken. I just did not reconnect seamlessly. A sense of not belonging seeped into my consciousness. Eddie and I did not resume the leisure-time activities we'd pursued prior to emigration. Instead, we intermittently attended several ethnic or international clubs in central London, which were meeting places for expatriates spending time in the crowded, bustling metropolis. We favored the Australian, Swedish and Swiss clubs perhaps in an effort to convince ourselves that we were now men-of-the-world

Most of the Aussies we talked to in their club bar, over the freely flowing Foster's, appeared to find it a necessity, while still young, to make a one-or-two year odyssey to Britain, via many far-flung points. So many of their ancestors had come from here that new generations seemed to respond to an instinctual need to return like salmon to spawn in the river tributaries of their birth.

On 4 October 1957 I was one of the two shorthand writers on duty for the evening shift. Unfortunately, it had been another day where I'd felt unwell, lethargic, and my concentration wavered. These days were increasing in frequency. The phone rang in one of the booths where we received oversea calls and it fell to me to respond. I put on the earphones and punched the button to connect with the caller. Through mild static the person at the other end identified himself as Reuters' Moscow correspondent. The time zones between London and the Russian capital meant he was still in his office at midnight, somewhat unusual. He said he had a hot story I needed to get to the desk editor as quickly as I could transcribe it. Off he charged with a piece that very soon had me stumbling and straining. I got down his first sentence about a government release announcing the launching that day of a "spudnit" into earth orbit. At first I thought the Soviets had launched a diseased pomme de terre to ruin the crops in capitalist countries. These Russian words, interspersed with unfamiliar technical terms, quickly had me asking him to repeat phrases and spell words. My general malaise and difficulty with focusing my thoughts, compounded by my usual embarrassment, made for a tense situation. Soon I heard the anger rising in his voice. Apparently he had a world-class headline story but fate had connected him with a shorthand-writing world-class simpleton.

After several attempts the now thoroughly irritated Moscow correspondent led me by the hand to understand that the "spudnit" was Sputnik I, an artificial spherical satellite that now circled the earth every 95 minutes at 18,000 m.p.h. Requiring 32 rocket boosters to push the satellite to its orbit, its flight altitude ranged from 143 to 584 miles. It contained a two-frequency transmitter, sported four trailing antennae, and its Russian name translated to "traveler." Sputnik I had been launched from Russia's primary space camp at Baikonur on salt flats in Karagand Basin, south Kazakhstan.

The effect on American public opinion of this small 184-lb. sphere, less than two-feet in diameter, demonstrated it punched in the heavyweight class. It alarmed American space scientists that the U.S. lagged behind. Department of Defense top brass worried because of its potential military applications. Historians now credit the Russian achievement on that day as marking the start of the space age. Here I was, present at the dawn of a new age, feeling lousy, inadequate, unenthusiastic and desperately sad.

By this time I'd reluctantly given up the idea of moving to Paris. My confidence and life gusto had evaporated to a degree where I accepted such an undertaking as being ludicrous. It pained me immensely, but the plunge represented a too frightening prospect to handle. Even though I'd abandoned a permanent relocation to Paris, in late October Eddie and I headed there. I wanted to at least see the City of Light. I feared a ferry crossing would be rough this late in the year, and we decided to fly. Ever wanting to save pennies, we used a start-up company that flew a couple of ramshackle planes, each capable of carrying not more than 10 passengers. It operated out of Lydd, on the Kent coast, to Le Tourquet, on the French coast, about 15 miles south of Boulogne. Flight time was 45 minutes. A bus, equally ramshackle, took us the 125 miles to central Paris where we secured, to put it politely, a less than fancy hotel room.

In the French capital we visited many of the more popular sights. We were well outside the tourist season and the places of interest were noticeably uncrowded. Because it was already cool, we sat inside Champs Elysee cafes to watch through the window the world go by. This certainly would have been more fun in the spring when the girls wouldn't be hidden in topcoats. At that stage of life, food didn't occupy an important place in our lives. We stupidly missed our opportunity to find out if French fine cuisine was really that fine. Instead we chose to eat at plain, workaday cafes where the standard fare was "biftek et pommes frites." In fact, we discovered the French eat nearly as many French fries as do the British.

We were booked on a return flight from Le Tourquet to Lydd for the late afternoon. A delay for mechanical repairs didn't help our apprehension about flying in what I believe was WWII military surplus aircraft. It had been dark for several hours by the time our plane rumbled and shook down the runway, lifted off clumsily, and shortly banked toward the nearby Channel. The single line of blue runway lights, and then a few coastal road lights, could be seen briefly out the starboard windows before low clouds blotted them out. We flew in darkness over the English Channel, the watery grave for many brave flyers in the war. Our pilot and co-pilot, not enclosed in a forward compartment, were eerily illuminated in the luminous glow of control panel dials and gauges. Albeit austere, this was my shaky introduction to commercial aviation.

When we arrived over the Kent coast in the Dungeness area, visibility worsened because of a bank of November fog. I am certain the aircraft didn't have instrument-landing radar, and it might not even have had radio contact with the ground. The young pilot was probably flying by the seat of his pants. Yet somehow he knew or guessed the fog hugged the ground too low to attempt landing and announced we'd go into a holding pattern. We spent a tense 30 minutes circling the area. Encased in the fragile vintage craft, flying through a black void, with the thundering of the engines easily penetrating its soundproof-less fuselage worked on the nerves. Then the man who controlled our fate called out, over his shoulder, he would attempt a landing. He directed us to put hands on head, and lean forward in our seats as low as spines permitted. I'm pretty sure the aircraft wasn't equipped with lap belts.

We learned later that the plane descended to about 50 feet above the field and still no runway guiding lights could be seen. The pilot chose to abort the approach, put full power to the engines, and raised the nose. For what seemed minutes we sensed the engines had stalled and the shuddering plane just hung in space. Then engines roared in response to the pilot's desperate action, and the old WWII veteran lurched and bucked like a rodeo entrant. Every passenger sucked air and gripped their armrests with white-knuckle intensity. The engines slowly settled into a steady, consistent rumble, and we headed to the alternate small Manston airport, inland from Ramsgate. In the 50 years since then, I've done a reasonable amount of flying in commercial aircraft, across oceans and over continents, but I know that my first was the one that came closest to being my only flight.

None of the various attempts I made during 1957 to secure a job that would satisfy my image of myself bore fruit. One try involved the British Broadcasting Company when I responded to an advertisement for an editor in their North America news department. It resulted in a courteous interview with a charming female personnel officer. I pleaded that my reading and travels qualified me for such a position, but she was not allowed to consider anyone without a degree.

It is reasonably clear to me now, after so many years, I set myself up for my own fall. Manifestly, this emergence in me of such a strong need for a prestigious position was quite at odds with my notably ordinary background. So why did I have this obsessive and inflated idea that I had to have a job that would hold my interest and reflect me in a special light? I choose to believe that my greedy and passionate reading of novels and adventure books since my early teens raised my feet off terre firma and my head went into the clouds. My grip on reality weakened. I craved the glamorous, or what I perceived as that, through a distorted life vision. And, most regretfully, I suspect the well-recognized Napoleon complex had its own strata in the various layers of my complex personality. My father had been partially right when once he said I read too much. Reading is a great good, but it must be in balance between fact and fiction.

Eddie began to talk of returning to America. I began to tell myself that if I didn't obtain a "special" job and had to spend my life working in a routine one, I'd prefer to do it in America where the sun shone more often and the wages were better. Always in the back of my mind were the words of one British expatriate when we discussed the merits of living in either country. This man advised me one needed to think clearly about where one would be, in material terms, at the end of working life in Britain versus the USA. I had to agree the scale tipped in favor of the USA.

The contortions I put myself through over a job were also increasingly performed against a backdrop of moods characterized by sadness. At times a cold numbness penetrated to my core. Nothing fired my enthusiasm and certainly nothing gave pleasure. These sensations perplexed and frightened me. They also caused me shame, and mostly I kept them to myself. The spirited side of me that wanted to be seen as someone with the courage to leave home and go out into the world seemed to have evaporated. Only a deflated, confused, and frightened remnant remained.

By the end of 1957 Eddie had made up his mind to return to the U.S. in early 1958. I struggled pathetically with what I should do. We even made lists of the pros and cons of life on either the east or west side of the Atlantic Ocean. My indecision became chronic. Rather than face reality, I'd tell myself I'd think about it tomorrow and make the big decision then. But I couldn't make tomorrow come. Yet an important reality would not be removed for all my confused dithering: under U.S. immigration law of the time, a resident alien with a green card could be absent from the country for a total of 12 consecutive months and still re-enter the USA under an original permit. If I stayed out longer, I would have to start over again. That meant I had until 31 March 1958 to get back on US soil. By now I had concluded I was not going to get a job that would satisfy my presumably unrealistic hopes. This made me favor returning to the United States to at least earn higher wages. Yet I seemed to be literally paralyzed with indecision. Years later I learned my parents worried I could be going insane.

What made me make up my chaotic mind finally involved me only in an indirect way. About this time, Roy made up his much clearer mind that he wanted to go on with his education to become a civil engineer. He had done some research into the possibility of achieving this in England, and found the prospects limited. Based on my comments about how easy it seemed to go to college in America, Roy began talking of doing that. Eddie's plans to return were underway, and with Roy newly indicating he wanted to try it, I finally made the decision to head for the U.S. again, even though my level of anxiety and doubt made it highly questionable as to its wisdom. Ignorance and pride still prevented me from seeking professional help.

My family: L to R: Dad, Mom, Roy, Vera, Reg. Photo taken in 1957 during my first confused visit to London. Their smiles might stem from my anticipated announcement I'd be returning to America in 1958.

CHAPTER 33

The year 1958 evolved to be the first with more passengers crossing the North Atlantic by air than by sea. This benchmark is considered one of the indicators the age of mass tourism had started. But it remained true at the time floating steerage across the world's second biggest ocean came cheaper than taking to the wing. Eddie and I, of course, chose the less costly mode. Thus when we headed back to America in mid-March —within a couple of weeks of the expiration of our permanent entry visas —we resorted again to another solidly dependable Cunard Line steamship. Compared with my previous ships, the "Ivernia II" was only three years in service and offered a relative level of elegant modernity.

Although March can serve up some ferocious weather in the North Atlantic, our crossing proved relatively serene. Each evening the ship offered entertainment in the form of dancing, to the accompaniment of a three- or four-man band, and even a fancy dress ball. We attended a number of these and met two nurses from Essex County who were going to Toronto to work and travel for a year. Eddie eventually married one of these nurses, but that occurred some years in the future and is a story for another to record.

On this crossing, the ship made port first at Halifax, Nova Scotia, the historic capital of the maritime province. The city, founded by British settlers in 1749, played a major role in Canada's story. It capacious natural harbor, which remains ice-free year round, ensured the area's early military importance. Today, Halifax is the country's biggest eastern commercial port and its primary naval base.

Next day, when we landed again on American soil, the goal of these two reformed world drifters meant arriving back in California as soon as possible. There we would get serious about life by settling down to join the quietly desperate majority of the 9-5 population and live happily ever after. To this end, we didn't intend to engage in any sightseeing en route. Our wanderlust desires were to be forever expunged. Well, almost.

Some large cities in America had agencies that matched drivers with automobile owners who needed their vehicles in far-off locations but didn't want to undertake long road journeys themselves. A New York City phone book and a few calls soon had Eddie matched with the older female owner of a recent Ford Fairlane sedan, who wanted her car in San Mateo, just south of San Francisco. She had concerns about crossing the continent while winter lingered, especially in the Midwest. We received no payment and had to provide all gasoline, except for an initial tankful. We also had to follow the most direct route between pick-up and delivery points, and not abuse the vehicle. These conditions suited us well. We avoided bus, train or plane fare, while giving us a large automobile in good mechanical shape to convey our worldly possessions and us. We'd already driven across this continent once on a road not yet paved for hundreds of miles. We assured the agent that winter conditions didn't faze us.

Eddie did most of the driving on this journey. At that time my own experience with this essentially boring activity was limited, I didn't have a license, and Eddie seemed to enjoy being behind the wheel. In flat Kansas we encountered heavy snow. Somewhere between Salina and Hays, the Ford skidded on the snow-packed road, turned sideways to our direction, and slid across the shoulder with the back wheels going into a snow-hidden rain ditch. Kansas can experience cloudburst rains in summer months, and roads need large gullies to let them drain speedily. We clambered out for a quick inspection, which fortunately revealed the vehicle hadn't sustained exterior damage. But now its hood pointed skyward as it sat at a 45° angle. Novice-like, we tried to get the car out ourselves with Eddie gunning the motor, rear wheels spinning aimlessly, and me pointlessly pushing. We soon realized we were in that ditch to stay until professional help arrived. Almost miraculously we didn't have too long to wait before a tractor rattled and swayed noisily towards us. The good-Samaritan farmer stopped to offer assistance. He fastened a heavy chain to the car's front chassis tow hook, and we were soon back on the road, engine idling cheerfully. This good friend-of-the-road would not accept a gratuity, and advised us we needed to put on snow chains as we still had the western half of Kansas to cross and weather conditions were worse in that part of the state. Later I seem to remember hearing that it's something of a Midwest tradition for farmers in their tractors to head out in inclement weather to help passing motorists.

We'd noticed the car's owner had snow chains stowed in the large trunk and presently buried under our suitcases. We clambered in and headed west again, but at a more conservative pace. At the next roadside service station we pulled in and parked at the rear away from pump traffic. Neither of us had ever installed snow chains and were at a loss. Once more our luck held. A solid-looking Midwesterner emerged from the station, saw the obviously clueless pair, and demonstrated on one wheel how the approximate four-foot-long, two-track chain with crossties spaced about six inches apart, wraps around the tire, and then sutures tightly on both sides of the wheel with wire clips. Doing one at a time, the trick is laying them on the ground and rolling the car until each wheel is properly placed. We again heartily thanked this American succoror, our second in one day, and set to on the other three wheels trying to follow his example. We were glad he hadn't stayed around to watch us because it took us inordinately longer at the task. With the help of a little Cockney cussing, they eventually all seemed to be mounted properly. At last we took off again on the ultra straight road crossing the seemingly endless plains of Kansas, which were again being buried even deeper by swirling, heavy snowflakes arriving from jostling gray clouds.

Although now aware of the dangers of driving too fast in these conditions, because we wanted to make up lost time we grew more heedless as the miles passed. With snow chains, the car tracked straight and appeared to brake well. So on we went, hour after hour. At some point that afternoon we became aware of a steady thump coming from the front of the car. Where exactly we didn't know, but it seemed to emanate from the engine compartment on the passenger side. The motor, however, sounded normal and no dashboard warning lights blazed. At some point we checked if an object had caught under the car that could be causing this noise as it dragged along. We saw nothing. Interested in getting the rest of our lives on track as soon as possible, we decided to ignore this mysterious but certainly constant sound. Thus we pushed on through Kansas and into eastern Colorado, the first 200 miles of which is part of America's vast interior plain stretching from Canada to Mexico. But by the time we reached Denver, on the eastern lower slopes of the Rocky Mountain range, we were at 5,280 feet above sea level. We stopped for gas in the south suburbs of this state capital. I remember getting out of the car and noting the temperature felt quite comfortable.

Although we were still in March, at this altitude the sun warms the thin air effectively to make for cheerful conditions.

A pleasant young man in his shirtsleeves pumped the gas and cleaned our windshield. After hearing our accents, he drew us into a conversation about nationalities, birthplaces, and destinations, both the immediate one and life's. As he wiped dry the glass, he wistfully expressed his desire to travel and see the world, a common theme with people encountered. Many express a yearning to break free and randomly roam, perhaps revealing an instinctual hankering from the earliest days of man. Yet relatively few make the break from their familiar surroundings. So many prefer the security and comforts of home.

From Denver we climbed roads with stunning views of the Rocky Mountains, to traverse high, windy passes at elevations averaging 11,000 feet. The surrounding peaks were snow covered and the white stuff packed all clefts, ledges and niches of the majestically rugged terrain. Yet the roads were drivable because Colorado liberally applies men and machines to keep them open through the winter. When we completed the approximate 200-mile-long slide down the western face of the Rockies to the border with Utah, snow no longer softened the landscape. But the thump still persisted. In fact, now that the roads were clear, the thump sounded more like a clang. At this late stage, we two non-mechanical types thought to remove the chains. The mysterious sound that had accompanied us up and down America's continental divide turned out to be a broken crosstie, separated on one side, which had been flailing the upper wheel well housing with every rotation. This broken crosstie had flogged the housing directly above the tire with such power and persistence it had cut an elongated hole through the sheet metal. When snow had been packed in the wheel well, the sound had been muffled to a thump, but once the snow melted, the sound became a clunk. Our ignorance caused damage to a car in excellent condition. It remained for us to complete the last one thousand miles to San Francisco without inflicting further outrage to this lady's automobile. We assumed the car would be inspected upon delivery, the damage discovered, and we'd incur a hefty repair bill. Our driving during this final phase would be noted for its conservatism.

Back in San Francisco we bedded down at the Turk Street YMCA, in the grungy Tenderloin district, where we'd started our first incursion in the city. This time, however, we decided to find reasonable accommodation before we launched a job search. Both felt we didn't want to return to the boarding house scene because of our earlier unsatisfactory experiences. We agreed to split the costs of an apartment, sharing the cleaning and cooking between us. Although readily acceding to this arrangement, I was full of reservations, which I kept to myself. It was more than just my ingrained reluctance to perform domestic chores. To my distress, my strange, embarrassing mental malaise, characterized by doubts and indecision, still persisted. I'd fervently hoped that once I'd made this big decision on where to spend the rest of my life, my emotions would stabilize and I'd emerge from this debilitating timidity and indecisiveness. To my deep distress, my strange condition still persisted.

Within days we'd found a modern, airy, furnished apartment at a manageable price for this high-cost city. Located on a hill in the Twin Peaks district, it overlooked Noe Valley. It barely qualified as "furnished", however, as it lacked easy chairs or a couch. Furthermore, its single bedroom, with only one bed, was the major detraction. Neither of us liked the idea of sharing a bedroom and bed, but anything bigger came with a much higher tab. Fortunately, the king-sized bed afforded plenty of room.

The job search didn't go as fast or smoothly as the hunt for accommodation. Although I'd told myself many times I returned to California to settle down in a routine job, my desire for a writing career still pushed me to first try San Francisco's two independent newspapers for work in their news departments. This attempt met with the same response I'd garnered three years earlier. Stepping down a notch, I fruitlessly tried a magazine publisher, which I saw as a pale substitute for newspaper work. A number of the large corporations with appropriately sized towers in the downtown financial district were the next targets. But it seemed these well-paying business giants didn't use male shorthand typists any more, if they ever had. For any other type of position they demanded a college degree.

After about four weeks, I concluded San Francisco is not an easy city for securing work because of the constant influx of newcomers with solid qualifications. Jobs go quickly, and the plentiful supply of labor tends to suppress wages. Although I remembered my two years in railroad freight rate work as tedious and unexciting, next I applied at Southern Pacific

Railroad, the major line headquartered in San Francisco. But they weren't hiring. False pride stopped me from reapplying at the Santa Fe Railroad, but it saved me embarrassment as I later learned of their policy of not re-hiring anyone who had quit.

One day I wandered into the British Airways' small sales office, on fashionable Union Square. I wasn't responding to an unemployment office lead or a newspaper ad. The manager chose to see me in his office and asked questions about my experience and general background. He said he needed someone to call on travel agents in San Francisco to make the case for routing people on BA, and asked if I'd be interested? Before I gave his question even a little consideration, my pathologic lack of confidence flooded over me like a Bay of Fundy tidal wave. To my life-long regret, I told the manager I didn't think I could handle such a job. He said thanks, and sent me on my way.

As a major port and commercial center, San Francisco hosts consulates from numerous countries. It was in this low-pay niche of the local economy that I obtained a position as an administrative assistant in the Press Office of the Consulate General of India with offices in the downtown financial district. The Consulate's monthly paltry pay of $215 was only helped by the fact the work was vaguely connected with the press world, but this required a good stretch of the imagination. However, because my new employer was a foreign government, I paid no federal or state taxes. And we did not work on the national holidays of either India or America. Eddie enrolled full-time as a student at a court-reporting school to master the stenotype machine to record live court proceedings. He intended to live on his savings, supplemented by returning to evening and weekend work at the up market men's clothing store on Union Square where he'd worked during our first year in the city.

My position at the Consulate included a few duties of modest interest, but much more of dull routine. The Consulate subscribed to the bigger west coast newspapers, particularly those in California, Washington, Oregon and Arizona. I had to peruse them and clip out anything with an Indian connection. Very soon I became more ardent to find items pertaining to Britain which I clipped for myself. I didn't then have enough understanding of human psychology to realize the subconscious wish this indicated.

I knew from the start I hadn't found work that gave me a chance of any progression. I decided I needed to obtain a college degree if I ever hoped to secure satisfying work. This meant I first had to acquire a high school diploma. By the time I'd made this decision, the school summer vacation had begun and it would be August before I could register at Mission Dolores Senior High School, which offered diploma night classes. Because my education record in America was confined to the two night classes taken when I lived in the city in 1955/6, my application caught the school admission counselor's eye. During an interview with her, she asked me about prior formal education. I explained that really the only worthwhile record I could offer was confined to night classes in England and Canada. After hearing my history, she expressed her opinion that my learning was totally lopsided in favor of language and literature. She prescribed remedial work in arithmetic, natural sciences, civics, and history. I buckled down and the following summer gained my American High School diploma.

Eddie and I next purchased a used auto — another Nash Rambler — between us to lower its cost and running expenses, but it soon proved to be a source of disputes as our individual schedules diverged. We chose to let the apartment remain sparsely furnished. We didn't have television; he owned a radio, I didn't. Because we were both occupied in the evenings and portions of the weekend with homework, I felt the less distraction, the better. Cooking, cleaning and doing laundry in an automatic laundromat on the now well-known Castro Street, only five blocks from our accommodation, consumed other leisure hours. At that time, Castro Street was not remarkable as anything but one more neighborhood thoroughfare with small shops and a slight Hispanic flavor. Since then it has evolved into one of San Francisco's large and vocal Gay communities.

Mission High School issued me a diploma on 29 May 1959. I stayed at the Consulate during that summer and enrolled at San Francisco State College to enter in the fall. I hoped to embark on a serious, four-year effort to give myself a chance in the real world. Once more I vowed to sever my umbilical connection to fiction and started to read general books on economics and sociology. Responding to the nervous Nellie in my make-up, I simultaneously experienced strong feelings of regret I'd indulged myself for so long on fiction. Such thoughts increasingly dominated my mind during bouts of sleeplessness.

September 1959, the month I started college, witnessed an unprecedented event when Nikita Sergeyevich Khrushchev, Premier of the Soviet Union, officially visited the USA. During his 12-day tour he traveled to San Francisco and stayed at the well-appointed Mark Hopkins Hotel on Nob Hill. His hotel departure time was announced publicly for a Saturday morning, and I went to glimpse this shoe-pounding, rambunctious personality.

Emerging from the hotel main entrance, and before climbing into an awaiting State Department limousine, Khrushchev walked across the forecourt and through the local police cordon to greet the small crowd lined up on the Mason Street sidewalk. Security, to say the least, was then far more relaxed. My viewpoint at the rear of the throng didn't let me shake his hand, but I did get a good view of the Russian brave enough to denounce Stalin. Although he wore a summer-weight, rumpled, light-gray, single-breasted suit, white shirt and red tie, I visualized him in Russian peasant garb scything wheat on the boundless steppe.

Only about 5'3" tall, he appeared to be the same wide. With his beefy body, large head, baldpate, and distinctive splattering of pimples bestride a broad nose, he could be fairly described as "the common man." I like to think I set eyes on a dynamic Russian who played a seminal role in 20th century history. Some thirty years after Khrushchev's American visit, other Soviet leaders received credit for bringing down the communist empire. But never Khrushchev. Surely, however, the first crack in the hitherto seemingly impregnable Soviet monolith came when, in 1956, Khrushchev publicly denounced the prolonged, horrific cruelties of the state under Joseph Stalin?

Eddie went every day to his court-reporting school, I believe from eight to four. On the evenings he worked at his clothing sales job, he went straight there. He also worked most Saturdays. On some days my classes were over by 2 p.m., and Eddie didn't return until 10 p.m. I had the apartment to myself for hours on end. At first I thought it was great and tried to study hard during this quiet time. And even when we were both there, after the evening meal, we chose to study in different rooms. As a result, I spent much time alone, and I began to find it increasingly difficult to ignore this loneliness. I remembered hearing a statement, and believed it true at the time, dismissing loneliness as a figment of the imagination. Suddenly loneliness seemed no mere whim; it hurt physically.

To escape the silent apartment, I started to attend a few weekend Sierra Club hikes, mainly in Marin and Sonoma Counties, north of the city. The Sierra Club, founded in 1892 is one of America's earliest groups dedicated to saving threatened natural resources, scenic areas, and wildlife. Today, it is represented in all 50 states and has developed into a powerful advocate. The San Francisco chapter hikes in public areas were often well attended. On several Saturday hikes I joined there were about 100 participants spread out along a hill trail like refugees fleeing a war-torn city. We hiked under California's crystalline blue skies amid sylvan surroundings. But even on these uplifting, social hikes, among so many interesting, intelligent and diverse people, I tended to walk alone. Inside I ached for companionship, but didn't have even the little confidence required to break out of my own self-absorption. On one hike, a girl from Switzerland, with whom I had talked briefly at the assembly point, caught up with me and asked why I walked in such noticeable isolation without talking to anyone. I acknowledged a life-long shyness to myself, which seemed to be getting worse. But I would never publicly acknowledge or accept it. In my abysmal lack of self-understanding, I tried to explain my behavior with the rationale that I believed we should only talk when we had something really worthwhile to say. How ridiculous! If this were so, humanity would be struck dumb!

CHAPTER 34

Now I joined Eddie as a full-time student. The counselor's comment about my lopsided education at the time I enrolled at Mission High School night classes still rattled me. I intended to rectify this deficiency at mach-scale speed. Displaying far more ambition than common sense, of the five courses I selected, two were straight mathematics, one was math-related, and the two others were business administration and human psychology. Five courses for a full-time student is a modest load, and would not faze an emotionally stable student with a balanced academic background. I didn't fit either description. I needed course selection counseling. Far too reticent and withdrawn, I never asked and never received such guidance, setting myself up for yet another fall. My intentions were good, but we all know where good intentions lead.

Still a stiff British citizen, I felt uncomfortable among my fellow students who were thousands of America's confident, boisterous youths, mostly 18 years old. Among all those 11,503 vibrant young people on campus for the fall 1959 semester, I mostly withdrew into myself in a quite unnatural manner. Everyone scurried between classrooms intent on arriving on time to meet his or her daily course schedules. Yet, during longer intervals between classes, individuals found each other, like migrating birds, forming animated groups sprawling on lawns to squeeze every drop of pleasure from their free time. I sat alone, propped up against a tree, head buried in a textbook. But the words went in one eye and out the other while my mind mostly registered sad solitariness.

My problem with concentration intensified no matter how I fought against it. My brain would not absorb the materials I read. Mathematical principles and formulas were especially elusive. Learning is said to be a matter of throwing so much mud against a wall in the hope some will stick. Very little stuck for me. A sense of desperation became more and more prevalent. With all this mental turmoil, it negatively impacted my sleep. Now I often started awake after just a couple of hours, mostly to remain awake until shortly before the 6 a.m. alarm. I'd drag myself out of bed, every step getting ready becoming a major effort. Then, somnambulist-like, I'd descend the 17th Street hill to catch the college-bound tram on Market Street. On those grim mornings, I hoped to secure a seat and nap to restore some clarity to my sluggish brain.

I felt I was slipping into a kind of dysfunctional mental state, although I didn't understand it, and certainly didn't accept it. I dropped the Mathematics and Human Affairs courses to lessen my load. A desperate step. Enough time had passed to count them as failures in term grades. To help distract from my sense of despondency, I signed up with the college office that matched students with local part-time employment. I did, indeed, land a few temporary jobs that helped combat the loneliness by bringing me into contact with people, but not much money.

At first I spent a few afternoons working for one of the college's administrative lady deans typing correspondence. She dictated letters to me, which I captured in shorthand and transcribed. A local lawyer offered a slightly better hourly rate and bit more on-the-job excitement. He and his wife held a party at their swank city residence for professional acquaintances and personal friends. He wanted a male bartender. Although I knew little about that trade, the Consulate's Italian chauffeur, who'd once worked as a waiter, bequeathed me a white linen jacket with silver buttons. With such livery, I reckoned I was half way there. A library book provided the nomenclature and ingredients of some popular mixed drinks. I exaggerated my experience to them, and mentioned the snazzy white coat. They were sold.

Arriving an hour before the invitees, I found the self-service food buffet table set up in the den/living room which extended almost the length of the home. The lawyer's wife advised she'd re-supply the food trays. My job as barman was to take individual drink orders from people arriving, prepare their choices in the kitchen, and bring them to the den. Drink glasses and an extensive collection of wines, spirits and mixes were set up on a table. She said I should come often to the reception room to pick-up discards and offer more to those with empty glasses. Drinking and driving was not yet an issue.

I was soon absolved of my primary concern of not knowing the ingredients of unusual fancy cocktails, such as the grasshopper, Rob Roy, or Singapore sling. Many of the men drank bourbon with a mixer and a few scotch and water, while the ladies tended to select wine. But the hostess also offered a peach juice punch in a huge silver bowl centered on a separate table with a glittering pyramid of upturned stem glasses around it. Champagne and a liqueur had boosted the peach juice. Peach halves and ice cubes jostled each other in the mixture. Its taste transported the drinker to scented evenings on tropical isles and quickly became the most popular choice among the ladies. Even I could handle ladling this divine nectar. But addiction to sweet almost became my literal downfall. For every glass filled, I took a generous gulp of the expensive ambrosia. This small theft, according to my devious reasoning, supplemented the modest hourly wage. Such was the demand, quite soon I didn't find it effective trekking from the reception room to my workstation with individual glasses to top up. I decided to carry a tray with a dozen glasses filled with punch. People could pick a fresh one and plunk their empties on the tray. Efficient as a Japanese assembly line. After about another 60 minutes, I'd carried quite a few trays and sampled the punch to where I started to feel happy, uncharacteristically self-assured, and pleasantly tingly in my new white-jacketed, servant's role.

When I returned to the reception on the next refill run, carrying a tray of full glasses at chest height, my right foot, which doesn't lift off the ground quite like the rest of humanity's, stubbed the perhaps inch-high thresh-hold. I lurched heavily forward, accelerated my pace with arms outstretched to steady the tray, like a scene from a Keystone cops movie, and hoped desperately to avoid falling flat on my face. The section of den carpet over which I staggered was miraculously clear of guests. My good fortune and balance held. Even so, my stumble ended just short of a group of ladies in their party finery. My mind instantly filled with the image of me colliding with them, sticky punch cascading down their very best gowns. Those who'd witnessed my brief gravity-defying performance now stared at me with looks of horror or disbelief. Another one of my paralyzing surges of mortification swept through me. I was instantly sober and didn't touch another sip that evening.

These few casual jobs did provide some company that eased the immediate loneliness. But nothing helped my inability to concentrate. I had a foreboding sense of crashing at the first term examinations, set for January 1960. And I did. I earned failures in both remaining math courses, and only a "C", or satisfactory pass, in business and psychology.

Early in February I received a stenciled form letter from San Francisco State College (now University) informing me I was academically disqualified to continue. A kick in the gut more shattering than anything before.

Nearly 28 years old, I'd flunked my first college attempt. Long burdened by a sense of personal failure, it was now proven beyond doubt. I'd been unable to secure a worthwhile job since returning to San Francisco. I'd hoped getting a college degree would solve that problem. Now I was back on the street with this new humiliation burned into my record and psyche.

This devastating development, however, seemed to fly in the face of the true circumstances. I believed I'd made a conscientious effort to study hard by devoting the time. Once the psychology professor, an Asian-American lady, said I appeared to be one of the most intent students in her class, focused and paying close attention. In fact, I made extensive shorthand notes of what seemed important material in the textbooks. In time this meant I'd copied whole pages in shorthand into an exercise book, thinking this method would help adhere some of that mud. It didn't. What I didn't then understand my brain would not absorb much no matter the hours devoted or the methods used. But my greatest mistake was I did nothing to find out why. If you believe in the old maxim of a silver lining in every cloud, as I now do, I believe the silver lining in this pitiful episode was it introduced me to human psychology.

As a reader of quality fiction, I'd gained some insight into the human condition. But it required the formal study of psychology for me to begin, ever so tentatively, to understand the mechanics of this all-important subject. I don't remember the name of the female professor who taught this course, but I still have the class textbook. In it are five drawings by Boris Artzybasheff depicting the neurotic behavior of some people in response to anxiety.

When I first gazed on these caricatures, it jolted me to see something of myself in each. From then on I became an avid reader of books on psychology in an effort to better understand my own inadequate adjustment to life. But I still didn't grasp that my problems emanated from within. However, I'd launched on what has proved to be a lifelong voyage of self-discovery in pursuit of the advice, attributed both to Aristotle and Socrates: to "know thyself."

Confirming the rightness of this path, many years later Lee Iacocca, former president of both Ford and Chrysler companies, in his own autobiography, said he considered the psychology courses, required in his degree in industrial engineering, to be the most useful for him in his life.

My understanding of human psychology at the time was insufficient for me to know my poor showing manifested a depression, which had been building over years. Further, even if I'd realized it, my vanity wouldn't have accepted it. I simply blamed my own inadequacy; the task needed more vigorous application on my part.

Without work or school to occupy me, for the first week I felt I didn't belong in human society. Each day I took a long, lonely walk through wonderful Golden Gate Park to the Pacific Ocean and back to divert my rigid thought patterns. At that time, during the workweek, I had the park almost to myself; nowadays I might have to share it with a large, camped-out homeless population. But I disliked being idled. Almost in spite of myself, I had a work ethic that made idleness uncomfortable. Now I faced finding a job with my already low self-confidence further battered, and a rampant physical and mental malaise.

My next job materialized from a leftover lead from the college employment office. I believe I portrayed myself as a student still enrolled in college, and secured a temporary, part-time position with Blyth & Company Inc., then a smaller New York-based investment banker with wholesale and retail client brokerage operations. I joined half-a-dozen young men, all enrolled in local colleges, who spent some hours performing simple computations of interest payments for clients holding coupon (bearer) bonds. Someone taught me the formula on the huge desktop calculator, which I executed automaton-like without understanding the process.

The college letter advising of my disqualification ended with something to the effect that I could re-enroll if I produced proof of academic redemption. While my spirit lay face down in sewer muck, I clung to the belief that if I had any economic future at all, I needed to get back into college. With this in mind, and despite my flagging spirit, I enrolled for the spring semester for two evening courses at the University of California (Berkeley) at its Extension Center located in San Francisco. I selected the course "Recent European History" believing I might garner a decent grade since I'd lived through some of its more grim moments. My second choice was "Principles of Accounting." For the history course I earned a respectable grade "B," but only a pitiable "D" in accounting principles. These results didn't come as a surprise. I'd felt comfortable in the first class, but had known for weeks I struggled in vain to keep up with the pace of the accounting class. My tattered psyche and surging self-pity gave rise to an array of negative feelings and a few incidents of childishness. I became excessively concerned about the equal assignment of the household chores between Eddie and I. By the fall, the friendship between us had taken on a quality of hostile competitiveness, and I accept the blame.

I remember feeling that, rather than the normal strengthening bonds of a friendship over time, ours had just worn itself out. We decided to leave our shared apartment, and sold the jointly-owned Nash. Yet I harbored a great reluctance to be completely alone. On those nights when I started from sleep in the wee hours, my daylight hours' resolve would dissipate like an elected politician's promises. As things transpired, however, our break up turned out quite well. Eddie rented a room in the home of a long-time bachelor acquaintance we knew from our previous sojourn in San Francisco. I sub-rented a bedroom from a divorced guy who worked in the computer room at Blyth & Company. The location of his small house in Twin Peaks made it convenient for taking the streetcar downtown. .

The temporary position at the stockbrokers soon came to an end and I was again looking for work. After several contacts with the California Employment Department, another break came along in September 1960. Ford Motor Company operated an assembly plant in Milpitas, about 50 miles from San Francisco, at the southern end of its Bay. It needed a male stenographer in the production control office. The job involved liaison with various Ford manufacturing plants for urgently needed parts to keep the Milpitas assembly line smoothly flowing. I pounded a typewriter producing lists of parts numbers and descriptions for dispatch to other plants. I knew the work would prove tedious, but it came with a good salary. The job interview included a physical by a company doctor. During his examination, the young doctor asked me if I'd come to America alone. When I explained I'd come with a friend, he said it still required considerable courage. Then, as an after thought, he added that London's residents had displayed a lot of bravery during WWII. When he listened to my heart through his stethoscope it wasn't sensitive enough to detect a heart full of a cold deadness and a brain full of fear.

I could entertain the idea of working in Milpitas only because of my recent purchase of a car, the first in which I held 100% ownership. It represented a new effort on my part to lead a more normal life. The right price of $575 had led to a small, used English Morris Minor. Its four-cylinder engine proved almost dangerously underpowered for San Francisco's steep hills. Yet its light gray color, convertible top, and white-walled tires showed it aspired bravely to fit into the California scene.

I had no enthusiasm for moving from San Francisco. I now knew a few people in the city, but at the far end of the peninsula I'd be totally alone. Once again I felt pulled powerfully in two directions. When I thought about this rationally, my reluctance to move made no sense in light of my record of discarding my British family so lightly. Now, in strange contrast, a few friends loomed large. Human insight comes at great cost! But move I had to because it enabled me to obtain a relatively well paid job, the very reason I'd returned to America.

I found a room without board in a quintessential suburban home in Mountain View, close to the Bayshore Freeway, State Highway 101, then the principal expressway north to San Francisco. I returned there each weekend, and followed this routine for the time I held the Ford job. My San Francisco landlord generously let me retain my room there at a reduced price. Driving back to Mountain View each Sunday evening brought back memories of my military experience of returning to camp at the end of each weekend spent in London.

The Ford workday was from 7:30 a.m. to 4:00 p.m., with 30 minutes for lunch. Because I had no board, I mostly went without breakfast, ate lunch at the plant cafeteria, spent time at the local library after work before having dinner at a restaurant en route to my room. For the rest of the evening, I'd lie on the bed reading. I was still adhering to my abstinence from fiction, so choices were social and business subjects, and even one or two science books. But my inability to concentrate still plagued me. In truth, I understood only small amounts of the contents, and retained less. My erratic sleep patterns continued, perhaps even worsened. I began my old routine of regularly popping awake after only a few hours, to stay awake until just before the alarm clock jarred for another workday. I'd arrive at my desk feeling fatigued, foggy brained, and generally out-ofsorts. Focusing on all the ten-digit parts numbers, many with add-on trailer codes, took every bit of my tenuous concentration. Only after lunch would I begin to feel halfway human and in control enough to keep on doing the job which proved demanding in volume if not intellectually. In truth, however, had the work presented a challenge to the brain, I know with certainty I couldn't have risen to it. If the job failed to meet my high-falutin' ideas of stimulating content, my performance must have failed to meet Ford's expectations. In December 1960, after only three months, I was terminated. The company kindly told me it had become necessary because of a business downturn. I believe, however, it must have been my performance inadequacies. After all, America's economy recorded its longest-sustained boom, lasting almost the entire decade from 1960-69. Meanwhile, once again, I was out on the street on my ear.

Just like a real blue-collar workman, having been laid off a few weeks before Christmas by America's second largest auto manufacturer, I was now entitled to draw California unemployment benefits in the amount of $29 weekly. Not a sum that permitted luxuries, but in those days $5 filled the standard 17"x12"x7" brown-paper grocery sack.

I didn't stay a state burden too long. Its employment bureau came up with a job in the first month of 1961. Schenley Industries Inc., one of America's larger manufacturers and/or marketers of distilled spirits, wines, and liqueurs, needed a "clerk-cum-warehouseman." Then headquartered in the Empire State Building in New York City, it had a west coast office in downtown San Francisco. It also had a non-bonded warehouse, in a predominantly light industrial area in the city's southeast.

Fierce competition reigned among the half dozen major American distillers and marketers to get the biggest share of the then estimated $4 billion annual liquor sales. Of the many advertising mediums used, primary was the placement of thematic materials in liquor store windows and grocery store aisles. At the time I worked there, the fashionable displays were large cardboard cut-outs of masterful male golfers and intrepid skiers, all handsome, healthy and smiling, who got that way simply by frequent imbibing of Schenley's brands.

My job involved clerical duties for the display manager in the branch office and also stock-taking and record keeping at the warehouse. The number of one-paragraph inter-branch memos dictated by the manager were so few, I never could understand why they'd wanted a male stenographer. While my salary was little more than half I'd earned during my brief stay at Ford, the workload was light. The main perk to this job, because I sometimes had to travel to the warehouse, was company-paid downtown parking only two blocks from the office. Downtown parking was already prohibitive.

One company practice in which I soon participated was a Friday late-afternoon gathering of the salesmen returning home from their weeklong jaunts around northern California pushing the company's products. They were given samples with which to win friends and favors. Often they returned with a few leftovers and would break a seal or two while bringing each other up to date on their accounts. Any of the Schenley administrative staff, willing to stay after office hours, could wander into the main sales office and imbibe a few. I became a frequent imbiber.

For the first time in years I was no longer attending evening classes and had time on my hands. Unused to distilled spirits and drinking on an empty stomach, I sometimes drove my Morris Minor home with little recollection next day of how I managed it. If luck never seemed to take my side in the job market, the good lady must have perched on my shoulder for a few of those Friday night commutes. But with a macho hangover, and no responsibilities to rouse me out of bed, it would often be noon before I showed my face to Saturday. These bouts of over indulgence helped bring brief moments of a form of happiness.

My brother, Roy, now at a technical college studying for a civil engineering degree, was in a program requiring six months of college courses followed by an equal period of full-time work. He proposed spending the next work portion in San Francisco, accompanied by a college friend. They had already determined they could obtain temporary U.S. work permits. In eager preparation, I soon moved from my Twin Peaks room, to which I'd returned after my Ford debacle, to a small, basement apartment in a private home. The monthly rent was $75. Now with my own automobile and accommodation, even though both of most modest dimensions, at last put me a little more in concert with the average among American bachelors.

Allowing this epiphany to progress to its next logical stage, I started dating a Cuban girl I'd met at the international social club. Not quite the Swedish blonde of my dreams, this girl from Castro's island and I hit if off. She had been in the U.S. for about 10 years during which she'd lived in several different cities, and now rented a room off Van Ness Avenue. She'd lost some of the conservatism that immigrant Latin girls often exhibit. She had a passionate side that for me represented a new, intensely exciting level of romantic experience. At least in her company, I'd forget my life woes. But she soon talked marriage. Rightly or wrongly, and despite my loneliness, I would not entertain the idea because I felt my job prospects and income were inadequate. We broke up without acrimony, and I remember her fondly. She might have made a wonderful wife. Not too long afterwards she married a U.S. Marine. I hope she found happiness.

Roy and Brian Asquith, his college friend, arrived in mid-April. They flew inexpensively London-New York via Iceland on that country's national airline. With the benefit of Eddie's advice, they obtained a vehicle from a ferrying agency for delivery to the San Francisco area, undergoing an adventure of their own, which remains to be related. They spent the first few weeks at my small apartment, Roy sharing my double bed and tall Brian bravely bunking on the living room's short couch. Roy quite soon found a job as a technical draftsman; Brian took a few more weeks to land something similar. From the start their visit proved successful. For five months I was sufficiently distracted to push aside all my concerns about academic failure and my inability to secure a fulfilling job. Eddie joined the group and we all, I believe, enjoyed ourselves. I refused to think about Roy's eventual departure.

We went skiing in Squaw Valley, its mountain pine-forested slopes still snow-blanketed, under cloudless, azure skies. The area, quieter now after hosting the winter Olympics the year before offered plenty of slopes for beginners to the speed demons .We golfed often. Day-trips took us to geyser-heated, mineral-water swimming pools at Agua Caliente and Calistoga in Sonoma and Napa Counties north of San Francisco. But our fun was not confined just to the weekends. A workday evening card game at my small apartment became a fixed activity of our busy social agenda. The four of us, supplemented by one or two other guys, assembled weekly. Taking advantage of my employee discount, I'd pick up a couple of fifths of Ancient Age, Schenley's most popular bourbon. We'd split the cost among the players. Our banter and laughter flowed freely, and the volume increased in direct relation with the input of liquor. These evenings contrasted so sharply with my usual lonely lifestyle.

As a grand finale, Eddie and I took a week off and, in his larger American car, drove south to Los Angeles and San Diego where we hit the highlight tourist spots. We golfed in Palm Springs, the ritzy winter resort. We were there late in August, on an especially hot day, and I have a vague recollection we were the only foursome on the course. One night we crossed the border into Mexico and drove the few miles to Tijuana, the disheveled, dirty town, whose sole purpose seems to be relieving gringos of their Yankee dollars. Our "taste of Mexico" included a visit to one of the many "girlie shows" where almost naked dancers, mostly short, plump, and seedy, nearly gave themselves heart attacks as they gyrated to canned music.

At the end of this wonderful week, our four-person tour group split. Roy and Brian boarded a Greyhound bus at Riverside for the four-day ride across America to New York to catch their Atlantic flight. Eddie and I headed north to San Francisco, Eddie to his nearly completed court reporter course and me to my dissatisfying job and seemingly bleak future.

The under-powered Morris Minor and me outside my small ground-floor apartment, constructed in part of the garage, in Noe Valley, San Francisco (1961).

CHAPTER 35

I stayed in touch with Eddie via telephone and occasional outings. He had continued his friendship with the English nurse we'd met on the "Ivernia II" when returning to America in March 1958. She'd since spent a year in Toronto, returned to England for a while, and then worked a year in Boston, only to return again to her native land. She advised Eddie she wouldn't again permanently leave the country of her birth. They seemed to be getting serious about each other, but now the wide Atlantic Ocean separated them.

About this time, Eddie's landlord told him of a former Santa Fe Railroad stenographer who'd left San Francisco for a job in Spain with the American construction company contracted by the U.S. Government to build the runways for a U.S. airbase at Torrejon de Ardoz, just east of Madrid. When construction was completed and the USAF began flight operations there, this stenographer accepted a U.S. Civil Service position with the Department of the Air Force at the base. As a government employee, he was well paid in U.S. dollars, plus he enjoyed the privilege of using the on-base medical facilities and subsidized commissary and exchange, in one of Europe's lowest-cost countries. It gave him a good living and interesting life in an international and cosmopolitan capital. He'd since indicated he would stay in Spain until he retired or the job ended whichever came first.

Learning this guy's history gave Eddie the idea to try something similar. Eddie made inquiries and ascertained the U.S. Air Force used U.S. Civil Service court reporters for courts martial and official investigations. Under an agreement with the United Kingdom government, there were no less than 14 American air bases/stations dotted around the English countryside. Five of these were active flying bases with various squadrons assigned. Air Force military personnel stationed in the country then totaled about 25,000, excluding family dependents. In fact, Britain had been described as an American aircraft carrier anchored off the European coast waiting in the event the cold war turned hot. Eddie, now a U.S.

citizen, returned to England to try to secure a civil service court reporter position with the USAF. If the English nurse wouldn't come west, he'd go east. It might turn out he could have the best of both worlds. Several months passed before I received his letter advising he'd not been successful in landing a court-reporter position, but had obtained a lower-grade administrative one at the 322nd Air Division, U.S.A.F., at RAF High Wycombe, about 30 miles west of London. He was within easy visiting distance of his nurse friend and his extensive family. I indulged my emotions of envy.

After nearly five years in Washington D.C., Robert Banting, the New Zealander whom I'd met in Toronto, had finally moved to San Francisco. He secured a low-pay clerical job with the Bank of America on Market Street. He now filled a big void for me after Eddie left. My life dissatisfaction and low-grade sadness persisted but I tried to keep this condition to myself. I found almost no pleasure in anything, even the occasional hike with the Sierra Club and jaunts to local scenic spots in my low-powered Morris Minor.

A few months into 1962, I wrote to Eddie asking the chances of my landing an American job with the USAF in England. Incredibly, I'd started to toy with the idea of again moving across the Atlantic. If Eddie could do it, why not me? But this simple reasoning didn't make much sense because Eddie was blessed with an optimistic personality while I struggled with the pessimistic type. Eddie's disposition apparently allowed him to undertake and survive these violent directional changes in life. Mine tore me asunder. While I continued reading human psychology, I still didn't associate my more-or-less continuous low-ebb state as an illness. I continued to assume it stemmed from character weakness.

When Eddie's reply arrived, he predictably said there were no certainties. There were only a limited number of positions, but a few vacancies came up each year. The wives of assigned active-duty military personnel, whose usual tour of duty in England lasted three years, filled most of the low-grade civil service clerical jobs. Long-term stateside employees of the Department of the Air Force who applied for overseas duty filled the more senior civilian positions. My appearance on the scene would represent a gamble. Regardless, and almost unbelievably, I now seriously contemplated my fourth relocation across the Atlantic Ocean. Each time I'd been seeking a magical happiness that so far had been elusive. This next uprooting had an air of raging desperation not previously felt. From the reaction of a few people I told, they gave the impression they viewed me as irrational.

Despite my fears, and contrary to the advice of people who said working for the US military in Europe had to be viewed as temporary, I started preparing to leave San Francisco again. My application for American citizenship moved rapidly. The process must have been far speedier when it favored people from northern Europe than today. I attended a swearing-in ceremony in June 1962 at San Francisco's Federal courthouse.

For this second return to England, I elected a less expensive flight to New York City on a four-propeller Constellation even though the jet age had arrived. Because of lower cost, for the ocean-crossing portion of the trip I switched from air to sea. For the first time, I selected a French Line ship rather than fish-and-chips tourist Cunard. Was this evidence of an increased sophistication? This crossing even proved pleasant because of a tranquil Atlantic. In fact, since I never once became seasick, almost certainly none of the other thousand-plus passengers had inner-ear problems either. For seven days I tried to put my troubled, messy life to the side and enjoyed the days of reading and the evenings in the stateroom for entertainment.

But as soon as my feet touched terra firma at Southampton, my mind switched instantly, and with a jolt, back to my reality. I was not on a vacation, but on one more of my erratic efforts to find a position that would meet my demands. My parents were at dockside to meet me. Kind as ever, they must have been wondering just how many more times they'd have to drive to a port to pick up their now middle-aged, maladjusted son. Once again, however, Mom and Dad did their best to make me feel at home.

They no longer lived in Forest Gate, from which I had first emigrated to Canada, but now shared a large house with Vera and Reg in Goodmayes, Essex, with sufficient rooms for both families to live fully self-contained. In the intervening eight years I'd bounced back-and-forth across the Atlantic Ocean like a tennis ball in a rally. But even though each relocation had been the result of my own will, I felt somehow the capricious decisions were not a matter over which I had control. Some kind of irresistible subconscious force dictated my actions.

Within a week I made the trek across sprawling London to visit South Ruislip, site of the 3rd Air Force. This was the primary headquarters of U.S. Air Forces assigned in the United Kingdom, under the command of U.S.A.F-Europe, in Germany. All American-citizen applicants for civilian positions with the USAF in the UK had to be processed at 3AF. A reflection of the cold war, much of the work and resulting records at American bases overseas carried a security classification. US law required people employed in these fields had to be American citizens.

The first documents I had to produce at 3AF were my crisp, new Certificate of Citizenship and green-colored U.S. passport with its embossed eagle emblem. A little irony was that the efficient lady who interviewed me was as British as they come. She had worked for the American military since the 1949/50 build-up in Britain reversed their withdrawal during the years immediately following WWII. Pleasant though she was, she didn't have a job to offer me. Clerical positions to be filled locally by Americans, she smiled in patient explanation, normally occur when current incumbents move back to the US. Sometimes this happened unexpectedly, so I should stay in touch. Eddie had obtained a job fairly quickly. Now I hoped to repeat his feat.

Meanwhile, since I was interested only in a job with the US forces, I had time on my hands. In fact, I had far too much of it to ponder my tenuous situation. In something of a panic, I wondered what I'd do if nothing came along. Would I once again head back to the USA, but now a jobless college failure? These persistent thoughts agitated me and soon sleep became as disrupted as it had ever been. I resorted to sleeping pills. They helped only partially, and my nerves wound themselves tighter and tighter. In my obsessive thinking I came to view my latest gamble as containing the possibility of destroying any chance of achieving a normal life.

To try to divert my mind, I practiced shorthand by taking dictation from the British Broadcasting Company's Oxford-accented radio announcers. I thought about trying to increase my speed to qualify as a court reporter. Realistically, however, I knew my best hope was for a stenographic position that, unfortunately for my sensitivities, came classified as "secretary" in Civil Service nomenclature.

The days became weeks, and the weeks, months. As it suggested, I stayed in touch with the 3AF Civilian Personnel Office. In fact, several times I took the long subway ride across London on the red-coded Central Line to keep my face in front of them. Nothing came of it. They advised me that the large USAF European Headquarters at Wiesbaden, Germany more often needed secretaries. My first reaction was negative: I'd come back to get a job in England, nowhere else. As time passed, my distress increased. Ensconced again in my own family, I felt very much an intruder. These emotions emanated from within and weren't attributable to external causes.

Eddie understood my sense of disharmony and kindly invited me to stay with him on several weekends. Since taking up his job at the 322nd Air Division, Eddie had found accommodation less than 10 miles from the base at Bourne End, a pretty village on the River Thames. He rented an ensuite room in a large Victorian-era home, not quite entitled to the "manor house" status. There were, in fact, several such units available for rent there, preferably to well-heeled Yanks.

Luck appeared to be on my side when, in September, I obtained a month-long, temporary civil service job at High Wycombe with the 322nd AD, substituting for someone who went to the US on emergency leave. To relieve me of accommodation expense, Eddie let me stay with him. The month afforded me a brief exposure to the work atmosphere in the USAF that, I soon learned, generated a large amount of paperwork in the performance of its mission to scare off the Russian bear. The 322nd AD, I learned later, had bomber squadrons assigned to it, even though Wycombe was not an active flying base. I assumed the 322nd functioned as a forward operating element to plan the arrival and assignment of targets for nuclear-armed bombers flying in from the US if the cold war went hot.

My temporary job mostly involved typing hand-written memos concerning routine administrative matters that carried no security classification. Eddie's work was similar, but he had received a security clearance and, presumably, at least some of his work had more significance and interest. The position I obtained carried the federal government grade of GS4, at the then current annual salary of $4,110. As it transpired, I was becoming involved with the federal government during the period when its pay rates enjoyed some of their best ever percentage increases. President Kennedy, shortly after taking office, authorized a series of more liberal government annual pay raises than normal. He did this on the basis that "if America was to be a leading player in the world of nations, it needed an educated and motivated Civil Service." During the first half of the 1960s, his philosophy resulted in federal salaries more approaching those paid in the private sector. For me, a lucky fluke.

Although I'd hoped the person whose job I filled would decide not to return, she came back, and I was terminated in late October. Although there were still no opportunities elsewhere in England, I was told that several positions at Headquarters USAFE in Germany were then open. Two world events had conspired to increase activity for the Air Force, apparently including its typing load. The 1959 border dispute between India and China flared up again in 1962. The discovery of Russian missiles, aimed at the USA, installed in Cuba, only 90 miles from the United States, resulted in a military showdown in late October. Yet I still cooled my heels for another month hoping something would open up in England. It didn't. At last on 2 December 1962 I went by Channel ferry and train to Wiesbaden for a job interview.

Wiesbaden, the capital of the large Land (State) of Hesse on the southern slopes of the Taunus Mountains, is about 25 miles west of Frankfurt. In addition to the Landtag (state parliament), it contained several state and federal activities. It surprised me to find it also a pleasant spa town with thermal baths, a ritzy casino, and elegant hotels, restaurants and shops. Wealthy businessmen had built imposing homes in the adjacent hills in the past half-century. Later I learned that when American Forces took control of their Zone of Occupation, as established by the victorious Allies in the defeated Germany of 1945, it selected the most extant real estate in attractive locations available for its military headquarters. The Army chose Heidelberg; the Air Force, Wiesbaden.

For my first overnight stay in Germany (in 1947 I'd only transited the country on the train to Prague) I went to a small hotel in central Wiesbaden near Lindsey Air Station, site of the USAFE headquarters. Not until I went to bed did I notice the absence of blankets. My inability to speak a word of German, and diffident to use the telephone, saw me spend the night on top of the duvet with my raincoat over me. Only on the second night did I fathom out one crawled under the thick eiderdown cover. What a difference it made in an especially cold December!

Next morning I interviewed at the Civilian Personnel Office and found only one position left from the several open earlier. This was in the

High Explosives Weapons Division, Munitions Directorate. This division kept control of conventional weapons storage sites located around the European Theater of Operations. I suspected the job was still available because the office itself occupied a section of the basement of the large DCS/Materiel building. The only natural light came through a couple of heavily grilled rectangular windows not much bigger than shoeboxes. They were at the level of the road in front of the building. All day long occupants saw the footwear choices of passersby and sucked in vehicles' exhaust fumes. If it weren't for the interior brick walls' coat of light yellow paint, I'd have felt like a city jail prisoner. Furnaces and boilers were in the space next to this office.

I had to be interviewed by the Air Force Lieutenant Colonel, an ex-bomber pilot, who headed this office. He seemed to have trouble believing a male, especially one with a British accent, was interested in a secretarial job. He called the Personnel Office to ensure I had US citizenship and then gave me a shorthand and transcription test to see if I was for real. I suspect that what the gung-ho ex-pilot really wanted was a cute, young girl to brighten his office. But I also suspected that any such candidate fitting that description might well have shied away at the prospect of spending eight hours a day in a dungeon. In the end, I believe he was a bit desperate, and I was a lot desperate. He said I'd done OK on the test, offered me the job, and I accepted. He also mentioned that one other civilian clerk worked in his office but she had taken two weeks off for the coming Christmas season.

I went through the PO in-processing the next day, so when I returned on 17 December I could start work right away. This included completing a long, detailed questionnaire about my life for the background check needed to receive a security clearance. During my return journey to London, over the same route, I encountered the English Channel at its most inhospitable. Winter storm-generated waves washed over the ferry's bow and ran inches deep along the decks. . Nearly everyone sought refuge in the interior common areas, but soon needed bathrooms because they could not hang over the safety railings when their unhappy stomachs erupted. The rest rooms started to look like a military field hospital during war.

Soon I'd vomited so much I went into spasmodic dry heaves. After a period of this unpleasantness, I began to lose it from the other end. It took a while to secure a vacant stall in the men's, and once inside, I stayed put. Water covered the floor, necessitating the frequent raising of one's feet, as it sloshed back and forth with each roll of the vessel. Desperate men banged on the door for me to surrender my haven, but I was beyond caring and the sea had me again hoping for death. My first voyage to Canada made me just as ill. But this Channel crossing lasted only two hours versus the 10 days of the Atlantic agony.

I returned to Wiesbaden in a week to start as a new US-citizen civil servant. I hadn't secured the hoped-for equivalent position in England, but I preferred moving to Germany rather than the USA where, during the last four years, I'd failed at college, failed to secure what I deemed a worthwhile position, and continued to experience my seemingly endless malaise.

A civil service civilian employee of the military overseas is entitled to subsidized accommodation. However, I presented the authorities with one problem. USAFE headquarters employed dozens of American secretaries, all females. They lived in a type of hotel run for them by the military. Now along I came to join their ranks, but my sex differed. They wouldn't give me a room in that hotel. My starting Civil Service grade of GS4 made me the military equivalent of a corporal. Yet I could not live in the barracks occupied by single corporals because of my civilian status. A dilemma solved to my advantage. They assigned me a room in the bachelor officers' quarters, called the American Arms. Thus I became the lowest ranked man in this hotel tower. While a majority of people wouldn't be bothered by this situation, indicative of my over-sensitivity and fragile ego, once again I harbored a feeling of not belonging that caused me discomfort.

With Christmas just five days away, I learned that only a skeleton crew would be on duty over the holiday. Not knowing anyone, I dreaded the prospect of spending Christmas alone in my American Arms room, pleasant though it was. So many of the Americans, military and civilians, used holidays to explore Europe. I rushed to the on-base American Express travel bureau. All the regular tours were already filled. I signed up for a package ski trip to Sankt Anton in Klostertal, on the Voralberg slopes in western Austria. This was a down-home ski resort, the prices right, and the charm boundless.

When the tour group met at the Wiesbaden train station for our evening departure, it comprised a couple of American military members, schoolteachers, secretaries, and a delegation of employees from the then Air Force Europe Exchange Service. The Exchange people ran the on-base department stores which, I learned much later, was the equivalent of the United Kingdom's Navy, Army, and Air Force Institute (NAAFI), although the American version was far more extensive and sophisticated as I knew from my RAF days.

This Christmas trip introduced me to the joys of skiing in the glories of the Alps. Transiting the snow-capped granite mountains and seeing the colorful valley villages breathing quietly under a mantel of white, represented visual magnificence. Sankt Anton itself seemed to incorporate a way of life that proved sheer joy and pleasure. I am sure a closer inspection would reveal drawbacks common to all human habitats, but for a few days as an outsider it seemed as close to a heaven as there is on planet Earth. But in addition to my discovery of the Austrian winter wonderland, for me a true Shangri-La, during this Christmas ski trip I also became acquainted with Eugene Bryerly, an Exchange manager. He would play an important part in the course of my by now extremely confused, erratic and peripatetic life.

CHAPTER 36

When I returned to work during the first week of January 1963, I found the other low-grade civilian in this office to be a feisty Floridian already in her mid sixties. As a young woman, Minnie Drees had never worked outside the home after marrying her same-age, high-school sweetheart upon graduation, and soon filling it with a quartet of children. Following 30 years of quintessential American middle-class life, her husband, while still in his forties, died from a massive heart attack. Minnie lived with the thought she inadvertently aided this tragedy with their "all-American, uninterrupted diet of steak, eggs, butter-soaked pancakes, and ice cream." Public Health Service warnings against excess saturated fats were just beginning about the time I met Minnie.

Following a period of mourning appropriate for a Southern lady and with her children grown, Minnie enrolled in a local secretarial school to learn typing. After the six-month course, she applied at a nearby USAF base and became a civil servant. Much to her own surprise, and especially that of her children, Minnie took an unexpected pleasure in her new life as an independent government girl Friday. When a personnel bulletin advertising federal overseas openings crossed her desk several years later, she applied, was accepted and, in her 63rd year, marched off to Hqs. USAFE in Germany. The reaction of Minnie's children was alarm and concern. Minnie, however, had the confidence of a teenager and the enthusiasm of a born-again evangelist.

Although my own security clearance didn't come through for perhaps two months, it took me about that time to learn the ropes in the arcane world of military administration with its special extra dimension of national security. There were specific procedures for unclassified material and strict routines for classified documents. The investigative work required to obtain a security clearance is done individually by the four military services. I assumed the process involved, among other things, checks with police departments wherever one had lived. Certainly the

Federal Bureau of Investigation would be sounded. In my case, an RAF officer, on behalf of the USAF, went to my parents' house to question them as to my status and character. However, aside from the voluntary overnight stay in the Williams, Arizona, jail when Eddie and I hitchhiked across America, I'd never tangled with the authorities on either side of the Atlantic.

At Hqs USAFE I found these elaborate security requirements necessitated extra administrative staff all by itself. I couldn't remember ever handling a classified document in the RAF but, as I was about to learn, a lot of the messages and correspondence generated in this office required a security classification. Each such document had to be accompanied by a dedicated routing form affixed at the front of the package. This described the document's subject (without revealing sensitive information), its originator and addressee(s), and was assigned a unique identifying number. Each recipient had to control the package until it moved to the next addressee or returned to originator. Preparing and maintaining these routing forms was intended to insure knowledge of the item's whereabouts at all times. The approved method for normal destruction of classified documents required witnessing by several disinterested officers who had to attest to this occurrence on a section of the routing form. These control procedures added a sizeable paper-shuffling workload.

Our daily work consisted primarily of typing messages and letters written in longhand on government, lined yellow pads by the three officers and five NCOs, all munitions specialists, in the office. The Lt. Colonel and his deputy, a Major, had both been aircrew before losing their flight status because of changes in their health, necessitating a switch to new career paths, so they could serve out the required number of years to qualify for military pensions at retirement.. A Lieutenant assigned to the office, who had a degree in chemistry, seemed to me the most technically competent. The NCOs had all spent hands-on time performing grunt work at military munitions sites. Our communications were mostly directed to the four conventional weapons storage sites in four principal countries in the NATO alliance. These were at Greenham Common, England; Saint Mihiel, France; Moerbach, West Germany; and Livorno, Italy.

My shorthand ability was virtually never called upon. None of the military men were comfortable trying to dictate. So they laboriously wrote communications in script and Minnie or I turned them into a typed format. I soon became bored with just straight copy typing of munitions codes and parts numbers. In time, Minnie came to my rescue. She didn't mind just pounding her typewriter to produce these scribbled epistles full of munitions' identifying numbers and military-approved name abbreviations in the Air Force's prescribed formats. I preferred preparing and controlling their accompanying routing forms for the classified items, especially composing the subject synopsis, which represented a smidgen of creativity. From such diverse backgrounds, we two improbable individuals in this dungeon environment came to complement each other quite well.

Despite the functioning persona I tried to publicly display, my emotions were jagged, sleep poor, and concentration erratic. Feelings of inadequacy never let me forget the job I held made me the lowest-ranked American Arms' resident. Each evening before dinner many of the lodgers, mainly young, single lieutenants and captains, gathered at the bar for a nightly happy hour. I joined them on one or two occasions in an effort to blend in. But my lack of confidence made me feel as out-of-place as a male ballet dancer in the Dallas Cowboys' shower room. I began stopping at the base library after work to kill two hours so the bar activity would be over when I arrived at the Arms. .

Almost in spite of myself, however, I did soon strike an acquaintance with Marlyn Pauley, a Captain, who was himself a bit of a loner and also an aspiring skier. The winter of 1962/3 produced an excessive snowfall in central Germany. On several Saturdays and Sundays he drove us to the U.S. military hilly golf course at Rheinblick in the suburbs of Wiesbaden toward the Rhine River. In summer season it was difficult to get a tee time, but now deserted and gloriously quiet, it let us novices practice out of sight. For hours we arduously climbed up on skis and slithered down, without much grace, its undulating terrain. This beginning skiing whetted my appetite for more, and the physical activity seemed briefly to lift my spirits. When Marlyn mentioned the local chapter of a German-American ski club, I soon joined.

In the spring Roy wrote and asked if I'd act as best man for his planned May wedding. The prospect of having a role in a church white wedding, with blushing bridesmaids, organ music, and the invitees all togged out in their Sunday best, somewhat terrified me. My shyness had reached the point where I felt most comfortable as a recluse. I'd struggled in the first few months of 1963 to maintain a facade of normalcy. In spite of these personality deficits, there was no question of refusing my brother who would marry Marie Blowers, a petite, pretty nurse, to whom he'd been introduced by Eddie's girlfriend, some 18 months earlier.

Marie's historic hometown of Colchester, site of the Roman municipium Camulodunum, about 65 miles east of London in Essex County, would be the venue. A few days before the event, I took a Lufthansa 90-minute flight from Frankfurt to London. Once again, my parents collected me at the airport, and accommodated me at their home. My sister had been long married, and she and her husband seemed to be successfully raising their son, now 12 years old. My brother had just launched his career as a professional civil engineer, and was about to take a wife. On the other hand, as I perceived it, my latest geographic relocation had resulted in just another menial, dead-end administrative job. I seemed to be the family misfit.

On the wedding day, despite acting and looking rather stiff, as the official photos show, I managed to hand the ring over at the proper time. Everyone performed his or her parts smoothly and the church ceremony went off without mishap. Roy and Marie headed to the rural flatlands of East Anglia for their honeymoon. The next evening, a Sunday, I flew back to Frankfurt. Taking leave of my parents proved emotional. The plane, fortunately only about a quarter filled, let me sit alone at a window seat toward the last row. As the medium-sized Boeing jet climbed into the low clouds above Heathrow airport and we lost sight of the night galaxy of London's lights, the emotional dam inside broke. I started crying.

Like the hurricane that builds far out over the ocean eventually moves devastatingly onshore, the sadness I'd felt for some years at the edges of my universe now roared in to over-power me. Shamed, I attempted to stifle my sobs, but tears flooded my face. I tried to control myself when I saw flight attendants bringing snacks or drinks, but couldn't. Even though I turned away pretending to look out the porthole, attendants are trained to notice distressed passengers. They asked if I needed assistance. I thanked them and declined, my pain far too complex even for efficient Lufthansa cabin crew.

I felt I'd messed up my life, was alone in the world, and had to return to an environment to which I didn't belong. When the plane rolled to a halt at the terminal, I had calmed myself to dam my tears, but exited with a choke in my throat, eyes downward, convinced my personal dignity lay on the cabin floor with all the detritus of the flying public.

I managed to show up for work the next morning, but it took my last dregs of will-power. I was in such distress; I knew my performance was inadequate even for my low-level position. I pretended to be normal although I felt anything but. The days after returning from England resulted in several almost sleepless nights, and I withdrew into myself ever more.

The next weekend, for which I had no plans, the loneliness filtered down to my lifeless soul. I stayed in bed for 48 hours. I hid, sleepless, in the one place I felt I could just cope. Under the blankets I didn't have to interact with anyone, which had become fearful and painful. I saw myself as a complete oddity, but lacked resolve to take action. On one of the subsequent horrific mornings, when I forced my feet over the side of the bed, my will power balked. I slumped back and pulled up the covers. Just getting to work, let alone performing the job, seemed beyond me. In desperation, I tried to assess the situation.

I felt total fatigue, physical and mental. Remorselessly I flagellated myself in my thoughts over my perceived life missteps like religious fanatics inflict physical self-abuse. Nothing seemed to interest me. Nothing provided pleasure. In the midst of this black hopelessness and icy fear, for the first time, I recognized and, more importantly, accepted my state must represent a heavy depression. I'd bandied the dreaded D-word about for some time, but without ever acknowledging it applied to me. I couldn't stop my mind going round-and-round on the theme I'd lived in four countries, switched jobs about three times that number, and hadn't had the backbone to attempt the writer's life, my youthful, over-reaching dream. Now I'd washed up on German shores working for, of all improbable employers, the American military. Perhaps more significant, I seemed to have lost my health and a good chunk of my mind. What had happened to the boy who had once been told he had "life's divine spark?" The bedside phone made it so easy to pick up, dial the office number, and say "...sorry, I won't be at work today, I don't feel well."

On the third day I pulled this stunt, after about an hour, the

Lieutenant called and asked in an icy voice the nature of my problem. Despite my desperation, I still couldn't bring myself to disclose I suspected depression. So I stuck to a feeble mantra: "I just don't feel well."

The sharp, precise Lieutenant, with his science degree and third in the office chain-of-command, obviously didn't buy it. He said I needed to get myself to the USAF hospital and obtain a doctor's certificate attesting to my medical condition. He was correctly attempting to protect the government from what he saw as a slimy malingerer. This exchange represented a new low. I felt like a fox cornered by a pack of hounds. I panicked that my "condition" put in question my ability to hold on to even this obtuse job. But perhaps the Lieutenant's patent, black-leather military shoe that had landed a kick on my scrofulous backside actually helped me. I did rally enough to see a doctor at Wiesbaden's large military hospital. But, again, I dodged the issue. I reported my problem as insomnia, and he prescribed sleeping tablets. They let me stay asleep perhaps an extra hour or two, but I continued popping awake well before dawn and couldn't return to sleep until just before the alarm rung. Then, zombie-like, I dragged myself out of bed, and the day's agony began again. This scenario had been dragging on seemingly forever.

On one such morning, I sat on the bed's edge and let my mind float darkly among suicidal thoughts. Life had become unbelievably painful and pointless. For a person who had tried to improve himself from age 14 onward, I felt I'd metamorphosed into a scumbag. Despite my efforts, nothing seemed to have worked out for me. Suicide would be a scary undertaking, but I'd be joyously free from all the pain, shame and fear. As I write these words I don't really understand why I didn't put thought into action. Certainly I lacked the raw courage to select a violent method, wrist-slitting or hanging. Or was it simply I didn't have a large bottle of aspirin at bedside? Hopefully, despite my utter desolation, a single, unrecognized atom of hope still coursed through my body and stayed my hand. Regardless of how low I'd sunk, I managed to remain glued together and make it through the summer.

I even forced myself to join the Wiesbaden American Ski Club, organized and run by ski enthusiasts stationed in Wiesbaden, both military and civilians. I've long felt, somewhat ironically, it took my move to Germany for me to get to know Americans. In the U.S., I had, of course, worked with Americans, but the few friends and acquaintances

I'd known tended to be immigrants. Now in Germany, we were a small group of American expatriates pushed together by the foreignness of our surroundings.

The season's highlight ski trip came in the last week of November to Switzerland. Club members were going to receive high-quality, but price-discounted, professional ski lessons available just before the official Christmas season began, when resort instructors must qualify for annual certification. With tourism and skiing so important to the Swiss economy, authorities don't let unqualified people present themselves as instructors. We received a week's lessons from an experienced instructor at about half his normal charge. Attending ski lessons just before the season opening in December risked having cloudy days and meager snow. However, the trip was to St Moritz that, at just over six thousand feet, normally enjoyed an adequate snow pack by late November. This resort offers a number of excellent ski runs, and has become one of the most popular resorts in Europe. Selected as the site of the 1948 Winter Olympics, it hosted that first meeting following the 12-year suspension for WWII,

The 20 ski-club members assembled one evening at the Wiesbaden train station for the overnight journey in sleeper berths on the clean, punctual Bundesbahn (German Railway). Because I was new to the group, I'd paid extra for a single berth, which proved worthwhile. I had trouble falling asleep and read well past midnight as the train plunged through the night. This would not have endeared me to whoever might have shared the compartment. Even so, I still woke early to the gray light of dawn to find our train twisting through passes and diving into long tunnels in a spectacular snow-covered landscape qualifying it as a winter wonderland.

We were booked into a rather modest hotel by St Moritz standards, but it served the unadorned demands of the majority of our group for whom the skiing was paramount. We ate only breakfast at the hotel, had lunch at restaurants at the top of chair lifts, and took the evening meal in different gemutliche, gaststatten (cafes with atmosphere.)

Yet regardless of our magnificent setting in the Engadine, the upper part of the River Inn Valley, with its exhilarating alpine resort ambience, the black curse of a debilitating, soul-destroying depression hunted me down. Just as surely as a tornado can flatten a prairie community, depression flattens an individual. This invisible malediction had followed me to this heavenly spot where fun was part of the natural ambience. It had slithered around the grizzled, majestic mountains, through their productive valleys, along the bustling, festive streets of Saint Moritz, and under the door of my small, unpretentious hotel room. Several mornings I started awake before dawn, instantly sensing defeat from depression's insidious errant brain chemistry sucking out my life spirit to leave a pathetic, hollow apology for a human being.

Barely functioning at breakfast, I had to force myself to eat the fresh, crusty rolls with jam, something I'd always loved. We then trudged through the jostling, ski-totting crowd on its way to the day's activities. Everyone registered on my consciousness as animated, enthusiastic, and full of happiness. I, in excruciating contrast, slunk along among them like a cowering, irritable, mangy cur. My emotions were madly contradictory; my every fiber yearned to be part of that joyful throng of radiant skiers; my mood had me in the frozen grip of a painful despair. Humiliation and shame destroyed all semblance of self-confidence.

I struggled through the mornings. At lunch I sat among these friendly comrades and almost never joined in the conversation. People in the ski club must have looked upon me as, at best, reserved, at worst, a snob. My sense of being the misfit, the outcast, the oddball, dominated my thoughts. Now in this glorious mecca of good times and healthy fun, finally my downcast state was something I could no longer ignore, or resist, or hope to ameliorate, without professional assistance. The pain was so intense, and I so desperate, I at last resolved to seek help. The very first workday after our return, I called the hospital to make an appointment with a psychiatrist a few days later.

When we met, I gave him some background details as to my take on my problems/symptoms. He told me the hospital was not staffed to provide counseling, and could treat depression only with pharmaceuticals, which were still limited in December 1963. He prescribed 75 milligrams of Tofranil daily, which came in small red 25mg tablets, produced by Geigy, the Swiss company. Tofranil might have been one of the first anti-depressants approved by the Food and Drug Administration for sale in the U.S.

The doctor advised me the medicine could take two to three weeks, or occasionally more, to start working. That seemed strange. As far as I knew, medications worked in hours or days. I'd also been surprised to find the Air Force psychiatrist looked young and athletic, and sported no facial hair. I wondered if he was really qualified to treat my obscure condition, and essentially held little hope for Tofranil's efficacy.

With another Christmas just three weeks ahead, and the medication not yet showing signs of changing my condition, a quandary arose. Could I face another ski trip in my misery, or should I elect lonely hibernation by remaining at the American Arms? With considerable trepidation, I signed up for another ski trip with the club, rationalizing that, if I'd survived a week in fashionable St Moritz, I could manage three days in rustic Sankt Anton, in the less-elevated Voralberg region of Austria. During the next 14 days the little red tablets produced no noticeable effect beyond a dry mouth and constipation. Then, within a few days of our departure for Austria, I noticed I'd begun sleeping longer, not startling awake following only two or three hours. After a couple more good nights, I awoke one morning like a new man. I felt willing, even eager, to face the day. The little red tablet had produced a gigantic miracle that, for me, matched any delivered to pilgrims to Lourdes. I'd marked the onset of my emotional problems to September 1956, now just over seven years earlier, after Eddie and I emerged from our Mexican detour during our hitchhiking jaunt across America. At first I'd assumed the strange condition to be caused by the intestinal upheavals I'd suffered. That had cleared up while my mood swings grew steadily in their severity. Now I felt so well. Suddenly I had confidence I'd never had even before slipping into my long malaise. Simply put, life had become worth living!

I had a 15-minute appointment with the psychiatrist the day before we left for Austria. To say I was already a passionate advocate for the chemo-biological treatment of depression is far too mild. In fact, I was disappointed the doctor didn't display my unbounded enthusiasm for this medicine. In depression, the sufferer certainly knows best the pain; and this sufferer now had a keen appreciation of the efficacy of this relieving agent. I told the doctor that I felt like the 90-lb. weakling at the seashore who'd always had sand kicked in his face by a beach bully. Then this little guy takes a Charles Atlas muscle development course. Returning to the beach, he beats the holy bejeesus out of his tormentor. And that, I concluded, was just how I felt. It produced a laugh from the doctor.

No one in the ski-club enjoyed our Christmas 1963 Austrian trip more than I did. During the next couple of years I took quite a few ski trips to both Switzerland and Austria, generally preferring less sophisticated resorts of the latter. I've since wondered if my partiality came from the fact it was during my first Austrian outing I felt so well as to be able to at last experience the sensation of human happiness after so long.

Playing best man at Roy's and Marie's wedding (1963). Me at left.

CHAPTER 37

During the early months of 1964 I continued to enjoy this miraculous sense of well being. It simply seemed too good to be true. I harbored a strong suspicion it wouldn't last. My fear had me awaking one morning to find myself back in a depression that filled me with sadness, stole my self-confidence, induced childish irritability, and blocked all sense of enjoyment. These had been its persistent manifestations during a seven-year period. Horrible waves of ice-cave cold regret pulsing through me. Now after medical science threw the Tofranil life-preserver ring to this drowning man, I found I could think, almost without emotion, about my life and not be overwhelmed by debilitating remorse. I still knew, of course, I'd made numerous poor life decisions, but their recall didn't destroy my sense of self. This palliative feature of the medication for me represented something extraordinary. .

Trying to restore some purpose to my life, I decided to resume my slow, erratic pursuit of a college degree through night classes. I enrolled in two University of Maryland courses, Business Law and German Language I, conducted in a Department of Defense school at the Wiesbaden American housing area. The UOM had a contract with the DOD to offer college level courses at bigger American military bases throughout Europe. Military personnel had their tuition fees paid by the government, but civil servants did not. In choosing Business Law, I finally accepted I had to forget the far-out dream of becoming a writer, and head for a degree in business administration, the achievement of which would still require years. Some knowledge of German would hopefully enable me to live more appreciatively in my current land of residence.

My transformation into a new man was not confined just to things of the mind. On Saturday mornings I started to regularly run three miles around the cinder sports track at the Wiesbaden Air Base (later an Army helicopter facility) with two DOD male teachers with whom I'd become acquainted at the American Arms. After running, we used exercise machines at the gymnasium, lifted weights, and performed other exercises. Then we enjoyed a steam sauna. These activities went on until mid-afternoon, when we returned to the American Arms to prepare for our separate Saturday evenings. I enjoyed the camaraderie of these intelligent men. As an additional bonus, within a few months, I felt the healthiest I'd been in years.

My drug-induced metamorphosis even included the social side. I suddenly found I had not just a repaired self-confidence but, more accurately, a new self-confidence. I had always tended to shyness which I felt had increased during my teen years. Even as an adult, and before the onset of my depressive symptoms, I lacked what I perceived as a normal level of social ease. Now, the miracle medication seemed to have given me a new backbone. Women no longer terrified me. As a result, I had a number of dates with females I met through the ski-club. My dates were as varied as an older German-born American secretary, an attractive U.S. military airwoman, an English girl visiting her sister who was married to an American, and one German girl who worked for the Air Force Exchange. This unprecedented spate of social activity didn't, however, qualify me as a womanizer.

Now that much of my former energy had been restored, I organized my evenings and weekends rather rigidly. On the two evenings at school, which started at 7 p.m., I walked the three-mile round trip to and from my lodging. I mostly devoted the other weeknights to studying or leisure reading. With Saturdays fully occupied, I used Sundays for my most important study time. But because I didn't want to spend so many hours alone in my room, I chose to study at the Lindsey Air Station library that opened from 1 to 9 p.m. On Sundays I enjoyed a late breakfast, and departed about noon to make the approximate three-mile, one-way walk across town to the library. I'd study until 5 p.m. when the AFEX cafeteria served reasonably priced, but decidedly unexciting, dinners. I'd return to the library until it closed, and hike back across town to the American Arms. When I crawled into bed around 10:30 p.m., I savored the satisfied feeling of a day well spent.

As testament to the restoration of my mental health, in early July, I took a two-week vacation in England and drove there in my left-hand-drive Opel. Assuming there'd be others interested in a reasonably-priced way to London, I advertised at the base exchange for paying passengers. Almost instantly I had two female fellow travelers to London: Barbara, an American secretary who wanted the cheapest way to the British capital; and Sylvia Redmond, wife of a Briton working for the AFEX, who wanted to visit her sister in west London.

We left Wiesbaden after work on a Friday, following a route through Germany into Holland via Aachen. At that time, west European nations, other than Germany, didn't have freeways. Night driving through Holland to Zeebruggee, west of Antwerp, on second-class roads, noteworthy for lack of directional signs, proved challenging. We reached the port only around 9 a.m. for the ferry sailing an hour later.

So long as daylight persisted, we three strangers cautiously outlined our life histories. I noticed that Mrs. Redmond was the most reserved and revealed the least. But even allowing for her British fusty conservatism, she struck me as pre-occupied, withdrawn, and nervous. Once it grew dark, Barbara fell asleep and stayed so through much of the night. Then conversation died away, mainly from our mutual introversion and partly out of respect for our sleeping partner in the rear. But the older Mrs. Redmond dozed only intermittently, spending much time just staring through the windshield into the night, repeatedly clasping her hands in her lap to rub their palms together. I formed an impression she was nervous and unhappy.

During the unusually smooth Channel crossing my passengers had breakfast in the ferry's cafeteria and I relished an hour's sleep on the back seat of the Opel stowed on the bottom deck. In the Dover Customs control, we three joined the lineup with the secretary first, myself second and the English woman last. When asked, the secretary and I both advised the Customs officer we had nothing to declare. Maybe she didn't, but I had a couple of cartons of Exchange cigarettes, costing about a third of their price in Britain, which I'd give to family members. The customs officer scrawled his chalk check mark on our suitcases and waved us through.

When he directed the same question to Mrs. Redmond, she responded in a quavering voice from a nodding head that "yes, she had cigarettes she wanted to share with her sister, Renee, and husband, Vincent, and a few close friends. But I won't name them because I've not yet decided who should get them." She promptly started to undo the straps securing her old-fashioned portmanteau that I'd hoisted onto the counter for her. The officer stared intently and quizzically at Mrs. Redmond for perhaps 30 seconds and then, slowly, distinctly and very deliberately, said: "Now, you don't have anything to declare, do you, madam?"

"Yes, officer, as I said, I have cigarettes for relatives. Oh, and few friends. Shall I say their names again?" She had undone one strap, and now turned her flustered attention to the other, seemingly eager to reveal her contraband. The officer's face had taken on a certain nonplused expression. He inhaled hugely through expanded nostrils, narrowed his eyes and, with a conspiratorial tone, almost hissed:

"Madam, for the last time, you don't have anything to declare, do you? Do you?"

By now everyone, apparently except my older lady passenger, realized he wanted to hear her simply say she had "nothing to declare" so he could, in good conscience, place his chalk clearance mark on her portmanteau. It seemed a child-like naiveté prevented her understanding this. I moved behind her and whispered that "nothing to declare" was all she needed to say.

"Oh, no, officer, absolutely nothing! Not a single, little thing," chirped Mrs. Redmond at last, turning the color of beetroot. The day would be long for that Customs Officer.

We reached London in the late afternoon, and dropped Barbara off at a hotel near Marble Arch. Mrs. Redmond had come from Slough, Berkshire, where her sister still lived, so there we headed. She alone would make the return trip with me. By now I was some 25 miles west of London so I next headed to Marlow, where Roy had secured a civil engineer position with Buckinghamshire County Council. I spent some days with Roy and Marie, who now had a baby girl of just a few months, before driving across London to spend the balance of my vacation with my parents in Essex. We had a week together, making a few visits to points of interest. They commented it was good to see their son upbeat and not struggling under a burden of melancholy. Early one morning, following the week with my parents, I again found my way to Mrs. Redmond in Slough to take her back to Wiesbaden. If her reticence had been noteworthy during the outbound journey, her new garrulousness now astonished me. Sylvia, as she asked me to call her almost before we left her driveway, had struck me as a demure, proper Englishwoman. She seemed to have transformed into a common gossip. Her subject matter, however, was not relatives, friends or AFEX employees, but her husband! My surprise was so great I couldn't help wondering if perhaps I picked-up a sufferer of multiple personality. It seemed to me something must have happened to turn this quiet, possibly repressed, woman into this talkative machine-gun on the passenger side of my car's front bench. I speculated she'd had the ear of a sympathetic sister for two weeks and now just couldn't stop the out-pouring. Whatever it was that launched Mrs. Redmond into her tirade, it quickly became clear she considered herself the grievously injured victim of an unhappy marriage. At that time I'd not met Lionel Redmond, her husband.

Here I should explain how this solid Brit came to work for the Americans in Germany. The Air Force was formed as a separate service from the Army in September 1947 as part of a major reorganization of the United States' armed forces (nearly 30 years after Britain took the same step.) It would have been logical, both economically and organizationally, if the existing Army Exchange Service had continued providing its welfare support to both the now divorced Army and Air Force. After all, soldiers and airmen puffed the same cigarettes, and soap lathers identically in men's hands no matter the uniform worn. But probably driven by individual service jealousies, after a period of political jockeying with the organizational set-up, a separate Air Force Exchange Service, or AFEX, was established.

A comment is needed here to mark the elaborateness, even plushness, of the Exchange Systems. They are one of several large, widespread support activities, providing clear evidence of how well America treats its military personnel. In the late 1940s and early 1950s, during the significant bolstering and re-positioning of American Air Force assets within Europe, North Africa, and Turkey, the new AFEX headquarters moved alternatively to these three regions. In early 1953, with much of the U.S. Air Forces-Europe now positioned in England, AFEX headquarters was established in London. Its location, a block from Piccadilly, says much about the financial clout of the American forces at that time. During these early days of the Cold War, the AFEX workload increased with the arrival of more permanently based fighter and bomber squadrons, with their human complements of crews, support personnel, and their families.

AFEX needed to hire local native citizens in all the various countries in which it then operated. As a result, while in London it recruited British civilians to fill its manpower needs. But in 1955 it moved again, this time to a commandeered German kaserne (camp) in Kastel, between Wiesbaden and Mainz, close-by the USAFE headquarters. Its British middle managers were offered the option of moving with the organization, and some elected to do so. Among them, Lionel Redmond. When I eventually met him, he proved to be a man of medium height and proportionate weight, with a small, neat mustache, and salt-and-pepper, straight-back hair with center parting. With his strict business uniform of dark suits and dress shirts, he could hardly be more the epitome of lower middle-class, white-collar London suburbia. Only his oral need for frequent filtered cheroots indicated the possibility of not being the complete master of his own subconscious. He had an insurance employment background in which he'd worked consistently since early youth. AFEX hired him as a section manager in its own insurance branch. Although I can't cite ages, he was not a young blood when he joined in 1953. What made this seeming pillar of London commuter suburbia in later middle age throw in his lot with an American quasi-military outfit? Was it something hidden and complex, or simply the more generous American pay scales?

Surprisingly, Mrs. Redmond started out, as we meandered through the well-to-do outskirts of Slough toward the road to the coast, by telling me a joke about the woman whose husband went to a neighborhood corner grocery for a loaf of bread on Friday evening and hadn't returned until Monday morning. The distraught woman asked a friend what to do? The response: "Send out for another loaf!" I found the joke most amusing, but it was not the sort of witticism I expected from this straight-laced lady who had displayed such naïveté at the Dover Customs checkpoint. I was confused as to whether to laugh out loud or restrain myself. Then Mrs. Redmond warmed to her subject and opened her own dam's floodgates.

Her husband had, she claimed, gone out for numerous loaves of bread during the last few years. I was confounded by her frank confession. It seemed downright weird that this older woman, with two grown sons, would reveal to me, a younger male and virtual stranger, such a sensitive secret about her marriage. I went slack-jawed as I struggled to think of a suitably compassionate, gentle if not priest-like, response to soothe her perturbed soul. Whatever I dredged up to say, she must have found it consoling, even encouraging. For mile after mile she anguished how her husband's decision to move to Germany with AFEX had ruined her life. How she thought she had been a good wife. How she suffered as she saw her marriage dissolve to something meaningless. As a result, she now hated AFEX and, especially, Germany. However, I don't recall her saying specifically she hated her husband. She even cited statistics on the middle-aged, single women in Germany's population. So large a number of German men had perished in WWII, the country was awash with lonely women.

Apparently her blackguard husband had linked-up with one of these feme sole in Frankfurt. This industrial center, about 30 kilometers east of Wiesbaden, served as headquarters for the U.S. occupation forces from 1945 to 1955, and would have been the rubble-strewn setting for many such bi-national human liaisons during that time. Mrs. Redmond's long, painful harangue must have exhausted her. She fell into a rather fitful sleep, and I relished the silence as we progressed through Belgium and on to the German autobahn in a southerly direction. .

I did sympathize with this rather unworldly woman for whom the sanctity of her church union was paramount. This had been destroyed by the infidelity of her husband, but with whom I could also empathize. Mrs. Redmond, I suspected, just might have been a singularly desiccated diva in their bedroom. When we reached our destination that night, and bid each other goodbye, I thought we'd probably never meet again. But my life was to involve both her and her husband in a way I certainly couldn't have then imagined.

Despite the separation of the Army and Air Force in 1947, in the United States the Exchange Service remained a joint activity serving both military branches. While this period saw a great deal of centralization of its basic internal operations, such as accounting and purchasing, and it emerged as the Army & Air Force Exchange Service, or A&AFES, instead of Army Exchange Service. In Europe, however, even after all the organizational jockeying since 1947, the Exchange Service survived as two separate entities. It was the next logical step that exchanges in Europe should be re-united after 17 years as independent entities. The Defense Department directed just that. When negotiations started to accomplish this re-joining, A&AFES was then headed by a one-star Air Force general. The European Exchange Service had a one-star Army General. One one-star was not about to permit another one-star to tell him what to do. Neither would conduct business at the other's headquarters as it could be interpreted as kowtowing.

A classic DOD internal turf power-struggle erupted to send intestinal-like rumbles rolling through Pentagon corridors. As a result, like bickering dukes of petty principalities, they agreed only to meet on neutral territory at a U.S. Navy base in Bermuda, then still a British colony, in the Atlantic, off Florida. Damn the expense, full speed ahead!

Egos assuaged, AFEX merged into EES at its headquarters in the historic Palace of Justice building in Nuernberg, site of the 1947 War Crimes Trials. This north Bavaria city was a major political power center during the rise of the National Socialist Party (Nazis), and later the site of Hitler's propagandizing mass rallies at the infamous stadium built on Zeppelin Field. The Allies had selected Nuernberg for the trials partly because it had been a focal point for Nazism. Now the people who sold toothpaste and condoms to the GIs roamed some of the palace's hallowed hallways. Was that poetic put down, or not?

By the time it moved to Nuernberg, I knew several AFEX people through the ski club, including Eugene Bryerly. He and I had, in fact, made a few long weekend excursions to highlights such as Copenhagen, Vienna and Rimini, Italy. Both single, we had a few interests in common. I would drive long distances' which he didn't like. I was sorry to see my acquaintances leave Wiesbaden, but once more my assumption we'd never meet again proved wrong. Bryerly frequently returned and moved into my life in a more important way. Or I into his.

The AFEX relocation to Nuernberg concluded by the beginning of 1965. Since most AFEX employees owned autos, were entitled to Army Quartermaster gasoline at little more than cost prices, some of them on weekends were soon burning up the approximate 160 autobahn miles back to Wiesbaden —Eugene Bryerly in particular. He'd left behind an assortment of international female friends — Americans, Germans, and one English girl — who magnetically drew him back, although he wasn't, as far as I knew, serious about any of them. He'd stay at the American Arms on a space-available basis, where I'd see him from time to time. About this time, Eugene Bryerly also came into the Lindsey AB library on several Sundays and found me bent over my Maryland University textbooks. He and the weekend's girlfriend had been to the matinee show at the base movie theater and he was killing time before heading back to Nuernberg.

In his ever-affable way, he'd come and shake my hand and we'd chat for a couple of minutes. On one occasion I was transcribing my shorthand notes from the classroom lectures, and he commented on my apparent conscientiousness. Over time I've come to think people who have not studied shorthand are sometimes more impressed by this arcane dictation method than need be. They are amazed someone can make sense of all these chicken scratches.

We next met at the American Arms one Friday evening when Bryerly called me from the lobby phone and invited me for a drink in the bar. The AFEX merger with EES and its move to Nuernberg, he said between sips of his Chianti wine, had caused personnel changes in the small Plans & Programs Branch, part of the Plans & Management Office. His former branch chief was moving to head a different entity, and he'd been designated to become the new P&P chief. This meant the other two planning technicians would each move up a notch, leaving open the bottom slot. He offered to champion me for the position. The job carried a GS-9 grade, although he said he wouldn't be able to offer that initially because of my lack of a college degree; but he believed he'd be able to get me in to the grade later provided I performed well.

When I questioned him about future prospects, he said it would all depend on my efforts on the job. My male ego certainly disliked being a humble (now GS-5) stenographer. It did appear I had few prospects in the Civil Service without that confounded degree. He speculated that if I stayed with the Exchange Service I'd eventually face rotation to its main office, then in New York City. At the time I remember thinking that wouldn't be bad: I knew America's west coast a little, and would like to have exposure to the eastern side. It didn't take me long to give him a positive answer. If I got the job I would, as if by magic, metamorphose from secretary into, if not having my very own, at least a one-third interest in the secretary who worked for the three planning technicians.

Eugene Bryerly must have pulled a few levers because I received a firm offer from EES to join the organization in April 1965 at a grade level of ASP-9, a mid-level pay scale. (The Annual Salary Plan, better than the clerical local national scale, but not up to the GS management scale). In retrospect, shedding the secretarial status was for me the most joyous aspect of joining EES and moving to Nuernberg. And it came just in time: I was now 33 years old, and the market for aging male secretaries had died. In truth, the offered annual salary of $5,200 was exactly $35 more than I received as a civil servant. But things worked out well. After completing my three months' probation, I was converted to a GS-7 at $6,050. Moving to the management scale brought with it a monthly housing allowance and a paid U.S. home leave after two years. Exactly a year after joining EES, I earned the assigned GS-9 grade at $7,479 annually of my position. As the joke goes, yesterday I couldn't spell engineer, today I are one.

I rented a small, box-like apartment in a utilitarian, post-war, six-story tower in a decidedly working-class area just outside and north of the Nuernberg historic city wall. To improve on its most Spartan furniture, I treated myself to an armchair and my very first black-and-white TV. I usually walked the 1.5 miles from the apartment to EES headquarters in one half of the Palace of Justice. My route took me through the old city along cobbled, narrow streets with buildings offering ornate stone facades fronting the narrow sidewalk. Most of these had been destroyed or severely damaged in the war, but the hard-working Germans had faithfully restored many to their original specifications while others were underway.

My new work involved collecting customer statistics on the ever-changing number of U.S. military personnel and their dependents stationed in Europe. These were used for budgeting by the Comptroller and stock planning by merchandising elements. The statistics were mostly obtained from classified documents (on the military) prepared by the Pentagon and the services' headquarters in Heidelberg (Army) and Wiesbaden (Air Force). The Exchange Service is required by military department regulations to prepare annual master plans and quarterly fiscal budgets. They are intended to keep the organization on the right track toward achieving its financial goals. Exchange profits, after paying for all operating expenses, are returned to the military services for use in welfare programs not covered by congressional appropriations.

In those days, planning for military field exercises usually carried a security classification. Because the P&P branch possessed the only safe at EES that met military security specifications, we received advance information on exercises, and they mostly wanted exchange service support. These cloak-and-dagger considerations meant that the P&P Branch was primary for arranging exchange support for deployed military personnel. All other branches had varying numbers of Germans nationals working in them, and couldn't handle classified materials.

I found this work interesting, even stimulating, and for the first time in years, I felt I had a job which paid well and met my exaggerated inner needs! My self-image greatly improved. But the move to Nuernberg was not all advantage: there was one major shortcoming. In the mid 1960s there were about 9,500 Army troops in the greater Nuernberg area spread among 13 camps. This compared with about 4,250 Air Force personnel in Wiesbaden at two locations. The UOM found it far more difficult to offer degree-programmed night classes in the Bavarian city. Despite having an American population of double the size compared with Wiesbaden, there just was not the same level of interest in continuing education among Army troopers. I'd always been impressed with the intelligence I discerned among the young airmen, but it was not repeated in this Army-dominated area. Several times I signed up for UOM classes, only to have them canceled because of insufficient participants: a class needed only 10 students to convene. I'd have to be more socially active to fill up spare time.

CHAPTER 38

After five months with EES I helped run a field exchange in support of a joint Air Force and Army deployment in Norway, site of NATO's combined northern headquarters. My only retail experience thus far had been as a customer. Two squadrons of F-4 Phantom fighters were flying in from North Carolina, plus about 500 troops from U.S. Army units in Germany. One squadron was going to Orland NAFB, some 250 miles northwest of Oslo; the other to Rygge NAFB, near Bodo, another 300 miles up the west coast, and just above the Arctic Circle.

The exchange war plan was that an Air Force lieutenant and a tech sergeant, both assigned to EES, would head our teams at the two locations. Another civilian employee would assist the lieutenant at Orland with me assisting the sergeant at Rygge. We met at the exchange at Evreux AB, near Paris, which had assembled 14,000 lbs. of merchandise for shipment on two MAC C-130 turbo propeller Hercules. With crates loaded late one day, we departed the next at 7 a.m., flying in tandem along the Belgian and Dutch coasts, then over the North Sea to Norway.

The flight was routine except for failure of the heating system, making for a bracing trip over northern Europe in late October. Fortunately, I wore ski clothing, the warmest practical gear I owned. No guidance had come from the military as to appropriate dress required by civilians while blocking a theoretical Soviet feint from the Kola Peninsula across the top of Norway. I felt I needed to pinch myself to wake up. Just a few months ago a lowly government clerk: now, as if by miraculous transformation, I was en route to personally engage the big, bad Russian Bear!

In time, the other C-130 banked to the right and sloped away to Orland, while we lumbered on along Norway's craggy, indented coastline, arriving at Rygge in the early afternoon. As soon as we stopped in front of flight operations, more excitement than I really sought began. A message awaited the sergeant that a family member had taken sick and he must return to Germany immediately. We shook hands and he disappeared into operations to make arrangements. I was sorry for him, but felt almost as sorry for myself. I'd be running the field BX alone. The exercise hadn't even begun, and EES-Bodo had sustained 50% casualties! As I stood in shock, a snappy-looking Air Force lieutenant colonel, wearing his squadron-unique silk scarf, came and introduced himself.

"I'm in charge of the squadron's morale and welfare. We've been on the ground for a couple of days already. These Norwegians eat fish at all three squares. My men are getting a little tired of this seafood passion. Need the BX open on the double." His tone sounded as though this subject was closed to further debate. While the crates were forklifted aboard a trailer hitched to a warehouse tractor, I was given 10 minutes to sign myself in and stash my bag in the adjacent guest quarters. I would then join the crates on the flatbed for the ride to a distant hangar designated for F-4 maintenance, with a side room allocated for the BX.

A biting wind from the nearby Atlantic Ocean compressed and channeled by the Salt Fjord, burst across the airfield's open spaces. Although it had not yet snowed, the battleship-gray sky threatened. As we trundled along the lengthy runway, I watched the operations building slowly recede. I paid little attention to our route, however, as I just knew the Air Force would assign a chauffeured, warmed staff car to take me back once I'd completed my bit for its morale.

An American Staff Sergeant and a Norwegian equivalent met us as we approached the hangar, its enormous automatic doors both wide open. Air Force mechanics swarmed over three Phantoms parked inside this cavernous garage. All of the building lights were on because at this latitude daylight faded fast even though not yet 3 p.m. Handing me the key, the Norwegian led me to a room where the BX would operate, a space about 20' wide and 80' long, running along one of the hangar walls. The interior entrance was a double door, and there were no exterior doors or windows. He said I was the only one with a key to the room, and I'd be in charge of this Norwegian real estate during the United States' presence. Surely this national representative status required my presentation to the Norwegian King as for a newly arriving Ambassador? But no kingly invitation arrived.

The American drove the trailer into the hangar and then maneuvered the crates on a forklift into the room, stacking them at one end. The NATO duo departed and I was alone and in sole charge of EES' northernmost BX. Armed with a small crowbar, wire cutters and two box blades brought from Evreux, I set quickly to work. The colonel's word still rumbled around in my head. There was a good supply of folding tables that I set up in the center for product display. Numerous times, as I opened cases, I discovered merchandise with a relationship to something already laid out, and I wound up rearranging displays over and over. I worked as fast as I could, but I made slow headway, and time passed quickly. Soon the men working outside learned that the "BX guy" was on board and they started to appear at the door asking when the store would open. At first I enjoyed the idle chitchat. Then I realized my progress had slowed badly and I still had many boxes to empty. So I taped a sign to the doorjamb proclaiming, "BX opens tomorrow." Know what? Mechanics don't read. The bodies and questions just kept coming and I grew steadily more concerned and agitated. It was already 8 p.m. A management decision had to be made. I used my honorary key, symbol of great power, and locked the heavy double-door. This stopped the interruptions, but the room's temperature rose and I had to strip off several layers.

Although my productivity leaped impressively, it took me another three hours to finish. When I placed the cash register on a table near the door, and counted and hid the change fund, it was well past 11 p.m. I was down to my T-shirt. I took a last walk through the facility (actually around the tables) like a real exchange manager, and confess to feeling pleased with myself. I believed the boys would really appreciate my efforts when I opened for business at 9 a.m. next morning. Air Force morale and welfare were intact!

I clicked off the lights of my little Arctic BX, unlocked the door, and stepped out — into a total, silent blackness. The huge hangar doors were closed; all lights off. Everyone gone. They hadn't thought about the little BX guy literally sweating away in his underwear on their behalf. I was crushed. I wondered if the Russian military would treat its exchange people so callously — but I didn't know if the Russians even had a BX.

Of course, I hadn't a clue how to open the hangar's automatic doors. Even if I found their controls they were certainly alarmed. A finger's touch would activate bells and whistles all over the installation. Vicious German shepherds would arrive faster than Olympic short-distance jocks. I'd be torn to shreds before I could explain that I was merely trying to get *OUT* rather than *IN*.

Exchange planning had overlooked shipping flashlights. (Readers should know they've been stocked religiously at all subsequent exercises!) There weren't even any red-glowing "exit" signs, or whatever the Norwegian word is. I began weighing my options. One would be to sleep in my room, but there was no furniture. Although I had plenty of empty cardboard boxes, such homeless housing was not then in vogue. I was angry, dirty, tired, and a little scared. Now I wished I hadn't been so hasty and locked out all those friendly GIs. Some company would feel good right now. Then I vaguely recalled seeing a regular-person door along one of the hangar walls. Of course, the chances of it being left unlocked seemed utterly beyond hope, given how close all those evil Russians were. But it was worth a try to escape the pitch-dark prison of which I was the sole inmate.

Feeling my sightless way along the wall, I intended to circle the entire hangar searching for that uncertain door. I moved with the slowness of the sleepwalker. Suddenly my mind fixated on the possibility that careless armament riggers had left ordnance lying around. Images flashed of newspaper headlines reading "Lost BX Manager Dies by Stepping on Fragmentation Bomb." While I wanted to do a good job, dying seemed beyond the pale!

My imagination now ran rampant. As I felt countless square inches of the cold, damp metal walls, I remembered the Norwegian rat, the largest on earth. It brought the bubonic plague to Europe in the 1300s. Naturally, they still thrived in the millions in their native land. Think about how often the military can't account for supply inventory. These losses had to be attributable to the Norwegian rat's appetite for engine parts.

After a terrifying, tedious 90 minutes, my hand touched something like a door latch. Unbelievably, it moved down and the door swung out! Rygge NAFB was all around me. Just imagine the entire western world of capitalism could have been enslaved that night by the communist Soviet Empire because a lone airman, American or Norwegian, forgot to lock this 36" wooden door! But I was ecstatic! I would live, grow old, and get pensioned!

My problems, however, weren't over just yet. This prison escapee didn't know the way or how far to his quarters. I hadn't paid attention to the tractor's outbound direction. Then, in the distance, through the soft night mist, I saw a cluster of lights. I asked aloud for a measure of assistance from the Norse god on duty that night.

During the long walk down Norway's longest runway, my brain, my biggest enemy, now started worrying what if a Norwegian armed guard found this lone infiltrator in dusty, disheveled ski garb, loose on a supposedly heavily-defended NATO installation. Don't forget it wasn't so long ago these people were bloodthirsty Vikings, rampaging all over. But proving that even exchange managers occasionally get lucky, the cluster of lights were from the operations building complex. The guest quarter's clerk, who spoke good English, wondered why I was coming in so late without baggage or uniform. I somehow didn't have the stomach to clarify my circumstances.

And for the rest of the time there, sharp at 5 p.m. each day I locked the store, and got out of that hanger. But in the end my contribution to NATO obviously counted. After all, we won the cold war!

The practical experience I gained in Norway, or at least some of it, helped me in the Plans and Programs Branch to be more effective. My job self-confidence improved and I was given responsibility for arranging several more field exchanges during 1966, these staffed by others. I also developed enthusiasm for my other major endeavor — collecting by location, and compiling by exchange areas, the numbers of military personnel and their dependents in the European theater of operations. After a while, one fact of possible historical interest emerged from this work. The U.S Army personnel were primarily stationed at former German Army kasernes. Army camps in the USA are few in number but large in capacity, garrisoning 30,000-plus troops. The German kasernes, on the other hand, never held more than about 1,000 personnel, were widely dispersed throughout West Germany, often with several in different quadrants of major cities. It seemed inefficient from the logistical viewpoint to supply so many locations. It appeared likely, I concluded, that Hitler had purposely spread his Army thinly but widely. An uprising among the civilian population could be quickly doused wherever it occurred. This might help explain, in part, why there were no popular uprisings among German civilians once they awoke to the fact that Hitler was leading them to ruin. Incredibly, after so many crummy jobs, I now had one keeping my interest and giving pleasure! But my good fortune was about to get even better.

The Plans & Programs Branch American secretary left in early January 1966, to return to the US with her young soldier husband who was leaving the service. The wives of soldiers were the source for many of the EES secretaries and general clerks, but they were frequently of short tenure because of continuous rotation of their husbands to the States in the days of military selective service. Mr. Bryerly told me he had interviewed several Americans and a local national woman for a replacement. Finally, he accepted the German in the hope she'd give his branch some longevity. Unfortunately, she couldn't start until 1 February, so we'd be without secretarial help for nearly a month. Our replacement had to provide her employer — the new German Heer (Army) in Mittenwald, her Bavarian hometown — with a month's notice. He talked highly of her qualifications. She spoke English fluently, wrote shorthand in both languages, and typed 70 wpm. Her English had something of an authentic lilt. This came about, I was to learn later, because she had lived in London for about three years as an au pair. In this role, she'd lived with, and worked half days for a family, and went to school the other half. It turned out she'd studied at Pitman's College — which I'd attended for about two years — but at its main campus on Southampton Row in Central London. We eagerly awaited the arrival of the new secretary, and questioned the wisdom of Mr. Bryerly's decision to leave us so long without one. He insisted his selectee was worth it, and when she showed up on 1 February, she didn't disappoint.

Juliane Fuerst proved to be a pleasant, helpful woman, whose 29th birthday had been during the previous month. She was attractive, shapely, and yet engagingly modest. With collar-length brown hair, good features, and alluring blue/green eyes, she had considerable appeal. I noticed she used cosmetics sparingly, and was conservative in her jewelry choices. Once she had caught on to the administrative ways and clerical procedures of the branch, she worked conscientiously and produced quality documents. Mr. Bryerly wanted our external communications to be of a high level, and sometimes made changes to my flowery offerings which, in the days before computers, meant a lot of tiresome re-typing.

Mr. Bryerly also believed that the provision of exchange support to the military's field exercises captured the essence of serving the frontier cavalry troopers of a hundred years earlier. When EES provided such support, he liked to get an article published in the organization's newspaper, EXCHANGE POST, about such endeavors. This was, of course, good public relations for his branch, which could only be career beneficial for him. But it just so happened that, in me, he found an eager scribe for such pieces because, at least partially, they satisfied my desire to be identified as a writer. Furthermore, the paper's editor was no go-getter, and this permitted me to get articles printed under my by-line.

At the time Ms. Fuerst started at the office, I was preparing an article about the Norwegian exercise I'd gone on, although I didn't mention my brief incarceration in the black, bolted hanger. Our new secretary cooperated by staying late to type this; such work wasn't really in our branch's domain. While this endeavor went on, another field exchange became necessary which had even greater attention-getting, newsworthy qualities.

On the morning of 17 January 1966, a Strategic Air Command B-52 eight-engine Stratofortress collided with a KC-135 aerial refueling tanker as they tried to hook-up at 30,500 feet while approaching the thinly populated coast of southeastern Spain. The Stratofortress broke up and four thermonuclear bombs dropped out. Three of the bomber's seven-man crew died. The tanker crashed and burned, killing its four-crew members. The nuclear cores of the H-bombs had not been activated and thus did not detonate when they fell to earth. (World history since then, most assuredly, would have been quite different had that happened!).

Of the four bombs, equipped with a series of parachutes to slow descent, two landed on the remote, arid, hilly coast near fishing villages in the province of Almeria. The third fell within the limits of Palomares, a village of 2,000 people. But the fourth proved elusive. A search, almost instantly mounted by the American 16th Air Force at Torrehon AB, Madrid, found one bomb just before dark on the day of the accident; two more on the following day. The fourth remained missing. The U.S. government, concerned about negative international publicity, ordered an all-out recovery operation. It also carefully controlled all press releases

The search team quickly grew to some 700 U.S. Air Force and civilian personnel, plus about 200 Spanish police and military. Reaching the search site, some 350 miles from Madrid involved traversing mountainous terrain on curving, narrow roads. The last five miles of the route required transiting a rutted, twisting, and dirt road. Coastal villages hereabouts lacked telephone connection. Indeed, electricity reached the area only eight years before in 1958!

EES early on received a request for limited exchange support for the searchers. A tent city sprang up at the site with a large one assigned as a field exchange. Because of the poor roads, EES could not use its 18-wheel tractor-trailers, but relied on smaller seven-ton trucks to bring in the snacks, sodas, cigarettes, candy, magazines, etc., from Torrejon AB's Exchange. The intensive hunt for the 4th bomb continued.

A local fisherman had reported seeing an object fall into the sea. Meanwhile, Sandia National Laboratories' scientists studied the projectile's probable trajectory based on the heading and speed of the aircraft and prevailing wind velocities. They calculated the bomb to be on the adjacent ocean floor. The recovery effort switched from land to sea. A veritable armada of ships from the American Mediterranean 6th Fleet joined in. The USN brought in three submersibles. When found, the bomb ensnared in its parachutes, rested precariously on a steep slope of an undersea ravine, at a depth of 2,550 feet, and five miles offshore.(1)

Mr. Byerly wanted this operation reported in our newspaper despite the fact we didn't have much detail early on. He thought it important because of its "doomsday overtones" with "EES to the rescue." Again, Ms. Fuerst cheerfully worked on this with me notwithstanding her considerable load of routine duties.

During these extra work assignments, I took the opportunity to find out more about our new delightful and genial secretary. Her home village, Mittenwald, located in the Bavarian Alps, close to the Austrian border, ensured she learned skiing as a child. The sport was now my passion. I also found out an avid reading habit started much earlier in her life than in mine.

At one of our little confessionals, she told me her mother, as Juliane approached her teens, encouraged her "to learn something so you can be something." Mrs. Fuerst didn't want her daughter to unquestioningly accept the life of a rural housewife. I guessed that this made Juliane's mother something of a freethinker. So, despite her father's disapproval, Julie, as I now called her, went to Munich at the age 16 to work part-time, attend a commercial school, and live in a home for girls run by Catholic nuns. Life in the city hadn't been easy in the immediate post-war years.

Afterwards Julie continued self-improvement by going to England to learn the language, also against her father's wishes. Returning to

Germany, some three years later, she didn't go back to Mittenwald, but went to Hamburg, Germany's major commercial port, to work two years as a translator for Marubeni, the large Japanese trading house. During her time in the north of the country, she'd had to make several long visits to Mittenwald when her mother developed cancer.

I also soon found out Julie enjoyed the outdoors. She liked to hike, as do many Europeans. A day's skiing for her when young involved carrying skis on her shoulders for the three-hour slog to the top of local mountains and making one run down. There were no cable cars, chair lifts, or even draglifts on her nearby mountains at that time. But after the climb, she said, the single run down was like a happy dream. I liked Fraulein Fuerst!

As the days and weeks passed, I was struck by the comparability of her life with my own. In fact, it intrigued me that our choices and experiences had tracked each other's in a number of significant ways, even though she'd been born into a picturesque, Alpine setting while I added to the hubbub of over-crowded, stratified London. Although we'd been randomly placed by life on fiercely opposed sides in WWII, both of our childhoods were impacted negatively by the global conflagration. She was, however, only a toddler compared to my seven years when it broke out in 1939. As a result, my so-called "formal education" had been disrupted far more than hers. Despite the war, she still received a solid grounding and, after 1945, attended a school taught by nuns recognized for their conscientiousness.

Both our fathers served in their country's army. Mr. Fuerst was called up in 1940. Severe varicose veins kept him out of combat units. Never stationed outside Germany, he enjoyed leaves at home, which he supplemented with several unauthorized trips to his family, risking his very life had he been caught. My father wasn't drafted until June 1942. But after six months, went overseas to never return until June 1946.

Julie left home at age 16; I didn't make my break until I'd attained my majority. She had bounced around a little since then, and I'd bounced around a lot. I'd vaguely justified it because many writers led a peripatetic existence, holding numerous jobs as they trolled life for a bountiful harvest of experience. But now I'd abandoned the writing dream, my record looked merely irresponsible.

Meeting this intelligent woman, whose life story reflected

something of mine, gave me a sense of redemption. By now I'd come to feel comfortable around her. I wanted to ask Julie out for dinner, but Mr. Bryerly knew this and had already let me know he didn't want his male staff dating females who worked in our division, let alone the same branch. He was the only other bachelor in the branch, and scrupulously obeyed his own rule. I owed him my loyalty for his effort in getting me hired into a job I liked so was torn over his ruling. In return, however, I felt I worked hard compared with others in our division, especially with my largely extra-curricular production of pieces for the POST. Eventually I wrote a total of ten.

Then about this time, one of the American bachelors in the Systems Division asked me what I knew of Ms. Fuerst. Immediately I suspected his inquiry indicated interest beyond the casual. This guy was fishing and likely intended to ask her for a date. For once, I didn't want to be beaten to the punch and, regardless of my boss' caution, I invited her for a Sunday afternoon drive and dinner. She accepted.

Julie had already told me of her great enjoyment of classical music, including opera. Although such music meant nothing to me, I sought to demonstrate my sophistication on our first date by visiting Bayreuth, site of the annual summer Wagner Festival. This is Europe's oldest yearly music gathering for the country's champagne-sipping bourgeoisie. Britain's comparable elegant summer opera season is Glynebourne.

When I asked for directions to pick her up at her rented room in the house of a German couple, a 20-minute walk from the office, I was taken aback when she indicated I shouldn't drive to the front door. Julie had told her landlord she worked for the Americans, and he'd made it plain he lacked enthusiasm for the species. He must have been one of the Nuernbergers, mostly among the older generation, who still regretted Germany's defeat under the psychopathic Adolph Hitler. I felt affronted by Julie's request and my gut reaction signaled to hell with her landlord. This issue, however, revealed to me Julie's gentle disposition and dislike of confrontation. Living accommodation was acutely scarce in the city, and she needed her modestly priced room, but above all she wanted to avoid any "unpleasantness." I, of course, didn't want to cause her any, so I lowered my neck hair and waited for her on a side street two blocks away. On the big day, Julie arrived on the minute of our scheduled meeting time; my introduction to her life-long punctuality.

Bayreuth's festival concert hall, built especially for the annual Richard Wagner summer fete, sits atop a low hill at the north end of town. The renowned summer event was still several months away and we found the festival concert hall closed. We walked in its gently sloping grounds admiring several statues of the human figure. As compensation for our disappointment over the closure of Wagner's concert hall, we toured Bayreuth's lavish Markgrafluekes opera house, built in the 1790s by the noble family of Franconia, then a separate duchy. Its sumptuous baroque interior with extensive gold-leaf features, large crystal chandeliers, wall murals, and ornate furnishings, overwhelmed my plebeian taste.

We broke the 40-mile return journey at Pegnitz, overlooking the river of the same name, for dinner at a typical Bavarian restaurant with heavy wood tables and benches, an interior decorated with old farming implements, and macho beer steins standing in niches. Its exterior walls, veined with massive wood struts, were painted with idyllic murals, with window boxes burdened with blood-red geraniums. At a corner table, as far from the counter as possible, we continued our animated conversation. I found out more of Julie's background and interests. I soon decided she was a serious person with a worldly outlook. An early passion for books had tended to make her dissatisfied with life at home. In this, perhaps more than anything else, I felt we'd trodden the same mine-strewn path.

No doubt hoping to make a favorable impression on Julie, I ordered a bottle of wine with our dinner. This we consumed slowly and rather daintily. I refilled our glasses when the conversation seemed to be slowing. We stayed in the restaurant for almost three hours, nothing exceptional in Europe, but certainly out-of-character for me. Our middle-aged, dirndl-clad waitress must have observed how absorbed we were in our long parley and, I believe, tried to take advantage of our abstraction. Some Germans perceived Americans as big, even careless, show-off spenders. Some American GIs deserved this reputation. When the bill came, the total price seemed too high. I don't remember now whether I'd been charged for two bottles of wine instead of one, or if the waitress doubled the price of our one bottle over that stated on the wine list. The waitress's reaction when I challenged her told me without a doubt that she'd tried to pull a fast one. I usually get angry when I'm a scam victim, but this time I worked to control my temper and avoid a rumpus. I didn't want to spoil what I hoped was Julie's good impression of me.

CHAPTER 39

We repeated our day-long first date on the next few weekends. We motored to the Franken Hills about 50 miles west of Nuernberg, to visit Rothenburg-on-the-Tauber (river) and the following Sunday to Bamberg, both towns offering well-preserved Middle Ages' architecture, and nowadays big tourist destinations. Julie's company generated a feel-good mood in me. As we strolled through these historic towns with their venerable buildings resplendent in autumnal colors, we exchanged more details of our backgrounds.

Both her father and grandfather, she told me over coffee and cake, attended the Bavarian state violin-making school in Mittenwald to become makers of handcrafted violins and violas. Because the earnings from this pursuit were limited, the family also operated a smallholding. Summer months were occupied working on their few acres growing hay and tending a few animals. They devoted the long winters, when alpine snowfall buries the area making movement difficult, to producing string instruments in a home workshop. Her only brother had completed his training at the violin school and secured a position there as a master. He worked along side his father on the smallholding, which he would one day inherit.

I quizzed Julie particularly about the views of her parents toward the Nazis. They had never been members of the Nazi party she told me, with both hands around a coffee cup, as if seeking warmth, and, in any case, were devout Roman Catholics, the predominant faith in Bavaria. Their faith was vital to them, and joining the party meant forswearing religion. As a child, Julie had been required to attend church weekly, undergo the various Catholic rights of passage, and had accepted the teachings completely. I discerned in her a sincere desire to be a kind, warm and generous human being. Yet I gained the impression that events in her life had fractured her once strong belief. I'd told her of my lack of faith and we left the subject there. Since she accepted my offer of subsequent dates, I assumed my attitude didn't matter.

Julie's father, George, had spent WWII in the Army as a guard at prisoner-of-war camps. As one of his duties, he traveled to some Axis-occupied countries escorting military prisoners back for detention in Germany. Julie regaled me with several amusing vignettes showing her father as one of the less enthusiastic members of Germany's armed might. George hadn't concerned himself with politics, and never believed Hitler's policies were the solution to Germany's problems. He had a run-in with authority early in his military career. Just as the British were brainwashed by photos of the Monarch hung in public places, the same process prevailed in Germany. A mandatory, ubiquitous image of the Fuehrer, glowering at his most messianic, hung above Private Fuerst's top tier bunk at boot camp. He objected to this propaganda symbol above his bed. When it had bugged him long enough, he turned the Fuehrer's face to the wall. Quickly Private Fuerst stood before the camp commandant to account for this outrageous display of disloyalty. Said George, by way of explanation: "Our great leader's eyes are so penetrating I can't sleep." The commandant accepted George's reasoning, but warned another instance of disrespect would be dealt with harshly.

By 1943 Germany had lost so many men it was desperate. Army bureaucrats searched among those once declared unfit for combat, and Private Fuerst found himself once again before his commandant. The Army dangled a promotion and, incidentally, assignment to a front-line combat unit in Russia, in front of George. The wily private wanted no part of that. During the intelligence assessment phase of the interview, a question was posed as to how George would recognize senior officers: "By the amount of gray hair growing in their ears." Despite the Wehrmacht's dire straights, it decided to do without him on the Russian front.

On another occasion, Julie's father had to escort a single POW from Austria to an internment camp in central Germany. Their official railroad ticketing took them through Mittenwald. Cool George decided to treat himself to an unauthorized 48-hour break at home, even though his small town happened to be the site of four camps housing the Army's tough mountain brigades. Once home, George secured his prisoner by locking him in a bedroom and boarding its one window with plywood nailed outside. Fortunately, the prisoner, probably thankful for the delay in arriving at his final destination, gave no trouble, and George got by with this infraction of the rules. In reality, had her father been caught pulling this stunt, he might well have faced a firing squad

Julie also told me of the brave action of a young cousin and its terrible outcome. As their situation deteriorated in the war, the Nazi authorities commandeered cast iron, especially private gates, railings, weather vanes, etc., for smelting into armaments. By 1944 they were also confiscating church bells. A small unit of soldiers and civilian workmen arrived unannounced in Mittenwald to relieve the town of its three bells in the tower of its 1737 Baroque parish church. The town's faithful were outraged, but opposition to the government received swift and severe punishment. During the night, however, Julie's 16-year old cousin, with youthful rashness, slashed the Army truck's tires. Caught in the act, he was instantly drafted into the Army, sent to the eastern front, and never heard from again.

As the Allies closed in on Germany from the east and west, Hitler, in another sign of desperation and inhumanity, ordered the call-up of boys who were 14 years or older to defend the Fatherland. Julie's brother, small for his age, had just qualified. He soon received the doomsday assignment to report for rifle training. Their courageous mother flew to the town hall and screamed her opposition. Her son was too young to even raise the heavy weapon to his shoulder. Her husband, even with diseased legs, already served the nation. One family member was enough. The authorities excused 14-year-old Andreas Fuerst. All credit must go to his mother because thousands of other 14-year-olds were thrown into the final battles of WWII. Many did not survive. They could not have changed the outcome of the conflict in the slightest, but Hitler stole their young lives anyway. By now I felt convinced Julie's parents were not Nazi sympathizers.

The relationship between Julie and I passed quickly from reserved shyness, conflicted with office considerations, to one of warm friendship. I attributed this development to the fact we seemed to enjoy many of the same things. I found her maturity appealing, and I had a respect for her as a person. Of course, it helped hugely that I found her attractive and it didn't hurt that she possessed a shapely figure. And she was a good sport!

Julie enjoyed walking as much as I did, which is nothing unusual for ordinary Europeans born before the 1960s. We started to participate in the German national pastime of walking in local parks and woods on Saturday or Sunday. Said to be motivated by claustrophobia engendered in the limited living space of the average apartment, hordes of Germans flock to nearby public open spaces to escape those in-pressing four walls. Despite our proclivity for walking, I found one aspect of this activity on which we didn't see eye-to-eye. For most Germans, their weekend walk in the park is occasion to put on their Sunday best. For the men, it even included a tie. I couldn't understand their reasoning. Casual clothes are a must for a ramble. In my mind it's an insult to nature when one is dressed like an office clerk. Julie had some trouble with this, but acquiesced with my sloppy appearance. It was another instance of Julie avoiding confrontation. Now I see my attitude was part immaturity, part stubbornness, but still the right one!

The fact soon emerged in our association neither of us was involved with anyone else. Most evenings and each weekend I was available and I soon discovered this also applied to Julie. As the months went by, I began to deduce from Julie talking about her life in Hamburg, that she'd known considerable loneliness. Yet she chose not to return to Mittenwald, cognizant of her record for quickly feeling dissatisfied and confined by her home surroundings. Although her loneliness represented pain, it was not sufficient to outweigh the sense of limitation induced in her childhood environment. I felt I could relate so much to that aspect of her life. We again fused.

On a date not long after I returned from a week's vacation in "go-go" Spain, booked before she came to EES, Julie decided to disclose something about herself that, as she told me later, she thought would bring things between us to an abrupt halt. Towards the end of her second year in Hamburg, Julie had fallen into a severe depression. She returned home to her father and stepmother. But the change of scene did not help and she made an attempt on her life. She was committed to a Munich psychiatric hospital. She felt her life was over. Julie remained at the hospital for two months.

After recovery, she returned home and found a secretarial job with the German Ministry of Defense in the supply administration at one of the Mittenwald kasernes. During her two years there she resumed social activity, including dating, hiking, skiing and even rock climbing. Her job bored her, but paid reasonably well, and was conveniently located. She could walk to work and home to lunch.

As the shattering experience of her depression receded in her memory, she found herself becoming restless again. Someone told her of the possibility of working for the Americans, which would utilize her hard-learned English language skills. She traveled to Nuernberg seeking a position with EES where our different paths, yet similar experiences, crossed.

Julie's concern this revelation might end our friendship proved needless. Perhaps it would have if I'd never experienced the insidiousness of depression myself. Although my depression had been comparatively mild, it had, unbeknown to me, fundamentally dictated my life decisions for seven years, some of which had been irrational, flying in the face of my own best interests. Learning of her worse depression, rather than causing me to run away in fear, generated a tender empathy toward her. I felt great tenderness for her because of my own journey through that black, bleak, rotting landscape. After this, we began to spend just about all of our free time together. .

By now we had exchanged all of the significant information about ourselves. Julie's honesty and modesty impressed me deeply. I knew I was dealing with a woman for whom I felt great respect. After living so much alone for so many years, frequent and close human company represented an immeasurable pleasure. It made me feel a more complete person. I was nervous about using the word "love," being so uncertain how to define the condition.

Because of our concern about repercussions in EES, we had always tried to be discrete and keep our friendship a secret. It had worked well because our activities tended to be different from the majority of the Americans at EES. The organization was a Department of Defense agency, and I was beginning to learn that the military services are some the most conservative Federal elements, perhaps necessarily so. But, as a result, we avoided the officer clubs and I never went to the Nuernberg Army golf course. Our time together now started to include Julie staying with me for the rest of the weekend after our Saturday night date. With our relationship having moved technically to the status of an affair, we felt the need to conceal it from the office even more.

Each return-to-work-and-reality Monday morning, I would drop off Julie on a quiet street blocks from the rear entrance of the Palace of Justice. She would then walk alone to that entrance while I drove to the building's front car park. This little subterfuge succeeded for some weeks but, inevitably, on one morning just as Julie alighted from the vehicle, weekend bag in hand, an older EES executive secretary rounded a corner and spotted us. As far as I know, and to her everlasting credit, she said nothing at work. Our new and exciting situation led to a discussion of the possibility of our cohabiting. Had we done this in 1966, however, there would have been, I believe, a chance of being fired from our jobs. We were probably 10 or 15 years ahead of our time. Now 34 years old, I had to hold on to my interesting and satisfying job for dear life. And for the first time ever, I felt I earned sufficient income to contemplate marriage. So around the end of September, Julie and I resolved to take all of our personal bonding to its logical conclusion: we would marry.

CHAPTER 40

Having lived a spartan bachelor life so long without any family members nearby, I wanted our decision executed with the least fuss. I didn't want a church ceremony. From my austere viewpoint, much of a church white wedding, with its self-boosterism rituals, smacks of human vanity, on which commercial interests have cleverly capitalized. I favored a garden-variety, down-and-dirty Nuernberg Town Hall civil marriage. The law required two witnesses, and that's all. My family hadn't even met Julie, and I'd gone once only with Julie to meet her father and stepmother. His conclusion, as she later told me, was that I "seemed civilized." Furthermore, partly because neither of us had family geographically close, I didn't see the point of holding a reception.

Somewhat surprisingly, Julie went along with all of this. I believe I didn't give credit at the time to Julie's accommodation of my viewpoint. Was it more of her avoidance of confrontation? Perhaps. Did my attitude represent excessive egoism? Yes. An inadequate defense is that too many years of living alone had me uncomfortable with some of life's social protocols. But I did buy Julie a modest diamond ring and we announced our engagement in the office. She had to relinquish her position in the Plans and Programs Branch. Conveniently, another opened in a branch in the same division just along the hallway. Magically, this somehow made us legit.

I never made a bended-knee proposal. Julie, I'm sure, had reservations about me as a life-partner. My lack of religion must have caused her concern and possible unhappiness. The most I felt comfortable doing was to admit to and acknowledge a God in the physical universe, similar to Native American beliefs. Probably this didn't suffice. Also my impatience and tendency to not always conform to some of society's norms were likely a source of troubling doubts for Julie. But I believed we both harbored a deep, core loneliness of long standing; we needed soul-mate companionship.

For my part, a mild reservation was on a different plane. Simply, even though I knew her family had been anti-Nazi, the truth is I still wondered about marrying someone from the nation that had been the principal opponent in two devastating world wars. Although 21 years had passed since the end of WWII, and 48 since WWI, undoubtedly there were residual feelings in some Britons and Americans of dislike of, or distrust for, Germans. But I knew such thoughts would not be found in my own immediate family. Beyond that, I told myself, it didn't really matter. I had now lived in Germany for four years and through EES met numerous ordinary Germans who were pleasant, polite and considerate. Most of them had a work ethic that I greatly admired and which often put ours to shame. What's more, I felt reassured when I remembered the British Monarch had married Philip of Battenburg, whose veins flowed with German blood. His relatives even included someone who reportedly dropped bombs on England during WWII. If he'd been acceptable to the Royals, surely gentle Julie, a child during those horrific years, wouldn't offend anyone?

Ever ready to attribute global significance to my personal situation, I eventually convinced myself that by marrying a citizen of our former enemy I would play a small part in reconciling the rift between Britain/America and Germany. The uniting of Julie and I would symbolize the healing of war wounds. Ours wasn't going to be some run-of-the-mill marriage. Ours would contain trappings of national rapprochement; anyone can marry for love! The date was set for Thanksgiving Day, 24 November 1966, a public holiday for EES employees.

That day turned out to be gray, windy, cold, but not wet. We asked Londoners Lionel and Sylvia Redmond, the lady I'd driven to England two years before, to be our mandatory witnesses. When I thought of what she'd revealed about their marriage, I realized this choice might be questionable. But they were willing, and I hoped she knew her secret was safe with me (as long as she lived.)

We met at the city hall, in the center of Nuernberg, half an hour before our mid-morning nuptial appointment. The Redmonds arrived in their car. Julie came by taxi. En route she bought a small bunch of assorted flowers at the open market in the adjacent square. Rising that morning as though going to work, I was ready early and had plenty of time. Despite it being my wedding day, I walked the couple of blocks from my apartment to take advantage of a 25-cent streetcar ride to city hall. Does that qualify for the Guinness Book of Records?

The formalities were conducted in German. Julie came to my rescue with whispered translations. The rituals consumed all of ten minutes and had a production-line quality because some 20 other couples were processed that morning. But most of those would also participate in subsequent church weddings. For poor Julie, this was it! After collecting the marriage certificate, the four of us headed out the chambers into the corridor, all focused on a champagne lunch reserved at a close-by Yugoslavian restaurant.

A short way along the passage, a middle-aged, plump, bespectacled woman in a worn, beige topcoat, sat on a wall bench, pad and pen in one hand, a 35mm camera in the other. As our foursome drew abreast, she rose and introduced herself as a reporter with the *Nuernberg Nachrichten*, the city's evening newspaper. She explained in German to Julie the paper, in its weekend edition, ran a short, general-interest feature entitled "Bridal Pair of the Week." When she reviewed the city's manifest of couples undergoing the civil ritual that week, she had selected us as her choice because of our disparate backgrounds. She invited us to sit on the wall bench while she posed a few questions, and recorded our answers: what we liked about each other; if it had been love at first sight; what we hoped for in an international marriage; etc., etc.

Julie answered these wide-ranging questions with a couple of succinct, sage comments. When it came to me, I turned on my best bureaucratic verbosity. As a result, in the city where Nazi sympathizers still lingered, I'm quoted in their evening newspaper with the following declaration: "I wish others would follow our example. Marriage between different nationalities is one of the best and surest ways of promoting understanding among nations of the world. I would hope that families related by marriage would not fight each other with real weapons. Kitchen plates would be OK." Hitler must have turned in…oh, no, sorry, he had himself burned up.

The reporter wanted a picture of us on the sidewalk with the entrance to the city hall as the backdrop. Outside, she said Julie's extra height, exaggerated by high heels, wouldn't look right for the "bridal pair of the week." So she photographed us from the knees up, with me standing on the sidewalk and Julie in the road. On such an important occasion, I unthinkingly played a part in upholding the world's prejudice against short men. Had I been quicker witted, I should have declined to begin our married life with a lie. It didn't augur well!

Yet 2005 A.D. finds us still married with grown offspring. Although I never did achieve a college degree, our two daughters have them. Nor did I make it as a writer outside of some newspaper and small-time magazine articles over a long period. I shakily hung on to my job with AAFES, retiring at age 60, at the lower end of mid-level management. But Julie and I continue to walk, with me ever sloppily dressed, and our noses are still in the books!

End

On our wedding day in Nuernberg outside its City Hall. The person with back to camera is reporter from local evening newspaper. (November 1966).

EPILOGUE

This book represents my mea culpa. As a highly motivated 15-year-old, I started on life's path. For the reasons I hope already elucidated, it didn't take long before I lost sight of my target and strayed off course. Now, looking back, this journey can be primarily noted for its many erratic directional changes. In fact, once I gave up the idea of attempting a full-time writer's life, my early record now looks no better than the garden-variety drifter.

A far nobler justification for this endeavor is as a plea for greater recognition of the suffering inflicted by war on innocent children. Since the WWII hostilities that affected me, there have been major-armed conflicts in Korea, Vietnam, Balkans, Iraq, Ireland, Mid-East, and several areas of Africa and Latin America. These violent disputes have engulfed millions of innocent children, leaving many dead and many more physically and psychologically scarred. Such savagery must be ended for the sake of the world's innocent children. These conflicts have endured during much of my life and, it seems to me, have mostly failed to solve the original problems. But this book is likely to reach so limited an audience as to render my plea a voice in the wilderness.

As to my own experience in WWII, I believe the psychiatrist who conjectured it might have been the basis for the onset of my dysthymia. Almost certainly this malaise had taken hold of me by the time I reached puberty. I think it retained this obscure format until my questionable choices of hitchhiking across America and our so-called expedition in Mexico. These adventures probably overloaded my less-than-robust nervous system and I buckled.

Nearly a decade later, as testament to my mental state following acquisition of a job engendering a sense of worth and the wholesome feelings of marriage to a soul mate, I stopped taking the anti-depressant. In fact, I felt "normal" and assumed myself cured of the weird condition stalking me for so long. But during the following five years I steadily slipped back and, after another year of resisting acceptance because of the old false pride, went again to a psychiatrist. I resumed the same medication and soon emerged from my encompassing psychological torment, although not with the miraculous zing I enjoyed first time. I've taken that same medication ever since, and now use its generic equivalent.

But how I twisted and wriggled on the barbed hook of depression during 1956-64, only slowly coming to accept my condition. Because of my false pride, it had to almost break me before I would recognize the symptoms I displayed and acquiesce with reality. So one should have compassion for sufferers of this illness, even oneself. Its masked, insidious nature is difficult to grapple. Even the highly intelligent and successful British actress, Vivien Leigh, refused to accept the judgment of several leading psychiatrists who diagnosed her as manic-depressive. She elected alcohol and tobacco to help lessen the effects of this furtive mental illness and greatly undermined her long-term general health.

I now know depression ran on my mother's side of our family, and my father may not have been free of it. They never talked on this subject, at least around their children, and it's likely they never understood it. They might have endured the pain in a heroic silence, perhaps even from each other. But during one of my last visits to Mom, a year or so before she died at age 89, she mentioned, in an amazingly casual way, that rarely a day passed in her life without feeling the depression demon. After all those years of suppression! Depression needs to be discussed openly if it plagues your family, and professional guidance sought.

The other perplexing conundrum of my life is why I, a person of almost no formal education, so early and eagerly entertained the improbable dream of being a writer. I suspect I became addicted to this goal as a result of youthful enthusiasm for literature, hooked almost from the moment I delved among the pages of my first adventure novel. Did the discovery of books, and the far-flung worlds to which they can transport the reader, serve as my magic carpet escape from the perceived dullness of home life? Was it merely an empty, innocent, thirsty brain soaking up exotic atmospheres like a marathon runner absorbs water?

As the years went by, during many of which I slaved to get spare-time travel and general pieces published in newspapers and magazines, my writing dream increasingly struck me as preposterous. In fact, I read an English author who compared this to an Epicurean who loves gourmet food and assumes he can produce such heavenly kitchen offerings without completing an apprenticeship. More doubts about my writing dream invaded my being when I read the words of Jean-Jacques Rousseau, France's 18th century philosopher, a man who is reported to have suffered guilt and inferiority feelings, who wrote: "In my youth I thought I would meet in the world the kind of people I had come to know in my books, but I was seeking what did not exist, and little by little I lost the hope of finding what I sought." For the longest time I felt my ache to be a writer could not have been valid. Then I read Pablo Picasso's life and he seemed to ponder the very same question when he said: "What, after all, is a painter? He's a collector who wants to make a collection by doing the paintings he saw in other collections. That's how it starts, but then it becomes something else...".

During my now 70+ years, I swung from a youth with a passionate desire to be a writer to a weak-kneed, doubting wimp, often ready to throw in the pen. But in more recent years I've found myself swinging back to the positive end of my small-time literary spectrum. I submit this book, a work of eight years in the writing, for the review of anyone kind enough to read it. Please, you be the judge of whether I made it as a writer. Today I support the sentiments of Dr. Benjamin E. Mays, President of Morehouse College, Atlanta, Georgia, USA, who said: "The tragedy of life doesn't lie in not reaching your goals. The tragedy lies in having no goals to reach. Not failure, but low aim, is a sin."

ENDNOTES

Prologue.

(1). *The Complete Poems of Emily Dickinson.* Editor: Thomas H. Johnson. Publisher: Little, Brown & Co., Boston. (cVarious).

Chapter 2:

(1). *The Mismeasure of Man* by Stephan Jay Gould. Publisher: Norton. (c. 1981).

(2). The London *Observer* newspaper's 1973 article series entitled "The New British."

(3). *London's Burning* by Constantine Fitzgibbon. Ballantine Books Inc. (c. 1970).

Chapter 3:

(1) Ibid. Chapter 2 (2).

(2) The London "WEEKLY TELEGRAPH" newspaper, September 1999.

(3) The Evacuation: A Very British Revolution, by Bob Holman. Publisher: Lion Publishing plc. London. (c1995).

(4) Ibid. (3).

(5) "War and Children" by Anna Freud and Dorothy T. Burlingham. Publisher: Medical War Books, New York. (c1943).

(6) Ibid. Chapter 2 (3).

Chapter 4:

(1) "The Cotswolds" by R.J.W. Hammond. Publisher: Ward Lock Ltd., London. (c1974).

(2) "Burke's Genealogical and Heraldic History of the Peerage, Baronetage and Knightage, Privy Council and Order of Precedence of the United Kingdom." Publisher: Burke. (c1949).

(3) Ibid. Chapter 2 (2).

(4) Ibid. Chapter 2 (3).

(5) Ibid. Chapter 3 (3).

(6} Ibid. (1).

(7) Ibid. Chapter 2 (3).

(8) " " "

(9) "The World Book Encyclopedia." Publisher: Field Enterprises Educational Corp., Chicago. (c1974).

(10) Ibid. (2) and Ampney Crucis Parish Council letter, 15 October 1976, to my mother from Council Clerk, Mr. P. C. White.

Chapter 5:

(1) Ibid. Chapter 2 (2).

(2) From Boys' Brigade website.

(3) Ibid. Chapter 2 (3).

Chapter 6:

(1) British Ministry of Defence letter, dated 28-01-1999, giving my father's Army record (Ref: 98/60357/CS (RM) 2b/6).

(2) From "Commander's War Diaries" on file at the Public Record Office, Kew, Richmond, Surrey, England, UK.

(3) Ibid. (2).

(4) " "

(5) " "

(6) Recollections of my father at home after the war.

(7) Ibid. (2).

Chapter 7:

(1) "Britain in the Century of Total War: War, Peace and Social Change 1900-1967" by Arthur Marwick . Publisher: Little, Brown & Co. Boston. (c1968).

Chapter 8:

(1) Pamphlet from Juno Beach Center, Burlington, Ontario, Canada, a non-profit organization preserving the gifts of valor and freedom for future generations.

(2) Weapon information obtained at Imperial War Museum exhibits of WWII, London SW, England.

(3) Ibid. (2).

(4) " "

(5) "Inside the Third Reich" by Albert Speer. Publisher: Macmillan, New York, NY (c1970).

Chapter 12:

(1) "Cambridge: A Brief Guide for Visitors." Publisher: Cambridge City Council (c1983).

(2) Ibid. Chapter 4 (9).

Chapter 15:

(1) RAF Henlow and the Radio Engineering Unit historical information obtained at RAF Museum Library, Hendon, London NW.

Chapter 17:

(1) Ibid. Chapter 7 (1).

(2) Ibid. Chapter 2 (2).

Chapter 18:

(1) *Chronicle of Aviation.* Publisher: Chronicle Communications Ltd., London. (c1992).

(2) *The Anatomy of Britain* by Anthony Sampson. Publisher: Harper & Row, New York, NY. (c1962).

Chapter 21:

(1) The London *Weekly Telegraph* newspaper article, (June 2003).

(2) Cunard Line—Cunard Heritage. From Web site http://www.cunardsteamshipsociety.com/.

Chapter 23:

(1) Ibid. Chapter 4(9).

Chapter 26:

(1) Ibid. Prologue (1).

Chapter 32:

(1) Ibid. Chapter 2 (2).

Chapter 38:

(1) *America's Lost H-bomb* by Randall C. Maydew. Publisher: Sunflower University Press, Manhattan, KS. (c1997).

524343

Made in the USA